An Excursion into the Paranormal

An Excursion into the Paranormal

George Karolyi

The
Paranormal Phenomena
Research Foundation

Published in Australia by The Paranormal Phenomena Research Foundation
PO Box 84, Upper Sturt, South Australia 5156
Copyright © 2003 George Karolyi
First published August, 2003
Revised edition January, 2009
National Library of Australia Card Number & ISBN 1 921008 83 0
Printed in China

Contents

Introduction and Acknowledgements	Page 1
Chapter 1 The Ancients	Page 3
Chapter 2 Fields and Particles	Page 7
Chapter 3 Waves – Relativity – Quanta	Page 31
Chapter 4 In Pursuit of the Human Aura	Page 59
Chapter 5 Corona Discharge Photography	Page 83
Chapter 6 The Exact and the Probable	Page 101
Chapter 7 The Normal and the Paranormal	Page 117
Chapter 8 Extrasensory Perception	Page 121
Chapter 9 Psychokinesis	Page 146
Chapter 10 Bioelectric Phenomena – Biofeedback	Page 172
Chapter 11 Survival Related Phenomena	Page 213
Chapter 12 Parallel Universes	Page 225
Chapter 13 Epilogue – Moral Issues	Page 235

Contents

Appendices to Chapter 2   Page 243

Appendices to Chapter 3   Page 256

Appendices to Chapter 6   Page 273

Appendices to Chapter 9   Page 280

Appendix to Chapter 13   Page 283

Any part of the contents of this book may be copied for personal use, provided that the source is acknowledged. The text of the book is also available on the internet at the website: www.paranormalphenomena.org

Introduction and Acknowledgements

Paranormal phenomena encompass all phenomena that cannot be explained in terms of currently prevailing scientific knowledge, but which nevertheless can be shown to exist to a high degree of probability by accepted scientific methodology, or which are frequently reported by numerous reliable observers in a consistent way.

The author is aware of the extensive work done by many others in the various areas of the paranormal, and realises that his contributions constitute a tiny fraction of the total.

This book is not an attempt to describe paranormal phenomena in an all-inclusive or systematic way. Rather, the book is a description of the author's own selective venture into the field of the paranormal, and presents the author's own results in particular areas. Nevertheless, these areas cover a wide range of the overall field, and include topics such as the human aura, corona discharge photography, extrasensory perception, psychokinesis, survival related phenomena, correlations between bioelectric variables and paranormal abilities, and attempts to enhance paranormal abilities via biofeedback.

The work described in this book is scientific research covering a period of some 25 years. Much of the work was carried out at the University of Adelaide, in South Australia, where the author lectured in electrical engineering for over thirty years. After the author retired from that university, the investigations continued at the Paranormal Phenomena Research Foundation Inc., in South Australia, which was specifically established for that purpose. Some of the results presented exhibit an exceptionally high level of statistical significance.

The book is intended for readers interested in the paranormal, who consider it worthwhile to spend the necessary time and effort in perusing it.

However, the presentation goes beyond being merely descriptive, and aims to provide the reader with quantitative understanding, while attempting to keep the necessary mathematics as simple as practicable. Correspondingly, the body of the text relies solely on arithmetic, while fuller explanations to be found in the appendices rarely go beyond simple algebra. Furthermore, Chapters 1, 2, 3, and 6 aim to provide some basic historical and scientific background for the benefit of those readers who have no prior scientific grounding, or who welcome some revision of their prior scientific studies. Readers with a suitable scientific background may bypass these chapters.

While at the University of Adelaide, the author was fortunate to have received help with the investigations from two associates, namely Dorisami Nandagopal and Hugh Wigg, whose valuable contributions, primarily in the fields of the human aura, corona discharge photography, and bioelectricity, are gratefully acknowledged. Thanks are also due to some members of the university technical support staff for much help rendered, and perhaps to a dozen students, who worked in related areas as part of projects for their final year theses under the author's supervision.

Investigations into paranormal phenomena are greatly reliant on the cooperation of people acting as subjects in tests and experiments. Without such cooperation the work could not have been undertaken. In the descriptions of various tests performed, and results obtained, the subjects of the tests are referred to by initials only. The following is a list of the names and initials of people whose results are presented in the various chapters.

Introduction

The author owes profound thanks to Aaltje (Anne) Dankbaar (A.D.) who took part in many experiments during the 1980s, 1990s, and early 2000s, some of which led to the best results obtained by the author.

Many thanks are also owing to Dani Morena (D.M.) for her participation in a considerable number of tests during the 1990s, some of which yielded excellent results as well.

The author is greatly indebted to a group of four ladies who jointly took part in numerous experiments during the 1980s and early 1990s, namely: Gladys Brown (G.B.), Pat Beck (P.B.), Mary Barnard (M.B.), and Maurine Spinks (M.S.).

The extensive participation of Ray Dodson (R.D.) in a large number of experiments is gratefully acknowledged, which substantially contributed to the overall work program.

Other people to whom the author owes thanks for taking part in experiments, and whose results appear in the text are:

Norman Barber (N.B.), John Bartlett (J.B.), Alex Bulatovas (A.B.), Volkert Dankbaar (V.D.), Ildiko Gulyas (I.G.), Jolanda Karolyi (J.K.), Marie Kernot (M.K.), John Markl (J.M.), Colin Mitchell (C.M.), and Debbie Smith (D.S.).

A further five subjects, whose results appear in Chapter 8, and who are referred to as (J.X.), (K.X.), (L.X), (M.X.), and (N.X.) because they did not offer their surnames for the record, are also thanked for their contributions.

Some experiments involved the application of hypnotic suggestions. The author is thankful for the valuable assistance rendered in such experiments by hypnotherapists Brian Perry and Carla Schadlich.

In some tests the author and his associates acted as subjects, in which case they are referred to by their initials, namely George Karolyi (G.K.), Dorisami Nandagopal (N.D.), and Hugh Wigg (H.W.).

Thanks are also owing to dozens of people who took part in one or more experiments, but whose results have not reached sufficient statistical significance for inclusion in the book, and are referred to in general terms only.

Many thanks are due to Ibolya Viragh for extensive help rendered with numerous routine calculations.

Finally, the author wishes to express great appreciation to Adrienne Twisk and Edwin van Ree for typing the text and drawing many of the diagrams.

Readers are begged to excuse errors in the text, which may have escaped detection during proofreading. It is hoped that few errors would be of scientific nature, but rather word processor errors such as missing, misspelt, or mistaken words.

It is also hoped that some readers would be induced to replicate the work described, leading to further verification of the results presented.

Chapter 1
The Ancients

Humans have long been intrigued by events taking place in their environment, and continually tried to find explanations for the phenomena observed by them. Early in human history, most explanations were based solely on belief. The development of sets of beliefs relating to the origin of the world and humankind, beliefs relating to the causation of various observed phenomena, together with rules for correct and incorrect conduct, led to the birth of the various religions. However, with the passing of time, some observers learnt to distinguish between belief and fact. A systematic search for explanations based on fact marked the beginnings of the scientific approach.

High in importance amongst events observed by humans at the dawn of history were the apparent motions of the sun, the moon, and the stars. As the earth appeared to be both flat and motionless, it was considered to be a flat disk fixed at the centre of the universe. This flat, disk shaped earth was considered to be surrounded by a celestial sphere, on which the sun and the stars were fixed, and which made a complete revolution around the earth once per day. This seemed to explain the movement of the sun and the stars across the sky, and also the alternations of day and night.

However, this early flat earth model failed to explain the movement and the phases of the moon, and also the movements of five starlike objects, which later turned out to be the five planets readily observable by the unaided eye. It also failed to explain why the point of sunrise on the horizon, and also the sun's path in the sky, went through a cyclic variation once per year, that clearly appeared to be connected with seasonal variations. So, here one had an early scientific theory, which in terms of the current state of knowledge is false, but which in its time explained some observed facts, while it left others unanswered. However, false theories can be improved by modifications and additions, so as to enlarge the extent of their validity, or increase the number of observed facts they explain, or do both.

In the 5th century B.C., Anaxagoras noted that while the celestial sphere, presumed to carry the sun and the stars, made one revolution per day around the earth, the moon's appearance went through phases suggesting that it made one revolution around the earth approximately in every 28 days. He proposed that the moon was a dark spherical object visible only by virtue of reflecting the light of the luminous sun, and since only half of the moon could be illuminated by the sun at any one time as the moon circled the earth, different portions of the illuminated half were visible from the earth at different times. Anaxagoras had thus correctly accounted for the phases exhibited by the moon.

This in turn led to an understanding of the eclipses. A solar eclipse would result when the moon came between the sun and the earth, and the moon blocked the sunlight from reaching part of the earth's surface. A lunar eclipse would be the result of the earth coming between the sun and the moon, and so blocking light from reaching part, or all, of the moon's surface.

In the 4th century B.C., Aristotle argued that if the earth were a flat, round disk, then a lunar eclipse around midnight would cast a shadow on the moon which was part of a circle, but a lunar eclipse near sunrise or sunset should cause a shadow on the moon in the form of a narrow, rectangular strip. Since the earth's shadow on the moon was always part of a circle, Aristotle came to the conclusion that the earth, like the moon, had to be spherical.

Chapter 1 – The Ancients

In the 3rd century B.C., Aristarchus noted that when the moon was in its quarter phase, that is, half of the moon was visible from earth, the lines joining the moon to the earth and the moon to the sun had to be perpendicular to each other, or the triangle with the earth, moon, and sun at its apexes must have had a right angle (90°) at the moon. This is shown in Figure 1.1, which is not drawn to scale.

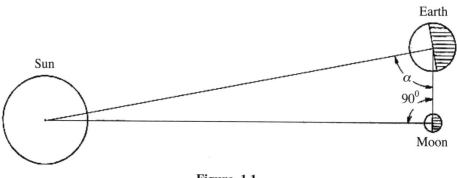

Figure 1.1
(Not to scale)

Aristarchus measured the angle α between the lines joining the earth to the moon and the earth to the sun, and found that this angle was very close to a right angle. Hence, he concluded that the sun was much further away from the earth than the moon was. In fact, from his measurement of this angle, he could estimate the ratio of the distances of the sun and the moon from the earth. Furthermore, since the sun and the moon appeared to be of comparable size in the sky, while the sun was much further away from the earth than the moon was, he could also conclude that the sun had to be much larger than the moon.

Aristarchus also noted that during a lunar eclipse, the moon took nearly three times as long to cross the earth's shadow as it took to move a distance in the sky equal to its own diameter. This indicated that the earth's shadow at the moon, and so the earth itself, had a diameter approximately three times the diameter of the moon. From this, he could estimate the diameters of both the sun and the moon relative to the diameter of the earth, within the accuracy of the rough methods of measurement available to him. The method employed by Aristarchus is illustrated in Figure 1.2, which is not drawn to scale.

With reference to Figure 1.2, the two triangles, having their apexes at the centre of the earth, and their bases equalling the diameters of the sun and the moon respectively, are similar. Consequently, the ratio of the diameters of the sun and the moon, had to equal the ratio of their distances from the earth, that is:

$$\frac{\left(\text{Diameter of the Sun}\right)}{\left(\text{Diameter of the Moon}\right)} = \frac{\left(\text{Distance of the Sun from Earth}\right)}{\left(\text{Distance of the Moon from Earth}\right)}$$

Although Aristarchus' estimates were not accurate, he clearly established that the sun was much larger than the earth, while the earth was considerably larger than the moon. He also correctly deduced that the sun was much further away from the earth than the moon was. His estimates relied on the limited means available to him for the measurement of the angle α in Figure 1.1, which suggested that the above ratio was around 20, as compared with the currently known value close to 400.

Chapter 1 – The Ancients

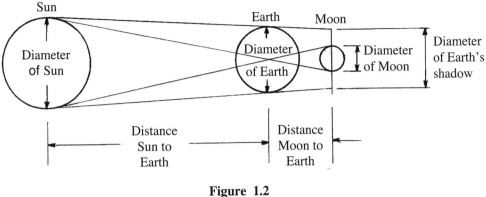

Figure 1.2
(Not to scale)

Then, also in the 3rd century B.C., Eratosthenes measured the circumference of the earth with remarkable accuracy. The method devised by Eratosthenes is depicted in Figure 1.3, which is not drawn to scale.

Eratosthenes noted that on a particular summer's day, the sun at noon was directly overhead at the ancient city of Syene (present day Aswan), as indicated by the rays of the sun penetrating a deep well without the walls of the well casting any shadow. On the same day in Alexandria, 800 kilometres north of Syene, when the sun reached the highest point in the sky, a vertical rod cast a shadow the length of which indicated that the sun's rays made an angle close to 7.2 degrees with the vertical. Since that angle is 1/50 of a full circle of 360 degrees, the polar circumference of the earth would have to be around 50 times 800 kilometres, that is, close to 40,000 kilometres. Eratosthenes' measurement was only 250 kilometres short of the currently accepted value for the polar circumference of the earth, involving an error of less than 1%. The validity of the calculation depended on two by then established facts, namely that the earth was a sphere, not a disk, and that the distance of the sun from the earth was so large that the sun's rays arriving at Syene and Alexandria could be regarded as parallel.

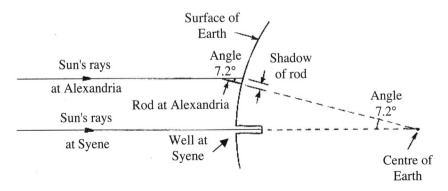

Figure 1.3
(Not to scale)

Chapter 1 – The Ancients

Having determined the circumference of the earth, and also the diameter of the moon as around one-third of the earth's diameter, the ancients were in a position to estimate the diameters of all three: the earth, the moon, and the sun, together with their relative distances from each other. The accurate determination of diameters and actual distances had to await a better understanding of the planetary system, as outlined in Appendix 6.2, and the development of instruments which could measure angles with a high degree of accuracy.

By the 3rd century B.C., observations indicated that, unlike the stars, the planets did not seem to move around the earth at a constant speed. Not only were the planets observed to move relative to the stars, but also occasionally they appeared to make retrograde motions. Aristarchus, and others, suggested placing the sun at the centre of the universe, with the earth and the planets moving around the sun. This would have explained the occasional apparent retrograde movements of the planets.

However, this would also have required an apparent yearly cyclic variation in the relative positions of the stars, as observed from an earth moving around the sun, the same way as an observer moving parallel to the line joining two posts would observe an apparent change in both the relative position of the posts, and the distance between them. This phenomenon is known as parallax, and in fact, the apparent relative positions of the stars are subject to parallax variations. However, the stars are so far away that this effect can only be detected with the aid of a telescope, which the ancients did not possess.

Nevertheless, the ancients had gone a long way. They deduced that the earth, the moon, and the sun were all spherical bodies, they determined the approximate sizes of these bodies, and also their relative distances from each other. So they showed that the notion of a flat earth with a revolving celestial sphere around it, to which the sun and the stars were fixed, could not hold. Yet, the vast majority of the people hung onto the concept of a flat earth at the centre of the universe, tooth and nail, for another 1800 years.

Religion is often blamed for this stubborn orthodoxy. Many believe that a similar situation could not exist in our modern times. But, in fact, such orthodoxy does still exist. Today's flat earth, for many, is the four-dimensional space-time continuum coming out of the theory of relativity. The problem is that while there are many demonstrably existing phenomena which do not fit into this continuum, most feel that whatever is not detectable with currently existing physical instruments, or that runs contrary to the tenets of currently held scientific principles, cannot possibly exist. Such phenomena have to be hallucinations, or just the imaginations of feeble minds.

The ancients could not detect the apparent cyclic motions of the stars relative to each other for the lack of a telescope, and wrongly concluded that the earth had to be the centre of the universe after all. Likewise today, the existing knowledge and instruments are insufficient to deal with many currently unexplainable phenomena, but this does not necessarily mean that such phenomena are nonexistent as so many assert. Subsequent chapters will argue that there is much beyond the presently known physical universe, and that the universe as currently perceived, is today's equivalent of the flat earth principle so firmly accepted in times gone by.

Chapter 2
Fields and Particles

Electric Fields

The ancient Greeks noticed, around 600 B.C., that when amber was rubbed with a piece of suitable cloth, it acquired the ability to attract small bits of matter. Objects acquiring this ability through rubbing are said to be electrified, or electrically charged. The term "electric" is derived from the Greek name for amber, namely "elektron".

In the course of time, two kinds of electrification became apparent. Two hollow glass beads electrified by rubbing with a silk cloth, and then hanged side by side with pieces of thread, were observed to repel each other. Hollow beads were used in order to make them light, so as to reduce gravitational effects on them that could mask the effects of the electrification. Again, hollow beads of hard rubber, or vulcanite, when electrified by rubbing with flannel cloth, and then suspended next to each other, were also found to repel each other. However, an electrified glass bead and an electrified vulcanite bead, suspended side by side, were observed to attract each other. This implied the existence of two kinds of electricity.

It came to be believed that electrification was due to invisibly small particles carrying "electrical charge", which were transferred from one substance to another during the electrification process. Arbitrarily, the proposition was accepted that as a result of such particle transfer, electrified glass became positively charged, while electrified vulcanite acquired negative charge. It follows from the above, that like charges, either both positive or both negative, repel each other, while unlike charges, one positive and the other negative, attract each other.

Toward the end of the 19th century it became apparent that the idea of electrification being due to particle transfer was indeed correct, and that the electrified vulcanite gained an excess of particles, while the electrified glass lost some of the same type of particles. Since by then the idea that as a result of electrification, glass became positively charged and vulcanite acquired negative charge, became firmly accepted, the transferred particles had to be regarded negatively charged. These negatively charged particles were eventually given the name "electron". Thus a negatively charged body has an excess of electrons, while a positively charged body has an electron deficiency. The discovery of the electron will be considered later in this chapter.

Only relatively small amounts of electric charge can be produced by friction, that is, by rubbing suitable surfaces with a piece of cloth, or a brush. Larger quantities of electrical charge may be obtained continually from "electric cells", or "batteries". The first electric cell was devised by Alessandro Volta in 1800. It consisted of a copper and a zinc plate with blotting paper soaked in sodium chloride (culinary salt) solution sandwiched between the plates. The copper and zinc plates were found to be continual sources of positive and negative charges respectively. It was also found that the effectiveness of the cell could be enhanced by constructing a voltaic battery consisting of a number of alternate copper and zinc plates, with blotting paper soaked in sodium chloride solution between adjacent plates. The copper and zinc plates could also be referred to as the positive and negative plates, while the outermost copper and zinc plates, being sources of positive and negative electric charges respectively, would be called the positive and negative terminals of the battery.

Chapter 2 – Fields and Particles

Now let a pair of flat metallic plates be mounted parallel to each other with air between them, as shown in Figure 2.1, and let the positive and negative terminals of a battery be connected to the left-hand and right-hand plates respectively, by means of metallic wires. The long and short lines depicting the battery in Figure 2.1 stand for the alternate positive and negative plates of the battery.

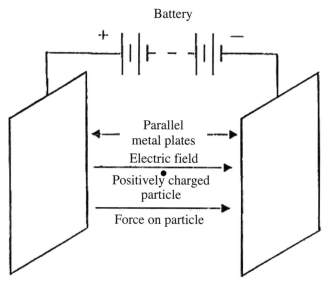

Figure 2.1

It is found that a small suspended glass bead carrying a positive charge is repulsed by the left-hand plate, and is attracted toward the right-hand plate. The left-hand and right-hand plates must therefore carry positive and negative charges respectively, which are transferred to them from the battery through the connecting metallic wires.

The charges on the two plates persist after disconnecting the battery from them, as can be verified by the presence of attraction or repulsion between small electrified objects and either of the plates. However, if after the removal of the battery, the plates are connected together by means of a length of metallic wire, the charges are found to vanish from the plates. This is shown by any attraction or repulsion between small charged bodies and the plates ceasing. So, it appears that the metallic wire enables charges to flow from one plate to the other, allowing the charges to reach and annihilate each other.

However, if after disconnecting the battery from the plates, the latter are connected together by means of a piece of dry string, the charges on the plates will be found preserved, which shows that the string does not allow charge transfer between the plates.

Materials that allow electrical charges to flow through them are called "conductors". Most metals are conductors. Conversely, materials that do not allow charge flow are called "insulators". For instance, while glass and vulcanite allow bound charges to be produced on their surfaces by rubbing them with a suitable cloth, they do not let such charges to flow through them, and are therefore insulators. Other insulators are dry wood, plastic, rubber,

Chapter 2 – Fields and Particles

and air. Nevertheless, under abnormal conditions, some insulators may break down and conduct electrical charge. For example, some insulators may break down when wet.

Since the first voltaic cell, many other more practicable cells were devised. The most often met ones nowadays are perhaps the "dry cell", the "alkaline cell" and the "lead acid cell", all of which may be series connected to form batteries.

It is also found that, different batteries connected to a pair of parallel metal plates some fixed distance apart, cause different amounts of charge to be placed on the plates. This is indicated by the force on a small charged body, suspended in some fixed position between the plates, changing when batteries are swapped, as indicated by a change in the deflection of the suspended charged body. In particular, two cells of the same type connected in series, constituting a two-cell battery, cause the force, and expectably also the charge, to double.

The ability of the cells to charge a pair of metallic plates is due to chemical processes within the cells, which cause positive and negative charges to be propelled to the positive and negative terminals of the cell respectively. This ability is designated by different names: "electromotive force", "potential difference", or just simply as "voltage". The magnitude of the voltage produced by a battery of cells depends on the chemical nature of the cells, and is proportional to the number of cells in series within the battery.

Considerations involving electrical quantities, such as voltage and charge, necessitate the establishment of units, in terms of which these quantities can be measured. Normally, some units are arbitrarily chosen, and from those the others follow. It is necessary to establish mechanical units first, and then build on these a consistent set of electrical units.

It could be helpful to read this chapter in conjunction with the discourse on often met rules and units listed in Appendices 2.1 and 2.2. When dealing with mechanical considerations, as discussed in Appendix 2.2, the units of length, mass, and time, are arbitrarily chosen to be the metre, the kilogram, and the second, respectively. From these, the units of other mechanical quantities follow, namely the units of velocity, acceleration, force, pressure, work, energy, and power.

When devising electrical units, one may choose either the unit of charge, or the unit of voltage arbitrarily. The rest of the electrical units then derive from mechanical units. In the following the unit of voltage is considered chosen arbitrarily, and is given the name "volt". A voltage of 1 volt may be based on the voltage produced by a particular cell, known as the Weston standard cell. However, for historical reasons, the currently accepted precise value of the voltage of this cell is not exactly 1 volt, but rather it is 1.0183 volts.

In the vicinity of an electrically charged body, where another charged body experiences a force of attraction or repulsion, an "electric field" is said to exist. If a small suspended electrically charged body is moved around in an electric field, it is normally found that the force acting on it varies in both magnitude and direction, as indicated by the size and the direction of the deflection of the suspended body. This shows that, in general, the electric field is a variable quantity, having both a definite magnitude and a definite direction at any point in the field, either or both of which may vary from point to point. The direction of the field is taken as that of the force acting on a small positively charged body. It follows from the foregoing that an electric field exists between a pair of parallel charged metallic plates.

Chapter 2 – Fields and Particles

Now let a pair of parallel metallic plates be mounted in air, and connected to the terminals of a battery as shown in Figure 2.1. Any mechanical support keeping the plates in place must be made of insulators. Investigations show that the force, acting on a small positively charged body between the plates, is constant in both magnitude and direction, regardless of the position of the small charged body between the plates, as long as the distance between the plates is small compared with the lengths of the edges of the plates, and the charged body between the plates is situated well away from the edges. Further, the direction of the force is perpendicular to both plates, and is directed from the positively charged plate to the negatively charged plate at all points between the plates well away from the edges.

This implies that the electric field between the plates, well away from the edges, is uniform, namely it is constant in both magnitude and direction, the direction being perpendicular to both plates, pointing from the positively charged plate toward the negatively charged plate.

If now the distance between the plates, that is, the plate separation, is doubled at a given battery voltage, one finds that the magnitude of the force on a small charged body is halved, and so is also the magnitude of the electric field. However, doubling the applied battery voltage at the new plate separation will restore the force, and thus also the electric field, to their original values. In general, the electric field, and also the force, will remain constant irrespective of changes in applied voltage and plate separation as long as the ratio of these two remains the same, or to put it differently, as long as the applied voltage per metre of plate separation remains unchanged. This suggests that the electric field is to be measured in terms of the applied volts per metre of plate separation, or simply in "volts per metre". So, if the plates have 10 volts applied to them, and their separation is 10 centimetres, or 0.1 metre, the electric field between the plates will be $(10)/(0.1) = 100$ volts per metre.

Next, it is necessary to find the unit in which the electric charge is to be measured. This requires the consideration of the unit of force. Again, with reference to Appendix 2.2, the unit of force is the "newton". A force of 1 newton is that force which when applied to a 1 kilogram mass that is free to move, causes the velocity of that mass to change by 1 metre per second in each second in the direction of the force, which direction is not necessarily the same as the direction of the velocity. Thus, 1 newton force causes a mass of 1 kilogram to accelerate at 1 metre per second per second in the direction of the force. In general:

(force acting on a mass, that is free to move in the direction of the force, in newtons)
= (mass in kilograms) x (acceleration in metres per second per second)

A readily observable force is the downward force of gravity at the surface of the earth. The velocity of a mass dropped from a tower is found to increase by 9.81 metres per second in each second, and so its downward acceleration is 9.81 metres per second per second. If the mass is 3 kilograms, the gravitational force acting on it is $(3) \times (9.81) = 29.43$ newtons.

Returning to the charged parallel plates, let the electric field between the plates be adjusted to 1 volt per metre, and let the charge on a body between the plates be so chosen that the force acting on it is 1 newton. Then, the magnitude of this charge is 1 "coulomb", which is the name given to the unit of electric charge. The coulomb is a rather large unit. A pair of coin sized parallel metallic plates, a few millimetres apart, when charged from a battery of a few volts, would carry a charge on each plate that is a tiny fraction of 1 coulomb.

Chapter 2 – Fields and Particles

The magnitude of the force acting on a charged body in an electric field is found to equal the magnitude of the charge multiplied by the magnitude of the electric field. In general:

(force acting on a charged body in an electric field, in newtons)
= (charge in coulombs) x (electric field in volts per metre)

The direction of this force is the same as that of the electric field.

So, a body carrying a charge of 0.1 coulomb, situated in an electric field of 100 volts per metre, would experience a force of (0.1 coulomb) x (100 volts per metre) = 10 newtons.

With reference to Appendix 2.2, when moving a body requires a force to be applied, or a force to be overcome, "work" needs to be done, or what is the same, energy needs to be expended. The work done equals the applied force times the distance moved in the direction of the force. If the force is 1 newton, and the distance moved is 1 metre, then the work done is 1 "joule", which is the name given to the unit of work, or energy. In general:

(work done, or energy expended, or gained, in joules)
= (force applied in newtons) x (distance moved, in the direction of the force, in metres)

If work is done in moving a body of a given mass, by overcoming an opposing force acting on it, without any energy loss due to friction, then the work done is converted into "potential energy". When the body is allowed to return freely to its original position owing to the same force acting on it, it will acquire velocity, and the potential energy will be converted into an equal amount of "kinetic energy" which, as shown in Appendix 2.2, is given by:

(kinetic energy in joules)
$= \left(\dfrac{1}{2}\right)$ x $\left(\begin{array}{c}\text{mass of object} \\ \text{in kilograms}\end{array}\right)$ x $\left(\begin{array}{c}\text{magnitude of velocity} \\ \text{in metres per second}\end{array}\right)$ x $\left(\begin{array}{c}\text{magnitude of velocity} \\ \text{in metres per second}\end{array}\right)$

Power is the rate at which work is done. Thus, if 1 joule of work is done every second, then the power developed is 1 joule per second, or 1 "watt", which is the name given to the unit of power. In general one has:

(power in watts)
= (work done in joules) / (time in which work is done in seconds)

The above is best understood by an example involving gravitation. With reference to the foregoing example, the vertical downward gravitational acceleration at the surface of the earth is 9.81 metres per second per second. The corresponding downward force acting on a 3 kilogram mass is thus (3) x (9.81) = 29.43 newtons. If this mass is raised 2 metres against the downward force acting on it, the work done, and the potential energy gained, is (29.43) x (2) = 58.86 joules. Upon allowing the 3 kilogram mass to fall freely through 2 metres back to its original position, its kinetic energy will thus be 58.86 joules. The magnitude of the velocity of the 3 kilogram mass, after falling through 2 metres, would equal 6.264 metres per second, since from the above expression for the kinetic energy one has: 58.86 = (1/2) x (3) x (6.264) x (6.264). Also, if the 3 kilogram mass is raised 2 metres every second, then the power developed is 58.86 joules per second, or 58.86 watts.

Likewise, when a charged body is moved some distance in an electric field in opposition to the electric field force, work is done that equals the force times the distance moved. This work is converted into potential energy, which may be reconverted into an equal amount

Chapter 2 – Fields and Particles

of kinetic energy if the charged body is allowed to move back freely to its original position under the action of the electric field force.

It is to be noted that when a body carrying 1 coulomb charge is moved 1 metre in an electric field of 1 volt per metre against the 1 newton force acting on it, it is moved through a potential difference of 1 volt. Thus, in general, the following holds:

(work done, or energy expended or gained, in joules)
= (force acting on charged body in newtons) x (distance moved against force in metres)
= (charge in coulombs) x (electric field in volts per metre) x (distance moved in metres)
= (charge in coulombs) x (voltage through which charge is moved in volts)

Returning to the previous example, a body carrying a 0.1 coulomb charge, located in a 100 volt per metre electric field, experiences a force of (0.1) x (100) = 10 newtons in the direction of the electric field. If the charged body is moved 0.5 metre against this force, the work done is (10) x (0.5) = 5 joules. This equals the potential energy gained by the charged body. If the charged body is allowed to move back freely to its original position under the action of the electric field force, it will do so with increasing velocity dependent on its mass. When back at the original position, the kinetic energy of the charged body will be 5 joules. If the mass of the charged body is 3 kilograms, its speed upon reaching its original position, from the above expression for the kinetic energy, will be 1.826 metres per second, since: 5 = (1/2) x (3) x (1.826) x (1.826).

Furthermore, if in the above example, 5 joules of work is done every second, then power is developed, or expended, at a rate of 5 joules per second, or 5 watts.

The electric field set up between a pair of electrically charged parallel metallic plates constitutes a special case. All electrically charged bodies produce electric fields around them that can be represented by directed lines of force. Electric field lines of force are lines that a small positively charged body would follow if it were free to move. The direction of the line is the direction of the movement of this positively charged body. Electric field lines always start on a positive charge and end on a negative charge. In the case of a pair of charged parallel plates, the electric field lines start on the positively charged plate, and end on the negatively charged plate. The lines are perpendicular to both plates and are directed from the positive plate toward the negative plate. This is true only between the plates, and well away from the edges of the plates. Near the edges of the plates the lines bulge outward which is referred to as fringing.

Now let the ends of a piece of relatively long and thin metallic wire be connected between the positive and negative terminals of a battery as shown in Figure 2.2, where the zigzag line stands for the wire. It is then found that a continual flow of charge results between the battery terminals through the wire. This would be expected from the fact that like charges repel, while unlike charges attract each other. Consequently, if both positive and negative charges were involved, then positive charges would be forced into the wire at the positive terminal, and removed at the negative terminal. Likewise, negative charges would be forced into the wire at the negative terminal and extracted at the positive terminal. Alternatively, the cause of the charge flow could be attributed to an electric field set up inside the wire, parallel to the axis of the wire, and having a magnitude equal to the battery voltage divided by the length of the wire. A continuous flow of charge is called an "electric current".

Chapter 2 – Fields and Particles

Prior to the discovery of the electron, it was assumed that positively charged particles were moving from the positive battery terminal, through the wire, to the negative battery terminal, as indicated by arrows in Figure 2.2. This direction is taken as the reference direction of the current even today, in spite of the currently known fact that actually negatively charged electrons flow in the wire in the opposite direction.

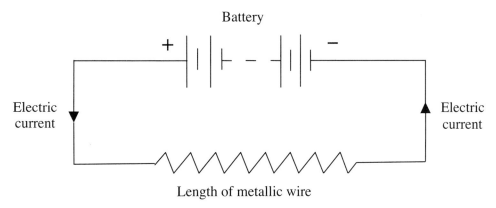

Figure 2.2

It is found that the electric current flow from a given battery diminishes as the wire is made longer, or thinner, or both. The wire thus offers a "resistance" to the current flow. This resistance increases with the length of the wire, and it also increases as the sectional area of the wire diminishes. The resistance also depends on the type of metal used, for example copper offers less resistance to electric currents than iron does. A length of metallic wire is often simply referred to as a conductor.

Let the applied voltage be chosen as 1 volt, and let the resistance of the wire be adjusted so that the charge flowing past any cross section of the wire is 1 coulomb in each second. Then, the corresponding current is 1 "ampere", and the resistance of the conducting wire is 1 "ohm", the ampere and the ohm being the names given to the unit of the electric current and the unit of the resistance respectively. In general, the current in a conductor equals the voltage applied between its ends, divided by the resistance of the conductor, that is:

(electric current in amperes) = (applied voltage in volts) / (resistance in ohms)

Thus, if the applied voltage is 10 volts, and the resistance is 5 ohms, then the resulting current will be (10 volts) / (5 ohms) = 2 amperes.

A current of 1 ampere flowing in a conductor with a voltage of 1 volt applied between its ends, is tantamount to 1 coulomb charge moving through a voltage difference of 1 volt every second. So, in terms of the above said, 1 joule of work is done in moving the charge through the conductor every second, amounting to power expended at a rate of 1 watt. In general, the applied voltage and the resulting current could have any values, and the power taken from the battery, and expended in the wire, would be proportional to both, or what is the same, the power would equal the product of the voltage in volts and the current in amperes, giving the power in joules per second, or watts. A battery is just one voltage source in a range of possible voltage sources. In general, the following relation holds:

Chapter 2 – Fields and Particles

(power transferred from a voltage source to a resistance in watts)

$$= \left(\begin{array}{c} \text{voltage developed by} \\ \text{voltage source in volts} \end{array} \right) \times \left(\begin{array}{c} \text{current drawn from} \\ \text{voltage source in amperes} \end{array} \right)$$

An electric current flowing in a conductor causes it to heat up. Heat is due to the basic units of matter, called the atoms, being in a continuous state of vibration. The higher is the temperature, the more violent these vibrations are. The moving electrons, constituting an electric current, collide with the atoms in the conducting wire, and cause them to vibrate more violently, which manifests itself as a rise in the temperature of the conductor. The electrical energy expended in the conductor is thus converted into heat energy this way.

Magnetic Fields

Certain solid bodies have the property of attracting small pieces of iron. In particular, near a place called Magnesia, in Asia Minor, a mineral was found that exhibited such properties. The mineral was named magnetite, from which the terms magnet and magnetic derive. Chemically, magnetite is an oxide of iron.

A soft iron bar can be magnetised by stroking it with a piece of magnetite, and so a bar magnet may be produced. The property of a bar magnet to attract small iron particles is strongest near the ends of the bar, which are termed the poles of the magnet.

When a bar magnet is suspended by a piece of string attached to its middle, so that the bar can swing freely in a horizontal plane, it will align itself approximately in the geographic north-south direction. The end of the bar magnet pointing north is called its north pole, and conversely the other end pointing south is referred to as its south pole.

Bringing the poles of two suspended bar magnets close to one another shows that like poles, either both north or both south, repel each other, while unlike poles, one north and the other south, attract each other.

The earth itself is a giant magnet with its magnetic south pole situated near the geographic North Pole, while its magnetic north pole is close to the geographic South Pole. A compass needle is essentially a small bar magnet, pivoted in the middle, so that it can turn in a horizontal plane. Such a needle aligns itself approximately in the geographic north-south direction since the needle's magnetic north and south poles are attracted toward the earth's magnetic south and north poles respectively.

Wherever a compass needle experiences a force causing it to align itself in a particular direction, a "magnetic field" is said to exist. The magnetic field, like the electric field, is a variable quantity in general, having both a definite magnitude and a definite direction at any point in the field, either or both of which may vary from point to point. The north pole of the compass needle points in the direction of the force acting on it, which by definition is taken to be the direction of the magnetic field, while the magnitude of the force is a measure of the magnitude of the field.

A strong bar magnet produces a magnetic field of its own, that in the vicinity of the magnet may have a magnitude many times that of the magnetic field produced by the earth. A

Chapter 2 – Fields and Particles

compass needle, at any point in the proximity of such a magnet, will align itself so as to indicate the direction of the field produced by the bar magnet at that point. The speed with which the needle aligns itself, when moved to a particular position, is a rough indication of the field's magnitude at that point. If the compass needle is moved around in the field of the magnet, it will be found that both the magnitude and the direction of the field vary from point to point.

While a stationary electrically charged body is acted on by a force in an electric field, the same charged body experiences no force in a magnetic field. If however, an electrically charged body is moving in a magnetic field with some velocity, a force is found to act on it. The magnitude of the force is proportional to the product of the magnitudes of all three: the charge, the velocity, and the magnetic field, while the direction of the force is perpendicular to the directions of both: the velocity of the charged body, and the magnetic field in which the body moves.

In the special case when the direction of the velocity with which the charged body moves is perpendicular to the direction of the magnetic field in which it is moving, the magnitude of the force acting on the moving charged body is found to be a maximum for a given product of the magnitudes of the three quantities: the charge, the velocity, and the magnetic field.

With reference to Figure 2.3, let a positively charged body be moving horizontally in the plane of the paper toward the right at constant velocity, while it is situated in a uniform magnetic field directed vertically downward. The charged body will then be acted on by a force that is perpendicular to the plane of the paper and is directed into it.

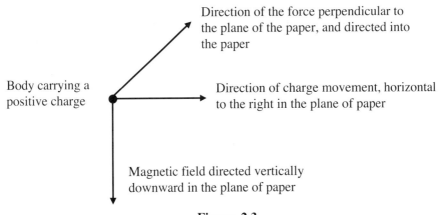

Figure 2.3

The above leads to the unit indicated for measuring the magnitudes of magnetic fields. In Figure 2.3, let the body carry 1 coulomb positive charge, and move horizontally in the plane of the paper toward the right with a velocity of 1 metre per second, while it is situated in a uniform magnetic field directed vertically downward in the plane of the paper.

Let the magnitude of the magnetic field be so adjusted that the force acting on the moving charged body is 1 newton, then the magnetic field has a magnitude of 1 "tesla", which is the name given to the unit used for measuring the magnitudes of magnetic fields.

Chapter 2 – Fields and Particles

When a charged body moves in a direction that is perpendicular to the direction of the magnetic field, then the following holds for the force acting on the charged body in general:

(magnitude of force in newtons)
= (magnitude of charge in coulombs) × (magnitude of velocity in metres per second) × (magnitude of magnetic field in teslas)

The direction of the force is perpendicular to both: the direction of the motion, and the direction of the field, as shown in Figure 2.3. If the charge is negative, or if either the direction of the motion or that of the field is reversed, so is the direction of the force.

An electric current flow in a metallic conductor represents electric charges moving in the conductor, and so a current carrying conductor located in a magnetic field is also subject to a force that depends on all four: the magnitude of the current, the length of the conductor, and the magnitude and the direction of the magnetic field.

With reference to Figure 2.4, let a length of metallic wire, forming a horizontal straight conductor in the plane of the paper, be connected across a battery so as to cause a current flowing toward the right, and let this conductor be situated in a uniform magnetic field directed vertically downward in the plane of the paper. A force will then be acting on the conductor perpendicular to the plane of the paper, and directed into it. If either the direction of the current, or the direction of the field, is reversed, so is the direction of the force.

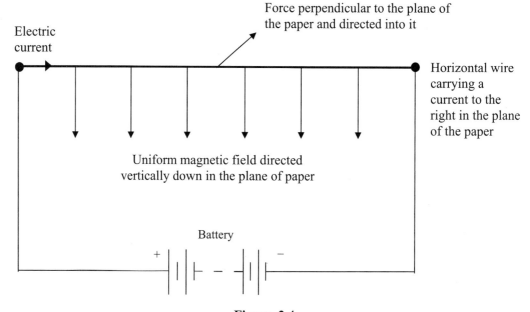

Figure 2.4

The magnitude of the force acting on the current carrying conductor above is given by:

(magnitude of force in newtons)
= (electric current in amperes) × (length of conductor in metres) × (magnitude of magnetic field in teslas)

Chapter 2 – Fields and Particles

This leads to an alternative way of deducing the unit for the magnitudes of magnetic fields.

If in Figure 2.4, the length of the conductor is 1 metre, while the current in the conductor is 1 ampere, and the magnitude of the magnetic field is so set that the force acting on the current carrying conductor is 1 newton, then the magnetic field once more has a magnitude of 1 tesla. The direction of the force on the conductor is perpendicular to the plane of the paper and is directed into it.

If in the above two cases, depicted in Figures 2.3 and 2.4, both the force and the magnetic field are the same, then the following must hold true:

(magnitude of charge in coulombs) x (magnitude of velocity in metres per second)
= (electric current in amperes) x (length of conductor in metres)

Theoretical considerations described further on in this chapter enable this relationship to be verified, as done in Appendix 2.5. As shown in Appendix 2.5, if a copper conductor is 1 metre long, has a cross sectional area of 1 square millimetre, and carries a current of 1 ampere, then the moving charge contained within the 1 metre of the conductor is 13,600 coulombs, moving with an average speed of 1/13,600 metres per second. In this particular case, both sides of the above equation equal unity.

Production of Magnetic Fields by Electric Currents

A compass needle placed close to a straight conductor carrying a steady electrical current is permanently deflected. This shows the presence of a magnetic field near the current. Mapping the field with the help of a compass needle indicates that lines along which the magnitude of the magnetic field is constant are concentric circles situated in planes which are perpendicular to the conductor, and that the centres of these circles are located on the middle line of the conductor. The magnitude of the field falls off with increasing distance from the conductor. The direction of the field is clockwise around the conductor if the latter is so viewed that the current appears to flow away from the observer.

Now let the wire be bent into the form of a plane circular loop, or alternatively let a plane circular coil be wound from the wire. In either case, let a steady current be passed through the wire forming the loop, or the coil. A compass needle placed at various points in the plane of the coil is found to align itself perpendicular to the plane of the coil at all points. This indicates that the current in the coil sets up a magnetic field, which in the plane of the coil is perpendicular to that plane everywhere.

The direction of the magnetic field is such that an observer situated on that side of the coil where the current in the coil appears to be clockwise, would see the field directed into the plane of the coil.

The magnitude of the field may be measured or calculated. As an example, a coil used for biofeedback purposes as described in Chapter 10, is wound with 1000 turns and has an average diameter of 40 centimetres. If the current passed into this coil is 1 ampere, the magnitude of the magnetic field at the centre of the coil is found to be about 3×10^{-3} tesla = 3 milliteslas. A magnetic field of 1 tesla is a rather large field, not often met in practice.

Chapter 2 – Fields and Particles

If by using a compass needle, or otherwise, one maps the magnetic field of a bar magnet, and also the magnetic field of a coil in which the current was suitably adjusted, one finds that at distances far enough from the magnet or the coil, the magnetic fields relative to the axes of the magnet and that of the coil are identical everywhere. This suggests that the magnetic field of a bar magnet originates from current loops, formed by circulating charges inside the magnet, in planes which are perpendicular to the axis of the magnet.

The magnetic field produced by a given current in a coil can be greatly increased by placing a soft iron bar inside the coil, and thereby converting it into an electromagnet. The increase in the field results from circulating currents produced in the soft iron bar.

The magnetic fields set up by electric currents in straight conductors, or in coils, constitute particular cases. In general, all electric currents produce magnetic fields which may be represented by directed lines of force. The directed magnetic field lines of force may be determined with the aid of a compass needle as described above, or as directed lines that a small magnetic north pole would follow, if it could exist by itself in separation from a south pole, and if it were free to move. Magnetic field lines always form closed paths. For instance, as stated above, in the case of a straight current carrying conductor, the magnetic field lines are circles, in planes perpendicular to the conductor, having centres on the centre line of the conductor. The directions of the magnetic field lines encircling the conductor are clockwise if so viewed that the current appears to flow away from the observer.

Also, as discussed above, a current carrying conductor, situated in a magnetic field, is acted on by a force. If the conductor is not physically restrained, it will move in the direction of that force.

Conversely, it is perhaps not surprising to find that a conductor, which is caused to move in a magnetic field, has a voltage induced in it. Normally, it is arranged that the conductor, the direction of the motion, and the magnetic field, are mutually perpendicular to each other. In Figure 2.5 the conductor is horizontal in the plane of the paper, the magnetic field is directed vertically downward in the plane of the paper, while the motion of the conductor is perpendicular to the plane of the paper and directed into it.

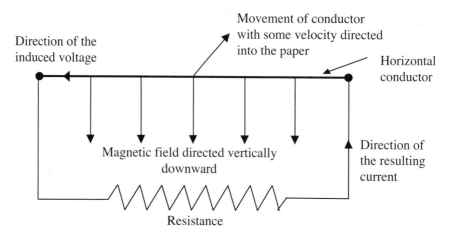

Figure 2.5

Chapter 2 – Fields and Particles

The induced voltage in the conductor is then directed toward the left, and its magnitude is found to be given by:

$$(\text{induced voltage in volts}) = \left(\begin{array}{c}\text{length of conductor}\\ \text{in metres}\end{array}\right) \times \left(\begin{array}{c}\text{magnitude of velocity}\\ \text{in metres per second}\end{array}\right) \times \left(\begin{array}{c}\text{magnitude of magnetic}\\ \text{field in teslas}\end{array}\right)$$

A resistance connected to the ends of the moving conductor, as shown in Figure 2.5, forms a conducting loop around which the induced voltage drives an electric current in an anticlockwise direction. The magnitude of the current equals the magnitude of the voltage divided by the resistance of the conducting loop. Since this current is situated in a magnetic field, then in view of Figure 2.4, a force will act on it directed out of the paper. This force must be overcome so as to make the conductor move in a direction into the paper.

Furthermore, it is now necessary to reconsider the situation depicted in Figure 2.4. If the conductor in Figure 2.4 is allowed to be moved by the force acting on it, then in view of Figure 2.5, a voltage must be induced in the conductor acting toward the left, and so opposing the current flow. The battery voltage must then overcome both: the resistance of the conducting loop, and the opposing induced voltage.

The above principles are utilised in electric generators and motors, both of which involve relative motion between magnetic fields and current carrying conductors acted on by forces, where all three: field, conductor, and force are arranged to be mutually perpendicular.

In generators, mechanical forces are applied to current carrying conductors so as to make them move in magnetic fields, which require the application of mechanical energy. The voltages induced in the conductors drive the currents in the circuits connected to them, and thereby produce electrical energy. Batteries can supply only small amounts of electrical energy. Large amounts of electrical energy are obtainable from electrical generators only.

In motors, the conductors draw electric currents from a voltage source, and so take electrical energy from the voltage source. At the same time, the forces acting on the current carrying conductors, due to being situated in magnetic fields, set the conductors into motion, and so produce mechanical energy.

Some electric meters used for measuring current, voltage, or electrical power, also utilise the forces acting on current carrying conductors in magnetic fields.

The Discovery of the Electron

In the late 1800s, it was found that electric currents could flow not only in metallic conductors, but also in evacuated space. This may be shown by means of an apparatus consisting of two metallic plates, called electrodes, sealed into a glass tube at the opposite ends of the tube, with metallic connections to the plates passing through the glass. Air may then be evacuated from the tube to a high degree of vacuum. If the electrodes are then connected to the terminals of a battery, or any other steady voltage source, producing a high enough voltage, an electric current is found to flow between the battery terminals, and also between the electrodes through the partially evacuated space inside the glass tube. The electrode connected to the positive terminal of the battery is called the anode, and that connected to the negative battery terminal is referred to as the cathode.

In 1897, Joseph Thomson devised an apparatus that showed that the electric current in evacuated space was carried by negatively charged particles having a finite mass, and a definite charge to mass ratio. Referring to Figure 2.6, the apparatus consisted of a glass tube with various electrodes sealed into it, and evacuated to a high degree of vacuum.

With a voltage V_1 applied between the anode A and the cathode C, making the anode positive relative to the cathode, any negatively charged particles emitted from the cathode were accelerated to the anode. Some of these particles would pass through the holes in the anode A and the baffle B, both holes being situated on the tube axis. The holes served to create a narrow beam of particles travelling at a constant velocity from the baffle B to the far end of the tube, where they caused a fluorescent spot at point P_1. The beam passed between a pair of horizontal plates. If a voltage V_2 was applied to these plates, making the bottom plate positive relative to the top plate, thereby creating an electric field directed vertically upward, the fluorescent spot at the end of the tube was found to move downward from position P_1 to position P_2. The particles in the beam being deflected downward toward the positive plate indicated that they must have been negatively charged.

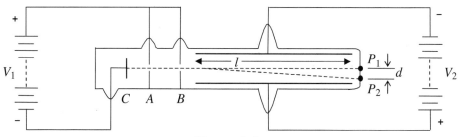

Figure 2.6

Also, two coils were placed on the two sides of the tube, not shown in Figure 2.6, one coil in front of the paper and the other behind it, with the plane of the coils parallel to the plane of the paper. The coils were so connected that the same steady electric current passing in both produced a magnetic field perpendicular to the paper, and also perpendicular to the electric field set up by the horizontal plates inside the tube. As the direction of the force, acting on a moving charge in a magnetic field, is perpendicular to both the directions of the motion and that of the magnetic field, the force could be arranged to act vertically upward through the appropriate choice of the direction of the current in the coils, and so to act in opposition to the force due to the electric field. By the correct choice of voltage V_2, and the current in the coils, the two forces could be made equal and opposite, and thereby cancel each other, which would be indicated by the fluorescent spot returning to point P_1.

Since the magnitude of the magnetic force, as given by the product of the magnitudes of the velocity, charge, and magnetic field, had to equal the magnitude of the electric force given by the product of the magnitudes of the charge and the electric field, it followed that the velocity of the particles had to equal the ratio of the magnitudes of the electric and magnetic fields. Then, from knowing the velocity of the particles, the length of the horizontal plates, and the size of the deflection of the fluorescent spot from P_1 to P_2 with the electric field acting alone, the ratio of the charge to mass of the negative particles could be deduced.

Chapter 2 – Fields and Particles

These negatively charged particles were given the name "electron". As shown in Appendix 2.3, if the electric field and the magnetic field are chosen as 1000 volts per metre and 0.0001 tesla respectively, then the speed of the electrons between the horizontal plates is expected to be:

(speed of electrons in metres per second)
= (electric field in volts per metre) / (magnetic field in teslas)
= (1000 volts per metre) / (0.0001 tesla) = 10,000,000 = 10^7 metres per second.

If the electric field of 1000 volts per metre is applied alone, and the horizontal plates are 20 centimetres = 0.2 metre long, while the distance from P_1 to P_2 = 3.52 centimetres = 0.0352 metre, then as shown in Appendix 2.3, one has:

(electronic charge in coulombs) / (electronic mass in kilograms)

$$= (2) \times \left(\frac{\text{distance } P_1 \text{ to } P_2 \text{ in metres}}{\text{electric field in volts per metre}} \right) \times \left(\frac{\text{electron speed in metres per second}}{\text{length of plates in metres}} \right) \times \left(\frac{\text{electron speed in metres per second}}{\text{length of plates in metres}} \right)$$

= (2) x (0.0352 / 1000) x (10^7/ 0.2) x (10^7/ 0.2) = 1.76 x 10^{11} coulombs per kilogram.

Thus, the Thomson experiment demonstrated that the electric current was carried by small negatively charged particles, eventually given the name electron, which carried a definite amount of charge and possessed a definite amount of mass.

With reference to Appendix 2.4, the value of the mass of the electron was determined in 1909 by Robert Millikan. The method was based on the fact that a negatively charged droplet of oil, situated in a vertically downward directed electric field, would experience an upward force, given by the product of the magnitudes of the charge and the electric field. Simultaneously, a downward force would act on the droplet due to gravity, given by the product of the mass of the droplet and the gravitational acceleration. By suitably adjusting the electric field, these two forces could be balanced against each other, in which case the droplet would neither rise, nor fall, but hover. If so, the following had to hold:

(charge on droplet in coulombs) x (electric field in volts per metre)

$$= \left(\begin{array}{c} \text{mass of droplet} \\ \text{in kilograms} \end{array} \right) \times \left(\begin{array}{c} \text{gravitational acceleration} \\ \text{in metres per second per second} \end{array} \right)$$

Hence, the charge on the droplet should be calculable in terms of the electric field, the mass of the droplet, and the gravitational acceleration.

However, the mass of the droplet could not be obtained by direct measurement. An indirect method had to be employed, which involved allowing the droplet to fall freely in air with no electric field applied. After a short period of acceleration, the droplet would fall with a constant terminal velocity, as determined by the viscosity of the air.

Measuring this velocity, and knowing the gravitational acceleration, the density of the oil, and the coefficient of viscosity for the air, enabled the radius of the droplet to be calculated, and so its mass deduced. Once the mass of the droplet was known, the charge on it was calculable as described above.

Since the droplet could carry any number of electrons, the calculated value of the charge would be a multiple of the smallest possible value occurring when the droplet carried one electron only. This smallest possible value would then be the charge of the electron.

With reference to Appendix 2.4, suppose that a droplet was observed to fall in the absence of an electric field with a speed of 10^{-4} metre per second. Its radius would then have to be 0.993×10^{-6} metre, and its mass would be 3.28×10^{-15} kilogram. If it was found that an electric field of 2000 volts per centimetre (200,000 volts per metre) was making this droplet hover, then in view of the above, the charge on it had to be 1.61×10^{-19} coulomb. Many experiments indicated this value as the smallest ever found, and so this value had to be the charge on one electron. The mass of the electron could now be calculated through dividing the value of the electronic charge by the charge to mass ratio found earlier:

$(1.61 \times 10^{-19}) / (1.76 \times 10^{11}) \approx 9.1 \times 10^{-31}$ kilogram.

More precise values deduced from many different experiments are:
Electronic mass = 9.109×10^{-31} kilogram,
Electronic charge = 1.602×10^{-19} coulomb.

The Nature of Matter – Atoms and Molecules

The Thompson and Millikan experiments have shown that physical matter contained small particles, called electrons, which had a definite mass, and carried a definite amount of negative charge. Since matter in its normal state was known to be electrically neutral, it had to contain equal amounts of positive and negative charges. The question then arose, as to how the equal amounts of positive and negative charges were arranged in electrically neutral matter, and also if matter contained constituents that were permanently neutral. It was also of great interest, how the masses of the positive, negative, and neutral constituents of matter compared to each other.

During the 18th and 19th centuries, matter underwent extensive investigations. It was obvious that matter belonged to one of three categories: solid, liquid, and gaseous. It was also clear that solids could be converted to liquids, and liquids to gases or vapours, by the application of heat. Further, it became apparent that some substances could be reduced to two or more constituents, while two or more different substances could be combined into a single substance with properties clearly different from those of its constituents. Substances that could not be broken into constituents were named elements, and those that were combinations of elements were called compounds.

For instance, it was observed that if metallic electrodes were connected to the positive and negative terminals of a battery, in this case called the anode and the cathode respectively, and then were immersed in water to which a small quantity of acid had been added, gaseous substances formed at the electrode surfaces. The gases, when collected and examined, were found to be elementary, that is not decomposable any further into constituents. The gas formed at the anode was called oxygen, and that formed at the cathode was called hydrogen. It was found that when these two gases were mixed together and ignited, an explosion took place, the end product of which was water. Therefore, oxygen and hydrogen had to be the constituent elements of water, which by the above definition had to be a compound.

Chapter 2 – Fields and Particles

Extensive investigations eventually identified 92 naturally occurring elements, which may combine with each other to form many compounds, of the order of a million or more. Some of the more frequently met elements, and the symbols assigned to them, are: Hydrogen (H), Helium (He), Beryllium (Be), Carbon (C), Nitrogen (N), Oxygen (O), Sodium (Na), Aluminium (Al), Silicon (Si), Sulphur (S), Chlorine (Cl), Calcium (Ca), Iron (Fe), Copper (Cu), Zinc (Zn), Silver (Ag), Gold (Au), Mercury (Hg), Lead (Pb), Radium (Ra), and Uranium (U).

It was found that elements combine in definite weight ratios to form compounds. For instance, 1 gram of hydrogen and 8 grams of oxygen combine to form 9 grams of water, while 3 grams of hydrogen and 14 grams of nitrogen form 17 grams of ammonia gas.

In seeking explanations for these definite ratios, it appeared that finite quantities of both the elements and the compounds had to be composed of small fundamental units, which were named "atoms" and "molecules" respectively, and that atoms of the elements combined with each other to form molecules of compounds.

Thus, one might expect that 1 atom of hydrogen combines with 1 atom of oxygen to form 1 water molecule, and since 1 gram of hydrogen combines with 8 grams of oxygen to form 9 grams of water, the oxygen atom would have to be 8 times as heavy as the hydrogen atom. However, it could also be possible for 2 hydrogen atoms to combine with 1 oxygen atom to form 1 water molecule, and since then 2 grams of hydrogen and 16 grams of oxygen form 18 grams of water, in this case the oxygen atom would have to be 16 times as heavy as the hydrogen atom.

To settle this issue, it is helpful to examine in what proportion by volume elementary gases combine to form compounds. For instance, it was found that 2 litres of hydrogen and 1 litre of oxygen combined to form water with no hydrogen or oxygen left over, while 3 litres of hydrogen and 1 litre of nitrogen combined to form ammonia gas with no hydrogen or nitrogen left over, provided that initially all gases had the same pressure and temperature.

In 1811, Amedeo Avogadro suggested that equal volumes of different gases at the same pressure and temperature contained equal numbers of atoms or molecules. This has become known as Avogadro's law, and its validity has been verified by many experiments since.

It then followed from Avogadro's law that 2 atoms of hydrogen must combine with 1 atom of oxygen to form 1 molecule of water, while 3 atoms of hydrogen combine with 1 atom of nitrogen to form 1 molecule of ammonia gas. Hence, it followed that the oxygen atom must be 16 times as heavy as the hydrogen atom, and that the nitrogen atom has to be 14 times heavier than the hydrogen atom.

The hydrogen atom was found to be the lightest atom, and most other atoms or molecules appeared to be a whole number of times heavier than the hydrogen atom. The number of times other atoms, or molecules, were found to be heavier than the hydrogen atom, were named their "atomic weight" or "molecular weight". So, the atomic weights of hydrogen, nitrogen, and oxygen would be 1, 14, and 16 respectively, while the molecular weights of ammonia and water would be 17 and 18 respectively. In practice small deviations are found to occur from these whole numbers, for reasons given later in this chapter.

Chapter 2 – Fields and Particles

It also followed from the above discussion that an amount of the various elements or compounds weighing as much in grams as their atomic or molecular weights, must contain the same number of atoms or molecules. These amounts are called one "gram atom", or one "gram molecule", or just simply as one "mole".

Thus, 1 gram of hydrogen, 14 grams of nitrogen, 16 grams of oxygen, 17 grams of ammonia, and 18 grams of water would all be expected to contain the same number of atoms or molecules. This number is known as Avogadro's number, knowledge of which would enable the actual weights of the various atoms and molecules to be determined.

While the above was found to be true, a further complication arose. Perhaps unexpectedly, at a given pressure and temperature, 3 litres of hydrogen gas and 1 litre of nitrogen gas were found to form 2 litres of ammonia gas, rather than 1 litre, as would have been expected from the above. This suggested that in the gaseous state 2 hydrogen atoms form a hydrogen molecule, and likewise 2 nitrogen atoms form a nitrogen molecule, so that 3 hydrogen molecules and 1 nitrogen molecule form 2 ammonia molecules. It was found that the atoms of most elementary gases tend to combine with each other. Thus, hydrogen, nitrogen, and oxygen gases all contain molecules made up of 2 of their atoms.

There are various ways of determining Avogadro's number, and so the number of atoms or molecules contained in one gram atom of elements, or one gram molecule of compounds. The method considered here makes use of the radiation emitted by radium.

Let a piece of radium be placed into the bottom of a narrow deep well in a lead container, as shown in Figure 2.7, so that any radiation from the radium could only issue from the top of the well, and initially move vertically upward. Let also two vertical parallel metal plates be placed on either side of the issuing radiation, and let the plates be oppositely charged from the terminals of a battery. The radiation is then found to be split into three component beams, one bending toward the negatively charged plate indicating that it consists of positively charged particles, the other bending toward the positively charged plate and thus consisting of negatively charged particles, and the third remaining undeflected showing that it is not carrying any electrical charge. The positively and negatively charged particles were named alpha (α) and beta (β) particles respectively, while the undeflected beam was called gamma (γ) radiation. The beta particles were eventually identified to be electrons, and the gamma radiation proved to be short wavelength electromagnetic waves akin to x-rays.

If the space between the charged plates is filled with a suitable gas, at a suitable pressure, then each alpha particle colliding with the atoms or molecules of this gas knocks electrons out of these atoms or molecules. Under favourable conditions, each alpha particle produces many electrons. These electrons are attracted to the positive plate, and produce a detectable current pulse in the battery lead. The number of current pulses per second, as counted by an electronic pulse counter, equals the number of alpha particles passing between the plates per second. This method is the basic principle of the Geiger counter. The alpha particles eventually meet and recombine with electrons to form neutral atoms of a gas identifiable as helium. If a sufficient number of helium atoms are collected in a vessel to form a determinable mass, then this mass, when divided by the corresponding alpha particle count, gives the mass of 1 helium atom as 6.63×10^{-24} gram, or 6.63×10^{-27} kilogram.

Chapter 2 – Fields and Particles

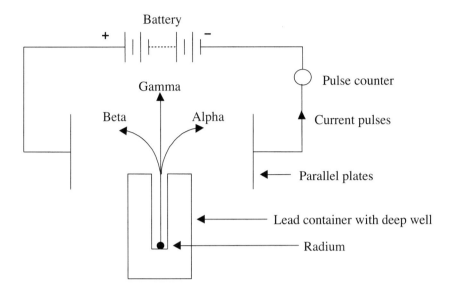

Figure 2.7

It may be mentioned in passing that when a radium sample sheds all of its alpha, beta and gamma radiation, it turns into the element lead.

One also needs to know the atomic weight of helium, before Avogadro's number can be deduced. Here again, reliance can be made on Avogadro's law, namely that equal volumes of different gases, at the same pressure and temperature, contain the same number of atoms or molecules. Now, while hydrogen gas contains hydrogen molecules, each made up of 2 hydrogen atoms, it is found that helium atoms do not combine with any other atoms, and so helium gas must be monatomic. Since 1 litre of helium gas is found to weigh twice as much as 1 litre of hydrogen gas at the same pressure and temperature, a helium atom must be twice as heavy as a hydrogen molecule, and four times as heavy as a hydrogen atom. Consequently, the atomic weight of helium must be 4. So, one gram atom of helium has a mass of 4 grams, which when divided by the mass of 1 helium atom, as deduced above, yields the number of atoms in 4 grams of helium as $N_o = 6.03 \times 10^{23}$.

This is Avogadro's number which gives the number of atoms in 1 gram of hydrogen, 14 grams of nitrogen, 16 grams of oxygen, or the number of molecules in 17 grams of ammonia, and 18 grams of water. It is now possible to calculate the mass of any atom or molecule. Thus, 1 hydrogen atom must have a mass of $1 / (6.03 \times 10^{23}) = 1.66 \times 10^{-24}$ gram, or 1.66×10^{-27} kilogram. Likewise, 1 atom of helium, nitrogen, or oxygen would have masses of 4, 14, and 16 times as much respectively.

Recalling the previously obtained value for the mass of an electron, namely 9.1×10^{-31} kilogram, the ratio of the mass of the hydrogen atom to the mass of an electron is: $(1.66 \times 10^{-27}) / (9.1 \times 10^{-31}) \approx 1820$.

Chapter 2 – Fields and Particles

Hence, it is seen that the mass of an electron is negligibly small compared with the mass of even the lightest atom, namely that of hydrogen. In general, the total mass of the positively charged parts and neutral parts of any atom very closely equal the mass of the whole atom.

One may also use Avogadro's number to calculate the volume occupied by one atom or one molecule. For example, 18 grams of water has a volume of 18 cubic centimetres, and contains 6.03×10^{23} molecules. Thus, the volume occupied by one water molecule is:

$18 / (6.03 \times 10^{23}) = 2.99 \times 10^{-23} \approx 3 \times 10^{-23}$ cubic centimetre $= 3 \times 10^{-29}$ cubic metre.

Since the above considerations involved the volume, pressure, and temperature of gases, it may be helpful to examine the interrelation of these quantities. It has been long known that the product of (volume) x (pressure) for a given amount of gas, say 1 gram, is constant at any given temperature. So, if the gas is contained in a cylinder with a movable piston, and its volume is reduced to half by moving the piston inward, the pressure would double, provided the temperature remained unaltered.

The molecules of a gas contained in a vessel continually move about in a random manner, and possess kinetic energy dependent on their mass and speed. Some molecules continually strike the walls of the vessel, and rebound from them, which is the source of the pressure exerted on the walls of the vessel. Pressure is defined as force acting on the walls per unit area. If, for a given amount of gas at a given temperature, the volume is measured in cubic metres, and the pressure is measured in newtons force per square metre area, then the unit of the product (volume) x (pressure) must be (newton) x (metre) which is the unit of energy, namely the joule. This indicates that the product of (volume) x (pressure) equals the heat energy of the given amount of gas at the given temperature, and equals the sum total of the kinetic energies of all the molecules contained in the volume of gas at that temperature.

It has also been established experimentally that for any given quantity of gas, the product (volume) x (pressure), that is the heat energy, is proportional to temperature provided that the temperature is measured from −273 degrees Celsius. Temperature so measured is called the absolute temperature. Thus, water freezes at 0 degrees Celsius or 273 degrees absolute, and it boils at 100 degrees Celsius or 373 degrees absolute. One may write for one gram molecule of gas in terms of its volume, pressure, absolute temperature, and Avogadro's number:

(volume in cubic metres) x (pressure in newtons per square metre)

$= \begin{pmatrix} \text{energy of one molecule per} \\ \text{degree of temperature} \\ \text{in joules per degree} \end{pmatrix} \times \begin{pmatrix} \text{Avogadro's number,} \\ \text{number of molecules} \\ \text{per mole} \end{pmatrix} \times \begin{pmatrix} \text{absolute temperature} \\ \text{in degrees} \\ \text{absolute} \end{pmatrix}$

In the above, the energy of one molecule per degree of temperature is called Boltzmann's constant after its discoverer. Its value is 1.38×10^{-23} joule per degree, and this value may be found from the volume, pressure, and absolute temperature of one gram molecule of gas, and Avogadro's number.

The above relation suggests that at a temperature of 0 degree absolute, or −273 degrees Celsius, the gas has zero energy, and all molecular motion ceases.

Chapter 2 – Fields and Particles

The charge to mass ratio of alpha particles may be determined from the observed bending of the paths of these particles moving with known speed in known electric and magnetic fields, as was done when finding the charge to mass ratio of electrons. Given that the mass of the alpha particle is already known, the positive charge on the particle can be deduced by multiplying its charge to mass ratio by its mass. The charge is found to equal twice the magnitude of the electronic charge. This indicates that a neutral helium atom must have 2 electrons, and also other parts carrying positive charges equal in magnitude to that of 2 electrons, and which are overall 4 times as heavy as a hydrogen atom. Likewise, all atoms must have negatively charged electrons, and much heavier components, carrying positive charges such that the magnitudes of the positive and negative charges equal each other.

The question then arises as to how the negative electrons and the positive constituents are arranged within the atom. Radium and uranium emit alpha particles with considerable speed, and so carry substantial energy. In 1911, Ernest Rutherford used such high energy alpha particles to bombard a thin gold foil. It was found that some alpha particles passed straight through the foil, while others were lightly deflected. However, some were turned back much the same way as a comet would be when entering the solar system and passing near the sun on one side, sweeping around it, and leaving on the other side after turning through a large angle. This suggested that the positive part of the atom was concentrated in a very small region, and alpha particles approaching this region closely were deflected through a large angle by the force of repulsion between two positively charged particles.

Soon after, in 1913, Niels Bohr proposed that an atom consisted of a positively charged nucleus, around which the negatively charged electrons revolved in orbits, being held in those orbits by the electric forces of attraction between the positive nucleus and the negative electrons, analogously to the way gravitational attraction keeps the planets in orbits around the sun. However, it was known that moving charges radiate electromagnetic waves, and so lose energy and consequently slow down. Bohr postulated that this did not happen in the atom as long as the electrons were confined to a relatively few discrete orbits, as indicated by experimental observations at the time.

Since both the nucleus and the electron have masses, there must also be a gravitational attraction between them. However, a relatively simple calculation shows that the electric force exceeds the gravitational force by a huge factor, of the order of 10^{40}. Thus, the role of gravitation within atoms is totally negligible.

Further advances were made in 1919, when Ernest Rutherford bombarded the atoms of nitrogen gas with alpha particles, which in light of the Bohr proposition would now be recognised as the nuclei of helium atoms. The result of this bombardment was oxygen atoms, and also some particles having nearly the same mass as the hydrogen atom and a positive charge equal in magnitude to that of the electronic charge. These particles were named "protons", and were recognised to be identical to the nuclei of hydrogen atoms.

Subsequently, other elements bombarded with alpha particles also yielded protons, and so it became apparent that protons were constituents of all atomic nuclei. Since all atoms in their normal state are electrically neutral, it must be true in general that the number of protons in the nucleus of any atom must equal the number of electrons orbiting it. Thus, a hydrogen atom consists of 1 proton orbited by 1 electron, while a helium atom has 2 protons in its nucleus, which is orbited by 2 electrons. However, since the helium atom is 4 times as heavy as the hydrogen atom, it must also possess an additional neutral mass in its nucleus closely equal to the mass of 2 protons.

It was not until 1932 that the nature of the neutral mass in atomic nuclei was unravelled through the work of Irene Curie, Frederic Joliot and James Chadwick. Beryllium atoms were bombarded with alpha particles, which led to carbon atoms and a stream of electrically neutral particles. Since the combined mass of a beryllium atom and an alpha particle is 13 times that of the hydrogen atom, while the mass of the carbon atom is 12 times that of the hydrogen atom, the mass of the neutral particle had to equal approximately that of the hydrogen atom. This neutral particle was named the "neutron", and was recognised as the electrically neutral constituent of atomic nuclei.

It thus became clear that all atoms are built of three types of particles, the proton, the neutron, and the electron. The protons and neutrons are contained in the nucleus, while the electrons orbit the nucleus. In neutral atoms, the number of protons must always equal the number of electrons. The identity of any one element is determined by the number of protons in the nucleus of its atoms, which is called the "atomic number".

Since the proton and the neutron are nearly equal in mass, and both are around 1820 times as heavy as the electron, protons and neutrons account for nearly all the mass of the atoms, and so also of all matter.

The atomic weight of any element, which by definition is the number of times an atom of that element is heavier than the hydrogen atom, could be expected to be a whole number. However, the atomic weights of many elements are fractional for three reasons.

Firstly, while the number of protons in the atomic nucleus determines an element's identity, the same element may have different numbers of neutrons in its nucleus. For example, all hydrogen atoms have 1 proton and 1 electron, but with nuclei containing either a proton only, or a proton and a neutron. These are called isotopes of hydrogen. The one having a neutron is called heavy hydrogen, or deuterium, which constitutes a small fraction of all hydrogen. Atomic weights are averages based on the relative abundance of isotopes.

Secondly, as the oxygen isotope with 8 protons and 8 neutrons is the most abundant atom on earth, it was proposed to take its atomic weight as exactly 16, and then relate all other atomic weights to it. The atomic weight of hydrogen then becomes 1.008.

Thirdly, the mass of a nucleus, consisting of a number of protons and neutrons, is less than the sum of the masses of the constituent protons and neutrons. While positively charged protons some distance apart repel each other, when a number of protons and neutrons are brought close enough to each other, a strong force of attraction takes over that binds the protons and neutrons together into a stable atomic nucleus. This process is associated with loss of mass, some mass being converted into the energy necessary for binding the nucleus together. The atomic weight is thus less than expected from summing its constituents.

Table 2.1 lists the more commonly met elements, together with their symbols, atomic numbers, and atomic weights.

Table 2.1

Element	Symbol	Atomic Number = Number of Protons = Number of Electrons	Atomic Weight based on Oxygen = 16.000
Hydrogen	H	1	1.008
Helium	He	2	4.003
Beryllium	Be	4	9.012
Carbon	C	6	12.011
Nitrogen	N	7	14.007
Oxygen	O	8	16.000
Sodium	Na	11	22.990
Aluminium	Al	13	26.982
Silicon	Si	14	28.086
Sulphur	S	16	32.064
Chlorine	Cl	17	35.453
Calcium	Ca	20	40.080
Iron	Fe	26	55.847
Copper	Cu	29	63.540
Zinc	Zn	30	65.370
Silver	Ag	47	107.870
Gold	Au	79	196.967
Mercury	Hg	80	200.590
Lead	Pb	82	207.190
Radium	Ra	88	226.025
Uranium	U	92	238.029

While the number of protons and neutrons in the nucleus determines the mass, and some other physical properties of the atoms, the electrons revolving around the nucleus are responsible for the chemical properties of the elements. It is not known how the electronic orbits are oriented in the atom. As will be discussed in Chapter 3, the evidence to hand indicates that electrons are revolving in concentric "shells", each containing a number of "subshells" of different radii, surrounding the nucleus. Also, as will be seen in Chapter 3, each shell and subshell may contain up to a definite maximum number of electrons but no more. In any subshell an electron has both: kinetic energy due to its orbital velocity, and also potential energy due to the electron being removed some distance from the nucleus against the electrical force of attraction exerted by the positive nucleus on the negative electron. The total energy of any electron is the sum of these two, and in view of relevant discussion in Chapter 3, this total energy can assume specific values only, leading to a number of possible, well identifiable shells and subshells.

Two or more atoms of different elements with partly filled outermost subshells may share their outermost electrons, which results in the atoms being bound together into a molecule. This way, elements may combine to form compounds. For example the water molecule consists of 2 atoms of hydrogen and 1 atom of oxygen, which is briefly expressed by the formula H_2O. Likewise, the ammonia molecule is made up of 3 atoms of hydrogen and 1 atom of nitrogen, and so its formula is NH_3.

With reference to the foregoing discussion involving electric cells and batteries, when a resistance is connected across the terminals of an electric battery, electrical energy is continually expended in the resistance. This energy results from chemical changes inside the cells, that is elements and compounds originally present, and having a certain amount of energy, being rearranged into some other elements and compounds, possessing a lower level of energy. The battery is exhausted when this chemical conversion is complete.

Whether an element, or a compound, is an electrical conductor or insulator depends on the electrons in the outermost subshells. Good conductors are normally metallic elements, the atoms of which have only 1 electron in their outermost subshell, such as copper or silver. This electron can easily detach itself from the parent atom, and move around in the solid metal. Furthermore, when in the presence of an applied electric field, it can also move due to the force exerted by the field, thereby producing an electric current.

Good insulators are normally compounds, the molecules of which have atoms with their outermost electronic subshells filled through electron sharing. In this case, all electrons are tightly bound to the molecules, and electron motion cannot be caused by moderate electric fields. However, in very strong fields insulators may break down and conduct as well.

Electrically charged particles, such as the proton or electron, can be accelerated to very high speeds in strong electric or magnetic fields, and then can be made to collide with each other, or other particles and atoms. Alternatively, matter may be subjected to alpha radiation such as emitted by radium. Such experiments resulted in the creation and identification of many particles, similar to protons, neutrons and electrons, as far as mass and charge go. Such artificially created particles are not normally stable, and convert into protons, neutrons, electrons, and gamma radiation after a brief existence.

Some of these particles are light and electron-like. In particular, the "positron" and the "neutrino" seem to have nearly the same mass as the electron. But, the positron carries a positive charge equal in magnitude to that of the negative electron charge. If positrons and electrons meet, they annihilate each other and are converted into gamma radiation.

The neutrino is electrically neutral, and as such is capable of passing through solid or liquid matter without any obstruction. Consequently, neutrinos are very difficult to detect. Much of the undetectable "dark matter" within the universe, which is noticeable through its gravitational effects only, is suspected to be due to neutrinos, or neutrino-like particles.

Other particles produced in collision experiments are heavy, proton or neutron like. Recent investigations suggest that the proton, the neutron, and other heavy particles like them, are not fundamental, but are combinations of component entities called "quarks", with definite mathematical characteristics, but whose physical existence is questionable.

The question as to what are the ultimate fundamental building blocks of matter still awaits elucidation.

Chapter 3
Waves – Relativity – Quanta

The phenomena of waves often play an important role in the physical universe. In what follows, three kinds of waves will be considered, namely: water waves, sound waves, and electromagnetic waves.

Water Waves

Let a cylindrical solid rod be placed in a pool of water, perpendicular to the surface of the water, and let it be moved vertically up and down in a periodic manner at a suitable rate. The periodic movement of the rod would often be referred to as a "vibration". The time for one complete cycle of upward and downward movement is called the "period" of the vibration, while the number of periods occurring in 1 second is the "frequency" of the vibration. For instance, a possible period could be 0.25 of a second, resulting in a frequency of 1 / 0.25 = 4 cycles per second.

Molecules in close proximity to each other often attract each other, due to the electrical forces exerted by the atomic nuclei in one molecule on the electrons of a neighbouring molecule. Such a force of attraction is called adhesion when occurring between dissimilar molecules, and cohesion when operating between similar molecules.

Hence, a cylindrical layer of water molecules just adjacent to the rod, is attracted to the rod by the force of adhesion, and consequently follows the motion of the rod. The next cylindrical layer of water molecules, further away from the rod, is attracted by the layer adjacent to the rod through the force of cohesion, and will follow the motion of that layer with some time delay. Likewise, each cylindrical layer of water molecules concentric with the rod, but progressively further away from it, will follow the movement of the adjacent layer closer to the rod with some time delay. Assuming that the process was started with an upward motion of the rod, the water molecules in such a concentric cylindrical layer some distance from the rod will still be moving upward at a time when the rod, and the layer of water molecules adjacent to it, reverse their motion and move downward. Thus, each cylindrical layer of the water molecules follows the motion of the adjacent layer closer to the rod with some time delay. This process results in water waves, having alternate crests and troughs travelling outward from the rod in concentric circles.

Now let the waves be observed at a point that is situated at some fixed horizontal distance from the rod. The crests and troughs of the waves travel past this point with a constant velocity that is called the "velocity of propagation" of the waves. The number of crests or troughs passing the point in each second is called the "frequency" of the waves, while the horizontal distance between two adjacent crests, or adjacent troughs, is the "wavelength" of the waves. The number of crests passing the point in one second, multiplied by the wavelength, is the total horizontal movement of the waves per second, and so equals the magnitude of the velocity of the waves, or simply the speed of the waves. The direction of the velocity in this case is in the plane of the water surface, and is directed radially outward from the rod. Thus, the speed of water wave propagation is given by:

(speed of water wave propagation in metres per second)
= (frequency in cycles per second) x (wavelength in metres)

Since each upward movement of the rod produces one crest of the wave, while each downward movement of the rod produces one trough of the wave, the frequency of the vibrations of the rod must equal the frequency of the waves.

The wavelength and the speed of propagation of water waves depend on various factors, including the gravity, temperature, density of the water, cohesive forces between the water molecules, and also any air movement or wind above the water surface. In the absence of wind, at a temperature of around 20 degrees Celsius, and a frequency of rod vibration of 4 cycles per second, the resulting wavelength is found to be about 0.1 of a metre. This gives a speed of wave propagation of around (4) x (0.1) = 0.4 metre per second.

At any fixed point some distance from the rod, the water molecules are expected to move vertically up and down only, so that only the disturbance, that is, the crests and troughs of the wave, move horizontally and radially outward from the rod.

Water waves are called transverse waves because the water molecules move in a direction that is perpendicular to the direction of the wave propagation.

The presence of air movement, namely wind above the water surface, or water flow as in a river, may cause some horizontal movements of water molecules in addition to the vertical ones. Such horizontal movements would affect the water wave propagation.

The "amplitude" of the wave is the vertical displacement of the crest above, or the trough below, the still water surface that would prevail in the absence of the waves.

The up and down motion of the water molecules, at any point some distance from the rod, is associated with kinetic energy. This energy is transmitted from the rod through the wave propagation. Thus in general, the waves carry energy. The amount of energy carried by the waves past 1 metre of water surface, perpendicular to the direction of the wave propagation, in each second, depends on both the amplitude and the frequency of the waves. As the waves move away from their source, namely the vibrating rod, in ever widening concentric circles, the amplitude falls, and so does the energy carried per second, past each metre of water surface perpendicular to the direction of the propagation. This is due to the energy of the waves being spread around the perimeters of ever-increasing circular areas.

Sound Waves

Sound waves are essentially vibrations of atoms or molecules in a gas, liquid, or solid. Sound waves in air are of particular interest. The main constituents of air are nitrogen gas 78%, oxygen gas 21%, and a number of other gases amounting to around 1%, including argon and carbon dioxide. These figures are percentages by volume. Nitrogen and oxygen are present in the air in a molecular form, two nitrogen atoms forming a nitrogen molecule, and two oxygen atoms constituting an oxygen molecule. These may be referred to as the molecules of air.

A common way of producing sound waves in air is by means of a loud speaker. The cone of the speaker is caused to vibrate by an alternating electric current passed into the voice coil fixed to the cone. The coil is located in the magnetic field of a permanent magnet with the field perpendicular to the coil current, and so causing a force to act on the coil parallel to its axis. The current, and the force acting on the coil and cone assembly, are

Chapter 3 — Waves — Relativity — Quanta

both reversing direction periodically, typically at frequencies between 100 and 10,000 times per second. This then causes the speaker cone to vibrate, that is move inward and outward, periodically changing the direction of its motion at the frequency of the current.

When the cone is moving outward, it pushes a layer of air molecules just ahead of it, which in turn presses on the next layer of air molecules further away from the cone with some time delay. As adjacent layers of air molecules progressively further away from the cone press on each other, a region of increased air pressure, or compression, is created that propagates outward from the cone with a finite speed. This situation is comparable to a line of toppling dominoes, which also takes finite time for the disturbance to pass along the line.

When some time later the cone is moving inward, it sucks air molecules backward, and creates a region of reduced air pressure, or rarefaction, which also takes a finite time to propagate outward from the cone.

The result is alternate regions of compression and rarefaction travelling away from the cone, with a definite constant velocity of propagation. At any point at some fixed distance from the speaker cone, the air pressure alternates between maximum and minimum values, which are the crests and troughs of the sound wave. The number of crests, or troughs, passing a fixed point per second is the frequency of the sound wave, while the distance between two adjacent crests, or troughs, in the direction of the propagation is the wavelength of the sound wave. The magnitude of the velocity, that is the speed of sound waves, as for water waves, is the product of the frequency and the wavelength:

(speed of sound wave propagation in metres per second)
= (frequency in cycles per second) x (wavelength in metres)

The velocity is directed radially outward from the speaker cone. Each outward movement of the speaker cone produces a crest, and each inward movement produces a trough. So, the frequency of the sound waves must equal the frequency at which the cone vibrates.

The speed of propagation of sound waves in air depends on a number of factors including the density, temperature, and pressure of the air. The speed of the sound waves in air at a temperature of zero degrees Celsius, and at normal atmospheric pressure, equalling the pressure produced by a 760 millimetre column of mercury, is very nearly 332 metres per second. Thus, if the speaker cone vibrates at a rate of 1000 cycles per second, then from the above relation the wavelength is (332) / (1000) = 0.332 metre.

Sound waves are called longitudinal waves, since the air molecules move to and fro in the same direction as the waves propagate. However, at any point, the air molecules vibrate about an equilibrium position, which the molecules would assume in the absence of any vibration. Thus, the air molecules do not travel with the wave, only the disturbance propagates in the form of alternate crests and troughs moving away from the source.

The presence of wind would cause a drift to be superposed on the to and fro motion of the air molecules arising from sound waves, and so affect the propagation of the waves.

The amplitude of the sound waves may be defined in two ways. Firstly, the "displacement amplitude" is the maximum departure of the air molecules from their equilibrium position, which the molecules would assume in the absence of sound waves. Secondly, the "pressure amplitude" is the maximum increase, or decrease, of the air pressure from the equilibrium pressure, which would prevail in the absence of the sound waves.

While water waves propagate in two dimensions, namely the plane of the water surface, sound waves travel in three dimensions. Since air molecules are set into motion at some distance from the source of the waves, and moving air molecules possess kinetic energy, sound waves carry energy. The amount of energy carried by sound waves per second through a square metre of area perpendicular to the direction of propagation depends on the frequency and the displacement or the pressure amplitude. As the sound waves propagate away from the source, both the amplitude and the energy of the waves crossing unit area, fall due to the energy of the waves being distributed over ever increasing spherical areas.

Sound waves can travel by the mechanism described above in any medium, gas, liquid, or solid. The speed of propagation depends on the medium. For example, the speed of sound waves in water, at a temperature of 4 degrees Celsius is 1480 metres per second, which is much faster than the speed of sound waves in air.

Electromagnetic Waves

Having dealt with water waves and sound waves, let now electromagnetic waves be considered, which are waves in electric and magnetic fields. Electric and magnetic fields represent forces acting on stationary and moving electrically charged bodies. Such forces apparently act over distances in empty space.

A possible mode of operation of such forces can be visualised through an analogy. With reference to Figure 3.1, consider two skaters, who are originally gliding side by side along parallel paths, at the same constant velocity. Let the skaters start throwing balls to each other, then both the act of throwing and the act of catching the balls will produce forces pushing the skaters away from each other, and so their paths will start to diverge.

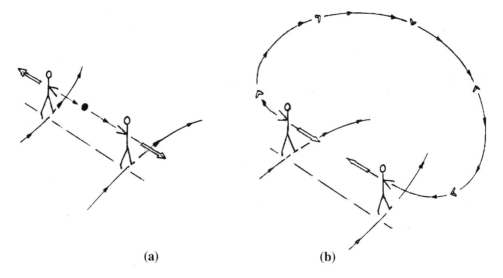

(a)   (b)

Figure 3.1

Chapter 3 — Waves — Relativity — Quanta

If, however, the skaters start throwing boomerangs to each other, in such a way that both the throw and the catch takes place on the side of each skater facing away from the other skater, then both the throw and the catch will produce forces pushing the skaters toward each other, and their paths will start to converge.

An observer, sufficiently removed from the skaters, will not see the exchange of the balls or the boomerangs, but will see the skaters diverging or converging, apparently caused by an invisible force acting between them over empty space.

Likewise, two electrically charged particles of the same type, say two electrons, initially moving parallel to each other with the same velocity, will start to diverge due to an invisible repelling force between them. This can be attributed to each charge being subject to a repelling electric field force due to the electric field produced by the other charge.

However, as the velocity of the like charges, such as those of the two electrons above, increases substantially, they are found to diverge less and less, which indicates an invisible force of attraction starting to act between them, partly counteracting the force of repulsion. The force of attraction is attributable to each moving charge being subject to a magnetic field force, due to its location in the magnetic field set up by the other moving charge. If the speed of the charges, moving in parallel paths side by side, closely approximates the speed of light, they cease to diverge and maintain a constant distance. This then indicates that, at the speed of light, the force of attraction between the moving charges due to the magnetic field equals the force of repulsion between the charges due to the electric field.

The forces associated with electric and magnetic fields are considered to be caused by the exchange of invisible messenger particles between the charges, in a way analogous to the exchange of balls and boomerangs between the skaters. Investigations suggest these exchange particles to be entities called photons, which are considered later in this chapter. However, just as the balls and the boomerangs, so the messenger particles would be expected to travel with finite speed, resulting in finite time being needed to establish electric or magnetic fields at some distance from the charges producing them.

Waves in electric and magnetic fields are normally produced by devices called antennae. With reference to Figure 3.2, a simple antenna consists of two conducting metallic rods of equal length, mounted end to end in the same straight line, with a small gap between them. A source of an alternating current is connected to the ends of the rods, adjacent to the gap. Such an antenna, consisting of two rods, is called a dipole. While the centre line of the rods may be oriented in any direction, they are usually chosen to be either vertical or horizontal, a vertical dipole being depicted in Figure 3.2.

Electrons from the alternating current source flow either downward in both antenna rods, or upward in both rods, periodically reversing direction at the frequency of the alternating current. As stated earlier, the conventional positive direction of the current is arbitrarily taken opposite to that of the electron flow. In one current cycle, the current increases from zero in a downward direction in the rods, reaches a downward maximum value, then drops back to zero, after which it increases in an upward direction in the rods to its upward maximum value, and then drops back to zero again, which completes the current cycle. The time for one current cycle is the period, and the number of current cycles per second is the frequency, of the alternating current.

Electric currents, being charged particles in motion, produce both magnetic and electric fields. It may be helpful to recall that the directions of magnetic and electric fields are defined as the directions of the forces acting on a small magnetic north pole and a small positive electric charge respectively.

With reference to Figure 3.2, when the current is flowing downward, an observer situated above the antenna would perceive circular, concentric, clockwise directed magnetic field lines near the antenna, in horizontal planes, and centring around the antenna rods. The magnetic field assumes a clockwise maximum value, when the downward flowing current passes through its maximum value.

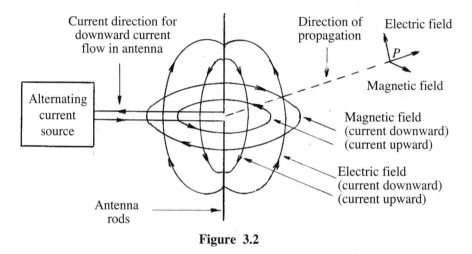

Figure 3.2

As a consequence of the downward current flow, eventually positive electric charges will accumulate in the bottom rod, and negative electric charges in the top rod. The observer would then perceive electric field lines, directed from the bottom rod to the top rod, in vertical planes passing through the antenna rods. At the same time, both the magnetic and electric fields would be found to propagate outward, and away from the antenna, at a finite speed as determined by the speed of the messenger particles.

When the current in the antenna reverses to an upward flow, it causes the magnetic field to reverse its direction near the antenna, so that when viewed from above, the magnetic field near the antenna would appear as circular, concentric, anticlockwise lines in horizontal planes, and centring around the antenna. The magnetic field reaches its maximum anticlockwise value, when the upward current passes through its maximum value.

The upward current flow in the antenna eventually produces an accumulation of positive electric charges in the top rod, and negative charges in the bottom rod, resulting in electric field lines directed from the top rod to the bottom rod in vertical planes through the antenna.

In the meantime, the fields produced by the previous downward current flow, namely the clockwise magnetic field, and the bottom rod to top rod directed electric field, will have progressed some distance further away from the antenna. This results in adjacent regions, in

Chapter 3 — Waves — Relativity — Quanta

which both the magnetic and electric fields are oppositely directed, and which propagate outward from the antenna with finite speed.

An observer at a considerable distance from the antenna, such as point P in Figure 3.2, would experience periodic variations and reversals of both the magnetic and electric fields, which are tantamount to waves in magnetic and electric fields sweeping past the observer. The line connecting the gap between the antenna rods to point P in Figure 3.2, is the direction of the wave propagation at point P. The observer would find that the directions of the magnetic and electric fields at point P are both perpendicular to the direction of propagation, and also perpendicular to each other, the magnetic and electric fields having their directions in horizontal and vertical planes respectively. Further, if the point P is far enough from the antenna, it would be found that the maximum values of the magnetic and electric fields occur at the same time, or using an alternative term, the two fields are in time phase. Arbitrarily, the maximum fields originally caused by the downward current may be labelled crests, while the oppositely directed maximum fields originally caused by the upward current may be called troughs. Since the magnetic and electric field waves are in time phase, that is, their crests and troughs coincide, and also since the two fields are perpendicular to each other, as well as to the direction of the propagation, the two waves are considered a single entity referred to as electromagnetic waves.

This relatively simple situation applies only at points sufficiently distant from the antenna. It does not apply at points in the close proximity of the antenna, where the relation between the magnetic and electric fields is more complex, and the two fields are not in time phase.

Thus, an observer at some sufficiently distant point from the antenna, such as point P in Figure 3.2, will perceive crests and troughs of electromagnetic waves sweep past at a constant velocity. The number of crests, or troughs, passing point P in each second is the frequency of the wave, while the distance between two adjacent crests, or troughs, is the wavelength of the wave. As for all waves, the magnitude of the velocity of the waves, that is the speed of propagation, is the product of the frequency times the wavelength, namely:

(speed of propagation of electromagnetic waves in metres per second)
= (frequency in cycles per second) x (wavelength in metres)

or alternatively:
(wavelength in metres)
= (speed of propagation in metres per second) / (frequency in cycles per second)

The direction of the velocity of the propagation, at any point P is outward from the gap between the antenna rods, and along the line connecting the gap to point P.

The frequency of the waves must equal the frequency of the alternating antenna current, since each cycle of that current produces one wave crest and one wave trough.

The speed of propagation of electromagnetic waves may be deduced from theoretical considerations, or may be determined by various practical tests. In free space, or in air, the speed is found to be 3×10^8 metres per second, irrespective of the frequency. Thus, from the above formula, a frequency of 1 million cycles per second corresponds to a wavelength:

(3×10^8 metres per second) / (10^6 cycles per second) = 300 metres,
which is a medium wave radiobroadcast wavelength.

Chapter 3 — Waves — Relativity — Quanta

Electromagnetic waves are transverse waves as the directions of the magnetic and electric fields are both perpendicular to the direction of the wave propagation.

The amplitudes of the electric and magnetic fields at any point, such as point P in Figure 3.2, are the maximum magnitudes attained by the two fields. The ratio: amplitude of the electric field in volts per metre, to the amplitude of the magnetic field in teslas, at points far enough from the antenna, is found to be constant and equal to the speed of propagation, namely 3×10^8 metres per second in free space or in air. In general, in free space or in air:

$$\frac{(\text{amplitude of electric field in volts per metre})}{(\text{amplitude of magnetic field in teslas})} = \begin{pmatrix} \text{speed of propagation} \\ 3 \times 10^8 \text{ metres per second} \end{pmatrix}$$

Electromagnetic waves sweeping past any fixed metallic conductor exert forces on the electrons in the conductor, and thereby set some electrons into vibrational motion inside the conductor. The electrons set into motion acquire kinetic energy from the electromagnetic waves, which must therefore carry energy. The energy carried past each square metre of area perpendicular to the direction of the propagation, in each second, may be calculated from theoretical considerations, or obtained from practical tests. It equals the product of the amplitudes of the electric and magnetic fields multiplied by (3.98×10^5). Thus one has:

$$\begin{pmatrix} \text{energy crossing 1 square metre area perpendicular to the} \\ \text{direction of propagation per second in joules per second} \end{pmatrix}$$
$$= (3.98 \times 10^5) \times \begin{pmatrix} \text{amplitude of electric field} \\ \text{in volts per metre} \end{pmatrix} \times \begin{pmatrix} \text{amplitude of magnetic} \\ \text{field in teslas} \end{pmatrix}$$

Hence, if at point P in Figure 3.2, the amplitude of the electric field is 1 volt per metre, then it follows from the above that the amplitude of the magnetic field must be $1/(3 \times 10^8)$ tesla, and the energy carried past 1 square metre area perpendicular to the direction of the propagation per second is: $(3.98 \times 10^5) \times (1) \times (1)/(3 \times 10^8) = 0.00133$ joule per second $= 0.00133$ watt $= 1.33$ milliwatts. This is a relatively strong electromagnetic field that could be expected only within a few kilometres of a powerful transmitter.

As the waves propagate out from the antenna, the energy of the waves is spread over ever increasing spherical surfaces, and so the energy carried per second past each square metre of area perpendicular to the direction of propagation must fall, and consequently the amplitudes of the electric and magnetic fields must fall also.

The antenna rods may be oriented in any direction. The above considerations will still apply, with the proviso that the magnetic field lines will be in planes perpendicular to the antenna rods, while the electric field lines will be in planes containing the antenna rods.

The ability of electromagnetic waves to produce oscillatory electric currents in metallic conductors, at substantial distances from the antennae producing the waves, is the basis for radio communications. The electromagnetic waves can be made to carry information, such as speech, music, or pictures, by modulation, namely by appropriately varying either the amplitude or the frequency of the electromagnetic waves.

The existence, and properties, of electromagnetic waves were predicted from theoretical considerations by James Maxwell around 1865, before the waves were first detected experimentally. So it was known, and later confirmed, that electromagnetic waves covered

Chapter 3 — Waves — Relativity — Quanta

an immense wavelength range: starting with kilometre wavelength radio waves, through television waves, microwaves, infra red rays, visible light, ultra violet rays, x-rays, down to gamma rays with wavelengths shorter than 10^{-9} metre. Maxwell's theory also predicted the speed of electromagnetic waves to be 3×10^8 metres per second in free space.

It is of historical interest that an early method of determining the speed of electromagnetic waves relied on light reaching earth from the planet Jupiter. The instants, when one of the moons of Jupiter just passed behind the planet, were noted for two cases: when the earth in its path around the sun was closest and furthest from Jupiter. These instants differed from what was expected from the measured period of revolution of this moon around the planet Jupiter. The difference, namely 997 seconds, had to be the time taken for light to traverse the orbit of the earth around the sun. The diameter of the earth's orbit, that is 299×10^9 metres, divided by the time difference of 997 seconds, gives the speed of light, and that of electromagnetic waves in general, as $(299 \times 10^9) / (997) = 3 \times 10^8$ metres per second.

In the foregoing, some characteristic quantities associated with waves have been considered such as wavelength, frequency, and speed of propagation. Another property of waves is the shape of the waves, which may assume many different forms.

The simplest and most fundamental wave shape is the "sine wave". The sine wave has a precise waveform, which is deducible from the motion of a point at constant speed around a circular path. The period in this case is the time taken for the point to move around the circle once, and the frequency is the number of times the point moves around the circle in 1 second. With reference to Figure 3.3, in order to deduce the shape of the sine wave, one may start by dividing the circle into a number of equal segments.

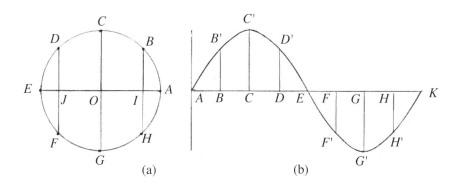

Figure 3.3

In Figure 3.3(a), eight equal segments were chosen as demarked by 8 equidistant points around the circle, namely points A, B, C, D, E, F, G, and H. Straight lines connecting the centre of the circle at O, to two adjacent points on the circle such as A and B, form a 45 degree angle with each other. This follows from a full circle containing 360 degrees, which when divided into 8 equal segments gives 360 / 8 = 45 degrees per segment.

One may set out the distances between the points A, B, C, etc., measured along the circle, on a horizontal straight line, as shown in Figure 3.3(b), so that the length of the arc AB in

Figure 3.3(a), corresponds to the length of the horizontal line AB in Figure 3.3(b), and so on. Note that points A and K in Figure 3.3(b) correspond to the same point A on the circle. Next, one needs to erect vertical lines, called ordinates, through points B, C, etc., in Figure 3.3(b), the heights of which are made equal to the corresponding heights of the points B, C, etc., in Figure 3.3(a), above the horizontal diameter of the circle. Thus, the ordinates B'B and BI in the two figures have equal height. Similarly one has C'C = CO, D'D = DJ, F'F = FJ, G'G = GO, and H'H = HI. Note that the heights of the ordinates through points A, E, and K, are zero. This now yields the points A, B', C', D', E, F', G', H', and K on the sine wave in Figure 3.3(b). For a reasonably accurate determination of the sine wave, the circle would have to be divided into considerably more equal segments, which would yield more points on the sine wave.

In Figure 3.3(b) the points A, B, C, etc., can represent points in space along the line of the wave propagation at a particular instant of time, while the ordinates B'B, C'C, etc., at these points in space, are proportional to the magnitudes of the electric and magnetic fields at that particular instant of time. The length of the line AK is the wavelength of the wave.

Alternatively, the points A, B, C, etc., in Figure 3.3(b), may represent instants of time at some fixed point in space, while the ordinates B'B, C'C, etc., at these instants of time, are proportional to the electric and magnetic fields at that particular point in space. The length of the line AK would then equal the time period of the wave, while the frequency of the wave would be the number of time periods occurring at that point in space per second.

The highest and lowest points on the wave in Figure 3.3(b), are the crest and the trough respectively. The vertical distance of the crest, or the trough, from the horizontal line AK, that is, the lengths of the ordinates C'C = G'G, are the amplitude of the wave. The crests and the troughs are often referred to alternatively as the positive and negative peaks.

Now let a particle move at a constant speed around a circle, and view the motion of this particle from a location in the plane of the circle, but which lies a relatively long distance outside the circle. The particle will then be seen to oscillate to and fro, along a straight line about the centre of that line corresponding to the centre of the circle. The displacements of the oscillating particle from the centre, along this straight line, at various instants of time, may once more be given by Figure 3.3(b), where points on the line AK represent instants of time, while the corresponding ordinates give the displacements of the particle from the centre, along the straight line, at those instants. This kind of oscillation is called sinusoidal, or simple harmonic, and when depicted as in Figure 3.3(b), it is called a sine wave.

The sine wave is the simplest possible wave. More complex waves may consist of a number of sine waves added together, for example a sine wave of a given frequency, called the "fundamental", to which are added any number of sine waves having frequencies that are integer multiples of the frequency of the fundamental, and the crests of which bear definite relations to the crests of the fundamental. These higher frequency sine wave components of the complex wave are called the "harmonics". The addition process involves adding the ordinates of the component waves at the same instants of time. The complex wave is still periodic, often having period and frequency equal to those of the fundamental component.

A simple example of a complex wave is shown in Figure 3.4, where a sine wave S_1 of a given frequency, and another sine wave S_3 having three times the frequency, are added

Chapter 3 — Waves — Relativity — Quanta

together, by adding their corresponding ordinates, along the same vertical lines, with due respect to sign, that is, negative ordinates must of course be subtracted from positive ones.

The lower frequency wave is called the fundamental, while the wave with three times the frequency is named the third harmonic. It will be noted that the period of the complex wave is still that of the fundamental.

Waves are often met that are not just the sum of a fundamental, and harmonics with frequencies a whole number times that of the fundamental, but which are composed of a continuous range of frequencies. Examples of such waves are sound waves carrying speech or music. The frequency of such a wave changes continually from one instant to another.

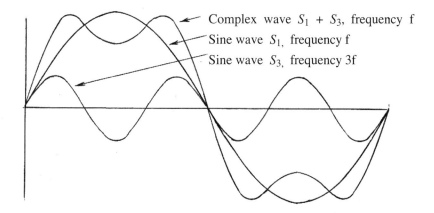

Figure 3.4

However, pure musical tones are single frequency sine waves. If the alternating current in an antenna is a sine wave, then so is the electromagnetic wave radiated from the antenna. Also, if the electromagnetic wave is to carry a time varying signal, such as speech, music, or television pictures, it must be modulated, which means varying either the amplitude, or the frequency, of the sine wave the same way the signal varies. It is also possible to transmit the ordinates of a complex wave serially in a digital form.

Relativity

Until the advent of the theory of relativity, it was believed that all waves had to rely on a medium for their propagation. Thus, water waves propagate in water, and sound waves do so in air, or any other material medium. So, it was assumed that electromagnetic waves also propagated in a medium, called the ether, even though such a medium could not be detected physically.

The velocity of wave propagation is found to be constant relative to the medium in which the propagation takes place, as long as relevant physical factors, such as temperature, pressure, and density remain unaltered. This is so, irrespective of whether the source of the waves moves relative to the medium, or whether the medium itself moves, as air moves with the earth in its path around the sun.

Chapter 3 – Waves – Relativity – Quanta

But if an observer moves relative to a medium in the same direction as the waves do, then, the speed of the waves relative to the observer will be the difference of the speed of the waves relative to the medium, minus the speed of the observer relative to the medium.

For example, let a stationary source of sound waves, such as a loud speaker, be switched on at a particular instant. Further, let the air temperature and pressure be such as to result in a sound wave velocity equal to 330 metres per second, which would be the same in all directions. Also, let a vehicle travel in a straight line due east, at 30 metres per second, and just pass the speaker at the moment it is switched on. Then, 1 second after the speaker was switched on, the sound wave front will be 330 metres east from the speaker, while the vehicle will be 30 metres east from the speaker. As a result, the sound wave front will be 300 metres east of the vehicle. An observer in the vehicle would then conclude that the sound wave front travelled 300 metres east relative to the vehicle in 1 second, or that the speed of the sound waves relative to the vehicle, in an easterly direction, is 330 – 30 = 300 metres per second.

The same holds if the speaker is mounted on the moving vehicle. The speed of the sound wave in air is still 330 metres per second, and the vehicle still moves at 30 metres per second in a straight line due east. Thus, 1 second after switching the speaker on, the sound wave front and the vehicle will have travelled eastward 330 metres and 30 metres respectively, and thus the sound wave front will be 300 metres east of the vehicle, and its speed in an easterly direction relative to the vehicle will still be 300 metres per second.

However, the wavelengths of the sound waves will be different in the two cases. If the speaker is driven from a 1000 cycles per second alternating current source, the speaker cone makes 1000 vibrations per second, and so the frequency of the sound waves will also be 1000 cycles per second.

In the case of a stationary speaker, there are 1000 wavelengths spread over 330 metres, and so a stationary observer perceives the wavelength of the sound waves as (330) / (1000) = 0.33 metre, and its frequency as 1000 cycles per second.

But, if the speaker is mounted on the moving vehicle, then the 1000 wavelengths generated in 1 second will be spread over the 300 metre distance between the vehicle and the eastern sound wave front, and the wavelength will have to be (300) / (1000) = 0.3 metre, while the speed of propagation past any fixed point will still be 330 metres per second. Thus, a stationary observer situated between the vehicle and the eastern wave front will experience sound waves sweeping past at a speed of 330 metres per second, but having a wavelength of 0.3 metre, and thus a frequency (330) / (0.3) = 1100 cycles per second. Consequently, the observer will perceive an increase in the pitch of the sound.

Now let the vehicle, and the speaker mounted on it, travel west at a speed of 30 metres per second. Then, 1 second after switching the speaker on, the vehicle will have travelled 30 metres west, while the east moving sound wave front will have travelled 330 metres east, and so at the end of 1 second the distance between the vehicle and the eastern wave front will be 360 metres. An observer moving with the vehicle will conclude that the sound wave front has moved 360 metres east in 1 second relative to the vehicle, and so its speed relative to the vehicle, in an easterly direction, is 360 metres per second.

Chapter 3 — Waves — Relativity — Quanta

If the loud speaker frequency is 1000 cycles per second as before, then 1 second after switch-on, 1000 wavelengths will be spread over the distance between the vehicle and the eastern wave front, which is 360 metres, and so the wavelength will be (360) / (1000) = 0.36 metre. The speed of propagation past any fixed point will still be 330 metres per second. Hence, a stationary observer between the vehicle and the eastern wave front will perceive sound waves sweeping past at 330 metres per second, but which have a wavelength of 0.36 metre, and thus have a frequency (330) / (0.36) ≈ 916.7 cycles per second. Consequently, the observer will perceive a reduction in the pitch of the sound.

The shortening or lengthening of the wavelengths of waves originating from moving sources is known as the Doppler effect. It applies to all waves, including electromagnetic waves, and so to light waves as well. The fact that light waves arriving at earth from distant galaxies have longer wavelengths than expected, led to the conclusion that all galaxies are moving away from each other, and that the universe is expanding.

Toward the end of the 19th century the view prevailed that since light was recognised as a wave, it had to propagate in some medium. Even though the medium could not be detected, its existence was assumed, and it was named the ether. Just as the speed of sound waves in air, relative to a moving observer is reduced in the direction of the observer's motion, and increased in the direction opposite to the observer's motion, it was expected that the speed of light waves in the ether, would also be reduced, or increased, depending on the direction of the observer's motion. Confirmation, or negation, of this proposition was essential for reconciling conflicting ideas and observations at the time.

To detect this effect, the speed of an observer moving with a light source had to be an appreciable fraction of the speed of light. Possibilities for substantial observer speeds are:

Rotational speed of the earth's surface at the equator ≈ 0.46 kilometre per second,
Speed of a satellite close to the earth's surface ≈ 8 kilometres per second,
Orbital speed of the earth around the sun ≈ 30 kilometres per second.

The last is the highest attainable speed to an observer on earth. Since the speed of light in air, or in free space, is 300,000 kilometres per second, an observer moving with the earth could expect, at best, the observed change in the speed of light to be 30 in 300,000, which is 1 in 10,000 or 0.01 percent.

In 1887, Albert Michelson and Edward Morley devised an experiment that could reliably detect such a small change. The apparatus, called an interferometer, was located in a laboratory, and was thus travelling with the earth, at earth's orbital speed of 30 kilometres per second. With reference to Figure 3.5, it utilised a light source producing a monochromatic light beam, that is a light beam having a single, well-defined wavelength. A semitransparent mirror M, placed at an angle of 45 degrees into the path of the beam, split the beam into two component beams, one travelling straight through the mirror in the direction of the earth's orbital motion, and the other deflected by the mirror through 90 degrees, and so travelling in a direction perpendicular to the earth's motion.

The first beam, travelling in the direction of the earth's orbital motion, passed through the semitransparent mirror M to mirror M_1 with an anticipated speed relative to the source of

300,000 − 30 = 299,970 kilometres per second, and then reflected back from mirror M_1 to mirror M with an expected relative speed of 300,000 +30 = 300,030 kilometres per second. Part of this first beam was then reflected by the semitransparent mirror M into telescope T.

The second beam, after being reflected by the semitransparent mirror M, was moving in a direction perpendicular to the earth's orbital motion to mirror M_2, and then reflected back to mirror M, with an anticipated speed closer to 300,000 kilometres per second, as this beam was expected to be affected by the earth's orbital motion to a lesser extent. Part of this second beam also passed through the semitransparent mirror M, and into the telescope T.

The anticipated times needed for the two beams to make the round trips, from mirror M to the reflecting mirrors M_1 and M_2 and back to mirror M, were calculated as the relevant path lengths between the mirrors divided by the expected speeds of the light beams relative to the moving apparatus.

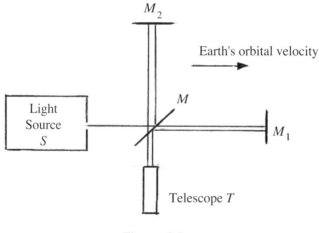

Figure 3.5

Supposing that in a replication of the experiment, the two round trips were arranged to be of equal length, then the expected time required for the round trip parallel to the earth's orbital motion would be longer than the time required for the round trip by the beam travelling perpendicular to it. Consequently, the crests of the two returning light waves should be shifted relative to each other. The telescope T would allow the detection of such a shift. If the lengths of the distances from mirror M to mirrors M_1 and M_2 were both 11 metres, while the wavelength of the monochromatic light was 550 nanometres (5.5 x 10^{-7} metre), then the expected shift in the crests of the two returning waves should be 1/5 or 0.2 of a wavelength. The calculations leading to this result are given in Appendix 3.1.

This experiment has been a landmark in physics, since neither the original experiment, nor the many repetitions of it, could detect any shift in the crests of the two returning waves. The far-reaching conclusion was that the speed of light was constant, irrespective of any motion of the source and the observer, and so the ether did not exist. This called for a revision of the laws of physics, as they prevailed toward the end of the 19th century.

Chapter 3 — Waves — Relativity — Quanta

After many attempts to find explanations, the special theory of relativity, put forward by Albert Einstein in 1905, proved to be the only one capable of offering non-contradictory explanations for all experimental observations.

The theory showed that two observers, moving in a straight line at constant speed relative to each other, could both measure the same speed of light, namely 3×10^8 metres per second, irrespective of the motion of the light source. However, this necessitated abandoning the universality of time, namely that time is the same for all observers anywhere in the universe.

The salient outcomes of the theory are:

(1) If an observer and a physical object are moving in a straight line at a constant speed relative to each other, then the observer would perceive the length of the object to appear shorter in the direction of its movement, compared with its length when stationary relative to the observer. The higher the relative speed, the shorter the object would appear. When the relative speed reaches the speed of light, the length of the object would appear to shrink to zero. The observed dimensions of the object perpendicular to the relative motion remain unaffected. In general, the apparent shortened length of the moving object equals the unshortened rest length, divided by a factor β, which depends on the speed ratio:

(speed of the object relative to the observer) / (speed of light)

The relation between the speed ratio and the factor β is given in the table below:

Speed ratio:	0	0.1	0.3	0.5	0.7	0.9	0.99	0.999
Factor β :	1	1.005	1.048	1.155	1.400	2.294	7.092	22.371

Thus, if the relative speed is 90% of the speed of light, then a 1 metre long object would appear shortened to (1) / (2.294) = 0.436 metre.

(2) If an observer and a clock are moving in a straight line at constant speed relative to each other, then the observer would perceive the clock to run slow, compared with another clock which is stationary relative to the observer, the two clocks having been originally synchronised at the same location. The higher the relative speed, the slower the moving clock would appear to run. When the speed of the clock reaches the speed of light relative to the observer, the clock, as seen from the observer's position, would appear to stop.

Again, in general, any time period perceived on the clock moving relative to the observer, would equal the corresponding time period perceived on the clock at rest relative to the observer, divided by the factor β above. Thus, if the relative speed is 90% of the speed of light, and 1 hour is observed to have elapsed on the clock that is stationary relative to the observer, then the time perceived to have elapsed on the clock moving relative to the observer would be (1) / (2.294) = 0.436 hour.

The above may be briefly summarised as follows: If two observers move relative to each other in a straight line at constant speed, then each observer would perceive objects stationary relative to the other observer to shrink in the direction of the motion, and each observer would perceive clocks stationary relative to the other observer lose time and run slow.

It also follows that two observers, moving in a straight line at a constant speed relative to each other, would observe the same two events occurring at different locations in space, and with different space intervals between those locations. Furthermore, the two observers would also observe the same two events occurring at different instants of time, and with different time intervals between those instants. However, if the three dimensions of space and the one dimension of time are combined into a four-dimensional space-time continuum, then it is found that the four-dimensional space-time intervals perceived by the two observers between the same two events would be equal. This implies that the physical universe is essentially a four-dimensional space-time continuum.

(3) The mass of an object moving relative to an observer in a straight line at a constant speed appears to increase with speed, and approach infinity as the speed approaches the speed of light. In general, the moving mass equals the stationary mass, or rest mass, multiplied by the above factor β. Thus, a 1 kilogram mass at rest, would increase its mass, at 99% of the speed of light, to (1) x (7.092) = 7.092 kilograms.

(4) Mass is convertible into energy in accordance with the relation:

$$(\text{energy in joules}) = \begin{pmatrix} \text{mass in} \\ \text{kilograms} \end{pmatrix} \times \begin{pmatrix} \text{speed of light in} \\ \text{metres per second} \end{pmatrix} \times \begin{pmatrix} \text{speed of light in} \\ \text{metres per second} \end{pmatrix}$$

Thus, 1 kilogram of mass is equivalent to an amount of energy:

(1) x (3 x 10^8) x (3 x 10^8) = 9 x 10^{16} joules.

This is an enormous amount of energy, which a 1 kilowatt electric heater would take 3 million years to consume.

An example indicating the equivalence of mass and energy is the fusion of four hydrogen atoms into a single helium atom. The mass of the helium atom is less than the sum of the masses of four hydrogen atoms, and the mass lost in the fusion process appears as a large amount of energy, in the form of electromagnetic radiation, and the emission of high energy subatomic particles. This happens in the sun, and also in the hydrogen bomb.

A relatively simple algebraic treatment of the special theory of relativity is presented in Appendix 3.2.

The theory of relativity has important implications for electric and magnetic fields. As stated earlier, if two stationary bodies carry like electrical charges, either both positive, or both negative, then there will be an electric force of repulsion between them. If, however, the two charged bodies move in a direction perpendicular to the line connecting them, then a magnetic force of attraction will appear between them, acting opposite to the electric force of repulsion. But, there can be no such thing as two stationary charged bodies, the charged bodies would move with the earth around the sun, while the sun itself also moves as the galaxy rotates.

Chapter 3 — Waves — Relativity — Quanta

So, the above must be modified to say that if an observer is moving with charged bodies in such a way that the observer and the charged bodies are at rest relative to each other, then the observer perceives only electric fields and electric forces acting on the charged bodies.

However, if there is a relative motion between an observer and charged bodies, then the observer will perceive magnetic fields, and magnetic forces acting on the charged bodies, in addition to the electric ones.

Quanta

As has been discussed above, waves that propagate in material media, such as sound waves propagating in gasses, liquids, or solids, do so at constant speed relative to the medium, but not relative to a moving observer. However, electromagnetic waves do not behave this way, as they do not need a medium for their propagation. The speed of propagation of electromagnetic waves appears to be constant to all observers, irrespective of any movement of the source of the waves or the observers of the waves.

The behaviour of electromagnetic waves differs from the behaviour of waves propagating in material media in yet another way. One might expect that the amplitude, and so the energy carried by electromagnetic waves, may be varied continuously in imperceptibly small steps. However, toward the end of the 19th century it became apparent that electromagnetic waves did not behave this way.

It was noticed that when ultraviolet rays fell on certain metallic surfaces, electrons were emitted from those surfaces. Ultraviolet rays are electromagnetic waves that, like all waves, carry energy. The energy of the waves impinging on a metallic surface may be imparted to electrons just inside the surface, and may thus increase the energy of such electrons. If the increase in the electronic energy is sufficiently large, the electrons may overcome the electric forces of attraction exerted on them by the nuclei of their parent atoms, and so enable such electrons to escape from the metallic surface. This phenomenon has become known as the photoelectric effect.

It was found as expected, that the number of electrons emitted from a given type of metallic surface, per unit area per second, increased with the intensity of the rays, that is, with the amplitude of the electromagnetic waves. However, it was also found that if the frequency of the waves was decreased below a certain threshold value for any given type of metallic surface, no electron emission would occur at all, no matter how intense the rays were, that is, no matter how large the amplitude of the waves was. Albert Einstein proposed a possible explanation for this strange behaviour in 1905, the same year he put forward his special theory of relativity.

The proposed explanation postulated that electromagnetic waves were not continuous, but rather consisted of discrete quanta, possibly in the form of finite length wave trains, which were eventually named photons. A photon has a definite frequency and wavelength. It travels at the same speed as all electromagnetic waves do, namely the speed of light, that is, 3×10^8 metres per second in free space or in air. It is still true that the speed of the photon equals the product of the frequency and the wavelength of the photon. However, every photon carries a definite amount of energy proportional to its frequency, that is, an amount of energy equal to a constant number times its frequency.

Five years earlier in 1900, Max Planck came to the same conclusion, while searching for an explanation for the observed relationships between the intensity and the frequency of electromagnetic waves radiated from hot solid bodies, in the form of infrared, visible, and ultraviolet rays, at given fixed temperatures. Planck arrived at the conclusion that the observed radiation could be explained only by assuming that it consisted of discrete quanta, or photons, each quantum possessing a definite amount of energy equal to a constant times its frequency. The constant turned out to have the same value as the one found from the photoelectric effect, and has become known as "Planck's constant".

So, two quite different approaches led to the same conclusion, namely that electromagnetic waves consisted of discrete quanta, or photons, each photon carrying a definite amount of energy in accordance with the relation:

(energy of a photon in joules)
= (Planck's constant in joule seconds) x (frequency of the photon in cycles per second)

The value of Planck's constant was found to equal 6.625×10^{-34} joule second, which was confirmed by many different tests.

As an example, a photon within the ultraviolet region of the electromagnetic waves may have a wavelength of 200 nanometres (2×10^{-7} metre) and thus its frequency is:

(frequency in cycles per second)
$$= \left(\frac{\text{speed of light} = 3 \times 10^8 \text{ metres per second}}{\text{wavelength of photon} = 2 \times 10^{-7} \text{ metre}} \right) = 1.5 \times 10^{15} \text{ cycles per second.}$$

The energy of this photon is:

(energy of photon in joules)
$$= \left(\begin{array}{c} \text{Planck's constant} \\ 6.625 \times 10^{-34} \text{ joule second} \end{array} \right) \times \left(\begin{array}{c} \text{frequency of photon} \\ 1.5 \times 10^{15} \text{ cycles per second} \end{array} \right) \approx 9.94 \times 10^{-19} \text{ joule.}$$

The frequency dependence of the photoelectric effect may now be explained as follows. In order to liberate an electron from a given metallic surface, a definite minimum amount of energy is required. If the energy of each incident photon is less than this, no electron emission from the surface can occur, no matter how many photons strike unit area of the surface per second, that is, no matter how intense the incident electromagnetic radiation is, or what is the same, no matter how large the amplitude of the electromagnetic waves.

If the energy of a photon just equals the minimum required, an electron may be emitted with near zero kinetic energy. If the photon energy exceeds the necessary minimum, an electron may be emitted with finite kinetic energy, having a maximum possible value equal the difference between the actual photon energy and the minimum photon energy required for emission to take place. However, even if the energy of the photon exceeds the minimum required, emission will not necessarily occur, or if it does occur, the kinetic energy may be less than the maximum possible value. This is so since the emission and the kinetic energy depend on additional factors, one being the angle of incidence of the photon.

The photoelectric effect may be investigated, and the value of Planck's constant may be determined, using the apparatus shown in Figure 3.6.

Chapter 3 — Waves — Relativity — Quanta

As shown in Figure 3.6, a metallic cathode and a metallic anode are sealed into a partially evacuated glass tube. A voltage is applied between the anode and the cathode from a voltage source that enables the voltage of the anode relative to the cathode to be varied by means of a potentiometer, from positive values, through zero, to negative values.

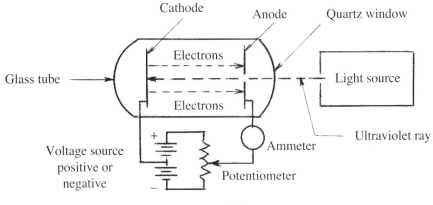

Figure 3.6

An ultraviolet ray, of a definite single frequency, is passed from a light source through the quartz window at the anode end of the glass tube, and also through a hole in the anode, after which it falls on the cathode at the opposite end of the tube. If the energy of the photons exceeds what is required for electron emission to occur from the cathode, and if the voltage of the anode is positive relative to that of the cathode, then the electrons emitted from the cathode will be attracted to the anode by the electric field force prevailing between the anode and the cathode, and the ammeter will record an electric current flow.

The electrons are emitted from the cathode with finite kinetic energy, and so with finite speed. The number of electrons reaching the anode per second, and so the electric current, may be reduced, and eventually be stopped, by gradually changing the voltage of the anode relative to that of the cathode from positive to negative values, and so producing an electric field repelling the electrons from the anode. As the frequency, and so the energy, of the photons is increased, so does the minimum negative anode to cathode voltage that is just sufficient to stop the current flow. As shown in Appendix 3.3, Planck's constant may be deduced from the slope of the line giving the variation of the stopping voltage with photon frequency, as Planck's constant equals the product of this slope and the electronic charge.

Photons possess energy but no measurable mass, yet they often behave as if they had mass. To throw light on this behaviour, it is helpful to consider the collision between two moving steel balls. The balls possess definite velocities, and kinetic energies, both before and after the collision. If the balls are elastic, so that no deformation of the balls results from the collision, and so no energy is lost in deforming them, then the sum of the kinetic energies of the two balls before and after the collision will be the same, even though the energies of the individual balls may change. It is said that the total energy of the two balls is conserved.

Now let an electron be considered, moving with a given speed and so having a definite amount of kinetic energy, to collide with a photon having some fixed frequency, and so possessing a definite amount of energy. (If the electron velocity is a substantial fraction of the speed of light, then the variation of the electron mass with electron speed would need to be taken into account.) It will be found that the sum of the energies of the electron and the photon before and after the collision remain the same, even though the energy of both the electron and the photon can change, as indicated by changes in electron velocity and photon frequency. Thus photons exhibit dual characteristics, they can behave both as waves and as particles possessing mass.

It was stated that the speed of light, or the speed of the electromagnetic waves in general, in free space or air, is 3×10^8 metres per second. In fact, the speed of light in air is less by a negligibly small amount, but in denser transparent media, such as water or glass, the speed of light is from 25% to 50% less than in free space. Furthermore, the speed of light in such media varies with the wavelength of the light as well. As a consequence of the speed of light, or the speed of electromagnetic waves in general, being lower in denser media, it is found that rays of light, or beams of electromagnetic waves, bend as they pass from a rarer medium to a denser medium, and vice versa, provided that the rays or beams impinge on the interface between the two media at an angle other than 90 degrees. The reason for the bending may be understood from the consideration of Figure 3.7.

In Figure 3.7, let P_1 and P_2 be two photons travelling parallel to each other in air. While photon P_1 is travelling in air from point A to point B, photon P_2 is travelling in water from point C to point D. Since photons travel more slowly in water than in air, distance C to D must be smaller than the distance A to B. Consequently, the directions of the two wave fronts CA and DB in air and water respectively, and also the directions of the propagation which are perpendicular to the wave fronts, will be different in the two media.

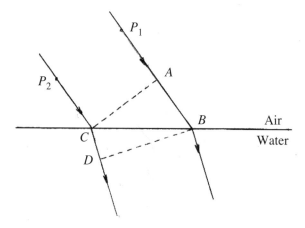

Figure 3.7

With reference to Figure 3.8, let now white light, from a source such as the sun, pass through a collimator tube, which by means of a slit and a lens at its opposite ends, produces a flat narrow beam of light, in which all photons travel parallel to each other. The beam is shown edgewise in Figure 3.8. Let this flat beam of light fall on one side of a glass prism, as shown in Figure 3.8, then the beam emerges on the other side of the prism with its direction bent, for reasons stated above.

Visible white light contains photons with a continuous range of wavelengths, ranging from 400 to 700 nanometres. It is found that red light having the longest wavelength, and the highest speed in glass, is bent the least, while violet light having the shortest wavelength, and lowest speed in glass, is bent the most. If the bent light rays are made to fall on a white solid screen, all colours of the rainbow will appear on the screen in the order of decreasing wavelength: red, orange, yellow, green, blue, and violet. Light having a single wavelength only is called monochromatic, while light having a range of wavelengths simultaneously present is referred to as possessing a spectrum of wavelengths.

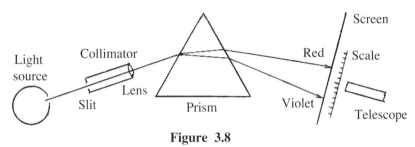

Figure 3.8

When examining the spectra of different light sources, it is found that hot solid objects, such as the filament of an incandescent lamp, or the sun, produce continuous spectra, in which all wavelengths are present. The continuous spectra are attributed to the atoms or molecules in solids being closely packed, and so continually interfering with each other's thermal vibrations.

On the other hand, hot luminous gases or vapours, in which the atoms or molecules are far apart, produce discontinuous spectra, in which only a relatively few discrete wavelengths are present. Collisions between atoms or molecules may result in some of the atoms or molecules temporarily gaining excess energies, which subsequently are given up as photons having discrete energies, and correspondingly definite fixed frequencies and wavelengths.

As an example, the sodium vapour lamp produces yellow light, which contains only two discrete wavelengths, so close to each other that for most practical purposes they may be regarded as a single wavelength. Thus, if in Figure 3.8, the light source is a sodium vapour lamp, then only a single yellow line would be seen on the screen, and the light produced by the lamp would be essentially monochromatic.

Determining, or measuring, the wavelength of monochromatic light is of prime importance. A simple arrangement allowing this to be done appears in Figure 3.9.

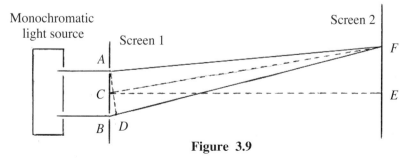

Figure 3.9

Let two flat, solid screens be placed parallel to each other, shown edgewise in Figure 3.9. Screen 1 has two narrow, horizontal, parallel slits, A and B, that are perpendicular to the plane of the paper. A monochromatic sodium vapour light source on the left illuminates the slits by producing parallel rays that reach slits A and B with their wave crests coinciding. Narrow slits cause light passing through them to be dispersed, and travel in all directions. In particular, two rays of light emerging from slits A and B in Screen 1 travel along lines AF and BF to F on Screen 2. If the difference between the lengths of the paths BF and AF, that is, $BF - AF = BD$, is one wavelength long, then the waves from the two slits reach F on Screen 2 with their crests coinciding, and so reinforce each other.

This will result in a bright line, or fringe, on Screen 2 at F. In fact, a number of lines, or fringes, will appear on Screen 2 corresponding to the cases when the distance BD is an integral multiple of the wavelength. Consequently, distance EF must be taken as the distance from E to the first bright line, or fringe. If the slit separation AB is large compared with the wavelength BD, so that the angle formed by the lines AB and AD is small, then it follows from the close similarity of the triangles ABD and CEF that the following holds to a good approximation:

(distance BD) / (distance AB) ≈ (distance EF) / (distance CF) ≈ (distance EF) / (distance CE)
from which it follows further that:
wavelength = (distance BD) ≈ (distance AB) x (distance EF) / (distance CE)

Thus, if AB = 0.1 millimetre, EF = 11.8 millimetres and CE = 2000 millimetres, then the wavelength = (0.1) x (11.8) / (2000) = 0.00059 millimetres, or 590 nanometres. More precise methods give the wavelength of the sodium vapour light as 589.3 nanometres.

A spectroscope is an instrument, the essentials of which appear in Figure 3.8, but with the screen replaced by a telescope, which can be moved relative to a graduated scale. This enables wavelengths within very narrow wavelength ranges to be picked up, and precise wavelength readings to be taken. The wavelength scales of spectroscopes need to be calibrated in terms of monochromatic light sources, the wavelengths of which have been precisely determined before.

A spectrograph is an instrument also based on the essentials shown in Figure 3.8, but in which the screen is replaced by a photosensitive film or plate. This enables a permanent record of the whole spectrum of a light source to be obtained in the form of a photograph. For example, the spectrum of hot self-luminous hydrogen gas, ascertained either by a spectroscope or a spectrograph, is shown in Figure 3.10.

Figure 3.10 shows the hydrogen spectral lines in the visible wavelength range only, but does not show the considerable number of lines in the ultraviolet region below 400 nanometres, nor any lines in the infrared region above 700 nanometres. The lines are not equally intense, as implied by their differing heights in Figure 3.10.

A model for the hydrogen atom was proposed by Niels Bohr in 1913, which was inspired by the spectral lines in the light emitted by hot hydrogen gas. The definite frequencies of these lines implied that in the hydrogen atom, the single electron revolving around the nucleus, could exist in one of a relatively few allowed orbits, and when in any one of these orbits, the electron had to possess a definite amount of energy appropriate for that orbit.

Chapter 3 — Waves — Relativity — Quanta

Now, in gases or vapours, atoms or molecules move about in a random manner, and collide from time to time. The hotter the gas or vapour is, the more violent are the random movements and the collisions. In hot hydrogen gas, the electron in a hydrogen atom may acquire extra energy from such a collision, and be forced temporarily from a lower energy orbit into a higher energy orbit. Soon after the collision, the electron falls back to a lower energy orbit, and the excess energy of the electron, which is the energy difference between the energies of the two orbits, is emitted as a photon having a definite frequency, and a corresponding definite wavelength.

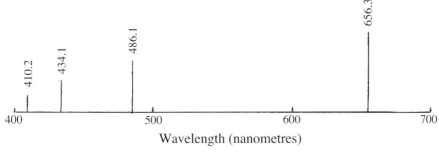

Figure 3.10

Bohr found that the wavelengths of the observed hydrogen spectral lines could be explained by satisfying the following requirement for any of the allowed orbits:

$$\left(\begin{array}{c}\text{mass of electron}\\\text{in kilograms}\end{array}\right) \times \left(\begin{array}{c}\text{orbital speed of electron}\\\text{in metres per second}\end{array}\right) \times \left(\begin{array}{c}\text{circumference of}\\\text{orbit in metres}\end{array}\right)$$
$$= (\text{an integral number } n) \times (\text{Planck's constant in joule seconds})$$

where the integral number n may be: $n = 1, 2, 3$, etc., each number corresponding to a possible allowed orbit.

A second requirement to be satisfied was that, since the electron had to be kept in its orbit around the nucleus by the electric force of attraction between the positively charged nucleus and the negatively charged electron, the electric force of attraction for any allowed orbit had to equal the force necessary for keeping the electron in that orbit.

From these two requirements it was possible to calculate for any one of the allowed orbits a number of quantities, namely: the radius and the circumference of the orbit, the speed of the electron in the orbit, and the total energy possessed by the electron while in that orbit.

The total energy of the electron, while in any particular orbit, would consist of two parts: kinetic energy associated with the electron's motion, and potential energy due to the electron being moved some distance from the nucleus against the force of attraction exercised by the nucleus on the electron. It was found that as an electron was moved further away from the nucleus to a more distant orbit, both the orbital speed and the kinetic energy decreased, while both the potential energy and the total energy increased.

If an electron fell from a higher energy orbit to a lower energy orbit, then from the known energies of these two orbits one could calculate the frequency and the wavelength of the emitted photon as the following relation was found to apply:

(energy difference between two energy levels in joules)
= (Planck's constant in joule seconds) x (frequency of photon in cycles per second)

from which:

(frequency of photon in cycles per second)
= (energy difference between two levels in joules) / (Planck's constant in joule seconds)

and also:

(wavelength of photon in metres)
= (speed of light in metres per second) / (frequency of photon in cycles per second)

In 1923, Louis De Broglie suggested that the apparently arbitrary requirement found by Niels Bohr, namely that electrons in allowed orbits had to satisfy:

(electron mass) x (electron speed) x (orbital circumference) = (integer) x (Planck's constant)

could be explained if the electron was assumed to move in a wavelike manner having a wavelength dependent on both its mass and its speed.

If wave motion is restricted to lie within certain limits, such as water waves in a rectangular swimming pool, then only an integral number of wavelengths can produce standing waves between such limits. Likewise one could expect that around any electronic orbit in an atom, only an integral number of electronic wavelengths could exist in accordance with:

(integer n) x (electronic wavelength in metres) = (circumference of orbit in metres)
where the integer n = 1, 2, 3, etc.

Thus, if in the Bohr requirement above, one replaces the orbital circumference by the product (integer) x (wavelength), it follows that the electron's wavelength, mass, and speed have to satisfy:

(electronic wavelength in metres)
= $\dfrac{\text{(Planck's constant in joule seconds)}}{\text{(mass of electron in kilograms) x (orbital speed of electron in metres per second)}}$

For example, an electron moving at 1/100 of the speed of light (3×10^6 metres per second) would have to have a wavelength:

$$\left(\frac{6.625 \times 10^{-34} \text{ joule second}}{(9.109 \times 10^{-31} \text{ kilogram}) \times (3 \times 10^6 \text{ metres per second})} \right) \approx 0.242 \times 10^{-9} \text{ metre,}$$

or 0.242 nanometre, which is within the x-ray wavelength range.

Because of the wavelike behaviour of electrons, streams of electrons can be focussed much the same way as light rays can, a property that is made use of in the electron microscope.

It would be expected that not only electrons, but all masses move in a wavelike manner, the wavelength being given as Planck's constant divided by the product (mass) x (speed). However, for masses and speeds met in everyday life, the wave nature of matter is not noticeable, because the associated wavelengths are imperceptibly small.

Calculations of numerical values for the hydrogen atom, based on Bohr's theory, are given in Appendix 3.4. Amongst others, it is shown that the 656.3 nanometre spectral line of hydrogen in Figure 3.10, is due to electrons falling from the third orbit ($n = 3$) to the second orbit ($n = 2$). It is also found that the diameter of the innermost orbit ($n = 1$) of the hydrogen atom is 1.058×10^{-10} metre, or 0.1058 nanometre, which may be considered the size of the hydrogen atom. Further, the speed of the electron in this orbit is 2.19×10^6 metres per second, or 0.73 % of the speed of light. Also, the circumference of this orbit is 3.32×10^{-10} metre, or 0.332 nanometre, which is exactly one electronic wavelength long, as would be expected from the foregoing discussion.

Elements, or compounds, whether solid, liquid, or gaseous, may all be heated to a high enough temperature, so as to bring them to a hot, self-luminous, vaporous or gaseous state. The spectra of the emitted light may then be examined over an extended wavelength range, including not only visible light, but also the ultraviolet and infrared regions.

The more electrons the atoms of elements have, the more numerous are the spectral lines in the emitted light. Each spectral line having a definite wavelength represents a transition of an electron from a definite higher energy level, to a definite lower energy level.

Soon after Bohr's theory was proposed, improved techniques in spectroscopy indicated that in the vicinity of the single wavelength hydrogen spectral lines, which were expected from Bohr's theory, a number of closely spaced lines existed, that could not be explained in terms of the theory. Furthermore, attempts to explain the spectra of multi-electron atoms in terms of Bohr's theory also failed.

An atomic orbital structure applicable to all elements was eventually arrived at as a result of extensive spectroscopic investigations of atomic spectral lines, with the aid of a new theoretical approach proposed by Ervin Schroedinger in 1926, which became known as quantum mechanics.

It appears from applying quantum mechanics to the observed spectra, that the electrons of multi-electron atoms are accommodated in a number of electronic "shells" surrounding the atomic nucleus. Within each shell there are a definite number of "subshells", and each subshell represents a definite discrete electronic energy level. Furthermore, each subshell can accommodate up to a certain number of electrons, but no more.

The shells may be numbered, or may be designated by capital letters, in increasing order of energy as: 1 or *K*, 2 or *L*, 3 or *M*, 4 or *N*, 5 or *O*, 6 or *P*, and 7 or *Q*. Each shell may contain as many subshells as its shell number. The subshells are designated by the lower case letters *s*, *p*, *d*, *f*, *q*, and *h* in increasing order of energy.

Table 3.1 shows only those shells and subshells which, for all the 92 naturally occurring elements, could contain electrons when all electrons are in the lowest possible energy levels. As a result of collisions between atoms or molecules, electrons could move temporarily into higher energy shells or subshells, such as 5*q*, 6*f*, or 7*p* for example. Table 3.1 also lists the capacities of the subshells, that is, the largest number of electrons each subshell may accommodate.

Table 3.1

Shells:	1/K	2/L		3/M			4/N				5/O				6/P			7/Q
Subshells:	1s	2s	2p	3s	3p	3d	4s	4p	4d	4f	5s	5p	5d	5f	6s	6p	6d	7s
Capacity	2	2	6	2	6	10	2	6	10	14	2	6	10	14	2	6	10	2

Only the heaviest of atoms, such as those of radium and uranium, would have electrons in the 7s subshell. Also, the electronic energies increase in the order as given in Table 3.1 for relatively heavy atoms only. For lighter atoms, the electron energies in the various subshells may assume different orders, as shown in Figure 3.11, where Z stands for the atomic number, that is, the number of protons in the atomic nucleus.

Table 3.2 shows the number of electrons in the various shells and subshells, for four of the elements, namely: hydrogen (H), oxygen (O), sodium (Na), and chorine (Cl), when these electrons occupy their lowest possible energy levels.

The outermost partly filled subshells are called valence shells. These are 1s for hydrogen, 2p for oxygen, 3s for sodium, and 3p for chlorine. Molecules of compounds are formed from the atoms of elements by an interaction of the electrons in the outermost partly filled valence shells of the atoms. Such interactions may be due to sharing the valence electrons by atoms, or it may be due to electric attraction between unlike charges.

As an example for electron sharing, the hydrogen (H) atom has a single electron in its 1s valence shell, which would be filled with 2 electrons. Normally 2 hydrogen atoms share their 1s valence electrons, thereby creating a hydrogen molecule, in which each hydrogen atom appears to have a 1s valence shell filled with 2 electrons through sharing. Since the hydrogen molecule consists of 2 hydrogen atoms, its formula is H_2.

As another example, 2 hydrogen (H) atoms may share their single 1s valence electrons with an oxygen (O) atom having 4 electrons in its 2p valence shell. In the ensuing water molecule, both hydrogen atoms appear to have 1s valence shells filled with 2 electrons, and the oxygen atom appears to have a 2p valence shell filled with 6 electrons. As the water molecule consists of 2 hydrogen atoms and 1 oxygen atom, its formula is H_2O.

An example for molecule formation through electric attraction of unlike charges, is the formation of the sodium chloride molecule from sodium (Na) and chlorine (Cl) atoms. The sodium atom loses its outermost 3s valence electron, and thereby becomes a positively charged sodium ion, while the chlorine atom gains the electron lost by the sodium atom as an extra 3p valence electron, and so it becomes a negatively charged chlorine ion. These ions are relatively stable since they have filled outermost subshells. The electrical attraction between the positively charged sodium ion, and the negatively charged chlorine ion, holds the sodium chloride molecule together. Since the sodium chloride molecule contains 1 sodium atom and 1 chlorine atom, its formula is NaCl.

Atoms form molecules because systems always seek a state of minimum energy, and the resulting molecule possesses less energy than the sum of the energies of its constituent atoms. Consequently, the resulting molecule is more stable than its component atoms.

Chapter 3 — Waves — Relativity — Quanta

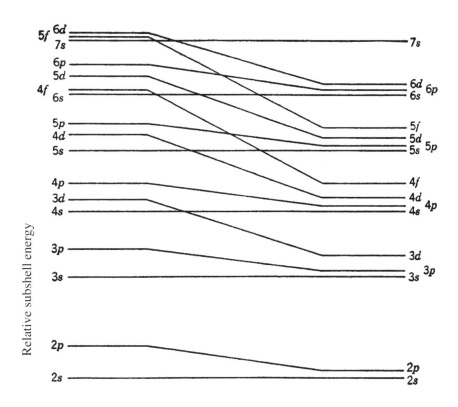

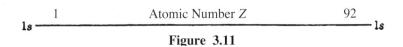

Figure 3.11

Table 3.2

Shells	1/K	2/L		3/M		
Subshells:	1s	2s	2p	3s	3p	3d
Capacity:	2	2	6	2	6	10
Hydrogen (H)	1					
Oxygen (O)	2	2	4			
Sodium (Na)	2	2	6	1		
Chlorine (Cl)	2	2	6	2	5	

The chemical processes taking place in an early electric cell devised by Alessandro Volta, consisting of a copper and a zinc plate, with blotting paper soaked in a solution of sodium chloride in water between them, can now be explained more fully than in Chapter 2.

The sodium chloride (NaCl), in the water (H_2O), separates into positively charged sodium ions and negatively charged chlorine ions. If the cell has an external resistance connected across it, the negatively charged chlorine ions give up their surplus electrons at the zinc plate, and form zinc chloride molecules ($ZnCl_2$). The sodium ions interact with water molecules, forming sodium hydroxide molecules (NaOH), and positively charged hydrogen ions. The positively charged hydrogen ions take up electrons at the copper plate, and become electrically neutral hydrogen atoms. Thus, electrons flow from the zinc plate through the external resistance to the copper plate. This process results in the copper and zinc plates of the cell acting as the positive and negative terminals respectively. The energy, expended in the resistance in the form of heat, comes from the energy difference between the starting and end products of the chemical processes. The cell is exhausted when the chemical transformations are complete.

With the passing of time, numerous more practicable cells have been devised. Of course, the constituent substances, and the chemical processes vary from cell to cell.

The essential difference between good electrical conductors and insulators is now also more fully explainable. Good electrical conductors are metallic elements, such as copper and silver, the atoms of which have a single electron in their outermost s subshells. Such electrons are only loosely bound to the atomic nuclei, they readily break away and move through the metallic crystal. When an electric field is applied, the resulting movement of these electrons leads to an electric current.

On the other hand, good electrical insulators are compounds having molecules composed of atoms with their outermost subshells filled through electron sharing. Consequently, in insulators, all electrons are tightly bound to the atomic nuclei, and so no electron movement or electric current is possible, even in the presence of moderately strong electric fields. However, in very strong electric fields, even insulators may have electrons pulled out of their valence shells, break down, and conduct.

Calculations relating to the structures of multi-electron atoms come within the domain of quantum mechanics. Such calculations entail the solutions of partial differential equations. Orbital radii and orbital electronic speeds are not calculable, only electronic energies and probable associated regions around the nucleus, namely, the shells and subshells are determinable.

Chapter 4
In Pursuit of the Human Aura

Historical Review

Investigations into the human aura extend back at least for a hundred years. In particular, Walter Kilner, a physician, had carried out extensive investigations into the human aura during the early 1900s, and presented his findings in a book titled "The Human Aura". The following is an overview of these early findings, and also of more recent claims.

It appears that only relatively few people claim to possess the gift of being able to see the human aura, although some profess to have acquired the ability through practice. Based on descriptions by such people, certain recurring properties of the aura are enumerated below.

The aura is not self-luminous, and is not visible in total darkness. It is best seen when the subject of the observation is placed around 30 centimetres in front of a dark background, and is illuminated by a dim, diffused light, such as indirect sunlight passing through a curtained window.

There appear to be three parts to the aura: the "etheric double", a dark space extending about 0.5 centimetre from the skin; the "inner aura", normally bluish, but may be any other colour, extending 5 to 10 centimetres from the skin; and the "outer aura", also coloured but fainter, extending some 20 centimetres from the skin. Occasionally rays are reported, usually originating on protuberances, such as the fingers. It is claimed that yellow colour in the aura is indicative of illness.

The aura is better seen on days when the air is clear, and is not misty or hazy. Temperature or humidity does not seem to affect the viewing. The perceiving of the aura may be aided by using coloured light for illumination, or viewing the aura through coloured glass screens, or various dye solutions contained in optical vessels with parallel quartz glass walls. Quartz glass is preferable, since it allows light with a wider range of wavelengths to pass through. Various shades of blue and carmine were found helpful, but the bluish alcoholic solution of dicyanine dye was reported to be particularly effective.

It is also claimed possible to sensitise the eyes by looking at diffused sunlight through dye solutions or coloured glass for a while, after which the ability to discern the aura by the unaided eye appears to be enhanced.

While illumination by coloured light, or viewing the aura through coloured screens, may improve the ability to see the aura, it also alters the perceived colours of the aura. In particular, using lightly coloured screens may help to distinguish the inner and outer auras, while dark coloured screens allow seeing the etheric double only.

The aura does not appear to be due to airborne particles or vapours emitted from the skin, since air movements near the skin leave the aura unaffected. It is also claimed that exposing the aura to certain gases or vapours alters the colour of the aura. Thus, exposure to chlorine gas turns the aura orange-green, bromine fumes make the aura bluish-green, while both iodine fumes and ozone gas cause the aura to turn reddish-brown.

Some subjects may learn to change the colour of their own aura at will, or may cause the emission of rays at will. Such voluntary colour changes are normally limited to the inner aura, but do not affect the outer aura. Hypnotising a subject would normally reduce the size of the aura.

It is further claimed that when a subject is placed on an insulated stool, and then electrically charged, the aura is reduced, or may disappear altogether. Positive charge is more effective than negative charge. Upon discharge the aura returns, and may be larger than normal for a whole day.

Individuals, who claim the ability to see the human aura, often also claim to be able to see an aura like mist around current carrying conductors, and between the poles of magnets. This would amount to having the ability of seeing magnetic fields, or the effects of such fields on the surrounding atmosphere. Furthermore, when a magnet is brought close to a subject, some observers see the auras of both the subject and the magnet intensify and join, and at times report rays produced between the subject and the magnet. The north and south poles of the magnet are equally effective, and so the aura does not seem to be pole sensitive.

The appearance and size of the aura appear to be dependent on the state of the nervous system. Nervous disorders, or impaired mental powers, and fainting, all reduce the size and the brightness of the aura. Finally, the aura completely disappears upon death.

Walter Kilner observed that the sensitising of his eyes with dicyanine dye screens required readjustment of his microscope for a sharp image, and so concluded that such sensitisation temporarily altered the focal length of his eyes. This suggested to him that sensitisation extended vision toward the ultraviolet region, while at the same time enhancing the ability to perceive the human aura. These together seemed to indicate that the human aura involved light at least partly extending into the ultraviolet region, and also that persons able to see the aura may have owed that ability to their vision extending into the ultraviolet, beyond the vision possessed by most people.

Recent Investigations

Extensive investigations were carried out by the author, and his associates, into the human aura over a period of years. The primary aims of the investigations were to ascertain if the aura was possibly due to incident light being reflected back by particles emitted from the skin, or perhaps the skin itself exhibited a low degree of self-luminosity within, or possibly outside, the wavelength range of light normally considered visible to humans.

With reference to Figure 4.1, the principal instruments used in the investigations were a "monochromator", and a "photomultiplier photon counting assembly" situated inside a darkroom, together with essential control and monitoring equipment to be described as the discussion proceeds. The dark room was constructed in the form of a double walled sheet metal cage, designed to minimise light leakage, and also to provide electrical shielding. Dense foam in its double walls served to enhance insulation against both light and sound.

In general, light is a mixture of a large number of electromagnetic waves of different wavelengths. Monochromators aim at isolating a single wavelength light beam from a multiple wavelength light source. However, due to practical limitations, the light produced by monochromators normally contain a narrow range of wavelengths, close enough to each other so that for practical purposes the light produced may be regarded as having a single wavelength only. Monochromators operate on the principle of the spectroscope, which was described in Chapter 3, and depicted in Figure 3.8. In a monochromator, light from a source having a wide range of wavelengths is focussed into a narrow flat beam, that is then allowed to fall on one side of a quartz glass prism, pass through the prism, and issue on the far side of the prism. Using quartz is essential, since it allows light of a wider range of wavelengths to pass through than ordinary glass does. With reference to Figure 3.8, light rays are bent both on entering and leaving the prism faces, light of different wavelengths being bent by different amounts. Thus, the light exiting from the prism is spread out into what is called a spectrum, in which light rays of different wavelengths are physically separated from each other.

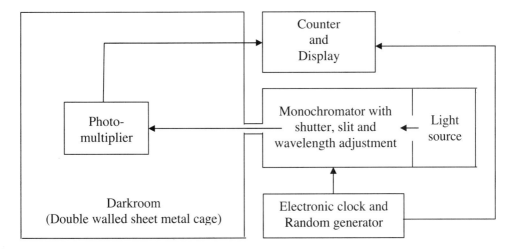

Figure 4.1

The prism in a monochromator can be mechanically rotated in such a way that the rays exiting from the prism are shifted relative to a narrow slit cut into a fixed non-transparent plate, which is placed into the path of the rays. This way, rays of any given wavelength may be caused to fall on the "output slit" in the fixed plate, and pass through that slit, while rays of other wavelengths would be blocked by the non-transparent plate. Rays emerging from the output slit would thus be nearly monochromatic, that is, they could be considered as possessing a single wavelength only.

The wavelength of the output light of the monochromator in Figure 4.1 could be set to any value from 200 to 2000 nanometres. Most observers normally see light only within the 400 to 700 nanometre wavelength region, the colour of the perceived light changing in the order: violet, blue, green, yellow, orange, and red, as the wavelength is increased from 400 to 700 nanometres. Consequently, the 400 to 700 nanometre wavelength range is referred to as the visible range. The invisible regions below 400 nanometres and above 700 nanometres are called the ultraviolet and infrared regions respectively.

The output light from the monochromator could be focussed into a narrow beam, so that at a distance of 2 metres from the output slit, the cross section of the beam was typically 0.5 centimetre wide and 3 centimetres high. Closer to the output slit, the sectional area of the beam would be proportionately smaller.

An essential feature of the monochromator was the ability to vary the intensity of the output beam, that is the number photons passing any cross sectional area of the beam per second, and in particular it was possible to reduce the intensity to zero. This could be arranged by adjusting the width of the output slit from about 0.1 millimetre down to zero.

62   Chapter 4 – In Pursuit of the Human Aura

In practice, the output light would always possess a narrow but finite wavelength range depending on the width of the output slit. Typically, a slit width of 0.02 millimetre would result in a wavelength range of about 1 nanometre wide. Thus, if the monochromator was adjusted for an output light wavelength of 500 nanometres, the actual output light intensity could be expected to peak at 500 nanometres, but with lesser amounts ranging on either side from approximately 499.5 to 500.5 nanometres. The monochromator would then be said to possess a resolution of 1 nanometre. For most practical purposes the output light could be considered monochromatic, that is, contain a single wavelength only. In general, a narrower output slit width would result in a narrower output beam sectional area, and a smaller output light wavelength range, signifying a better resolution.

Another essential device used in the investigations was a photomultiplier photon counting assembly. The heart of such an assembly is a photomultiplier tube, which is an evacuated glass tube with a number of electrodes sealed inside it, including a cathode, an anode, and up to 10 or more intermediate electrodes called dynodes. Such a tube having 10 dynodes is depicted in Figure 4.2.

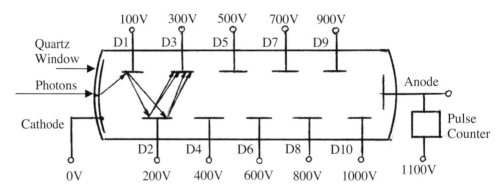

Figure 4.2

In a possible arrangement, the cathode could be connected to the negative terminal of a 1100 volt direct voltage source, while the anode would then be connected to the positive terminal of the same source through an electronic current pulse counter circuit. The voltage source must have voltage taps, at around 100 volt intervals, to which the dynodes would be connected in such a way as to keep each successive dynode 100 volts positive relative to the previous one. Thus, dynodes D1, D2, D3, ... D10 would respectively be 100, 200, 300, ... 1000 volts positive relative to the cathode, while the anode would be 1100 volts positive relative to the cathode. As a result, electric fields are established between the cathode, the successive dynodes, and the anode. The cathode normally is constituted in the form of a semitransparent electron emitting coating on the inside of a quartz window.

Now, consider a photon to fall on, and pass through, the quartz window to the semi-transparent electron emitting cathode coating. If the photon has sufficient energy, it may cause an electron to be emitted from the cathode. The emitted electron would then be accelerated to dynode D1 by the electric field force, set up due to the voltage difference between the cathode and dynode D1. In this process the electron acquires an increasing amount of kinetic energy, and when it hits dynode D1, it may cause a number of electrons to be emitted from the surface of dynode D1. These are then accelerated to dynode D2 by

Chapter 4 – In Pursuit of the Human Aura

the electric field force, set up between dynodes D1 and D2 due to the voltage difference existing between them. When these electrons impinge on dynode D2, each of them may knock a number of electrons out of dynode D2. Thus, the number of electrons emitted from successive dynodes would rapidly increase. If each electron hitting a dynode causes four electrons to be emitted, then at successive dynodes the number of electrons emitted is quadrupled, in which case each electron emitted from the cathode would result in over a million electrons impinging on the anode. A burst of a million electrons reaching the anode constitutes a detectable electric current pulse in the anode. The number of such current pulses, occurring in a given time period, may be counted by an electronic current pulse counter circuit in the anode lead.

As the cathode is sensitive to photons in the sense that photons falling on the cathode may cause electrons to be emitted from it, the cathode is often referred to as the photocathode. However, not all photons falling on the cathode cause electron emission from the cathode. Thus, the count in a given time period equals the number of those photons which, upon passing through the photomultiplier window to the cathode, are energetic enough to cause the emission of an electron from the cathode to take place. Less energetic photons falling on the cathode, without causing electron emission from the cathode, are not counted.

Consequently, in any given time period, the number of electrons emitted from the cathode is always a fraction of the number of photons impinging on the cathode. This fraction is called the "quantum efficiency", a quantity which is dependent on the photon wavelength, the window material, and the chemical composition of the electron emitting cathode coating. The quantum efficiency is determinable from practical tests. Figure 4.3 shows how the quantum efficiency depends on the photon wavelength for the photomultiplier employed in the work described here.

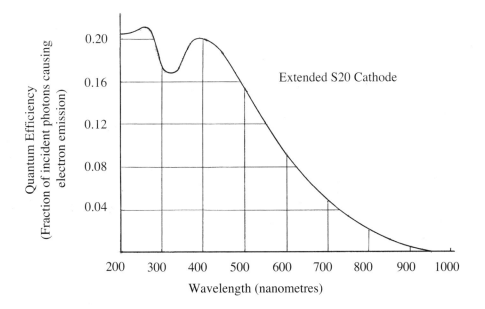

Figure 4.3

It will be noticed that the wavelength range in Figure 4.3 extends from 200 to 950 nanometres. The curve falls to zero at 950 nanometres because the cathode coating of the particular photomultiplier used in the investigations, did not emit electrons in the infrared region beyond the wavelength of 950 nanometres. On the other hand, in the ultraviolet region, the coating did emit electrons at wavelengths well below 200 nanometres. But, the ability of the quartz window to allow photons to pass through it, falls sharply below 200 nanometres. Consequently, the useable wavelength range of the tube extended from 200 to 950 nanometres.

It is notable that while the count equals the number of electrons emitted from the cathode in a given period of time, from this the number of photons striking the window in the same period of time can be deduced if the quantum efficiency is known. The electron count is often loosely termed as photon count, and the apparatus is often called a photon counter.

It may be helpful to note that since the photocathode is normally a semitransparent coating on the inside surface of the photomultiplier window, the effective window area is essentially the same as the cathode area. Further, it may be worth noting that a small fraction of the photons falling on the photomultiplier window is absorbed by the window, and does not reach the photocathode. This small effect is taken account of by the quantum efficiency curve in Figure 4.3, and in what follows the terms: photomultiplier window, photocathode, or just window, or cathode, are used interchangeably.

In the work described here, it was imperative that only photons from the intended source, such as a human subject, or a monochromator, reached the photocathode, and any other "stray" light was totally excluded. In order to achieve this, the photomultiplier photon counter assembly was housed in a darkroom, essentially a double walled sheet metal cage, that itself was located in a windowless room. The output light beam of the monochromator was then passed into the windowless room, and the cage, from the adjacent laboratory, through a lightproof coupling, and allowed to fall on the photomultiplier window at right angles to the beam, with the window typically 2 metres from the inlet point of the beam. The diameter of the circular cathode area was 4.5 centimetres, that could accommodate the light beam falling on it, which had a sectional area of 0.5 by 3 centimetres or less.

An undesirable property of photomultipliers is that they produce "dark" current pulses, and corresponding dark counts, even when no light falls on the cathode. Such pulses are due to thermal vibrations of the atoms in the electron emitting coating of the cathode. Atoms colliding can knock electrons out of the atoms much the same way as photons impinging on the atoms can. It is essential to reduce the dark counts, in order to minimise any errors resulting from them. This was done by enclosing the photomultiplier in a cooled housing, that enabled the cooling of the photocathode to a temperature of around -30° Celsius. At this temperature the atomic vibrations, and consequent electron emissions, were reduced to a level yielding dark counts of around 10 per second, which was found acceptable for the investigations at hand. Further, the photomultiplier housing also needed to have a quartz window, through which photons could reach the photomultiplier window and the cathode behind it, over the full wavelength range of the photomultiplier.

For all the investigations described in the current chapter, the electronic current pulse counter circuit was designed to count the photomultiplier anode current pulses occurring in accurately measured 10 second periods, as determined by an electronic clock circuit. Counting could be done by one of two methods.

Chapter 4 – In Pursuit of the Human Aura

One of these methods of counting could be described as the "single count method". When using this method, a push button had to be pressed to initiate the counting process. The circuit would then count the number of anode current pulses over the ensuing 10 second period. Two short audible beeps were also produced, the onsets of which marked the beginning and the end of the 10 second count period. The number of current pulses, which have occurred during the 10 second count period, would then be shown on a numerical display after the second beep.

The second method of counting may be designated the "continuous count method". This involved an electronic clock producing short beeps, the onsets of which were accurately spaced to be 10 seconds apart. Counts were taken by the circuit during successive 10 second periods between beeps. A count taken during any particular 10 second period would be displayed during the next 10 second period. Thus, after every beep the display showed the count taken during the 10 second period preceding the beep.

The beeps were audible to the experimenter in the laboratory, and also to any subject in the cage through an intercom. The intercom also facilitated verbal communications between the experimenter and the subject.

It was also possible to either pass light from the monochromator into the cage, or block the light from entering the cage, during any randomly selected 10 second period between any two consecutive beeps, by means of a mechanical shutter, which was activated by an electronic random generator circuit coupled to the electronic clock.

While counts were always taken over 10 second periods, these were often divided by 10, so as to convert them into counts per second for calculating and stating results.

It may be helpful at this stage to consider a numerical example. Let the monochromator output light wavelength be set to 500 nanometres, and the output slit be so adjusted that the difference between the actual count (shutter open) and the dark count (shutter closed) is 200 per second. Then from Figure 4.3, the number of photons falling on the cathode per second must be:

(number of photons falling on the cathode per second)

$$= \left(\frac{\text{number of electrons emitted per second}}{\text{quantum efficiency at 500 nanometres}} \right) = \frac{200}{0.153} \approx 1310$$

The energy of each 500 nanometre photon is:

(Planck's constant) x (photon frequency)

= (Planck's constant) x (speed of light) / (photon wavelength)

$$= \frac{(6.625 \times 10^{-34} \text{ joule second}) \times (3 \times 10^{8} \text{ metres per second})}{(500 \times 10^{-9} \text{ metre})}$$

= 3.975×10^{-19} joule.

The energy delivered to the cathode by the number of photons falling on the cathode per second, in joules per second, is then:

(energy per photon in joules) x (number of photons delivered per second)

= $(3.975 \times 10^{-19}) \times (1310) \approx 5.21 \times 10^{-16}$ joule per second $\approx 5.21 \times 10^{-16}$ watt.

Note that since energy created, carried, or expended per second is called power, which is measured in watts, one may alternatively say that the power delivered to the cathode by the photons falling on it is 5.21×10^{-16} watt.

The procedure followed in investigating the aura of individual persons, usually referred to as subjects, may now be described. As stated earlier, the output light beam from the monochromator was passed into a lightproof metal cage, and allowed to fall on the photomultiplier window approximately 2 metres from the entrance point of the beam. The light beam on its way to the window was arranged to pass between a pair of parallel, horizontal prongs. The subject inside the cage was then positioned with various parts of her or his body, such as the head, hand, arm, and abdomen, in gentle contact with the edges of the prongs. This way the light beam could be made to pass parallel to, and at a known distance from, the surface of the subject's skin. This distance could be varied from 0.5 centimetre to 15 centimetres by appropriately adjusting the prongs relative to the beam.

It was expected that if the aura consisted of particles emitted from the skin, then some of the photons passing near the subject's body may be reflected back toward the source, or at least would be deflected, and so would be prevented from reaching the photocathode. Thus, at a given monochromator output beam intensity, one would expect the photomultiplier count to be lower with a subject near to the beam, than with a subject far from the beam. This would mean that observers of the aura see light reflected from aural particles, much the same way as observers seeing a physical object actually perceive light reflected from that object.

It could be that such reflections are more readily observable at certain wavelengths, and not necessarily at others. Also, if the light beam intensity were too high, then the number of photons in a given volume of space next to the skin could be large compared with the number of emitted particles from the skin, in which case only a small fraction of the photons would suffer reflection or deflection, and the effect would then go unnoticed. The distance of the beam from the surface of the skin could also be an important factor.

It was therefore necessary to carry out tests over a range of beam intensities, wavelengths, and beam to skin separations. Six subjects were tested repeatedly this way. In no case was a reduction in the count detected. Thus, it seems that the monochromator light beam passes near the human body unhindered, and so the aura is not seen as a reflection of light from any substance emitted from the skin within the 200 to 950 nanometre wavelength range.

In seeking further confirmation of this negative result, the photomultiplier was next placed adjacent to the entry point of the light beam into the cage. A non-reflecting collimator tube was mounted in front of the window of the photomultiplier housing, having such length and diameter, and so directed, that the photomultiplier could respond to scattered photons from the region where the beam passed adjacent to the body, but was not able to pick up any photons which may have originated from the skin.

Again various intensities and wavelengths were tried for different distances from various parts of the body. In no case could any scattered light be detected, leading once more to the conclusion that the aura has no detectable reflectivity, or scatter effect, in the 200 to 950 nanometre wavelength range.

The question then arose whether the aura perhaps possessed a low degree of self-luminosity. In order to test for this possibility, non-reflecting rectangular horns were mounted in front of the photomultiplier housing window. A typical horn aperture was 5 x 25 centimetres.

Chapter 4 – In Pursuit of the Human Aura

The long side of the aperture was positioned parallel to the body, and 1 to 5 centimetres away from it. This enabled photons to be gathered from a rather large volume of space adjacent to the body, but to exclude any photons originating from the skin.

Once again the results were negative, no self-luminosity could be detected adjacent to any part of the body. The conclusion was that the aura did not exhibit any detectable self-luminosity in the 200 to 950 nanometre range, within the sensitivity of the apparatus.

In the foregoing, the space adjacent to the human body, extending up to 20 centimetres from the skin's surface, was examined for reflectivity and self-luminosity with negative results. In these tests looking at the skin's surface was deliberately excluded. While the skin obviously reflects incident photons, the question arose if it exhibits detectable self-luminosity, that is, if it emits photons itself.

In seeking an answer to this question, a collimator tube was mounted in front of the window of the photomultiplier housing. The diameter of the collimator tube was 5 centimetres, and its length was 13 centimetres, while the photocathode lay 4 centimetres behind the housing window. This meant that parts of the human body placed just in front of the collimator tube were 17 centimetres from the photocathode, and also that photons reaching the photocathode could originate from anywhere within a 5 centimetre diameter area. Parts of the human body placed in front of the collimator included the fingers, palms, nose, forehead, eyes, chest, and the abdomen.

The counts taken indicated that all parts of the human body emitted photons, but that the fingertips were much more effective emitters than areas of flat skin. Consequently, initial investigations were carried out with three fingertips, namely those of the middle finger and the fingers adjacent to it, placed on a platform just inside the entrance to the collimator tube.

Alternate counts were taken over successive 10 second periods, with the fingers in place, and the fingers removed, yielding both active counts and dark counts respectively. The differences of consecutive active and dark counts yielded net counts, which were measures of the number of photons emitted from the fingertips over 10 second periods. As a rule, 10 consecutive net counts were averaged, and 1 such average was obtained every 10 minutes up to 3 hours. This was done for three different subjects. The results of these tests are shown in Figure 4.4, where the subjects are identified by their initials.

As seen from Figure 4.4, subject G.K. had the highest initial net count, over 1100 in 10 seconds, that is 110 per second, but the count decayed to about 1/3 in 3 hours, and remained close to that level up to 8 hours. On the other hand, subject P.B. exhibited a lower net count, which fluctuated, but showed little decay over 3 hours. Finally, subject A.D. yielded net counts lying between those for subjects G.K. and P.B. The dark count, obtained with the fingers removed, is also shown in Figure 4.4. The dark count was around 150 over 10 seconds, or 15 per second, and it exhibited next to no fluctuations.

The results given in Figure 4.4 are "all-pass", in the sense that photons of any wavelength within the photomultiplier wavelength range of 200 to 950 nanometres may have been present. The question arose that if the overall photomultiplier wavelength range is divided into a number of narrow subranges, how many photons are emitted within each subrange in a given period of time, and what is the energy associated with the photons within these subranges, or in other words how does the energy distribution depend on wavelength.

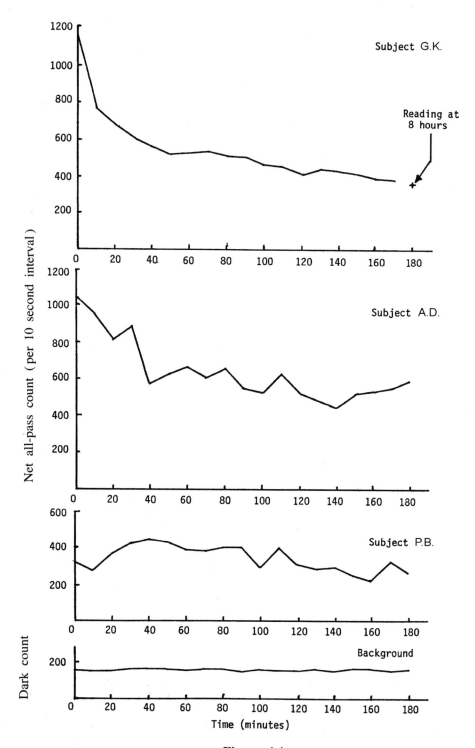

Figure 4.4

Chapter 4 – In Pursuit of the Human Aura

One way of obtaining this kind of information is by interposing optical filters between the fingertips and the window of the photomultiplier housing. A "band-pass" filter allows photons falling on it to pass through within a given wavelength range, while it blocks photons outside that wavelength range. Figure 4.5 shows a band-pass filter transmission curve. Such a curve gives the fraction of the incident photons that pass through the filter, in any given time period, at particular wavelengths.

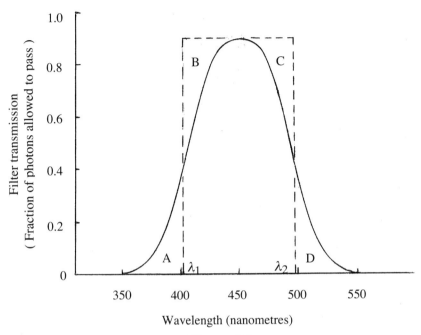

Figure 4.5

It will be seen, that as the wavelength of the photons falling on the filter increases, the change from blocking to passing and then back to blocking is gradual, and that 100% pass is never reached. The filter curve can be easily deduced, by obtaining net counts from a monochromator at various wavelengths, with the filter in front of the window of the photomultiplier housing, and also with the filter removed, and then forming the ratio of the two net counts. Net counts are the differences of monochromator counts less dark counts.

For the purposes of the investigations at hand, the filter curve can be approximated by a rectangle as shown in dashed lines in Figure 4.5, having the same height as the filter curve, and sides such that: area A = area B, and area C = area D. This yields an idealised pass range for the filter, given by the base of the rectangle extending from wavelength λ_1 to wavelength λ_2, within which the fraction of the incident photons transmitted is considered to be constant and equal to the height of the rectangle, and outside of which it is assumed that all photons are blocked. It may be worth noting that given the equality of the areas above, the area under the actual filter curve equals the area of the rectangle.

One may then insert the filter in front of the window of the photomultiplier housing, and so the photocathode, and take "active" counts from the fingertips, and also take "dark" counts with the fingers removed, over alternate 10 second periods. The average of the differences of consecutive active and dark counts is the average net count, from which the average energy reaching the photocathode over 10 seconds, from three finger tips 17 centimetres from the cathode, within the λ_1 to λ_2 wavelength range, may be determined.

In practice better results may be obtained by using "long-pass" filters which block shorter wavelength photons, and pass longer wavelength photons, with a gradual change from blocking to passing as the wavelength of the incident photons increases. The transmission curves of two long pass filters are shown in Figure 4.6, marked F_1 and F_2. These curves give the fraction of the incident photons transmitted by the filter, at all wavelengths of interest, in any given time period.

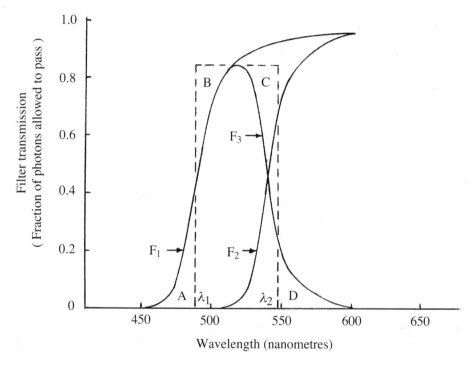

Figure 4.6

If active counts are taken from the fingertips through two long-pass filters over two consecutive 10 second periods, and the two counts are differenced, the result is the same as the net count which would be obtained with a single equivalent band-pass filter. The filter curve of this equivalent band-pass filter is the difference between the two long-pass filter curves, wavelength by wavelength, and is shown in Figure 4.6 marked F_3. One may thus obtain the same result with two long-pass filters as with a one band-pass filter, by using the idealised rectangular equivalent of the filter curve F_3 shown in dashed lines in Figure 4.6. The height of this rectangle equals the height of the filter curve F_3, while the base of the rectangle, $(\lambda_2 - \lambda_1)$, is determined by making: area A = area B, and area C = area D, the same way as was done in Figure 4.5. The fraction of the incident photons passed by the idealised filter within the wavelength range λ_1 to λ_2, in a given time period, equals the height of the rectangle, while outside this wavelength range all photons are blocked.

Chapter 4 – In Pursuit of the Human Aura

Using long-pass filters has two advantages. Firstly, there is no need to take dark counts, since when differencing two active long-pass counts, the dark count components cancel out. Secondly, the wavelength ranges λ_1 to λ_2 can be made narrower this way.

The average net count is the average of a number of differences of active counts taken with two long-pass filters consecutively over 10 second periods. From this average net count, the average energy reaching the photocathode over 10 seconds, within the λ_1 to λ_2 range, from three fingertips 17 centimetres from the photocathode, may be deduced the same way as for band-pass filters.

Using a combination of band-pass and long-pass filters, the overall wavelength range of the photomultiplier tube, namely 200 to 950 nanometres, was divided into 9 subranges as follows: 263 to 385, 382 to 484, 489 to 543, 529 to 574, 572 to 614, 612 to 660, 662 to 710, 703 to 763, 755 to 870, where all figures are in nanometres. It will be noticed that there are small overlaps and gaps between the subranges, which arose from the limited availability of suitable filters. Changing filters was greatly assisted by mounting the filters around the circumference of a wheel, so pivoted as to allow each filter to be rotated into position in front of the window of the photomultiplier housing, one filter at a time. A filter change could be accomplished within fraction of a second this way.

Let it be recalled, that at any one wavelength, only a fraction of the photons falling on the photomultiplier window cause electron emission from the cathode, and that this fraction varies from one wavelength to another as given in Figure 4.3. However, if the wavelength range λ_1 to λ_2 is small enough, then it may be assumed with little error that this fraction is constant within the λ_1 to λ_2 range, at a value applicable at the centre of the range.

Although counts were taken over 10 second periods for practical reasons, the energy reaching the photocathode within a given wavelength range would normally be calculated and given per second. To do this requires to work with the average net count per second, which is simply the average net count over 10 seconds divided by 10.

The energy actually reaching the photocathode per second through the idealised filters in Figures 4.5 and 4.6, suffers a reduction because these filters do not allow all photons to pass within their λ_1 to λ_2 pass ranges. The energy of interest is that amount of energy emitted from the fingers, which would reach the photocathode per second, 17 centimetres from the fingertips, within the λ_1 to λ_2 range of an ideal filter passing all photons within that wavelength range (100% transmission), and blocking all photons outside that range (zero transmission). The calculation of the value of this energy, from the average net count per second, involves the following steps:

(energy which would reach the photocathode per second within the λ_1 to λ_2 range at 100% transmission)

$$= \frac{\begin{pmatrix} \text{energy per photon at the} \\ \text{middle of the } \lambda_1 \text{ to } \lambda_2 \text{ range} \\ \text{in joules} \end{pmatrix} \times \begin{pmatrix} \text{number of photons which actually} \\ \text{reaches the cathode per second within} \\ \text{the } \lambda_1 \text{ to } \lambda_2 \text{ range through the filter} \end{pmatrix}}{\begin{pmatrix} \text{fraction of photons passing the filter in the } \lambda_1 \text{ to } \lambda_2 \text{ range} \\ = \text{height of the rectangle in Figure 4.4 or 4.5} \end{pmatrix}}$$

where one has:

(energy per photon at the middle of the λ_1 to λ_2 range in joules)

$$= \frac{\begin{pmatrix} \text{Planck's constant} \\ 6.625 \times 10^{-34} \text{ joule second} \end{pmatrix} \times \begin{pmatrix} \text{speed of light} \\ 3 \times 10^8 \text{ metres per second} \end{pmatrix}}{\left(\text{wavelength at the middle of the } \lambda_1 \text{ to } \lambda_2 \text{ range in metres} \right)}$$

and also:

$$\begin{pmatrix} \text{number of photons which actually reaches the cathode} \\ \text{per second within } \lambda_1 \text{ to } \lambda_2 \text{ range through the filter} \end{pmatrix}$$

$$= \frac{(\text{ net count per second within the } \lambda_1 \text{ to } \lambda_2 \text{ range })}{\begin{pmatrix} \text{fraction of the incident photons on the photomultiplier window} \\ \text{resulting in electron emission from the photocathode at the centre of the} \\ \lambda_1 \text{ to } \lambda_2 \text{ range} \end{pmatrix}}$$

For example, two particular long-pass filters used in the actual tests were Wratten 29 and Wratten 92. Working with the filter curves of these filters as shown in Figure 4.6, yielded the height of the idealised rectangle = 0.96, and the base $(\lambda_2 - \lambda_1) = (660 - 612) = 48$ nanometres with centre at 636 nanometres. From Figure 4.3, at 636 nanometres, the fraction of the incident photons on the photomultiplier window causing electron emission from the photocathode is 0.073 (or 7.3%). The average of 50 net counts with the above two filters was 370 over 10 seconds, or 37 per second. One then has:

(number of photons reaching the photocathode per second)

= (37) / (0.073) ≈ 507 photons per second,

(energy per photon at 636 nanometres)

= $(6.625 \times 10^{-34}) \times (3 \times 10^8) / (636 \times 10^{-9})$ ≈ 3.13×10^{-19} joule,

and so:

$$\begin{pmatrix} \text{energy reaching the photocathode per second within the 612 to 660} \\ \text{nanometre wavelength range at 100\% filter transmission} \end{pmatrix}$$

= $(3.13 \times 10^{-19}) \times (507) / (0.96)$ ≈ 1.65×10^{-16} joule per second ≈ 1.65×10^{-16} watt.

In what follows, the energy reaching the photocathode per second through a filter will be understood to mean, energy per second at 100% filter transmission, within the filter pass range of λ_1 to λ_2.

The "power density" is defined as power (energy per second) reaching the photocathode per nanometre wavelength, which is the energy per second within the λ_1 to λ_2 wavelength range divided by the range, namely $(\lambda_2 - \lambda_1)$. Thus for the above case:

(power density) = $(1.65 \times 10^{-16}) / (660 - 612)$ ≈ 3.44×10^{-18} watt per nanometre.

Using the same procedure, one may determine within the above wavelength ranges both the power (energy per second), and the power density (power per nanometre), reaching the photocathode, from three fingertips 17 centimetres from the photocathode. The results obtained are shown in Figure 4.7, for the same three subjects whose overall net count in the 200 to 950 nanometre photomultiplier wavelength range was determined before,

Chapter 4 – In Pursuit of the Human Aura

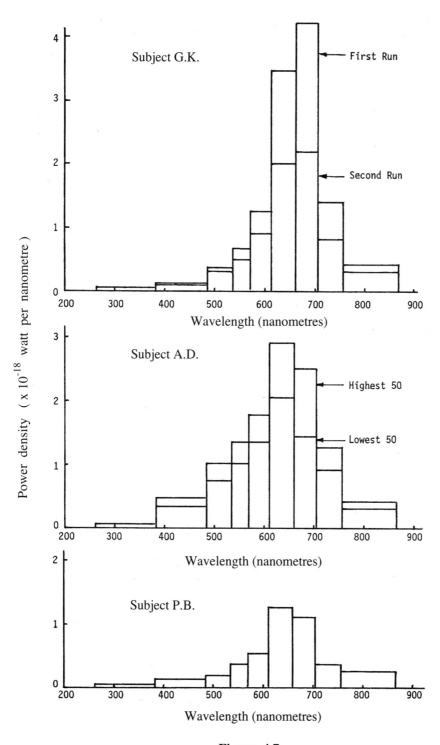

Figure 4.7

and presented in Figure 4.4. Each column in Figure 4.7 is the average of 50 readings, obtained from five experimental runs, conducted on five different days at least one week apart, with 10 readings per column per experimental run. It was stated earlier that there were small gaps and overlaps between the idealised filter wavelength ranges. In Figure 4.7 the filter range boundaries have been adjusted by small amounts, by placing the boundaries in the middle of the gaps and overlaps, and thereby facilitating their removal. (As a result of these adjustments, the 612 to 660 nanometre range in the above example becomes 613 to 661 nanometres, which has a negligible effect on the calculated results).

As shown in Figure 4.4, subject G.K. exhibited considerable decay of the all-pass count with time. Consequently, for this subject, in each experimental run, 10 net count readings per column were taken just after entering the cage, and another 10 one hour later, yielding two sets of results. In Figure 4.7, these correspond to the top of each column, and the horizontal line further down within each column, respectively. The difference shows the power density loss taking place within one hour. In particular, the above sample calculation for the 612 to 660 nanometre wavelength range, which yielded the power density figure of 3.44×10^{-18} watt per nanometre, is the result obtained for subject G.K. just after entering the cage, as inspection of Figure 4.7 would confirm.

Subject A.D. exhibited less decay with time, but more fluctuations of the all-pass count, as indicated in Figure 4.4. In order to demonstrate these fluctuations, Figure 4.7 gives two sets of results for subject A.D., based on the average of the 50 highest readings, and the 50 lowest readings, given by the top of each column, and the horizontal line further down within each column, respectively.

Since subject P.B. exhibited little decay, and only modest fluctuations of the all-pass count in Figure 4.4, only one set of results were obtained for this subject, as shown in Figure 4.7.

The area of any one rectangle in Figure 4.7 is the base multiplied by the height, and equals the power that would reach the photocathode from three fingers through the corresponding ideal filter, that is, if that filter passed all photons within its wavelength range, and blocked all photons outside that range. The total power reaching the photocathode, under these conditions, is the sum of all the rectangular areas in Figure 4.7.

So, in Figure 4.7, for subject G.K. just after entering the cage, with the filter wavelength ranges so rounded as to remove the gaps and overlaps, the sum of the rectangular areas may be estimated as:

$$(870 - 759) \times (0.5 \times 10^{-18}) + (759 - 706) \times (1.3 \times 10^{-18}) + (706 - 661) \times (4.3 \times 10^{-18})$$
$$+ (661 - 613) \times (3.4 \times 10^{-18}) + (613 - 573) \times (1.1 \times 10^{-18}) + (573 - 536) \times (0.7 \times 10^{-18})$$
$$+ (536 - 487) \times (0.3 \times 10^{-18}) + (487 - 383) \times (0.1 \times 10^{-18}) + (383 - 263) \times (0.05 \times 10^{-18})$$
$$= (55.5 + 68.9 + 193.5 + 163.2 + 44.0 + 25.9 + 14.7 + 10.4 + 6.0) \times 10^{-18}$$
$$= 582 \times 10^{-18} = 5.82 \times 10^{-16} \text{ watt.}$$

This is the power associated with the photons, which can reach the photocathode. However, the number of photons emitted from the three fingertips far exceeds the number of photons, which may reach the photocathode. Let it be assumed that photons emitted from the fingers travel in equal numbers in all directions, and only those following a straight line path from the fingertips to the photocathode actually reach the cathode, that is no photons can reach the cathode by reflection from nearby surfaces, such as the inner surface of the collimator tube. Then, since the cathode is 17 centimetres from the fingertips, one has:

Chapter 4 – In Pursuit of the Human Aura

$$\frac{\text{(total number of photons emitted from the fingers per second)}}{\text{(number of photons reaching the cathode per second)}}$$

$$= \frac{\text{(area of sphere with 17 centimetre radius)}}{\text{(area of cathode with 2.25 centimetre radius)}}$$

$$= \frac{(4) \times (3.14) \times (17) \times (17)}{(3.14) \times (2.25) \times (2.25)} \approx \frac{3630}{15.9} \approx 228$$

where $\pi = 3.14$ is the number used in calculating circular and spherical areas.

The foregoing assumptions may be subject to substantial error, and so the above figure must be considered an upper limit. However, it may be assumed with confidence that the total number of photons emitted from the fingers per second, could be around 100 or more times the number of photons reaching the photocathode per second. Thus, the total power radiated from three fingers would be of the order of 10^{-14} watt.

The obvious conclusion from the spectral distributions depicted in Figure 4.7 is that, apart from the very low power levels, most of the photon emission falls within the visible wavelength region, and is concentrated within the 600 to 700 nanometre wavelength range, corresponding to visible red light. Whether observers can actually see light emission at such low power levels is to be considered later on.

Photon emissions from other parts of the body, that is, other than the fingers, were found to be too low for spectral distributions to be determined by means of optical filters. However, unfiltered all-pass counts could be obtained as described above in conjunction with Figure 4.4. Such all pass counts were obtained with the 5 centimetre diameter collimator tube described earlier, inserted between the window of the photomultiplier housing and the body surface, ensuring that only photons originating from a 5 centimetre diameter circular body surface area could contribute to the all-pass count.

Average net counts were obtained from seven areas of body surface, centring on the palm, nose, forehead, right eye, left eye, chest, and abdomen. This was done for the same three subjects for whom results are given in Figures 4.4 and 4.7. The experimental procedure involved taking active counts over 10 second periods, with each of the above body surface areas placed in front of the collimator successively, and also taking 10 second dark counts between the active counts with the body surfaces removed. The differences between active counts and dark counts then yielded net counts. This procedure was repeated 10 times in an experimental run, so as to yield 10 net counts for each body surface. The times required for such experimental runs ranged up to 1 hour, depending on inevitable delays between successive 10 second count periods, and also on rest periods requested by subjects.

Five such experimental runs were arranged on five different days, typically a week apart, for each subject, leading to 50 net counts for each body surface of each subject.

The average net count per second equals the average net count in 10 seconds, as obtained above, divided by 10. Average net counts per second may be converted into estimates of energy emitted per second, that is power, by making the assumption that photon emissions from all body surfaces are concentrated in the 600 to 700 nanometre wavelength region as was found for the fingers. Thus, it may be reasonably assumed that all photon energies correspond to the wavelength at the centre of this range, namely 650 nanometres,

Chapter 4 – In Pursuit of the Human Aura

and also that the fraction of photons falling on the photomultiplier window, which cause electron emission from the photocathode, is the figure applicable to a wavelength of 650 nanometres in Figure 4.3, namely 0.067. One then has:

(energy per photon at 650 nanometres in joules)

$$= \frac{(\text{Planck's constant } 6.625 \times 10^{-34} \text{ joule second}) \times (\text{speed of light } 3 \times 10^{8} \text{ metres per second})}{(\text{wavelength } 650 \times 10^{-9} \text{ metre})}$$

$$= (6.625 \times 10^{-34}) \times (3 \times 10^{8}) / (650 \times 10^{-9}) \approx 3.06 \times 10^{-19} \text{ joule.}$$

Hence:

(energy reaching the photocathode per second in watts)

$$= \frac{(\text{energy per photon at 650 nanometres in joules}) \times (\text{average net all pass count per second})}{(\text{fraction of photons falling on the cathode causing electron emission at 650 nanometres})}$$

$\approx (3.06 \times 10^{-19}) \times (\text{average net all pass count per second}) / 0.067$

$\approx (\text{average net all pass count per second}) \times (4.56 \times 10^{-18})$ watt.

Thus, dividing the average net count per second by 0.067, gives the number of photons reaching the photocathode per second, and multiplying the average net count per second by 4.56×10^{-18} gives the average power in watts reaching the photocathode, via the collimator tube from selected 5 centimetre diameter areas of body surface. The results, rounded to two figures in Table 4.1, were obtained this way, except for the fingertip results, that were obtained by the more accurate method of summing the rectangular areas in Figure 4.7.

Table 4.1

Part of Body	Subject G.K.			Subject A.D.			Subject P.B.		
	Count per second	Photons per second	Power $\times 10^{-16}$ watt	Count per second	Photons per second	Power $\times 10^{-16}$ watt	Count per second	Photons per second	Power $\times 10^{-16}$ watt
Fingers	128	1910	5.8	126	1880	5.7	51	760	2.3
Palm	46	690	2.1	64	960	2.9	53	790	2.4
Nose	20	280	0.91	37	550	1.7	24	360	1.1
Forehead	14	210	0.63	26	390	1.2	12	180	0.54
Right Eye	18	250	0.82	21	310	0.95	15	220	0.68
Left Eye	16	240	0.72	17	240	0.77	16	220	0.72
Chest	7.9	120	0.36	6.8	100	0.31	4.0	60	0.18
Abdomen	5.1	76	0.23	2.9	43	0.13	6.0	90	0.27

The collimator tube was coated with a non-reflecting substance. Since emitted photons may travel in all directions away from the body surface, most of these photons would strike the non-reflecting collimator wall, and would be absorbed, with only a small fraction reaching the cathode through reflections from the collimator wall. Thus, arguing as for the fingers before, the number of photons emitted from 5 centimetre diameter circular body surface areas, could be up to 100 times the counts listed in Table 4.1.

Chapter 4 – In Pursuit of the Human Aura

Inspection of Table 4.1 indicates that after the fingers, the palm and the nose are the next most effective radiators of photons, while flat skin surfaces on the chest and the abdomen are the least effective. It may also be worth noting that subject G.K., with the highest photon emission, did not claim to possess paranormal abilities, while subjects A.D. and P.B., with lower photon emission, did claim to have psychic abilities, including abilities of healing. The results in Table 4.1 do not suggest any correlation between photon emission and claimed psychic abilities.

As stated in the historical review section of this chapter, an earlier investigator, Walter Kilner, proposed that the aura could be associated with light emission outside the visible wavelength region, and those able to see it, perhaps possessed vision extending beyond the normally visible range. However, Figure 4.7 indicates that photon emission from human fingertips is very low in the ultraviolet and infrared wavelength regions, and thus photon emission within those regions is an unlikely source of the aura seen by some observers.

Nevertheless, tests were undertaken aiming at comparing the "bandwidth of vision" of a number of subjects, that is the wavelength ranges within which various subjects can see light emanations. Subjects tested included some who claimed the ability to see the human aura, and some who made no such claim.

The essential items of equipment for these tests were the formerly described lightproof cage in a windowless room, a monochromator in the adjacent laboratory, with its output light passed into the cage through a lightproof coupling, and a photomultiplier photon counting assembly inside the cage. The light beam issuing from the monochromator output slit was arranged to fall, at right angles, on the window of the photon counting assembly inside the cage, situated approximately 2 metres from the light inlet point. The subject to be tested was seated with her or his head just below the window of the photomultiplier housing. A concave quartz lens, mounted in front of the light inlet into the cage, served to spread the cross sectional area of the inlet light beam. This area, in the plane of the photomultiplier window, had to be so large that the photocathode and the subject's eyes were exposed to the same light intensity, that is, the same number of photons crossing 1 square centimetre area per second. This had to be true even if the subject moved her or his head by small amounts. The concave lens was made of quartz glass so that it would pass ultraviolet light.

The monochromator enabled the wavelength of the light to be set to any value from 200 nanometres in the ultraviolet region, through the visible, up to 2000 nanometres in the infrared region. The output slit width of the monochromator was adjustable, which enabled the setting of the light intensity to selectable fixed values. As mentioned previously, the monochromator output light would normally contain a range of wavelengths in addition to the set value, however, these could be limited to lie within half a nanometre on either side of the set value, by keeping the width of the output slit small enough.

When deciding whether a subject can see light of a given wavelength and intensity, a simple "yes" or "no" statement from the subject cannot be relied on. It is necessary to adopt a statistical approach. The subject would hear short beeps delivered from an electronic clock through an intercom at regular intervals, typically 10 seconds apart. Between any two beeps, the light from the monochromator would either be passed into the cage, or blocked from entering the cage, by means of a light trap operated by an electronic random generator coupled to the clock. This meant that between any two beeps the passing or blocking of the light was randomly selected, much the same way as a tossed coin would normally land randomly "head" or "tail" uppermost. The subject was provided with two push buttons, designated "yes" and "no", the "yes" button to be pressed between any two beeps if the light was perceived, and the "no" button to be actuated between two beeps if no light was perceived. At any given wavelength and intensity setting, the subject was asked for 30 consecutive push button operations, which in general could yield a mixture of "yes" and "no" responses. Any of these responses could be correct or incorrect, in accordance with the Table 4.2 below:

Table 4.2

Light on or off	Button Pressed	Response
On	Yes	Correct
Off	No	Correct
On	No	Incorrect
Off	Yes	Incorrect

If at some set values of wavelength and intensity, a subject came up with 30 correct "yes" responses, then the subject was considered seeing the light clearly. If, however, out of 30 responses around 15 were correct, and 15 were incorrect, then the subject was considered guessing only, and one would have to conclude that she or he was unable to perceive the light. The probability of a given result being due to chance, or guessing, will be considered in Chapter 6 in some detail. For the present, let it be stated that the probability of getting 20 or more correct responses out of 30 attempts by chance, or guessing, is less than 5%. At this level of probability, it would usually be assumed that 20 or more correct responses out of 30 attempts are not due to guessing, but indicate the that the subject is perceiving the light, even if with some difficulty. On the contrary, 19 or less correct responses out of 30 attempts would be considered to indicate inability to see the light.

In order to cover the full wavelength range of the monochromator, it was found necessary to employ two different input light sources to the monochromator. A tungsten filament incandescent lamp was used for the long wavelength end of the spectrum including the infrared, and a mercury vapour lamp was employed for short wavelengths including the ultraviolet. A tungsten lamp radiates a continuous spectrum, that is all wavelengths present, and so any wavelength could be chosen for test purposes. On the other hand, the mercury lamp provides a discontinuous spectrum, with relatively few spectral lines of discrete wavelengths, and one thus could carry out tests at these discrete wavelengths only.

It was found that the bandwidth of vision of the subjects depended on the light intensity. It was therefore decided to work with the minimum light intensity, which all the test subjects could clearly see within the 400 to 700 nanometre wavelength range, generally assumed visible to humans. Using the tungsten lamp, the wavelength of the output light from the monochromator was set to 650 nanometres, and then its intensity was gradually increased by opening the monochromator output slit in small steps, until each of the eight test subjects achieved 30 correct responses out of 30 attempts.

This way it was found that, at 650 nanometres, all subjects achieved 30 correct responses out of 30 attempts at the rounded figure of 30,000 electron counts per second. Then, with the monochromator set to 650 nanometres, and its output slit adjusted to yield an electron count of 30,000 per second, each subject was tested as below. The wavelength was increased in 25 nanometre steps, and for each step the number of correct responses out of 30 attempts was determined as described above. The highest wavelength setting, which still yielded 20 or more correct responses out of 30 attempts, was considered to be the limit of vision of the subject under test, at the infrared end of the spectrum.

In order to determine the limit of vision at the ultraviolet end of the spectrum, the tungsten lamp was replaced with the mercury vapour lamp. Out of the numerous spectral lines of this lamp, six of the more intense lines were chosen for test purposes. Rounded to the nearest nanometre, these were 436, 405, 365, 334, 297, and 254 nanometres. Because of rounding errors, and also because no wavelength dial is 100% accurate, after having set the monochromator to any of the above listed wavelength values, small wavelength adjustments had to be applied at a suitably small slit width, in order to achieve maximum electron count per second. Only then was the monochromator correctly set to the desired spectral line.

Proceeding as for the infrared end of the spectrum, it was found that at 436 nanometres, all eight subjects achieved 30 correct responses out of 30 attempts at the rounded figure of 3000 electron counts per second. This was only 1/10 of the corresponding count at 650 nanometres. Likely reasons are that at lower wavelengths the photon energies, the quantum efficiency, and the eye's sensitivity are all higher. The test procedure involved setting the slit to yield 3000 electron counts per second at the 436 nanometre spectral line, and then determining for each subject the number of correct responses out of 30 attempts for each of the spectral lines listed above, in decreasing order of wavelength. The lowest wavelength spectral line, still yielding 20 or more correct responses out of 30 attempts, was then taken as the limit of vision of the subject under test at the ultraviolet end of the spectrum.

Out of the eight subjects tested, four claimed psychic abilities, including the ability to see the human aura, while the other four made no such claims, and were thus control subjects. The results of the bandwidth of vision tests for the eight subjects are listed in Table 4.3 giving the lower and upper wavelength limits of vision in nanometres for each subject.

Table 4.3

Psychic Subjects		Control Subjects	
G.B.	405 – 700	G.K.	405 – 700
M.B.	405 – 725	D.N.	365 – 700
P.B.	365 – 700	H.W.	365 – 725
M.S.	365 – 850	J.M.	297 – 700

When considering the results presented in Table 4.3, it is seen that the bandwidth of vision of the first three psychic subjects, and also the first three control subjects, was closely agreeing with the generally accepted visible range extending from 400 to 700 nanometres. However, psychic subject M.S., with vision from 365 to 850 nanometres, was able to see far into the infrared region, but not into the ultraviolet region, while control subject J.M. having vision from 297 to 700 nanometres perceived light far into the ultraviolet region, but not into the infrared region. Based on the results of psychic subject M.S., one might be tempted to consider that perhaps the human aura was associated with the infrared region. But, the fact that psychic subject G.B. was the most definite in claiming to see the human aura, while psychic subject M.S. was less certain, argues against such a consideration. The final conclusion seems to be that while some people see well beyond the normally accepted visible range, the bandwidth of vision of those claiming the ability to see the human aura is not wider than the bandwidth of vision of those making no such claim, and so the ability of seeing the aura does not seem to arise from extended vision into either the ultraviolet or the infrared regions.

Another question arising was, whether psychics claiming the ability to see the human aura, possessed sensitive enough vision that would enable them to see the emission of light from the human skin, as presented by the results in Table 4.1. Since psychic subject G.B. in Table 4.3 was the most positive in claiming the ability to perceive the human aura, it was decided to ascertain the "threshold of vision" of this subject, namely the minimum number of photons crossing 1 square centimetre area, at right angles to that area, per second, which subject G.B. could reliably perceive at the two wavelengths 436 and 650 nanometres.

The test procedure was similar to the one used for determining the bandwidth of vision of subjects, but altered so that at each of the two wavelengths 436 and 650 nanometres, the monochromator output slit was gradually reduced, until the subject only just got 20 correct responses out of 30 attempts, indicating that the threshold of vision had been reached. The test was repeated a number of times. The average of the differences between the electron counts with the light on, and the light blocked, at the threshold of vision, yielded the "net threshold of vision electron count per second" for psychic subject G.B., at the above two wavelengths. From these, a number of relevant quantities, as calculated over page, are listed in Table 4.4 below, where all values have been rounded to two figures.

Table 4.4

Wavelength in nanometres	436	650
Net threshold of vision electron count per second	250	3000
Quantum efficiency	0.19	0.067
Number of photons striking the cathode per second	1300	45,000
Cathode area in square centimetres	16	16
Number of photons striking the cathode per square centimetre per second	83	2800
Energy per photon in joules	4.6×10^{-19}	3.1×10^{-19}
Light intensity reaching the cathode and the eyes in watts per square centimetre, at the threshold of vision	38×10^{-18}	870×10^{-18}
Light intensity reaching the cathode from three fingers, 17 centimetres from the cathode, in watts per square centimetre	2.0×10^{-18}	35×10^{-18}
(Intensity at threshold) / (Intensity from fingers)	19	25

In Table 4.4, the net threshold electron count per second, divided by the appropriate quantum efficiency from Figure 4.3, gave the number photons falling on the photocathode per second. The number of photons striking the cathode per square centimetre per second was obtained as the number of photons falling on the cathode per second, divided by the cathode area in square centimetres. In Table 4.4, light intensity is understood to be energy carried by photons across 1 square centimetre area, perpendicular to the motion of the photons, in 1 second, and is measured in units of joules per square centimetre per second. But, since energy created, carried, or expended, per second is called power, light intensity may also be designated as power carried across 1 square centimetre area perpendicular to the motion of the photons, and measured in units of watts per square centimetre. Thus, in Table 4.4, light intensity reaching the photocathode, or the eyes, in watts per square centimetre, at the threshold of vision, was calculated as the number of photons striking the cathode per square centimetre per second, multiplied by the energy of 1 photon in joules at the relevant wavelength. This then gave 38×10^{-18} watt per square centimetre at the 436 nanometre wavelength, and 870×10^{-18} watt per square centimetre at the 650 nanometre wavelength.

These were then compared with the light intensity falling on the cathode from three fingers of subject G.K., 17 centimetres from the cathode, as given in Figure 4.7. Subject G.K. was chosen as the one with the highest photon emission. Now, unlike the vision tests, the photons reaching the cathode from the fingertips had a continuous wavelength distribution. To allow for this, the overall wavelength range was divided into two parts, namely:

Firstly, the power within the 263 to 536 nanometre wavelength range, which equalled the sum of the first three rectangular areas in Figure 4.7, and which for subject G.K. added up to 31×10^{-18} watt falling on the window, or upon division by the cathode area, yielded a light intensity of 2.0×10^{-18} watt per square centimetre.

Secondly, the power within the 536 to 870 nanometre wavelength range, which equalled the sum of the last six rectangular areas in Figure 4.7, and which for subject G.K added up to 551×10^{-18} watt falling on the window, or upon division by the cathode area, yielded a light intensity of 35×10^{-18} watt per square centimetre.

It is seen that the threshold intensity at 436 nanometres was 19 times the intensity falling on the cathode from the fingers within the 263 to 536 nanometre wavelength range, while the threshold intensity at 650 nanometres was 25 times the intensity reaching the cathode from the fingers within 536 to 870 nanometre wavelength range.

It had to be concluded that psychic subject G.B. could not be able to see the light emitted from three fingers at a distance of 17 centimetres, by a large margin. The question then arose, if light intensity arriving at the eyes of an observer from the whole body of a subject, at an increased distance, could be discernible to the observer. Now, light intensity is known to fall off with the square of the distance from the source of the photons. This means that if the fingers were viewed at 1.7 metres, instead of 17 centimetres, that is at 10 times the distance, the observed light intensity would be 1/100 of that seen at 17 centimetres.

Light intensity reaching the eyes of an observer from the whole body of a subject, viewed at some fixed distance, is rather difficult to estimate. A very rough figure could be deduced by estimating the whole skin surface area of the body, and with the aid of the information in Table 4.1, estimating the total power emitted by the whole body. Then, remembering that emitted photons travel not only in a direction perpendicular to the skin, but in all directions, and also that light intensity falls with distance, a rough estimate for the light intensity reaching the eyes of an observer, 1.7 metres from the subject, could be arrived at. An approximate calculation along these lines for subject G.K., relying on Table 4.1, yielded

10^{-17} watt per square centimetre, which has been rounded to the nearest order of magnitude. (Orders of magnitude are: 10^{N} or 10^{-N} where N = any whole number).

It has to be recalled that most photon emission from the skin occurs within the 600 to 700 nanometre wavelength region. Consequently, the above 10^{-17} watt per square centimetre intensity needs to be compared with the threshold of vision intensity at 650 nanometres in Table 4.4, namely 870 x 10^{-18} watt per square centimetre, or 10^{-15} watt per square centimetre when rounded to the nearest order of magnitude. Thus, it is seen that the above deduced light intensity of 10^{-17} watt per square centimetre is below the threshold of vision, as rounded to 10^{-15} watt per square centimetre, by a factor of 100, or two orders of magnitude. This leads to the conclusion that the observer would not be able to perceive the light emitted from the whole body of a subject at a distance of 1.7 metres.

Let it now be supposed that the observer's eyes are replaced by the photomultiplier, which then has an intensity of 10^{-17} watt per square centimetre falling on its photocathode. Since this intensity is approximately 1/100 of the threshold intensity, the corresponding net electron count per second would also be around 1/100 of the net threshold electron count of 3000 per second at 650 nanometres in Table 4.4, that is, approximately 30 per second, or 300 over a 10 second period.

It is to be noted that photomultipliers can be expected to yield good results only from small areas of skin, with the aid of collimator tubes excluding stray photons. Nevertheless, tests were carried out with the subjects standing in the cage, 1.7 metres from the photomultiplier at waist height, and no collimator attached. Dark counts, over 10 second periods, were typically around 300, increasing to around 450 with the subjects in front of the tube, yielding net counts around 150 over 10 seconds. The readings were thus greatly affected by background stray photons, partly due to exhaled air by the subjects, which was found to be a substantial source of photon emission, persisting for long periods after a subject has left the cage. Lower than expected counts may also be explained by the fact that many photons emitted by the subject strike the cathode obliquely, and consequently are less effective in producing electron emission. Nevertheless, the predicted and measured net counts were of the same order, they could not be considered contradictory.

It is claimed that the aura is best seen in subdued light, such as may be present in a curtained room. Any such subdued light would exceed the emission from the skin by many orders of magnitude, and completely swamp it, thereby rendering it invisible even if the observer could possibly see light emitted from the skin.

Furthermore, observers of the aura claim to see colours. Now, not only is the light emitted from the skin essentially visible red, but light of any colour seen at low levels of intensity, approaching the threshold of vision, appears greyish to all observers. The eye has the ability to distinguish colours only at much higher levels of intensity.

Thus, all indications are that observers claiming the ability to see the human aura do not perceive physical light, that is photons emitted or reflected. The claimed ability to see auras is akin to the claimed ability to see "ghosts". Such abilities, if real, constitute paranormal phenomena. The purported reality of such abilities, and their possible modus operandi, will be considered in a later chapter.

Chapter 5
Corona Discharge Photography

Although corona discharge photography was known of early in the 20th century, much interest was generated in it during the 1970s, through the work of Semyon and Valentina Kirlian, a Russian husband and wife team. In fact, the techniques involved in producing such photos are often referred to as Kirlian photography. It has been claimed that such photographs, when involving biological entities, such as plant leaves or parts of the human body, can convey information relating to physical illnesses and mental states. Some people believe that such photographs are photos of an "aura" surrounding living organisms.

In order to gain an insight into corona discharge photography, some underlying principles need to be examined in some detail. Briefly, electrons can be removed from, or attached to, the molecules of the constituent gases present in air. As a result, such molecules become ionised, that is electrically charged. In the presence of an applied electric field the ions are accelerated, and the resulting collisions between ions and neutral molecules can produce the emission of light. This process may come about in different ways, one of which is referred to as "corona discharge". Such a discharge may be photographed by various methods.

The constituent gases of pure dry air are by volume: nitrogen 78%, oxygen 21%, the remaining 1% being made up of inert gases: mostly argon, and lesser amounts of neon, krypton, and xenon. Air also contains a small amount of carbon dioxide, (0.03 to 0.04%), which being essential for all plant life, plays a rather important role.

The nitrogen atom contains 7 protons in its nucleus, orbited by 7 electrons, 2 in the innermost K shell, which is thereby completely filled, and 5 in the next shell further out, namely the L shell, that would be fully filled with 8 electrons. The corresponding figures for the oxygen atom are 8 protons in the nucleus, orbited by 8 electrons, 2 electrons in the K shell, and 6 electrons in the L shell. Thus, both the nitrogen and the oxygen atoms have partially filled L shells.

It is found that in air, the nitrogen atoms pair up to form nitrogen molecules, denoted N_2, each such nitrogen molecule being made up of two nitrogen atoms. Likewise oxygen atoms pair up forming oxygen molecules, denoted O_2, each such oxygen molecule containing two oxygen atoms. In these molecules the L shells interact, resulting in some L shell electrons being shared by the two atoms. The shared electrons could be thought of as orbiting both nuclei in the molecule. Such molecules possess less energy than the sum of the energies of the two individual atoms, which is the reason for the molecule formation. In general, all systems always seek the lowest energy state, just as a ball on an uneven surface tends to stop at the lowest available point, where its potential energy is a minimum.

It is also possible for three oxygen atoms to form a three-atom molecule through L shell electron sharing. The resulting three-atom molecule is denoted O_3, and is called ozone. Ozone is normally found in the upper atmosphere.

It may appear that nitrogen and oxygen atoms would readily combine to form molecules of various nitrogen oxides (denoted NO, N_2O, NO_2, etc). But, these molecules have higher energy states, and so nitrogen oxides form at high temperatures only. Such molecules tend to fall apart when the temperature drops, unless the cooling takes place very rapidly.

A carbon atom, with 6 protons in the nucleus, 2 electrons in the K shell, and 4 electrons in the L shell, can combine with 2 oxygen atoms through L shell electron sharing to form a carbon dioxide molecule (CO_2). Carbon dioxide in the air originates from the exhalation of animals, the decay of plants, volcanic eruptions, and the burning of carbon containing fuels. At the same time it is continually being removed from the air by plant growth.

Inert gases present in the air, either possess completely filled energy shells, such as neon, or possess fully filled subshells, namely argon, krypton, and xenon. For instance, neon has 10 protons, 2 electrons in the K shell, and 8 electrons in the L shell, and thus both of these shells are completely filled. For these reasons, inert gases do not form molecules, but remain in the monatomic state.

In a single isolated atom, the energy of the atom consists of the sum of the energies of all its electrons, each electron having an amount of kinetic energy due to the motion of its mass around the nucleus, and also an amount of potential energy due to the negatively charged electron being moved some distance from the positively charged nucleus against the force of attraction exerted on it by the nucleus.

In molecules formed of two atoms, such as the nitrogen and oxygen molecules, the situation is more complex. This is due to the fact that the two atoms may vibrate relative to each other along the line joining their nuclei, and the atoms may also rotate around a point on the line joining their nuclei. Both of these involve the motions of masses, and so are associated with kinetic energy. Consequently, the total energy of a molecule consists not only of the sum of the electronic energies, but also of the vibrational and rotational energies of its constituent atoms. Investigations show that the vibrational and rotational energies, like the electronic energies, may assume specific discrete values only.

Electromagnetic waves are made up of photons, each photon having a definite wavelength and frequency, and each having a definite amount of energy in proportion to its frequency. As one covers the higher frequency range of the electromagnetic wave spectrum, starting with infrared radiation, and moving in the direction of decreasing wavelength, and thereby toward increasing frequency and photon energy, one passes through the regions of infrared radiation, visible light, ultraviolet rays, x-rays, and γ-rays, in that order.

The atmosphere always contains small quantities of subatomic particles, in particular alpha particles, protons, neutrons, electrons, and neutrinos, together with any short wavelength electromagnetic radiation such as ultraviolet rays, x-rays, and γ-rays. These particles and radiation originate from radioactive substances in the ground, in the air, or enter as cosmic rays from outer space. While the cosmic rays arriving from outer space may be highly energetic, they lose much of their energy through collisions with molecules in the air, and so do not present danger to life on the surface of the earth.

When such particles, radiation, or cosmic rays, collide with molecules in the air, they can cause electrons to be removed from those molecules. If that happens, the affected molecules will suffer from electron deficiency, and will become positively charged ions. An electron removed from a molecule, may exist as a free electron for some time, but eventually may attach itself to a neutral molecule, and so form a negatively charged ion. As a result, a small fraction of the molecules in the atmosphere is always ionised into positively and negatively charged ions.

Chapter 5 – Corona Discharge Photography

A direct voltage source produces a voltage that does not vary with time. Let such a voltage source be connected to two physically adjacent metallic conductors, normally referred to as electrodes, with some airspace between them. The shape of the electrodes may be parallel plates, parallel cylindrical conductors, a pair of spheres, or the points of two needles. Depending on the intended application, some resistance would normally be inserted in series with the voltage source. Such an arrangement is depicted in Figure 5.1.

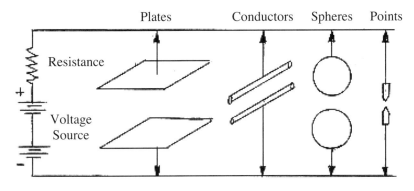

Figure 5.1

The applied voltage causes the electrode connected to the positive terminal of the voltage source to become positively charged, while the electrode connected to the negative terminal of the voltage source stores negative charge. As a result, an electric field is set up between the two electrodes. Consequently, positively charged ions between the electrodes will be driven by the electric field to the negatively charged electrode, while electrons, or negatively charged ions, will be propelled by the electric field to the positively charged electrode.

Positive ions reaching the negative electrode take up electrons from it, and so once more become electrically neutral molecules. At the same time, electrons, or negative ions, drawn to the positive electrode, supply electrons to that electrode, negative ions becoming neutral molecules in so doing. This process results in an anticlockwise flow of electrons, that is, an anticlockwise flow of negative charge, around the loop consisting of the voltage source, the resistance in series with the voltage source if any, the connecting wires, the electrodes, and the airspace between the electrodes. The resulting electric current around the loop is clockwise, since the conventional direction of an electric current is always taken opposite to that of the electron flow.

The ions and the electrons between the electrodes are accelerated to speeds which depend on the magnitude of the electric field. The magnitude of the field can be increased by raising the magnitude of the applied voltage, or by reducing the separation between the electrodes, or by doing both. If the ionic or electronic speeds, and the kinetic energies, assume large enough values, then an ion or an electron upon collision with a neutral molecule may knock an electron out of that molecule, and so produce an additional positive ion and an additional electron. This process is called ionisation by collision. If the two positive ions or the two electrons, the originals and the newly created ones, reach sufficient speeds, they can produce through collision with neutral molecules two additional positive ions and two additional electrons. At the same time, electrons can attach themselves to neutral molecules, thereby creating negative ions, which may upon acquiring sufficient speed, also produce further ions and electrons via collisions with neutral molecules. So, if the electric field is large enough, the number of ions and electrons attracted to the electrodes will undergo a rapid increase, resulting in a sharp rise in the electric current around the loop. Thus, the sudden increase in current is due to an avalanche-like increase in the number of ions and electrons, acting as charge carriers, and if this occurs the air is said to have suffered a breakdown. Also, since ions reaching the electrodes lose their charge, and are converted back into neutral molecules, the process may be referred to as a discharge.

The applied voltage at which breakdown occurs depends on the distance between the electrodes, the shape of the electrodes, and also on the pressure and humidity of the air. For example, if two metallic spheres situated in relatively dry air, at normal atmospheric pressure, are separated by 1 centimetre, and also provided that the diameter of the spheres is considerably larger than their separation, breakdown is found to occur at around 31,000 volts, corresponding to an electric field of 31,000 volts per centimetre, (3.1 million volts per metre). The breakdown voltage drops with air pressure and humidity, and is very dependent on the shape of the electrodes. For example in the case of sharp needlepoints, 1 centimetre apart, the breakdown voltage drops to around 13,000 volts. This is due to the fact that the electric field between needlepoints is not uniform, but is much larger near the needlepoints than half way between them.

Once breakdown has occurred, the resulting electric current may assume destructively high levels. Nevertheless, the current may always be limited to a safe level, suitable for the purposes at hand, by inserting sufficient resistance in series with one terminal of the voltage source.

However, not all collisions between ions and neutral molecules result in ionisation. Many collisions will only cause electrons in neutral molecules to be raised to higher unfilled energy levels, without removing them from the molecules all together. At the same time the collision would normally also result in the vibrational and rotational energies of some of the molecules being increased. The combined effect is likely to be an increase in the overall energy of the molecule. After a short time the electrons will fall back to a lower unfilled level, or possibly the lowest unfilled level, while the vibrational and rotational energies will also fall, and return, partly or fully, to their original levels. These transitions from higher to lower energy states are likely to occur in a number of steps. Each such step results in a drop of the overall molecular energy, and also in the emission of a photon, the energy of the photon being equal to the energy difference between the two energy states involved in the transition. The frequency, or the wavelength, of the emitted photon is thus given by:

$$\text{(energy difference between the two states in joules)}$$
$$= \begin{pmatrix} \text{Planck's constant} \\ \text{in joule seconds} \end{pmatrix} \times \begin{pmatrix} \text{frequency of photon} \\ \text{in cycles per second} \end{pmatrix}$$
$$= \begin{pmatrix} \text{Planck's constant} \\ \text{in joule seconds} \end{pmatrix} \times \left(\frac{\text{speed of light in metres per second}}{\text{wavelength of the photon in metres}} \right)$$

As a result, light would be produced continually, which may be in the visible region, or on either side of the visible range, namely in the ultraviolet or infrared regions. The intensity of the emitted light depends on the factors that may contribute to determining the electric

Chapter 5 – Corona Discharge Photography

field, that is: the applied voltage, the shape and the separation of the electrodes, and also the amount of resistance in series with the voltage source. Since the emitted light often appears as a bluish "corona" surrounding the electrodes, while ions are being discharged at the same time at the electrodes, the phenomenon is often referred to as "corona discharge". Ions impinging on the electrodes also produce both heat and audible sound. When large currents are involved, the discharge may take on the form of sparks or arcs. Lightning and thunder are discharges between clouds and the earth on a massive scale.

In the arrangement depicted in Figure 5.1, it is not necessary to work with a direct (d.c.) voltage, one may employ an alternating (a.c.) voltage just as well. In the latter case, while the two electrodes would be oppositely charged at any instant, the charge on any one of the electrodes would vary between positive and negative values periodically. This means that the direction of the electric field, and so the directions in which the positive or negative ions move, would also vary periodically. Collisions between ions, electrons, and neutral molecules would still occur, resulting in the production of further ions, electrons, and photons, and so the emission of light. Also, ions would still be attracted to oppositely charged electrodes, and would be discharged when reaching those electrodes.

The light produced by the corona discharge may be used to expose photographic film or paper, and so obtain photographs of various objects acting as electrodes, possible examples being coins, the leaves of plants, human fingertips, or other parts of the human body.

Corona discharge photographs are obtainable in two ways. One of these involves exposing the photographic film or paper, to the light produced by the discharge, by placing them directly into the discharge path. The other way relies on photographing the discharge by means of a photographic camera. One possible arrangement for the direct exposure of the film or paper, without reliance on a camera, is depicted in Figure 5.2. Such an arrangement was employed in some investigations by the author and his associates.

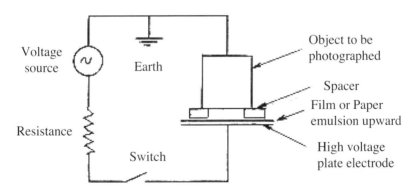

Figure 5.2

With reference to Figure 5.2, the voltage source provided an alternating voltage with an amplitude adjustable up to 30,000 volts, and a frequency adjustable between 10,000 and 30,000 cycles per second. This meant that the voltage could be made to vary periodically between positive and negative limits up to ± 30,000 volts, and that it could also be made to change from its positive maximum to its negative maximum and back to its positive maximum 10,000 to 30,000 times in each second.

One terminal of the voltage source was earthed, while the other terminal was connected to a metallic plate serving as a "high voltage" electrode. A piece of photographic film or paper was then placed on the high voltage plate, with the non-emulsion side facing the plate. The object to be photographed was placed on the emulsion side of the film, with or without a suitable spacer frame interposed, and the object was then earthed. The role of the spacer frame was to provide a layer of air, a fraction of a millimetre thick, between the film and the object, in which the corona discharge could develop. Without a spacer, corona discharge would form only around the edges of the object, and possibly also in pockets of air left between the object, and the film or paper.

While some airspace, between the emulsion side of the film or paper and the object, is essential for the formation of the corona discharge, it is important that no airspace should exist next to the non-emulsion side of colour films, in which a corona discharge could form. This is so since colour films can faithfully reproduce a coloured image only when exposed to light on the emulsion side. For example, while blue light on the emulsion side produces a blue coloured photograph, the same blue light on the non-emulsion side would produce an orange-red coloured photograph, which would clearly be a false result. It is thus imperative that no air pockets be allowed to exist between the high voltage plate and the non-emulsion side of the colour film.

The whole apparatus had to be situated in a darkroom, so that exposure of the film was due entirely to the corona discharge. However, when using a much less light sensitive photographic paper, good photos could be obtained in a dimly lit room. The need for a darkroom may be obviated by encasing the film in a lightproof envelope, exposure being produced by the corona discharge formed inside the envelope. Photos obtained this way, could be of doubtful value, due to the presence of the envelope in the discharge path.

The production of a photo involved adjusting the voltage, or the resistance in series with the high voltage source, or both, so as to yield a corona discharge which was bright enough, and yet which would not generate so much heat as to cause damage to the object, or the film, or cause discomfort when the object was a human fingertip, or some other part of the human body. The frequency of the voltage was not found to be critical, that is, it did not seem to affect the appearance of the picture obtained. Exposure was produced by switching on the high voltage, with the object in position, for a period found by trial and error to yield a good quality photograph, neither too dark, nor too light, and having optimum contrast. (It is not practicable to put a switch in the high voltage lead as shown in Figure 5.2. In the actual setup the high voltage source was the output winding of a step-up transformer, with the switch on the low voltage input winding side of the transformer).

The arrangement that was used for photographing corona discharge by means of a camera is shown in Figure 5.3. The quartz glass plate in Figure 5.3 had its bottom side coated with an indium oxide layer, which was transparent to light over a wide range of wavelengths including the ultraviolet, visible, and the infrared, and which was capable of conducting an electric current at the same time. One terminal of the alternating high voltage source was earthed, and the other terminal was connected to the indium oxide layer serving as the high voltage electrode. The object to be photographed was placed on the topside of quartz glass plate and earthed. A spacer frame was placed between the object and the glass plate if deemed necessary, depending on the application at hand. A camera loaded with colour film was then placed under the quartz glass plate, and focussed on the topside of the plate.

Chapter 5 – Corona Discharge Photography

With the voltage switched on, the corona discharge would form in the space between the object and the top side of the glass plate provided by the spacer, or around the edges of the object if no spacer was utilised. Light from the corona discharge passed through the quartz glass plate, and the indium oxide layer, to form an image of the corona discharge on the film inside the camera. Exposure would be made by keeping the camera shutter open for the duration of the discharge period, that is, the period while the high voltage was being applied. (As in Figure 5.2, so in Figure 5.3, the high voltage source was the output winding of a step-up transformer, with the switch located on the low voltage input winding side).

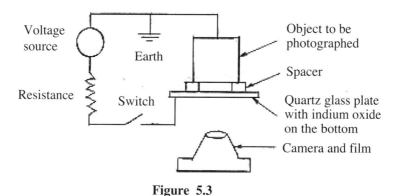

Figure 5.3

As with the direct method, the intensity of the discharge had to be limited by controlling of either the voltage, or the resistance in series with the voltage source, or both. This was necessary so as to avoid damage to the object, or undue discomfort to a human subject, caused by the generation of excessive heat. In fact, quartz glass was used not only because it passed a wider range of wavelengths, but also because for a given discharge intensity it was subject to less heating than ordinary glass would have been.

Taking photographs could be carried out in a dimly lit room, as long as the background light intensity was small compared with light intensity generated by the discharge itself, and provided that the camera shutter would be kept open for the duration of the discharge period only, the necessary period for best exposure having been determined by trial and error.

An advantage of using a camera was that light could not reach the non-emulsion side of the film, and so false pictures could not result. At the same time, any possible interaction between the object and the film, through heat or chemical reaction, was also avoided.

The arrangements depicted in Figures 5.2 and 5.3 would not function with direct voltage sources. This is so because a steady flow of ions, or electrons, could not pass through the photographic film or paper in Figure 5.2, or the quartz glass plate in Figure 5.3, and so could not pass from the high voltage electrode to the object acting as the earthed electrode. However, both arrangements work with alternating voltages because the ions and electrons could oscillate to and fro in the space between the object and the film, or the object and the glass plate. In so doing they could suffer collisions with neutral molecules, and thereby produce photons and also additional ions and electrons. In fact, when making corona discharge photos of human fingertips, or other parts of the human body, using alternating voltage sources, it was not even necessary to earth the human subject, because the human body was found to possess sufficient capacity to store and give up electrons as required.

Nevertheless, arrangements were devised which allowed continuous current flow in one direction, and thus enabled the photographing of corona discharges using direct voltage sources. Such arrangements were considerably more elaborate, and yet did not offer advantages over what was obtainable with alternating voltage sources.

Figure 5.4(a) shows black and white corona discharge photographs of two live plant leaves, obtained by direct exposure of negative film, as described in conjunction with Figure 5.2. From these, the positive pictures in Figure 5.4(a) were obtained by means of an enlarger and black and white bromide paper.

In Figure 5.4(a), the white spots, and the whitish areas, correspond to high discharge light intensity, while the dark areas represent low light intensity. This suggests that the whitish regions correspond to areas on the leaf where electrons are readily supplied or absorbed, or where the surface resistance of the leaf to electron flow is relatively low.

Figure 5.4(b) shows reduced sized corona discharge photos of palms and fingers of human hands, obtained by direct contact between the hands and black and white bromide paper.

In this case dark areas correspond to high light intensity, while white areas represent little or no light produced. The latter include areas of direct contact between the skin and the paper, with no airspace between the two, or alternatively, airspace between the skin and the paper that are too large for discharge formation. The dark areas are the result of corona discharge in the narrow airspace surrounding the edges of the actual contact areas. Some people claim to be able to diagnose illnesses from photos such as depicted in Figure 5.4(b).

Figure 5.4(c) depicts corona discharge photographs of a coin, and of a human fingertip, obtained by means of a camera on colour film, the method having been as described with the help of Figure 5.3. Whereas the original pictures were in colour, Figure 5.4(c) gives black and white reproductions only.

Since the process involved exposing negative film, which was then copied to positive paper, lighter areas correspond to higher light intensity, while darker areas represent low light intensity.

As the photos in Figure 5.4(c) are black and white reproductions of the colour originals, lighter and darker areas of grey in Figure 5.4(c) correspond to lighter and darker shades of blue on the colour originals. All colour photos obtained in these investigations were shades of blue with occasional violet tinges. Colours of red and orange were obtained only if the colour film was deliberately exposed to corona discharge on the non-emulsion side.

It is sometimes claimed that subjects with psychic healing abilities can produce orange-red photographs. Although a number of psychics claiming healing abilities were examined, all were found to produce photographs with various shades of blue only.

Some investigators also claim that if a small part of a plant leaf is cut away, the corona discharge photo still shows the whole leaf. This is called the "phantom leaf effect", and is supposed to be due to the "aura" of the cut-away portion still being present. Relying on the methodology described above, all attempts to replicate the phantom leaf effect failed. It seems that the cut edges of the leaf are a richer source of electrons than the rest of the leaf, resulting in a flare on the photograph, which masks the missing portion if the cut away part of the leaf is small enough.

Chapter 5 – Corona Discharge Photography

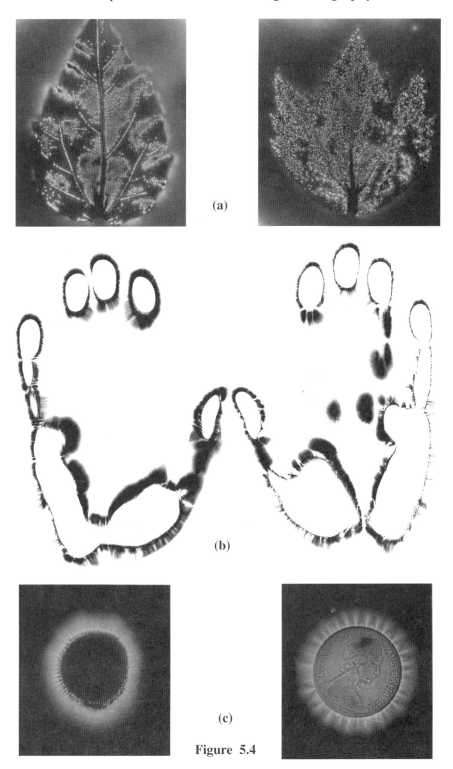

Figure 5.4

Chapter 5 – Corona Discharge Photography

Photography is not an accurate way of examining the colour content of the light produced by corona discharge. One would expect to obtain much more detailed information from the spectrum of the produced light, which gives information about light intensities for given values of wavelengths, over a wide wavelength range.

Such spectra were obtained by an arrangement similar to that shown in Figure 5.3, but in which the camera was replaced by a monochromator coupled to a photomultiplier, as shown in Figure 5.5.

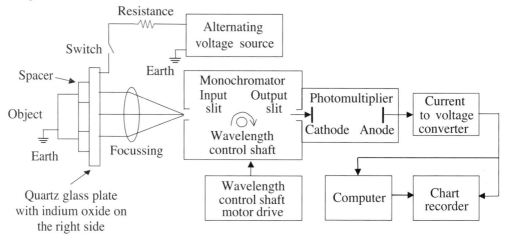

Figure 5.5

With reference to Figure 5.5, if the object was physically small it had to be earthed, but if it was part of the human body then earthing was not necessary, for reasons stated earlier. The light produced by the corona discharge passed through the quartz glass plate, and the indium oxide coating, after which it was focussed onto the monochromator input slit. The light issuing from the monochromator output slit could be adjusted to any wavelength component of the input light, within a range from 200 to 1000 nanometres. However, the light emerging from the output slit would normally extend over a small wavelength range, depending on the width of the slit. The output slit width actually used in the investigations restricted the output wavelength range to lie within ±0.5 nanometre of the set value.

At any given wavelength setting, the current in the photomultiplier anode lead would consist of a number of electric current pulses per second, depending on the number of photons striking the photomultiplier window per second, and so depended on the light intensity reaching the photocathode coating inside the window. The current to voltage converter in Figure 5.5, would then average the current pulses every few milliseconds, and produce a continually updated output voltage proportional to the prevailing average current, with selectable conversion factors of 1, 10, or 100 millivolts per nanoampere of anode current.

Light intensities produced by corona discharge are much higher than those met in the human aura investigations, as discussed in the previous chapter. As an example, a representative corona discharge light intensity could cause 1 million photons impinging on the cathode per second. If 10% of these cause electron emission from the cathode, and if the phototube multiplication factor from cathode to anode is also 1 million, then the number of electrons in the anode lead per second would be $(10^6) \times (0.1) \times (10^6) = 10^{11}$. Multiplying this

Chapter 5 – Corona Discharge Photography

by the charge of 1 electron, gives the anode current as $(10^{11}) \times (1.6 \times 10^{-19}) = 16 \times 10^{-9}$ ampere, or 16 nanoamperes. Working with a current to voltage conversion factor of 100 millivolts per nanoampere, the expected output voltage would then be $(16) \times (100) = 1600$ millivolts = 1.6 volts. As seen from this example, at any given wavelength setting, the output voltage from the current to voltage converter would be a measure of the corona discharge light intensity at that wavelength.

The objects of corona discharge investigations could be inanimate objects, such as metallic disks or coins, or they could be parts of living organisms, such as plant leaves or human fingertips. In all of these cases it was found that, if the monochromator wavelength setting was adjusted gradually, the converter output voltage, and thus the corresponding corona discharge light intensity, attained high levels within a relatively few narrow wavelength regions only, and dropped nearly to zero outside those regions.

A high light intensity occurring at a well-defined single wavelength, but not on either side of that wavelength, is called a spectral line. On the other hand, high light intensity prevailing over a well-defined narrow wavelength range, but not outside that range, is referred to as a spectral band.

Spectral lines normally originate from the transitions of electrons between specific energy levels in isolated atoms, which are not parts of molecules. On the other hand, spectral bands are a number of spectral lines very close to each other in wavelength values. Such bands originate from transitions between energy levels in molecules. As stated earlier, molecular energy levels consist of three parts, namely electronic energies, and also vibrational and rotational energies of the constituent atoms within the molecules. A spectral band arises from a transition between two electronic energy levels, but which in addition involves small vibrational and rotational energy sublevels, differing from each other by small but finite amounts of energy, leading to closely spaced spectral lines within the band. The highest intensity line within a band is called the "band head", which often occurs at a wavelength corresponding to one edge of the band.

Returning to the examination of the corona discharge spectrum, that is the variation of the corona discharge light intensity with the wavelength, as indicated by the variation of the converter output voltage with the wavelength, it became apparent that the corona discharge spectrum did not have a continuous wavelength distribution, but that it essentially consisted of spectral bands of molecular origin.

It may appear feasible, that the wavelengths of the various lines, bands, band heads, and also their relative intensities, could be determined by manually adjusting the wavelength control shaft of the monochromator, so as to locate the spectral lines, bands, and band heads, and then read the corresponding converter output voltages by means of an accurate voltmeter.

However, practical limitations arose from a number of factors. One was that in order to avoid damage to the photomultiplier, the number of electrons emitted from the cathode per second, and also the number of electrons reaching the anode per second, that is both the cathode and anode currents, had to be kept below specified maximum limits, by suitably limiting the light intensity falling on the cathode. This could be done either by limiting the discharge light intensity through adjusting the voltage applied to the indium oxide coating, or adjusting the resistance in series with the voltage source, or by interposing an adjustable diameter aperture between the discharge and the monochromator input slit.

Chapter 5 – Corona Discharge Photography

Another practical limitation arose from the fact that a corona discharge in the space between the object and the glass plate caused both to heat up. The larger was the voltage applied to the indium oxide layer, the more intense was the discharge, and the hotter the object and the glass plate became in a given period of time.

It was found that a typical discharge, intense enough for experimental purposes, may allow the discharge to take place for no longer than 5 to 10 seconds before the glass plate would get uncomfortably hot for human fingertips. But, even with metal objects, the discharge period had to be limited, in order to avoid damage to the glass plate through overheating.

Consequently, active discharge periods had to be interleaved with long enough discharge-off periods, to allow sufficient cooling to take place, which in the case of human subjects would have amounted to an unduly long and uncomfortable procedure. So, determining discharge spectra, as outlined above, would have been a lengthy and tedious process.

However, it was possible to obtain discharge spectra drawn on paper in a shorter time by scanning the spectrum. This was done by coupling the monochromator wavelength control shaft to the shaft of a constant speed electric motor, that allowed to sweep through the 200 to 1000 nanometre wavelength range within one continuous discharge period of 5 to 10 second duration. Alternatively, consecutive sections of the full wavelength range could be swept in a relatively few discharge periods, allowing for cooling periods in between.

As the monochromator wavelength control shaft was driven at constant speed, with the discharge on, the current to voltage converter output voltage varied with time. This time varying voltage was then applied to the drive mechanisms of a pen of a chart recorder. A chart recorder is an instrument, in which a continuous strip of paper is moving at constant speed, the paper being supplied from a reel. At the same time, a number of pens in contact with the paper are arranged to move in proportion to the voltages applied to their drive mechanisms, the pen movement being perpendicular to the motion of the paper. This way traces can be drawn on the moving paper showing how the pen voltages vary with time.

Since the monochromator wavelength setting, and the length of paper passing the pens, both increased at a constant rate, the pen to which the converter output voltage was applied drew on the paper a curve showing how the monochromator output light intensity varied with wavelength, which amounted to a plot of the corona discharge spectrum on paper.

But, as the chart paper moved, wavelength values also had to be recorded on the paper at regular intervals, so that the light intensity values could be associated with corresponding wavelength values. This was done by mounting a circular disk on the monochromator wavelength control shaft, so that the disk rotated with the shaft. The disk had a narrow slot cut into its edge. A stationary light source and a light sensor were mounted on the opposite sides of the rotating disk, in such a way that the light sensor was exposed to the light source only when the slot in the disk passed between them. The voltage pulses, resulting from the light falling on the sensor, were applied to another pen of the recorder, leading to narrow rectangular pulses drawn on the moving paper at regular wavelength intervals, each pulse corresponding to one full revolution of the monochromator wavelength control shaft.

The wavelength of the output light from the particular monochromator employed in the investigations increased by 20 nanometres for each complete revolution of the wavelength control shaft. This meant that successive rectangular pulses on the paper chart represented 20 nanometre wavelength increments.

Chapter 5 – Corona Discharge Photography

Figure 5.6 shows typical traces drawn by the two pens side by side, namely the discharge spectrum, and the wavelength indicator pulse train respectively.

Neither the monochromator wavelength dial, nor the wavelength indicator pulses on the paper chart, could be regarded as giving accurate wavelength readings. Both had to be calibrated, that is checked against a light source having well known spectral lines, namely light produced at well-known specific wavelengths only. The mercury vapour lamp has a rather large number of spectral lines of varying light intensities, whose wavelengths have been accurately determined many times in the past, and are listed in physical data books.

Calibrations of the monochromator wavelength dial, and also the paper chart wavelength indicator pulses, were carried out by applying the light from the mercury vapour lamp to the monochromator input slit. Accurate calibration could be achieved by relying on the easily identifiable stronger mercury spectral lines only. For example a strong mercury spectral line exists at 546.1 nanometres. If the monochromator wavelength dial read this line as 546.4 nanometres, then the monochromator wavelength readings near 546 nanometres would have to be corrected by subtracting 0.3 of a nanometre from them.

On the paper chart, accurate wavelength values needed to be assigned to the leading edges of the wavelength indicator pulses, that is, the edges first drawn by the pen on the moving chart paper. This could be done by using two pens, one for drawing the calibration pulses, and the other for drawing the mercury spectrum, side by side, as close to each other as practicable. One could then pick the closest known wavelength mercury spectral lines on the two sides of a calibration pulse leading edge, and then work out the wavelength value corresponding to that leading edge by proportion. The accuracy of the calibration could be enhanced by using three pens, and drawing two mercury spectrum traces, one on each side of the calibration pulse trace.

Figures 5.6 (a), (b), and (c), show three corona discharge spectral scans, the object having been a metal disk in the form of a coin, together with wavelength calibration pulses. The three scans correspond to three different sensitivity settings of the current to voltage converter, that is 1, 10, and 100 millivolts per nanoampere respectively. The 1 millivolt per nanoampere setting was suitable for determining the most intense spectral bands, the 10 millivolts per nanoampere setting was indicated for recording medium intensity spectral bands, while the 100 millivolts per nanoampere setting was necessary for picking up the lowest intensity spectral bands. The flat tops of the spectral curves resulting at higher converter sensitivities were due to intense bands "saturating" the current to voltage converter, that is, driving it to the maximum output voltage it could handle.

The triangular areas in Figures 5.6 (a), (b), and (c), represent the various bands. The bases of these areas are the wavelength ranges over which the bands extend, and the heights of the areas are the band heads. The individual lines within a band are not distinguishable on the scales employed in Figure 5.6, which is intended as an illustration only. For accurate wavelength determination of bands and band heads, charts were produced with extended wavelength scales, with the 200 to 1000 nanometre wavelength range spread out over a distance of 2 metres or more. This was done by storing a 5 second scan of the converter output voltage in computer memory, and then extracting it from the memory over a longer period, and transferring it to chart paper at a rate typically 1/20 of the original scan rate.

96 Chapter 5 – Corona Discharge Photography

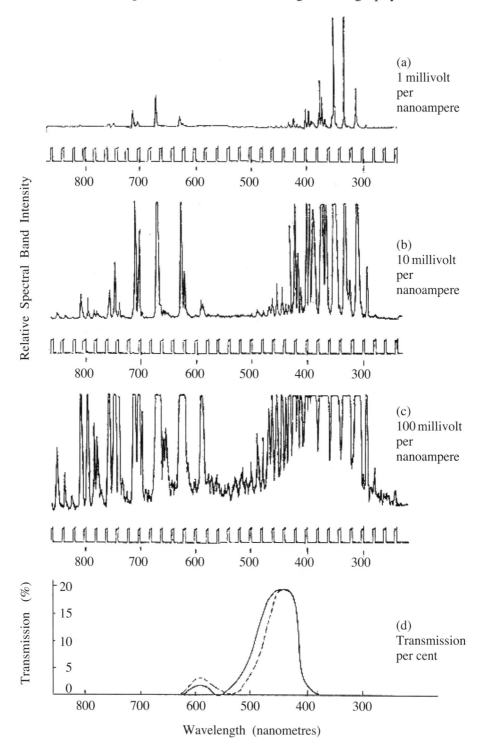

(a) 1 millivolt per nanoampere

(b) 10 millivolt per nanoampere

(c) 100 millivolt per nanoampere

(d) Transmission per cent

Wavelength (nanometres)

Figure 5.6

Chapter 5 – Corona Discharge Photography

A large number of scans drawn to an extended scale were obtained for each of the three types of objects used as electrodes, namely: metal disks, plant leaves, and human fingertips. Spectral bands and band heads in these large scale scans were reliably determinable to the nearest 0.1 nanometre. In addition, individual bands or band heads could also be verified by direct reading, involving manual wavelength control and a voltmeter as outlined above.

In order to identify the molecules, or atoms, responsible for the measured wavelengths of bands, band heads, or spectral lines, one needs to consult physical data books listing the wavelengths of molecular band heads, or of atomic spectral lines, associated with specific molecules or atoms, as determined by many investigations over many years in the past. There are hundreds of band heads listed for the nitrogen molecule N_2 alone, obtained under greatly varied conditions. However, only a fraction of these were found in the corona discharge spectra by the procedure described above.

These investigations led to the conclusion that the same 64 bands were consistently present in all scans, regardless of whether derived from metal disks, plant leaves, or human fingers. These were spread over a wavelength range extending from 297 to 866 nanometres. Out of these 64 bands, 43 were identified, or strongly suspected, as coming from the nitrogen molecules in the air. The remaining 21 bands were not identified with certainty, but their wavelength values, when checked against published data, suggested that they were very likely to have come from constituents of air other than nitrogen, such as oxygen, nitrogen oxides, carbon dioxide, argon, or unidentified impurities.

It may be worth mentioning that the whole spectrum appeared to consist of spectral bands. Spectral lines could be expected only from the monatomic inert gasses in air, such as argon. In fact, one or two unidentified narrow bands were suspected of being argon spectral lines.

Some bands were found occasionally other than the above mentioned 64. However, these were not consistently present in all metal electrode tests, or in all biological electrode tests. It appeared therefore that these extra bands originated from transient impurities in air, and as such they were ignored.

The 43 identified nitrogen band heads, and the 21 unidentified bands, that were detected consistently in all tests, are listed in Table 5.1. The 43 identified nitrogen band heads are given in nanometres to two decimal places as listed in data books. The 21 unidentified bands are given in nanometres to the nearest nanometre only, as most of these were found to be double or multiple bands close to each other in wavelength, which were not specifiable by single well defined band heads.

Since no differences could be found between the spectra resulting from various electrodes, whether metallic disks, plant leaves, or human fingertips, it appeared that the spectra originated solely from the constituents of the air in which the discharge took place. The spectra did not depend on the nature of the objects serving as electrodes irrespective of whether they were inanimate or biological.

Yet, in the case of biological electrodes, one might have expected that secretions from plant leaves or fingertips, could have found their way into the discharge path, and contributed spectral lines, or bands, which would not be present when using metallic electrodes. In particular sweat would be expected to contain sodium chloride, and the two well-known strong, yellow sodium spectral lines near 589 nanometres could be expected to show up in the spectrum. Nevertheless, all searches for these lines yielded negative results. However, when the fingertip was dipped into a 1% sodium chloride solution in water, and then allowed to dry partially prior to acting as an electrode, the sodium spectral lines did appear in the spectrum. These tests seem to confirm that uncontaminated biological objects acting as electrodes did not contribute to the discharge spectrum any bands or lines beyond those originating from the air itself.

The above tests also indicated the need for working with clean electrodes. The electrodes, animate or inanimate, were cleaned with water or alcohol, and dried prior to tests.

Table 5.1

Nitrogen band heads (nanometres):						
Ultraviolet:	297.68	313.60	315.93	326.81	328.53	
	330.90	333.90	337.13	344.60	350.05	
	353.67	357.69	364.17	317.05	375.54	
	380.49	389.46	394.30	399.84		
Visible:	405.94	414.18	420.05	426.97	434.36	
	435.50	441.67	449.02	457.43	464.94	
	472.35	481.47	491.68	590.60	595.90	
	625.28	632.29	654.48	670.48		
Infrared:	705.90	716.48	750,39	762.62	854.18	
Unidentified bands (nanometres):						
Ultraviolet:	355	359	369	377		
Visible:	412	440	446	463	470	657	660	672	675
Infrared:	714	733	760	781	798	810	839	866

With reference to Figure 5.6, by far the most intense bands in the discharge were found situated in the ultraviolet region, with relatively little contributed by the visible and infrared regions. It must also be borne in mind that the sensitivities of both the monochromator and the photomultiplier vary with wavelength, and so the height of spectral band heads in Figure 5.6 are not proportional to the actual light intensities responsible for those bands.

When considering the spectral bands in Figure 5.6, the important question arises as to how photography deals with the discrete spectral wavelength bands or lines when the discharge is photographed. This question can be answered by examining the colour compositions, or spectra, of actual corona discharge colour photographs. Positive transparency colour photographs of the corona discharge are suitable for such an examination. Such photos of coins, or of fingertips, display transparent bluish rings, or annuli, typically having about 1 centimetre inner diameter and up to 2 centimetres outer diameter, so that the transparent bluish region is a few millimetres wide.

The experimental arrangement used for the spectral examination of such transparencies is shown in Figure 5.7. The light source needed to have a wide wavelength distribution. In order to cover a wavelength range from 200 to 1000 nanometres, two light sources had to be used, a tungsten lamp producing light within the infrared and visible regions, and a mercury vapour lamp, or possibly a deuterium lamp, producing light within the ultraviolet and visible regions. An opaque plate, with two adjacent holes, was interposed between the light source and the monochromator input slit, in such a way that by sliding the plate within guides, either hole could be inserted between the light source and the monochromator input slit. The diameters of the two holes had to be equal, and small enough, so that one of the holes could be covered by the bluish annulus of the colour transparency fixed in front of it, while the other hole was being left free.

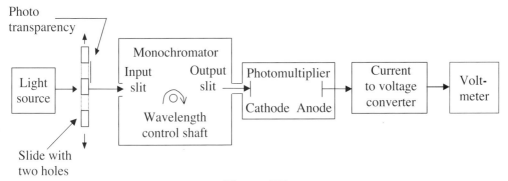

Figure 5.7

Thus, by means of the slide arrangement, at any given monochromator wavelength setting, either the hole covered by the transparency, or the uncovered hole, could be interposed successively between the light source and the monochromator input slit, and then the current to voltage converter output voltages read for both. The ratio of the two readings, that is, the reading through the transparency, divided by the reading through the open hole, gave the fraction of the light transmitted by the transparency at the given wavelength setting. Thus, if the ratio was found to be 0.2, then 20% of the incident light was transmitted by the transparency at that wavelength setting. A higher ratio indicated a lighter colour of the transparency, suggesting more intense light in the corona discharge at the given wavelength setting. Conversely a lower ratio suggested a darker transparency colour, and a lower light intensity in the discharge at the corresponding wavelength setting.

This procedure needed to be repeated for a relatively large number of wavelength settings, which led to a curve showing how the above ratio, and so colour intensity of the photo transparency, varied with wavelength. Figure 5.6 (d) shows two such curves obtained from two different corona discharge photographs, the wavelength scale being the same as for the scanned band spectra in Figures 5.6 (a), (b), and (c).

Comparison of the scanned band spectra, with the spectra of the photographs, clearly shows that the latter are smooth curves peaking in the visible blue region, with a much less pronounced peak in the visible red region. By visual observation, the photos would appear entirely blue, so that their red colour content could not be visually discerned. The spectra of the photographs are essentially continuous, containing wavelengths that are entirely absent from the band spectra. The effect of the photographs is to "bulldoze" the original spectral bands into smooth curves. Furthermore, photographic film or paper, intended for visible region photography, seems to miss almost completely the ultraviolet part of the band spectrum, which contains the most intense bands. Therefore, it appears that when the corona discharge is photographed, much of the information present in the spectrum of the discharge is lost, while the rest is drastically modified.

In conclusion, it may be stated that the light produced by corona discharge appears to be entirely due to the constituent gases, and possible impurities, present in air. It appears to be independent of the nature of the electrodes between which the discharge takes place, irrespective of whether the electrodes are inanimate metallic objects such as coins, or parts of living organisms such as plant leaves, or skin on the fingers or palm of the human hand.

The light produced consists of spectral bands, most of which are identifiable as originating from the nitrogen molecules in the air, but other constituents of the air also contribute.

In particular, secretions from biological electrodes do not seem to contribute to the light produced, unless artificially introduced in relatively high concentrations.

When examining the spectra of corona discharge photographs, it is found that photography flattens the spectral bands present in the actual discharge into a smooth curve, and thereby loses most of the information which the examination of the discharge spectrum could yield.

Further, contact photography that is not relying on the use of a camera, is also prone to the production of erroneous colours, unless great care is taken to prevent discharge developing on the non-emulsion side of the film.

The relatively small part of the foregoing chapter involving the use of a photographic film camera, would also apply to the more recent digital cameras with few exceptions, if any.

Claims have been made by a number of investigators, for corona discharge photography yielding information of physiological, psychological, and indeed of paranormal nature, enabling such photographs to be used as a diagnostic tool.

It is not the intention here to refute such claims, but merely to state that the extensive investigations by the author, and his associates, failed to find supporting evidence for such claims. However, as will be discussed in a subsequent chapter, photographs may be subject to psychokinetic interference. Some corona discharge photographs may have been affected by such interference, yielding photographs that are not explainable in terms of the foregoing discussion.

Chapter 6
The Exact and the Probable

Some branches of science may be regarded exact, while the exactness of others is doubtable. The exact sciences deal with phenomena which are quantitative, and accurately calculable, repeatable, and which when repeated always yield the same results. The physical sciences would normally be regarded exact, provided that observations are limited to a human scale, that is, neither too small, nor too large. Even in the exact sciences, the exactness breaks down for considerations of the very small, such as the field of the subatomic particles, or the very large, approaching the limits of the observable universe.

On the other hand, the life and mind sciences may be considered inexact, in the sense that accurate statements cannot always be made, since chance often plays a role. It is then only possible to state, to what level of probability a certain course of events may be attributable to particular causative factors, or alternatively, what is the probability for a certain outcome to have occurred by chance.

The boundaries between the exact and the inexact are not sharply definable. Even what may be considered exact today, may have gone through an inexact developmental stage earlier, since the various factors contributing to the presently known facts came to light gradually. Thus, even in the fields of the exact sciences, cursory observations have often resulted in erroneous conclusions in the past, due to the lack of full knowledge of the underlying facts, or the lack of instruments enabling the making of precise measurements and calculations.

Considering a simple example, originally it was believed that when objects of different sizes were allowed to fall freely, they fell at different speeds. However, observations eventually revealed that all dense objects, with relatively small surface areas, fell the same distance in a given time, and only light objects, with large surface areas, departed from this rule. It came to be suspected by some observers that this discrepancy was due to a retarding effect produced by the air, and that in the absence of air all objects would fall at the same speed. This was eventually proven correct when the facilities to create evacuated space were developed, so that the falling of objects could be observed in a vacuum.

It was also found that the speed of falling objects was not constant, but increased continually by the same amount in each second. This increase in speed per second was given the name "gravitational acceleration", and upon measurement, at sea level, it was found to be 9.807 metres per second in each second. At the surface of the sea, in the absence of air resistance retarding the fall, all falling objects always behave this way, and no departure can ever be observed from this rule. However, measuring the speed of falling objects is not easy.

As another example of a predictable and repeatable behaviour, which lends itself to easier measurement, let a small relatively heavy object, such as a small metal bob, be suspended from a fixed point by means of a light unstretchable cord. This arrangement is called a pendulum. If the bob is pulled to one side and then let go, it will keep swinging for some time. The maximum displacement of the bob from its rest position, namely the amplitude of the swing, gradually diminishes due to air resistance, and also due to friction at the point of suspension, until the bob eventually comes to rest. If air resistance and friction could be eliminated, the pendulum, once set in motion, would swing forever. But, in spite of the diminishing amplitude, the duration of one full swing, called the period, remains the same, provided that the maximum angle between the cord and the vertical is kept small, say less than 10 degrees. Examination shows that the period of one full swing increases with the length of the pendulum, as measured from the point of suspension to the centre of the bob. The period also depends on the earth's gravitational pull, that diminishes with height above sea level, and so for a pendulum of given length, the period is found to increase with height above sea level. Further, as the length of the suspending cord will in general increase with temperature, the period will also increase with the temperature. The effects of both height and temperature are small, and may jointly affect the period only to a small fraction of 1%. An easy way of measuring the period of a pendulum is to time a large enough number of full swings, say 20 swings, by means of a stopwatch, and then divide the result by 20.

A pendulum, which makes one full swing in exactly 1 second at sea level, has to be 248.4 millimetres long, as shown in Appendix 6.1. Anyone making a pendulum of this length will find its period of swing at sea level to be 1 second, with any error well within a small fraction of 1%. This phenomenon was found to be so repeatable, that pendulums were used for centuries to regulate clocks. Of course, in pendulum clocks, the amplitude of the swing must be maintained, which can be done by supplying the small energy loss per swing, due to air resistance and friction, from the energy stored in a wound up spiral spring, or a suspended weight which is allowed to descend slowly.

Another example for precisely determinable behaviour is the orbital motion of the planets around the sun. The speed with which a planet moves, and the time it takes to make one complete orbit around the sun, both depend on the gravitational pull exerted by the sun at the planet's location, that is, dependent on the mass of the sun, and also on the distance of the planet from the sun. If the location of a planet, and its velocity, namely its speed and its direction of motion relative to the sun, are determined from astronomical observations at a particular instant, its location and velocity may be accurately calculated at any future instant of time. A simplified version of the relevant calculations is given in Appendix 6.2.

As stated earlier, precise repeatability is a feature of the classical physical sciences, dealing with phenomena on a human scale. The very small subatomic particles do not obey precise rules, and only the probabilities of such particles behaving in particular ways are calculable. Thus, even in simple atoms, the positions and the velocities of the electrons relative to the nucleus are not determinable, only the probability of finding electrons in particular regions surrounding the nucleus is computable.

Likewise, biological phenomena do not conform to precise laws, and can only be handled in terms of probabilities. This normally requires the assembling and processing of numerical data in an orderly way, which is usually referred to as statistics. Only after such assembling and ordering can probability calculations be made.

The nature of the statistical approach can be illustrated by means of a simple example involving the throwing or tossing of a coin onto a flat, horizontal surface a number of times. Following any particular toss of a coin, one can be certain that it will fall flat on the surface with one of its sides facing upward. Since this happening is a certainty, the probability for the coin falling flat is 100%, or putting it differently, the probability of certainty is 100%. However, the coin may fall with either "head" or "tail" facing upward. If the coin is unbiased, that is, it has uniform density and perfectly even edges, and is so tossed that it is spinning in the air before landing, then the head or tail outcomes are equally likely. The probability of getting either the one or the other is 50% each.

Chapter 6 – The Exact and the Probable

Now let the coin be tossed four times in succession. Each toss may result in either head or tail facing upward, and the outcome of four tosses may be 1 out of 16 possible different combinations of heads and tails as listed in the columns of Table 6.1, where "H" stands for head, and "T" stands for tail.

Table 6.1

Column number	1	2	3	4	5	6	7	8	9	10	11	12	13	14	15	16
First toss	H	H	H	H	T	H	T	H	T	H	T	H	T	T	T	T
Second toss	H	H	H	T	H	H	H	T	T	T	H	T	H	T	T	T
Third toss	H	H	T	H	H	T	H	T	H	H	T	T	T	T	H	T
Fourth toss	H	T	H	H	H	T	T	H	H	T	H	T	T	T	H	T

For example, in Table 6.1, Column 3 represents 1 of the 16 possible outcomes, the four tosses yielding: head, head, tail, head, in that order. Since each column represents a possible outcome, and each outcome is equally likely, the probability for each possible outcome is 1 in 16, or 1/16, or 0.0625, or 6.25%. Consequently, the probability of obtaining in four tosses, either four heads or four tails is 0.0625 or 6.25% each, as there is only 1 column with four heads, and 1 column with four tails. The probability of getting either three heads or three tails is 4 times 1/16, namely 4/16 = 0.25 or 25%, as there are 4 columns with three heads, and 4 columns with three tails. Finally, the probability of obtaining two heads and two tails is 6 times 1/16, that is 6/16 = 0.375 or 37.5%, since there are 6 columns with two heads and two tails. Table 6.2 summarises these outcomes.

Table 6.2

Combinations	Probabilities	
Zero heads and four tails	1 / 16	6.25 %
One head and three tails	4 / 16	25.00 %
Two heads and two tails	6 / 16	37.50 %
Three heads and one tail	4 / 16	25.00 %
Four heads and zero tails	1 / 16	6.25 %
Total	16 / 16 = 1	100.00 %

Further, the probability of obtaining in four tosses, three heads or four heads, or what is the same three heads or more, is 5/16 = 0.3125 or 31.25%, since there are 5 columns with three heads or more. Likewise, the probability of obtaining two heads or more, is 11/16 = 0.6875 or 68.75%, since there are 11 columns with two heads or more. Finally, the probability of obtaining zero head or more, is 16/16 = 1 or 100%, since there are 16 columns with zero head or more. Thus, the sum of all the probabilities in Table 6.2 equals 1 or 100%, which is to be expected, since one of all the possible outcomes occurring is certain, and the probability for certainty is 100%. It is to be noted, that the probability for a number of alternative outcomes is the sum of the probabilities of the individual outcomes.

It is helpful to notice that 4 tosses yield 16 possible outcomes, and that the number 2 multiplied together 4 times equals 16, that is: 2 x 2 x 2 x 2 = 4 x 4 = 16. This is usually written in the exponential form as $2^4 = 16$, where the exponent 4 signifies that the number 2 is to be multiplied together 4 times. It is found in general, that the number of possible outcomes equals the number 2 multiplied together as many times as there are tosses. For example, 10 tosses result in a number of possible outcomes equalling the number 2 multiplied together 10 times, that is, 2^{10} which equals 1024, and so 10 tosses yield 1024 possible outcomes. Similarly, one finds that 20 tosses yield $2^{20} = 1,048,580$ possible outcomes, namely over a million outcomes, while for 100 tosses the number of possible outcomes equals 2^{100}, which exceeds 10^{30}, that is, a number consisting of the figure 1 followed by 30 zeros.

It appears that as the number of tosses exceeds 4, it soon becomes impracticable to find the probabilities for particular numbers of heads in a given number of tosses by means of tables such as Table 6.1. Probabilities for larger numbers of tosses are more readily found from the so-called "Pascal's triangle" shown in Table 6.3.

Table 6.3

Number of Tosses												Number of Outcomes
1						1	1					2
2					1	2	1					4
3					1	3	3	1				8
4				1	4	6	4	1				16
5				1	5	10	10	5	1			32
6			1	6	15	20	15	6	1			64
7			1	7	21	35	35	21	7	1		128
8		1	8	28	56	70	56	28	8	1		256
9		1	9	36	84	126	126	84	36	9	1	512
10	1	10	45	120	210	252	210	120	45	10	1	1024

With reference to Table 6.3, the triangular array of numbers may be formed from the top down, by adding two adjacent numbers in a line and writing the sum in the next line half way between the numbers added. So, adding numbers 6 and 15 in the sixth line, gives the number 21 in the seventh line. The column of numbers to the left of the triangular array lists the number of tosses, and the column of numbers to the right of the triangular array lists the number of possible outcomes. If the numbers in any horizontal line of the array are divided by the number of possible outcomes to the right of that line, one gets fractions that equal the probabilities for obtaining 0, 1, 2, 3, etc., heads in that order, in the number of tosses indicated to the left of that line. Thus, the fourth line yields Table 6.4 for 4 tosses. Similarly the tenth line yields Table 6.5 for 10 tosses, where the decimals and the percentages have been rounded. It will be noted that the sum of all probabilities, whether expressed as fractions or as decimals equals 1.0, and when expressed as percentages equals 100%, once more indicating that one of all the possible outcomes occurring is a certainty.

Chapter 6 – The Exact and the Probable

Table 6.4

Number of heads in 4 tosses	0	1	2	3	4
Probabilities expressed as fractions	$\frac{1}{16}$	$\frac{4}{16}$	$\frac{6}{16}$	$\frac{4}{16}$	$\frac{1}{16}$
Probabilities as decimals	0.0625	0.25	0.375	0.25	0.0625
Probabilities as percentages (%)	6.25	25.0	37.5	25.0	6.25

Table 6.5

Number of heads in 10 tosses	0	1	2	3	4	5	6	7	8	9	10
Probabilities as fractions	$\frac{1}{1024}$	$\frac{10}{1024}$	$\frac{45}{1024}$	$\frac{120}{1024}$	$\frac{210}{1024}$	$\frac{252}{1024}$	$\frac{210}{1024}$	$\frac{120}{1024}$	$\frac{45}{1024}$	$\frac{10}{1024}$	$\frac{1}{1024}$
Probabilities as decimals	0.001	0.010	0.044	0.117	0.205	0.246	0.205	0.117	0.044	0.010	0.001
Probabilities as percentages (%)	0.1	1.0	4.4	11.7	20.5	24.6	20.5	11.7	4.4	1.0	0.1

It is important to note that the word outcome may have two meanings. It may refer either to the result of a toss, or to the resulting number of heads in a given number of tosses.

Using Table 6.5, the probabilities can be obtained for various outcomes in 10 tosses. For example the probability of getting 7 heads is 0.117 or 11.7%, the probability of getting 8 heads is 0.044 or 4.4%, while the probability of 7 or 8 heads is 0.117 + 0.044 = 0.161 or 16.1%. Further, the probability of 7, or 8, or 9, or 10 heads, that is, 7 heads or more is 0.117 + 0.044 + 0.010 + 0.001 = 0.172 or 17.2%. Here again, it is to be noted that the probabilities for combinations of alternative outcomes is additive.

The information contained in Table 6.4 may be represented graphically as shown in Figure 6.1(a). The 5 equal segments on the horizontal base line in Figure 6.1(a) represent 0, 1, 2, 3, and 4 heads, each of which may be the outcome of 4 tosses. Rectangles are erected over these segments, such that the height of each rectangle equals the probability of the outcome represented by its base, that is, the segment on which it stands. If the bases of the rectangles are made 1 unit long each, then the probabilities will be given by both the heights and the areas of the rectangles, in which case the sum of the 5 rectangular areas equals unity, again indicating that one of all the possible outcomes occurring is a certainty.

In Figure 6.1(b) the same is done for 10 tosses. There are 11 possible outcomes in 10 tosses ranging from 0 to 10 heads, as marked by 11 segments along the horizontal base line. Once more, if the segments are 1 unit long each, and the heights of the rectangles are made equal to the probabilities of the outcomes represented by the base line segments on which they stand, then the probabilities will be given by both the heights and the areas of the rectangles. The sum of the areas of the 11 rectangles once more equals unity.

106 Chapter 6 – The Exact and the Probable

While it is feasible to work out the probability of obtaining any given number of heads in a relatively large number of tosses by the method used in deriving Tables 6.4 and 6.5, the work becomes increasingly tedious as the number of tosses increases.

For example in Figure 6.1(c), the heights of the rectangles equal the probabilities of obtaining given numbers of heads in 100 tosses. Probabilities are shown only for the range extending from 35 to 65 heads in 100 tosses, since the probabilities of getting less than 35 heads or more than 65 heads, in 100 tosses, are so small that they cannot be shown on the scale of Figure 6.1(c). If once more, the horizontal bases on which the rectangles stand are each 1 unit long, then the sum of the rectangular areas shown in Figure 6.1(c) equals close to 0.996, while the sum of those areas not shown equals about 0.004. These figures indicate that the probability of getting a number of heads anywhere between and including 35 and 65 heads, in 100 tosses, is 0.996 or 99.6%, and the probability of obtaining a number of heads outside this range is 0.004 or 0.4%.

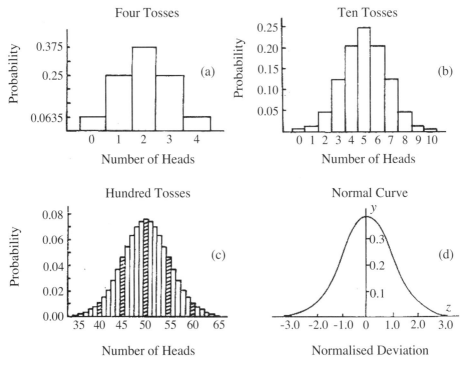

Figure 6.1

As the number of tosses increases, the number of rectangles also increases, and the stepped line formed of the rectangle tops in Figure 6.1(c) approaches a smooth curve as shown in Figure 6.1(d), provided that the number of tosses becomes large enough. It is possible to make the smooth curve in Figure 6.1(d) to be applicable to any number of tosses by "normalising" the horizontal base line as described in what follows.

The normalisation process involves three characteristic quantities that are calculable for any set of numbers. These are called the "arithmetic average" or "mean", the "variance", and

Chapter 6 – The Exact and the Probable

the "standard deviation". In order to avoid misunderstandings, it is helpful to designate the individual numbers in a set of numbers by the term "values", where a value may be a whole number or a fractional number, and it may be a positive or a negative number.

The "arithmetic average" or "mean" of a set of values equals the sum of the values divided by the number of values in the set. When summing values, positive values must be added, and negative values, of course, must be subtracted.

A "deviation" equals the difference between any value in the set and the mean. It may be positive or negative, depending on whether the value is larger or smaller than the mean.

The "square of a deviation" equals the magnitude of the deviation multiplied by itself, and is always positive.

The "variance" of a set of values equals the sum of the squares of the deviations, divided by the number of values in the set. It is always positive.

The "standard deviation" of a set of values is the "square root" of the variance, that is, the quantity which when multiplied by itself yields the variance. It is also always positive.

The square root is normally indicated by the symbol $\sqrt{}$. For example since $2 \times 2 = 4$, it follows that the square root of 4 is $\sqrt{4} = 2$. Using this symbol one has:
Standard deviation = $\sqrt{\text{variance}}$.

The calculation of these quantities may now be illustrated by means of a simple example, involving a set of five values, namely: 2, 3, 4, 5, and 6. The procedure is illustrated in Table 6.6.

Table 6.6

Values:	2, 3, 4, 5, 6
Number of values:	5
Sum of the values:	$2 + 3 + 4 + 5 + 6 = 20$
Mean of the values:	$20 / 5 = 4$
Deviations from the mean:	$-2, -1, 0, 1, 2$
Squares of the deviations:	4, 1, 0, 1, 4
Sum of the squares:	$4 + 1 + 0 + 1 + 4 = 10$
Variance of the values:	$10 / 5 = 2$
Standard deviation:	Square root of 2 = $\sqrt{2} \approx 1.4142$ Note that: $(1.4142) \times (1.4142) \approx 2$

Consider now the case of 10 successive tosses of a coin again, and suppose that the 10 tosses are repeated 1024 times, amounting to 10,240 tosses altogether. With reference to Table 6.5, since in each batch of 10 tosses, the probability of obtaining 0, 1, 2, etc., heads respectively is 1/1024, 10/1024, 45/1024, etc., one would expect, in the 1024 batches of 10 tosses, zero head to occur in 1 batch, 1 head to occur in 10 batches, 2 heads to occur in 45 batches, and so on. There would be all told $1 + 10 + 45 + ... = 1024$ values for the number of heads in the 1024 batches. One may work out the mean, the variance, and the standard deviation of these 1024 values relatively easily, if the problem is dealt with in a systematic way, as is done in Appendix 6.3. The result is: Mean = 5, Variance = 2.5, Standard deviation = $\sqrt{2.5}$ = 1.581.

Working a number of cases for different numbers of tosses per batch, one finds that the mean, the variance, and the standard deviation, is always given by the relations in Table 6.7 below. The relations in Table 6.7 apply to the number of tosses per batch of tosses, but do not depend on the number of batches. These relations can be calculated from any number of batches, yielding a number of values large enough to work with.

Table 6.7

Mean =	(number of tosses) / 2
Variance =	(number of tosses) / 4
Standard deviation =	square root of the variance = $\sqrt{\text{variance}}$

One may now use Table 6.7 for calculating the values of the mean, the variance, and standard deviation for 4, 10, and 100 tosses per batch, as shown in Table 6.8.

Table 6.8

Number of tosses	4	10	100
Mean	4 / 2 = 2	10 / 2 = 5	100 / 2 = 50
Variance	4 / 4 = 1	10 / 4 = 2.5	100 / 4 = 25
Standard deviation	$\sqrt{1}$ = 1	$\sqrt{2.5}$ = 1.581	$\sqrt{25}$ = 5

Let it now be recalled that Figure 6.1(c) applies to 100 tosses, and that it gives the probabilities for obtaining specific numbers of heads in 100 tosses. If the 100 tosses were repeated many times, the number of heads occurring in one particular batch of 100 tosses would be one value in a large set of values. It follows from the above, that this large set of values has a mean equal to 50, and a standard deviation equal to 5.

In Figure 6.1(c), 45 heads, or 55 heads, deviate from the mean of 50 heads by 5 heads, which equals 1 standard deviation. Likewise 40 heads, or 60 heads, deviate from the mean by 10 heads, which equals 2 standard deviations. This suggests that one may graduate the horizontal base line in terms of the number of standard deviations from the mean, which may be called "normalised deviation". Thus, for any number of tosses, the normalised deviation equals the actual deviation divided by the standard deviation, that is:

(normalised deviation) = (actual deviation) / (standard deviation)

Since actual deviations of values from the mean may be positive or negative, depending on whether those values lie above or below the mean, the corresponding normalised deviations may also be positive or negative. Furthermore, since the mean obviously does not deviate from itself, the normalised deviation of the mean must be zero.

Chapter 6 – The Exact and the Probable

As the number of tosses increases beyond 100 tosses, the stepped curve in Figure 6.1(c) approaches the smooth curve in Figure 6.1(d). This smooth curve is often referred to as the "normal probability curve". The horizontal base line in Figure 6.1(d) is called the z axis, which is now graduated in terms of normalised deviations measured from the mean at $z = 0$. The vertical line at $z = 0$, passing through the peak of the curve, is called the y axis, while vertical lines connecting given z values on the z axis to the normal curve are referred to as ordinates, or y values. Since values equalling the mean at $z = 0$ are the most probable, the normal probability curve must have its maximum value at $z = 0$, on the y axis.

The total combined areas of the rectangles in Figures 6.1 (a), (b), and (c) equal unity, representing 100% probability. Likewise, the total area in Figure 6.1(d), between the z axis and the normal probability curve, represents 100% probability, and consequently must also equal unity. As a result, in Figure 6.1(d), the maximum ordinate on the y axis, corresponding to the mean at $z = 0$, works out to equal 0.3989.

The normalised deviation z is a continuous variable, which may assume any value, that may be positive, negative, integer, or fractional. In what follows, specific values of the normalised deviation applicable to particular situations will be denoted by the capital letter Z. For given values of the normalised deviations, that is values of Z, statistical tables usually list the corresponding values of the ordinates, that is values of y, and also the areas P to the right of those ordinates, that is between those ordinates, the normal probability curve, and the z axis extending up to z equals infinity. Table A6.4, in Appendix 6.4, is such a table. Table A6.4 gives for any specific value of Z, the associated area P, which equals the probability of obtaining that Z value or higher, in a particular situation. Normalised deviations are also called z scores.

While values of the normalised deviation z may assume a continuous range of integer or fractional values, they need to be relatable to the number of heads in a given number of tosses, of which Figures 6.1 (a), (b), and (c) are particular examples. This requires that the horizontal base lines in Figures 6.1 (a), (b), and (c) are also considered having continuous scales, on which the bases of the rectangles occupy finite ranges that are 1 unit long. So, on the base line in Figure 6.1(a), one must consider 2 heads extending from 1.5 to 2.5, while 3 heads extend from 2.5 to 3.5. Also, on the base line in Figure 6.1(c), one has 60 heads extending from 59.5 to 60.5, while 60 heads or more, extend from 59.5 to 100.5, or from 59.5 up to infinity, that would normally be an acceptable approximation.

Now let illustrate the use of the normal probability curve by a few examples. As tossing coins by human agency may influence the outcome, such influence should be eliminated by employing a push button operated mechanical catapult. Let a coin be tossed 200 times by means of such a catapult. As a head or a tail result is equally likely in each toss, one might intuitively expect a result of 100 heads and 100 tails in 200 tosses, if chance were the only factor at work. However, even if all possible bias is eliminated, it is still unlikely that 200 tosses will yield exactly 100 heads and 100 tails.

The probability of obtaining a certain number of heads or more, in 200 tosses, may be calculated from the normal probability curve. For repeated batches of 200 tosses, the set of values for the number of heads, in 200 tosses, has the following associated quantities:

Mean = 200 / 2 = 100, Variance = 200 / 4 = 50,
Standard deviation = square root of 50 = $\sqrt{50}$ = 7.071.

Obtaining exactly 100 heads in 200 tosses, corresponds to a segment along the continuous scale of the base line extending from 99.5 to 100.5, that deviate by −0.5 and +0.5 from the mean of 100. The corresponding values of the normalised deviations are approximately −0.5 / 7.071 ≈ −0.07 and +0.5 / 7.071 ≈ +0.07. From Table A6.4 in Appendix 6.4, the shaded area P corresponding to a normalised deviation $Z = 0.07$ equals 0.4721, and so the area above the segment of the z axis extending from 0 to 0.07 is (0.5 − 0.4721) = 0.0279. The area above the segment of the z axis extending from −0.07 to +0.07 is twice as large, namely 2 x (0.0279) ≈ 0.056. Hence, the probability of obtaining exactly 100 heads in 200 tosses is approximately 0.056 or 5.6%. At this relatively low level of probability, obtaining exactly 100 heads in 200 tosses is rather unlikely.

Now let the probability be found for obtaining a number of heads anywhere in the range between and including 95 and 105 heads, in 200 tosses. The corresponding segment on the continuous scale of the base line extends from 94.5 to 105.5. The deviations from the mean of 100 are −5.5 and +5.5, which correspond to approximate normalised deviations of −5.5 / 7.071 ≈ −0.78, and +5.5 / 7.071 ≈ +0.78. From Table A6.4 in Appendix 6.4, the shaded area P corresponding to normalised deviation $Z = 0.78$ equals 0.2177, hence the area above the segment of the z axis extending from 0 to 0.78 equals (0.5 − 0.2177) ≈ 0.282, and the area above the segment of the z axis extending from −0.78 to +0.78 is 2 x (0.282) ≈ 0.56. So, the probability of obtaining a number of heads anywhere between and including 95 and 105 heads, in 200 tosses, is approximately 0.56 or 56%. One can conclude that, at this level of probability, obtaining a number of heads by chance anywhere between and including 95 and 105, in 200 tosses, is a rather more likely outcome.

However, it could happen that an actual experiment might yield 120 heads and 80 tails, in 200 tosses. For reasons stated below, let the probability be found for obtaining 120 heads or more, in 200 tosses, and not the probability for obtaining 120 heads exactly. The segment on the continuous scale of the base line then extends from 119.5 upward, the corresponding deviation from the mean being 119.5 − 100 = 19.5. This yields a rounded normalised deviation of 19.5 / 7.071 ≈ 2.76. Table A6.4, in Appendix 6.4, gives the area to the right of the ordinate at $Z = 2.76$, as 0.00289. So, the probability of obtaining 120 heads or more, in 200 tosses, is approximately 0.0029 or 0.29%.

At this relatively low level of probability, the result would no longer be accepted as the outcome of chance, but rather resulting from the coin being biased in some way, perhaps its edges are not even enough, or its density is not uniform, making one side heavier than the other. The probability calculation is not made for exactly 120 heads out of 200 tosses, but rather for 120 heads or more, out of 200 tosses, since more than 120 heads out of 200 tosses is even less likely, and would likewise indicate a biased coin.

Now let two coins be tossed simultaneously on a flat surface. Then, the two coins may both finish with the same face uppermost, that is both head or both tail, an outcome which one may designate a "hit". Alternatively, the two coins may land with different faces topmost, that is, one head and the other tail, an outcome which would then be called a "miss".

Once one of the coins has landed with either head or tail uppermost, the probability of the second coin landing with the same face upward is 1/2 = 0.5 or 50%, and the probability of the second coin landing with the opposite face upward is also 1/2 = 0.5 or 50%.

Chapter 6 – The Exact and the Probable

Consequently, the probability of obtaining some given number of hits, in a number of simultaneous tosses of two coins, is exactly the same as the probability of obtaining the same given number of heads, in the same number of tosses of a single coin.

When tossing two coins simultaneously, one coin could be thought of as "guessing" the outcome resulting from the other coin, yielding a hit if the guess is correct, namely, both coins finish with the same face upward, or leading to a miss if the guess is incorrect, that is, the coins land with different faces upward. This concept of hits and misses will be seen as useful in many situations.

The above principles apply not only to coin tossing, but to any situation where the result of any single action may be one of two possible outcomes, which are equally probable, namely have a probability of 0.5 or 50% each.

For example in an examination, each question may be supplied with two answers, only one of which is correct. The examinee is asked to tick the answer he or she thinks is the correct one. Ticking the correct answer yields a hit, while ticking the incorrect answer results in a miss. An examinee with little or no knowledge of the subject matter, and who guesses only as to which is the correct answer, would come up with nearly equal numbers of hits and misses, corresponding to around 50% probability. However, if the probability for the number of hits, out of the total number questions asked, having come about by chance is relatively small, then knowledge of the subject matter is indicated. The lower the probability is, the higher is the examinee's knowledge of the subject matter.

Up to this point, only such situations were considered where a single act could result in one of two equally probable outcomes. However, there are many cases where a single action may result in more than two equally probable outcomes. An example is offered by throwing or casting a die, the six faces of which carry spots ranging from one to six spots. When a single die is cast onto a horizontal, flat surface, the result could be one of six equally likely outcomes, namely, the die may land with any of the six possible numbers of spots topmost. It is essential that neither the die, nor the throwing technique should be biased. Bias in throwing may be eliminated by the use of a push button actuated mechanical catapult. In the absence of any bias, the probability of any particular number of spots coming topmost, for example three spots, is 1 in 6, or 1/6 = 0.1667, or 16.67%.

Now let two unbiased dice be cast simultaneously. It then could happen that both dice land with the same number of spots uppermost, for example both two spots, in which case the outcome would be referred to as a "hit". Alternatively, the two resulting number of spots could be different, for example three spots and five spots respectively, in which case the outcome would be called a "miss". Once one of the dice comes up with a given number of spots, the second die could come up with any one of the six different numbers of spots, each equally probable, out of which only one could produce a hit. Hence, the probability of a hit is 1/6 = 0.1667 or 16.67%, while the probability of a miss is 5/6 = 0.8333 or 83.33%.

Let the simultaneous throw of two dice be repeated 10 times, a procedure which could be designated a batch of 10 throws. The number of hits resulting from a batch of 10 throws could assume any one of 11 different values, namely: 0, 1, 2, 3, 4, 5, 6, 7, 8, 9, 10. By repeating the batch of 10 throws a large enough number of times, one could accumulate a large set of values, and calculate the three characteristic quantities associated with that set of values, namely: the mean, the variance, and the standard deviation.

Chapter 6 – The Exact and the Probable

When casting a die, there are six possible outcomes corresponding to the numbers of spots on the six faces. However, there are situations where a single action may result in any other number of possible outcomes. For example one may place ten tickets, numbered 1 to 10 in a jar, and draw out one ticket. In this case a single draw results in 1 of 10 possible outcomes. Here too, if two jars were each containing ten tickets numbered 1 to 10, and a draw were made from each jar, the two tickets drawn could bear the same number yielding a "hit", or they could have different numbers leading to a "miss". A batch of draws would then yield a value for the number of hits, and repetitions of the batch of draws would give a set of values for which the mean, the variance, and the standard deviation could be deduced.

When a pair of dice is thrown, or a pair of tickets is drawn from two jars, one can arbitrarily label these as the first and second die, or the first and second ticket. One may then argue that the result from the second die or ticket being the same as, or different from, that of the first die or ticket, "decides" whether the outcome is a hit or a miss. In a batch of throws or draws, each involving a pair of dice or a pair of tickets, as many "decisions" are made as there are throws or draws in the batch. A throw or a draw of a pair of dice or tickets, may also be referred to as an "attempt". Each batch yields a value for the number of hits. Repeating the batches of throws or draws a number of times yield a set of values. In general one finds that the mean, the variance, and the standard deviation of these values, in terms of the number of decisions or attempts per batch, are always given by Table 6.9.

Table 6.9

Mean = (number of decisions) x (probability of a hit)
Variance = (number of decisions) x (probability of a hit) x (probability of a miss)
Standard deviation = square root of variance = $\sqrt{\text{variance}}$

It is worth noting that in the case of the simultaneous tossing of two coins, the probability of a hit or a miss both equal 0.5, for which case Table 6.9 reduces to Table 6.7.

Returning to the case of two dice thrown simultaneously in batches of 10 throws, the probability of a hit is 1/6, while the probability of a miss is 5/6. Using Table 6.9:

Mean = (10) x (1/6) = 1.6667, Variance = (10) x (1/6) x (5/6) = 1.3889,
Standard deviation = square root of variance = $\sqrt{1.3889}$ = 1.1785.

These figures have been rounded to four decimal places.

One may now deduce the probability of a certain number of hits or more, in a given number of attempts, in cases where the probabilities for a hit and a miss are unequal. Using the simultaneous throw of two dice as an example, let the two dice be thrown 180 times. In the absence of bias, one would expect by chance alone (180) x (1/6) = 30 hits. Let it be supposed that an actual test yielded 40 hits, in 180 throws, and let it be required to find the probability for 40 hits or more occurring by chance alone. In this case one has:

Mean = (180) x (1/6) = 30,
Variance = (180) x (1/6) x (5/6) = 25,
Standard deviation = square root of variance = $\sqrt{25}$ = 5.

Chapter 6 – The Exact and the Probable

Now, on the continuous scale of the base line, 40 hits extend from 39.5 to 40.5, and 40 hits or more, extend from 39.5 upward. Thus:

Deviation from the mean = 39.5 − 30 = 9.5,
Normalised deviation = (actual deviation) / (standard deviation) = $Z = 9.5 / 5 = 1.9$,
Corresponding area from Table A6.4, in Appendix 6.4 gives $P = 0.02872$,
Hence: Probability for 40 hits or more ≈ 0.0287 or 2.87%.

At this relatively low level of probability, the result would not normally be accepted as the outcome of chance, but rather the dice, or the throwing technique, or both, would be suspected of suffering from some kind of bias.

The above principles may be applied to any situation where a single act may yield more than two equally probable outcomes. For example in an examination, each question could be followed by six alternative answers, only one of which would be correct. The examinee would then be asked to tick the answer believed to be the correct one. Ticking the correct answer would lead to a hit, while ticking an incorrect answer would incur a miss. An examinee guessing only would be expected by chance to tick the correct answers for 1/6 of the number of questions presented. For a higher number of hits, one may calculate the probability of that hit rate having come about by chance, as in the example above. A low figure for the probability would then indicate a high level of knowledge of the subject matter by the examinee.

The question now arises, at what level of probability does one start regarding that the outcome of a test, or of an experiment, has not come about by chance, but rather has resulted from an underlying causative factor.

In scientific circles it is generally, but arbitrarily, accepted that if the probability for any result having come about by chance is larger than 5%, then that result should be considered to have occurred by chance.

Should the probability for a result being the outcome of chance lie within the 1% to 5% range, that result would be regarded "significant", and it would normally be assumed that the result is not the outcome of chance, but that some underlying causative factor is likely.

Finally, if the probability for a result to have occurred by chance is 1% or less, that result is labelled "highly significant", and it is generally agreed that such a result should not be attributed to chance, but that some causative factor should be assumed and sought.

In Chapter 4 on the human aura, subjects were tested for the ability to perceive light outside the normally visible wavelength region, by randomly mingling periods with the light on, and the light off. The subjects were to press the "Yes" push button if they thought to have perceived the light, and the "No" push button if they have not. Here, 20 or more correct responses out of 30 attempts, were accepted as confirmation of the ability to perceive the light, since the probability of obtaining 20 hits or more, in 30 attempts by chance is almost exactly 5%.

In the life and mind sciences exact results are rarely attainable, and probability calculations have to be frequently relied on. An example may be provided by the following procedure, as a possible method for determining the effectiveness of a drug for a particular ailment.

Chapter 6 – The Exact and the Probable

The drug may be administered to a number of volunteer subjects who suffer from that illness, and through observation and questioning of the subjects, an attempt could be made to assess the drug's effectiveness. But, as it is well-known, if some subjects are given so-called placebos, such as starch pills with no medicinal effect, coupled with the suggestion that they are taking a proven beneficial drug for their condition, many will report and, in fact, actually show improvement. Since belief and other factors enter the drug evaluation process, it is necessary to devise test procedures, which eliminate or neutralise extraneous factors. This can be done by employing statistical methods.

The investigators may enlist the services of 100 volunteer subjects, randomly selected from a wide circle of persons for whom the drug may be beneficial. This way, the sample of 100 subjects may be assumed to be truly representative of all possible subjects. The drug would then be administered to 50 of the subjects, and a placebo to the remaining 50.

This would be best done by the so-called "double blind" method, whereby each subject would know that she or he has received either the drug or the placebo, but would not know which of the two, nor would the investigators know which subject had received the drug, and which received the placebo. Each subject would then have to be tested for the possible effectiveness of the drug in accordance with clearly established criteria. Only after securing the test results for all subjects, would the investigators and the subjects be in a position to know, which subjects were given the drug, and which received the placebo. The aim of this double blind arrangement is to eliminate any influence, which beliefs, suggestions, or prior knowledge may have on the test results.

One possible way of proceeding from this point would be to assign each subject to one of four groups:

   Group 1:   drug administered, found effective,
   Group 2:   placebo administered, found no effect,
   Group 3:   drug administered, found no effect,
   Group 4:   placebo administered, found effective.

Thus, Groups 1 and 2 yielded the expected or positive results constituting "hits". On the other hand, Groups 3 and 4 yielded negative results amounting to "misses".

Now, suppose that a particular investigation yielded 60 hits and 40 misses. Calculations based on the normal probability curve, show that the probability of this result occurring by chance is 2.87%. At this level of probability, some investigators may deem the result to be statistically significant, and therefore the drug to be effective, while others may still dispute its efficacy. Let it be noted that in order to regard the drug to be effective, a 100% hit rate is not expected. In the life sciences, results normally are accepted as positive or significant, if the probability for the results to have occurred by chance is 5% or less.

The demarcation between chance results and significant results at the 5% probability level, and also the demarcation between significant and highly significant results at the 1% probability level, are arbitrary figures. Nevertheless, the 5% and the 1% figures are accepted worldwide, and should therefore apply to all investigations regardless of whether the investigations fall within the generally accepted boundaries of orthodox science, or lie outside such boundaries.

Chapter 6 – The Exact and the Probable

Before leaving the subject of probability calculations from the normal probability curve, attention needs to be paid to the fact that all probability calculations from the normal curve are approximate. One reason for this is that the numbers of heads, tails, hits, or misses, are always whole numbers, leading to stepped graphs such as in Figures 6.1 (a), (b), and (c), while the normal curve is a smooth line approximation to those stepped graphs.

Another reason is the fact that the normal curve in Appendix 6.4 is not derived from the theory underlying Pascal's triangle in Table 6.3, but through generally accepted practice, from a mathematical expression that is given in Appendix 6.4, at the head of Table A6.4.

The errors resulting from these causes are relatively small for low values of the normalised deviation, but the errors can become substantial as the normalised deviation increases.

For example, if a coin is tossed 10 times, then the probability of obtaining 10 heads in 10 tosses from Table 6.5 is $1 / 1024 = 0.000977$ (≈ 0.001).

However, working from the normal curve one has:
Mean $= 10 / 2 = 5$, Standard deviation $= \sqrt{10/4} = 1.581$.

On the continuous scale of the base line, 10 heads extend from 9.5 to 10.5. The deduced normalised deviations, rounded to two decimal places, are: $(9.5 - 5) / 1.581 \approx 2.85$, and $(10.5 - 5) / 1.581 \approx 3.48$. The corresponding areas from the normal curve in Table A6.4, Appendix 6.4, are 0.00219 and 0.00023. The difference of these two areas should equal the probability of 10 heads in 10 tosses: $0.00219 - 0.00023 = 0.00196$, which is nearly twice the probability obtained from Pascal's triangle.

Similar calculations lead to the probabilities of 9 or more heads, 8 or more heads, and 7 or more heads, in 10 tosses, as given in rounded figures in Table 6.10:

Table 6.10

Number of heads or more	Probability from Table 6.5	Probability from the normal curve
10	$1 / 1024 = 0.00098$	0.00196
9 or more	$11 / 1024 = 0.0107$	0.0134
8 or more	$56 / 1024 = 0.0547$	0.0568
7 or more	$176 / 1024 = 0.1719$	0.1714

So, the error is seen to increase as the probability decreases, and the associated normalised deviation increases, that is, as one is moving toward the tail end of the normal curve.

An exact calculation for the probability of obtaining any number of heads or more, in any given number of tosses, or in general, any number of hits or more, in any given number of attempts, may be performed by using the so-called "binomial theorem" or "binomial expansion" given in Appendix 6.5, from which Pascal's triangle derives.

As stated above, the normal probability curve gives higher figures for the probability, than what would be obtained from Pascal's triangle or the binomial expansion. In general, the discrepancies increase, as the probability P for a number of hits or more in a given number of attempts or decisions diminishes, that is, as one moves toward the tail end of the curve. The discrepancies also increase as the probability of a hit p and that of a miss q in a single attempt, become more unequal. The normal probability curve underestimates the level of significance, and so it may be safely relied on.

When a large number of repetitive probability calculations are called for, as in some of the subsequent chapters, it may be helpful to work with letter symbols representing the various quantities involved as follows:

X = number of hits,
Y = number of misses,
N = number of decisions, or attempts, $N = X + Y$,
p = probability of a hit following a single decision,
q = probability of a miss following a single decision,
M = mean, $M = (N) \times (p)$, or simply $M = Np$,
S = standard deviation, $S = \sqrt{(N) \times (p) \times (q)}$, or simply $S = \sqrt{Npq}$,
Z = normalised deviation, corresponding to X, Y, N, and M above,
P = probability corresponding to the above value of Z or higher.

In the literature on probability and statistics, usually lower case letters are used for N, M, S, and Z. Here, and in subsequent chapters, upper case letters are adopted in the interest of improved clarity.

Now, X hits or higher, on the continuous scale of the base line, extend from $X - 0.5$ upward to infinity, corresponding to an actual deviation equal to $(X - 0.5 - M)$.

The corresponding normalised deviation is $Z = (X - 0.5 - M)/S$.

The corresponding probability P for the above value of Z may now be obtained from Table A6.4 in Appendix 6.4.

As an example, let these symbols be applied for finding the probability of 7 heads or more, in 10 tosses:

$X = 7$, $Y = 3$, $N = X + Y = 10$, $p = q = 0.5$,
$M = (N) \times (p) = (10) \times (0.5) = 5$,
$S = \sqrt{(N) \times (p) \times (q)} = \sqrt{(10) \times (0.5) \times (0.5)} = \sqrt{2.5} = 1.581$,
$Z = (X - 0.5 - M)/S = (7 - 0.5 - 5)/(1.581) = (1.5)/(1.581) \approx 0.95$.

Then, from Appendix 6.4, Table A6.4, for $Z = 0.95$, one has $P = 0.1711$. The corresponding figure in Table 6.10 is $P = 0.1714$. This small discrepancy is due to 7 heads or more, having been taken here as extending from 6.5 to infinity, and not from 6.5 to 10.5 as was done in Table 6.10.

Chapter 7
The Normal and the Paranormal

A phenomenon may be regarded as "normal" if for that phenomenon generally accepted scientific explanations exist, so that the phenomenon neither violates currently accepted scientific principles, nor goes beyond the boundaries of such principles.

Conversely, a phenomenon would be regarded "paranormal" if it is not explicable in terms of the currently prevailing state of scientific knowledge, or if it violates scientific laws currently believed to be valid, but which nevertheless is a phenomenon reported by many reliable observers in a consistent way, and can be shown to exist by the same scientific methodology that orthodox science employs for many of its purposes.

As science progresses, it gradually succeeds in explaining an ever-increasing number of paranormal phenomena, and as a result more and more such phenomena gain normal acceptance. Consequently, the range of paranormal phenomena shrinks continually, while the range of normal phenomena steadily increases. Thus, many phenomena, which would have been regarded as paranormal in the past, would now be considered as normal.

Numerous phenomena, that are still regarded as paranormal today, originate from human experiences reported from time immemorial. One of these is the often reported observation of immaterial human or animal forms, commonly referred to as "ghosts", or more rarely as "apparitions", which is a term preferred by investigators employing scientific methodology. The ostensible appearance of apparitions are considered by many as an indication of a non-physical, or discarnate, aspect of a human being, or of an animal, surviving physical death.

Toward the end of the 19th century, some investigators decided to subject the reality, or otherwise, of apparitions to systematic scrutiny. It was noted that many apparitions claimed to have been seen were those of people who were in the process of dying, the apparent aim being to inform interested parties of the impending death. In most cases it was impossible to ascertain whether the claimed appearance of the apparition of the dying preceded the time of the death, or whether it was subsequent to it. However, it became clear, that apparitions of living individuals were observed far more often than apparitions of the dead.

It was soon realised that the phenomenon of apparitions was very similar to the then newly recognised phenomenon of "telepathy", a concept claiming the possibility of direct information exchange between the minds of two living people without any sensory means. Apparitions and telepathy both involved the extrasensory transmission of information from a sender, usually referred to as the "agent", to a receiver, often called the "percipient".

During the early 20th century, investigations gradually shifted from apparitions, and the ostensible survival of physical death, to information acquisition by the human mind without reliance on the senses, which became known as "extrasensory perception". Extrasensory perception may thus be defined as the ability of humans or animals, to acquire information without reliance on any of the normal sensory means, that is: sight, hearing, smell, taste, or touch, and also without relying on any clues, or prior knowledge, which could enable deductions or inferences to be made, or any other means falling within the domain of orthodox science. When these conditions are met, the information acquisition may be designated extrasensory, and deemed to be paranormal.

Eventually, three distinct kinds of extrasensory perception became discernible, which were named: "telepathy", "clairvoyance", and "precognition" respectively.

Telepathy may be defined as paranormal information transfer between the minds of humans or animals. For example, an individual could become aware of the thoughts or intentions of another individual without sensory clues, or any knowledge allowing inferences to be made.

Clairvoyance is definable as paranormal awareness of objects or events. An example could be acquiring awareness of the location of a displaced or lost object without reliance on sensory means, or prior knowledge, or any information allowing to make inferences.

Precognition designates paranormal awareness of future events, again without any clues, or prior knowledge, enabling deductions or inferences to be relied on.

Sometimes a fourth category of extrasensory perception, called "retrocognition", is also distinguished, that refers to paranormal awareness of past events, once more without sensory clues, or prior knowledge, allowing the acquisition of the information by normal means.

A special case of extrasensory perception is called "psychometry", which is a combination of telepathy and clairvoyance. It entails the apparent telepathic information acquisition by a psychic practitioner from the mind of a client, aided by clairvoyant awareness of events associated with an object, which is the personal property of the client, and is handed to the practitioner while the consultation takes place.

Another phenomenon akin to apparitions, and which was claimed to have been observed from the earliest of times, involves unexplainable physical disturbances without any identifiable underlying objective causes. The most readily discernible example of these is the so-called "poltergeist" outbreak. The word poltergeist is of German origin, meaning "noisy spirit" or "rampant spirit". A poltergeist outbreak typically affects a single house, and lasts around a few months. The associated phenomena claimed to have been observed involve, amongst others, objects flying about, the production of sound and light effects, and occasional spontaneous ignition. Similar physical manifestations were also claimed to have been observed in the vicinity of so-called "physical mediums".

In the past such physical manifestations were often attributed to discarnate entities, namely the "ghosts" or "spirits" of the dead. However, investigations during the early 1900s eventually led to the conclusion that these physical disturbances originated from the unconscious minds of living agents, who were not consciously aware of their unconscious minds being the source of these disturbances.

The phenomenon was eventually designated "psychokinesis", a term which is of Greek origin, meaning motion caused by the mind. However, the term psychokinesis eventually came to cover all physical, chemical, or biological manifestations without detectable objective causes, and which are suspected of originating from the unconscious mind of living agents. A more complete list of observed or reported psychokinetic effects includes setting physical objects into motion, or influencing the motion of objects already moving, also "levitation", that is, the floating of physical bodies in defiance of gravity, the deformation of physical objects, the production of sound, light, and ignition, interference with the functioning of any apparatus, but in particular electronic equipment such as computers. Psychokinetic phenomena also include the effects of the unconscious mind on biological systems, such as influence on plant growth and psychic healing.

Chapter 7 – The Normal and the Paranormal

Further to the above, some observers claimed to have witnessed the dematerialisation of physical objects, and even of human beings, on rare occasions, and their re-materialisation, often at a different location which is referred to as "teleportation".

A special case of paranormal phenomena is "dowsing", which appears to be a combination of clairvoyance and psychokinesis. In dowsing, information acquired by the unconscious mind via clairvoyance about the location of objects, such as underground water, is transferred to the conscious mind by the unconscious mind psychokinetically causing twigs, or suitably bent pieces of wire, loosely hand held by the walking dowser, to move or swing when the correct location is reached. Alternatively, a change in the direction of the motion of a hand held pendulum is relied on by some practitioners for transferring the clairvoyantly acquired information from the unconscious mind to the conscious mind.

As investigations into extrasensory perception and psychokinesis progressed, it became apparent that most paranormal phenomena, originally attributed to discarnate entities surviving physical death, were in fact the products of the unconscious mind of living agents. However, a number of paranormal phenomena suggest that the possibility of discarnate survival of physical death cannot be dismissed with certainty. One such phenomenon is the "out of body experience", which is a sensation of consciousness separating from the body, and operating totally outside of it. This phenomenon has been reported often enough not to be ignored. Other phenomena suggesting survival include some cases of spiritualistic messages, a fraction of the cases involving apparitions, near death experiences described by people who have revived after being considered as having been clinically dead for varying short periods, utterances of people shortly before dying, and case histories suggesting reincarnation of discarnate beings into the bodies of newly born infants.

These survival related phenomena collectively suggest that the mind is a non-physical entity in its own right, distinct from the brain or the body, and while it normally functions in conjunction with the brain, it is capable of not only functioning outside the body, and independently of the brain, but also to survive the physical death of the body.

Paranormal phenomena, being essentially the products of the unconscious mind, are not normally producible or repeatable by the conscious will. Such phenomena can only be investigated when they occur spontaneously. This requires investigations over extended periods of time within which paranormal manifestations occur at random.

In the areas of extrasensory perception and psychokinesis, it is possible to devise strictly controlled laboratory experiments, the results of which can be evaluated by statistical methods. Such evaluations rely on showing that the probability of the results having come about by chance is so small that, in accordance with generally accepted scientific practice, chance should be dismissed, and the existence of some underlying causes being the source of the results should be considered as being beyond doubt.

The underlying causes of paranormal events would be paranormal themselves, that is, they would not be explainable in terms of current scientific knowledge, yet their existence should be accepted as proven if the calculated probability figures for chance occurrence were small enough. It is of course essential that investigations are not based on selected results, but that they include all results, and show that the overall results are not attributable to chance.

However, the orthodox scientific view appears to be, that no matter how carefully the investigations may have been conducted, in accordance with accepted scientific principles, and no matter how small the probability for the results having occurred by chance may be, the results must have been obtained either by chance or by fraud, since the phenomena violate currently accepted scientific laws, and therefore cannot exist.

The situation with survival related phenomena is even more tenuous, since such phenomena do not lend themselves to statistically calculable laboratory tests, but rely on the systematic evaluation of consistent observations by many individuals. All that can be said is that the systematic examination of a large body of accumulated evidence is strongly suggestive of the survival of the mind beyond bodily death. However, here again, no matter how large and consistent the accumulated evidence is, orthodox science dismisses it on grounds that it is subjective and anecdotal. Orthodox science holds that the mind is a manifestation of the brain, and must cease to exist upon the death of the body.

Paranormal phenomena are investigated under a number of different names. The most frequently used terms are: parapsychology, paraphysics, bioenergetics (suggesting that paranormal phenomena are inherent to biological systems in a hitherto unknown manner), and psychotronics (after a supposed fundamental entity, namely the psitron or psychotron, akin to subatomic particles and ostensibly responsible for psychic phenomena). None of these terms can be regarded as fully appropriate, since none of them convey the essentially multidisciplinary nature of paranormal events.

Some investigators have attempted to secure scientific acknowledgement for paranormal phenomena by replacing well-established terminology with terms that could be more acceptable to orthodox science. For example, the term "remote viewing" was proposed as an alternative to clairvoyance. However, it could be argued that it should not be necessary to pander to orthodoxy by name changing, and that the statistical results of well controlled experiments ought to be acceptable to all, regardless of the field of study or terminology.

The three main branches of paranormal phenomena, namely: extrasensory perception, psychokinesis, and survival related phenomena, are discussed in more detail in subsequent chapters, which also include the author's own investigations and results.

Chapter 8
Extrasensory Perception

As stated in the previous chapter, the paranormal phenomenon of extrasensory perception refers to the ability of humans or animals to acquire information without reliance on any of the senses, namely: sight, hearing, smell, taste, or touch. Furthermore, the process must also exclude making use of any clues, which would enable the acquisition of the information by deduction or inference, or any other means explainable in terms of currently prevailing scientific knowledge.

Let it be recalled that the various subcategories of extrasensory perception, as enumerated in Chapter 7, are: Telepathy, signifying non-sensory, and non-inferable, information transfer between the minds of two or more humans or animals; Clairvoyance, denoting information acquisition about an object or event, without reliance on the senses, clues, or inferences; Precognition, referring to information acquisition about future events, without any clues enabling deductions or inferences to be made; and Retrocognition, signifying the obtaining of information about past events, without prior knowledge, or clues allowing conclusions to be drawn. Retrocognition is not always listed as a separate subcategory.

These subcategories of extrasensory perception normally manifest together, and an individual human usually exhibits either all of them, or none.

In the case of telepathy, the individual from whom the extrasensory information originates is referred to as the sender, or "agent", while the individual acquiring the information is called the receiver, or "percipient". In the other cases, namely clairvoyance, precognition, and retrocognition, there are only percipients, but no identifiable agents.

The acquisition of extrasensory information is essentially an unconscious process. It is not possible to send, or receive, extrasensory messages by consciously wanting to do so. Conscious desire for information transmission, or acquisition, may or may not result in messages being transmitted, or perceived, through the agency of the unconscious mind. The existence of the unconscious mind is evident from the fact that information can be consciously acquired, then forgotten, and later recalled. Such forgotten information is not lost, but is stored in a part of the mind, that came to be called the unconscious mind. The forgotten information can be recalled from the unconscious mind sometimes instantly, but at other times only after considerable delay. After such delay, the information sought may emerge into consciousness suddenly, at a moment when it is not expected. The term "subconscious" is used at times as an alternative to "unconscious", however, the term unconscious seems to have become the preferred usage in recent times.

The most frequent way of acquiring extrasensory messages is by the information emerging into consciousness, much the same way as forgotten information is remembered. However, extrasensory information may also be acquired while the percipient is asleep, in the form of a realistic dream. For example, the whereabouts of a misplaced object, not remembered in the waking state, may be revealed in a dream.

In a relatively small number of cases, perhaps around 10% of all cases, the percipient may become aware of extrasensory information through sense impressions, which are internally generated in the brain without objective causes. It appears that regions of the brain, where normally the various types of information picked up by the senses are processed, may become activated in response to extrasensory messages received by the unconscious mind. This way, the percipient may, without physical causation, hear voices or other sounds; see apparitions, that is, immaterial forms of humans, animals, or objects; feel being touched; and experience smell or taste. As a result of such sense impressions, usually some extrasensory information is being imparted to the percipient.

Again, another way whereby extrasensory information may be acquired is by reliance on physical implements, such as hand held pendulums or dowsing rods, which are activated in particular ways, either by unconscious muscular activity, or by unconscious psychokinetic agency, thereby providing the information consciously sought by the percipient.

In the transmission of extrasensory information, either the agent, or the percipient, may assume an active role. Thus, if an agent has the desire to communicate some information to a percipient, that information may emerge into the consciousness of the passive percipient, and on rare occasions the percipient may hear the voice or see the apparition of the agent, so as to aid the delivery of the message. Conversely, if the percipient desires to receive some information from an agent, then once again that information may pop into the consciousness of the percipient, and in addition on rare occasions the voice or the apparition of the agent may also be perceived. While this communication takes place, the agent could be engaged in some conscious activity, without knowing that her or his unconscious mind is tapped, or that her or his voice is heard, or her or his apparition is seen, by the percipient.

When a percipient receives extrasensory information about an event, she or he may be able to give a fairly good description of the event, but the percipient is almost always uncertain of the location or the time of the event. The percipient may not even know if a past, present, or future event is being perceived. However, the location or the time of the event may often be surmised from the context of the perceived event. While the event is often correctly perceived, its location and timing, as deduced from the context, is often erroneous.

Much of the often correct information that clairvoyants deliver to their clients, is extracted by the clairvoyant from the client's conscious or unconscious mind. The clairvoyant is usually unaware of the source of the information so obtained. The client is often impressed, because the clairvoyant "could not possibly have known".

However, some people conversing with clairvoyants come to realise, that capable psychics can read their thoughts. This may well be an embarrassing experience, since some thoughts would be considered highly private. The thought reading ability of psychics may be frustrated by not dwelling on any particular thought for any length of time, but rather continually changing the objects of one's attention, while in the presence of a psychic. The objects of attention could be the attributes of items nearby, such as pieces of furniture, floor coverings, chandeliers, the colour of walls, and so on.

Also, once an unconscious mental link is established between a clairvoyant and a client, or another human individual, the clairvoyant may experience any pain felt by that individual. The clairvoyant would normally feel the pain in the same part of her or his body, as is felt by the other individual. Pain felt by animals may likewise be picked up by clairvoyants.

The question now arises, how one can statistically verify the existence of extrasensory perception. Early experiments in the 1930s relied on cards, dice, or coins. As coin tossing has already been considered in some detail in Chapter 6, let it now be considered how coin tossing may be applied so as to obtain statistical verification of extrasensory perception. It would be necessary to establish first, that neither the coin, nor the coin tossing technique, is biased in any way. As described in Chapter 6, the procedure may be assumed free of bias, if in the absence of an agent, 200 tosses yield a number of heads lying in the range 95 to 105. As found in Chapter 6, the probability for this to occur by chance is 56%, and at this level of probability the result is attributable to chance, indicating the absence of any bias.

A test for extrasensory perception would normally involve a percipient, an experimenter, and in the case of telepathy, also an agent. The experimenter, and the agent if any, would be located in one room, or a laboratory, while the percipient would be located in another room, or possibly in another building. It is, of course, absolutely essential, that the information to be transmitted to the percipient through extrasensory perception should not be able to reach the percipient through any normal means. The experimenter would toss the coin at regular intervals onto a flat surface, preferably by a push button operated catapult. Each toss may yield head or tail uppermost, the probability for either to occur being 0.5 or 50% each. The percipient would know the instants of time when the coin is being tossed, either because of an agreed time schedule, or via being informed by the experimenter pushing a button, and so delivering sound beeps to the percipient preceding the tosses. Between any two consecutive tosses, the percipient would then write down, or electronically record, the outcome of the toss, as perceived through extrasensory perception.

In the case of a telepathy test, the agent would observe the outcome of each toss, and would then try to transmit the information to the percipient by mentally contemplating "head" or "tail", as the case may be.

When testing for clairvoyance, there would be no agent involved, and in order to exclude telepathy, the experimenter would also be restricted from knowing the outcome of each toss, until after the percipient's decision has been made.

Finally, when testing for precognition, the percipient would be asked to make a decision regarding the outcome of the next toss, before each toss takes place.

For each toss, the percipient's decision may agree or disagree with the actual outcome, yielding "hits" or "misses" respectively.

In Chapter 6, hits and misses resulting from the simultaneous throw of two coins, or two dice, were considered. When testing for extrasensory perception, the situation is exactly the same, except that the percipient takes over the role played by the second coin, or the second die. If the test involves the tossing of a coin, then when the planned number of tosses is completed, the results of the test would be obtained by comparing the percipient's record against the experimenter's record, and counting the number of hits and misses. Using the probability calculations in Chapter 6, and Table A6.4 in Appendix 6.4, one may then deduce the probability of the results having come about by chance. For example, as shown in Chapter 6, the probability of obtaining 120 hits or more, in 200 tosses by chance, is very close to 0.0029 or 0.29%. Thus 120 hits or more, in 200 tosses, would constitute a highly significant result, and suggest extrasensory perception taking place.

However, when a subject is tested for extrasensory perception, the results of one test run of 200 tosses would not be acceptable as convincing proof. Normally 10, or even more, test runs may be considered necessary, typically one or two weeks apart, each test run involving 200 to 400 decisions.

Chapter 8 — Extrasensory Perception

Let it be supposed that a subject undertakes 5 test runs, each with 200 decisions, and that the subject performs uniformly with 110 hits out of 200 decisions in each test run. The probability for the running total of the results occurring by chance is listed in Table 8.1.

Table 8.1

Test run	Number of decisions (running total)	Hits (running total)	Misses (running total)	Probability (percentage) (running total)
1	200	110	90	9.01
2	400	220	180	2.56
3	600	330	270	0.80
4	800	440	360	0.26
5	1000	550	450	0.09

As Table 8.1 shows, if a relatively moderate performance is maintained over a number of test runs, the probability of the results having come about by chance continually diminishes. In particular, the probability of 550 or more hits, in 1000 decisions, occurring by chance is 0.09% or 0.0009, which is less than 1 in 1000. This is a highly significant result.

Let it now be supposed that the coin, or the coin tossing technique, is biased, so that in the absence of an agent, in a test run of 200 tosses, heads come up 120 times and tails 80 times. If a percipient were present, and the percipient were to decide that the outcome is head each and every time, then this would lead to 120 hits in 200 tosses. This would constitute a highly significant result, since as seen above, the probability for obtaining 120 hits or more, in 200 tosses by chance, is very close to 0.29%. While this is not a realistic example, it clearly indicates the need for avoiding bias in the test procedure.

Tests for extrasensory perception may also be carried out by means of casting a die. The procedure is the same as for coin tossing, except that the probability for a hit in a single throw is $1/6 = 0.1667$ or 16.67%, and the probability for a miss in a single throw is $5/6 = 0.8333$ or 83.33%. The probability calculation would then be carried out as described in Chapter 6, with the aid of Table 6.9, and the discussion relating to Table 6.9.

Yet another way of testing for extrasensory perception is by means of cards. In the simplest case one may use ordinary playing cards, half of the cards in a pack having red coloured symbols, and the other half black coloured symbols. Shuffling and cutting the pack may come up with either a red card, or a black card, the probability of either occurring being 50% each. The test procedure would be the same as with coins, except that "red" replaces "head", and "black" replaces "tail", or vice versa, while the shuffling and cutting of the pack replaces coin tosses.

Experimenters in the 1930s came to the conclusion that ordinary playing cards were not the optimal means of testing for extrasensory perception. It was felt that the cards should depict simple pictures with a definite number of easily identifiable features, or alternatively, each card should carry a clearly recognisable distinct symbol. In the end, five symbols were chosen, namely: square, circle, cross, star, and wavy lines. These are shown in Figure 8.1. Cards bearing these symbols are often called ESP (Extra-Sensory Perception) cards.

Chapter 8 — Extrasensory Perception

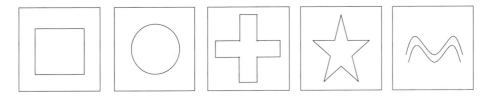

Figure 8.1

In a pack of ESP cards, each one of the above 5 symbols is carried by 5 cards, adding up to 25 cards in all. Shuffling and cutting the pack may come up with any one of the 5 symbols, the probability of getting any particular symbol being 1/5 = 0.2 or 20%.

The experimenter would keep shuffling and cutting the pack, preferably not by hand, but with the aid of a mechanical device. The percipient, in some other room or building, would attempt to become aware of the symbol resulting from each shuffle and cut, in accordance with an agreed time schedule, or a signal indicating when each cut of the pack has been made. For each shuffle and cut, the experimenter would record the resulting symbol, while the percipient would record a decision as to which of the five symbols is being perceived.

When testing for telepathy, an agent observing each shuffle and cut would attempt to transmit mentally the resulting symbol to the percipient. In the case of a clairvoyance test, neither the experimenter, nor anyone else, would know the resulting symbol until after the percipient has recorded a decision. Finally in a precognition test, the percipient would be asked for a decision before each shuffle and cut is performed. After the conclusion of the test, a comparison of the experimenter's and the percipient's test records would yield the resulting number of hits and misses.

The task is then to deduce the probability of the results having occurred by chance, that is, the resulting number of hits or more, in a given number of shuffles and cuts, having come about by chance. Below 0.05 or 5% probability, the results would be deemed statistically significant, while below 0.01 or 1% probability, the results would be regarded highly significant, and indicative of extrasensory perception taking place.

The probability calculations follow from Table 6.9 and the discussion associated with that table in Chapter 6, which deals with the situation where a single action may lead to more than two equally probable outcomes. When using ESP cards, each shuffle and cut may result in 1 of 5 equally probable outcomes, namely in 1 of the 5 symbols in Figure 8.1. Any one decision by the percipient, regarding the outcome of a particular shuffle and cut, may lead to picking the correct card yielding a hit, the probability of which occurring by chance is 1 in 5, or 1/5 = 0.2, or 20%. Alternatively, any decision by the percipient may result in picking the wrong card leading to a miss, the probability of which coming about by chance is 4 in 5, or 4/5 = 0.8, or 80%.

Let it now be supposed that a percipient, in an extrasensory perception test run employing a pack of cards with 5 symbols, comes up with 55 hits in 200 shuffles and cuts. The task is to find the probability of 55 hits or more, in 200 decisions, and whether this could be regarded as a chance result. Consulting Table 6.9, in Chapter 6, yields the values for the mean, the variance, and the standard deviation, applicable to this case:

Mean = (200) x (0.2) = 40, Variance = (200) x (0.2) x (0.8) = 32,
Standard deviation = square root of 32 = $\sqrt{32}$ = 5.657.

Working from here as in Chapter 6:

While 55 hits extend from 54.5 to 55.5 on the continuous scale of the base line, 55 hits or more extend from 54.5 upward. So one has: Deviation from the mean = 54.5 – 40 = 14.5, Normalised deviation = (Actual deviation) / (Standard deviation) = (14.5) / (5.657) = 2.56. Consulting Appendix 6.4, Table A6.4, a normalised deviation of Z = 2.56 corresponds to a shaded area P = 0.0052. Hence the probability is 0.0052 or 0.52%. As the probability is less than 1%, this would be a highly significant result, indicating that extrasensory perception taking place is very likely.

In testing for extrasensory perception, it is possible to replace coins, dice or cards by any one of a wide variety of targets, which may be pictures, or objects, with a number of specific features. The question then is how many of these features can the percipient correctly identify, correct and incorrect identifications constituting hits and misses respectively. It is always necessary that the test leads to numbers of hits and misses out of a given number of decisions, enabling probability calculations to be made.

When testing for clairvoyance, the experiment needs to be "doubly blind", so that neither the percipient nor the experimenter knows the target, that is the result of the tossing of a coin, casting a die, or shuffling and cutting a pack of cards, until after the percipient's decision is made and recorded. This is necessary so as to exclude information acquisition by telepathy, so that the results may be taken to have come about by clairvoyance only. Conversely, in telepathy tests it is always possible that the percipient acquires information via clairvoyance, and not through telepathy from the agent's mind. Thus one must always consider that telepathy test results may have come about through clairvoyance. But, if a given percipient, in a long series of test runs, performs persistently better in telepathy tests, as compared with clairvoyance tests, then the difference may be attributed to telepathy with some degree of confidence. In the cases of clairvoyance and precognition tests, there is no agent, only an experimenter and percipient, in which case the percipient could be referred to as the subject of the tests.

Many tests along the above lines were conducted from the 1930s onward, in particular by Joseph and Louisa Rhine, a married couple research team, but also by many others, which produced much in way of statistically significant results supporting extrasensory perception.

While tests for extrasensory perception by coin tossing, die casting, or card shuffling and cutting, if properly controlled, cannot be scientifically faulted, more elaborate electronically based methods may be readily devised. These rely on electronic random event generators, which produce randomly selected targets for identification by percipients.

When a radio receiver is switched on, but is not tuned to a transmitting station, one hears a hissing noise issuing from the loudspeaker. This noise is caused by an alternating voltage at the speaker terminals that varies between positive and negative values in a random manner. Such a random noise voltage is generated in all electronic circuits. An electronic noise voltage generator is specifically designed to produce an alternating noise voltage randomly varying between positive and negative values. The time elapsing between crossovers from positive to negative values, and then back to positive values, or vice versa, may be arranged

Chapter 8 – Extrasensory Perception

through appropriate design to vary randomly, typically within the range from 0.1 of a millisecond to 10 milliseconds. In terms of current scientific knowledge, it is not possible to predict if such a noise voltage will be positive, or negative, at any particular instant in the future.

With reference to Figure 8.2, the author's own work involved an electronic noise voltage generator, combined with an electronic clock, and a logic circuit. The clock produced short audible "beeps" at regular intervals, typically 7 seconds apart, and examined the noise voltage at the onset of each beep. If the noise voltage was found to be positive, the clock caused a green light to come on for a fixed period of time, not exceeding the length of the interval between beeps, and if the noise voltage was found to be negative, a red light was turned on for the same fixed period. Because positive and negative noise voltages were equally likely, the number of times the green and red lights came on over a large enough number of intervals was expected to be nearly equal, even though the light activated at each particular beep was randomly selected, and so was expected to be unpredictable according to orthodox scientific theory.

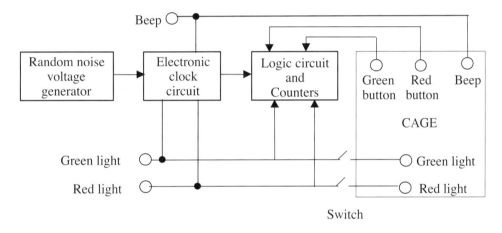

Figure 8.2

The random generator, the clock, the logic circuit, and any other associated equipment, together with the experimenter conducting the test, were all situated in a room serving as a laboratory. The percipient, or subject, to be tested for the ability to receive information through extrasensory perception, was situated in another room, inside a double walled metal cage with foam insulation between its walls, to provide both sound insulation and electrical shielding. In fact, the same cage was used as the one described in Chapter 4, in connection with testing for the human aura. The subject inside the cage would hear the short beeps produced by the clock, delivered via a loud speaker, and would thereby know when a new interval had begun, and that one of the lights was turned on when the beep was heard. The interval between consecutive beeps would be set in accordance with the wish of the subject. Experience had shown that most subjects preferred around 7 second intervals. The cage could be dimly lit, or totally dark, again in accordance with the wishes of the subject.

If the test was for telepathy, one of the two lights was arranged to come on for the duration of the beep only, typically no longer than 1 second, or about 10% of the interval between successive beeps. An agent would then attempt to mentally transmit to the percipient either the colour of the light coinciding with each beep, or one of two previously agreed symbols assigned to each of the two lights. The percipient would be requested to record decisions as to which colour, or symbol, was received from the mind of the agent, by pressing the appropriate push button out of two buttons provided, and marked green and red respectively. The duration of the randomly chosen light was made a small fraction of the interval between beeps, in the hope that this would encourage the percipient to obtain the information from the mind of the agent telepathically, and not from the state of the lights clairvoyantly.

In the case of a clairvoyance test, the light randomly selected at the beginning of each interval would be arranged to stay on for the whole interval, in the hope that this would aid clairvoyant perception. The subject would be asked to decide as to which light was on currently by pressing the appropriate push button. The lights were hidden, and could not be observed by anyone at all, at least from the beginning of each interval until after the subject had recorded a decision by pressing the appropriate push button. This was necessary in order to exclude telepathic perception.

When testing for precognition, the lights would once more come on only for the duration of the beeps, and the experimenter could be, but would not need to be, aware of the lights. The subject would be asked to decide as to which light would come on at the next beep, again by pressing the appropriate push button, but in this case before the next beep and associated light eventuated. Restricting the light to be on for the duration of the beeps only, was aimed at minimising distraction of the subject by the prevailing state of the light, and thereby help to direct attention to the light which was about to come on next.

While in the cases of telepathy and clairvoyance tests, the lights or other targets must of course be hidden from the subject, in the case of precognition tests, the subject may be allowed to see the lights, since they would see any particular light after they have already recorded their prediction as to what the colour of that light would be. Thus, for precognition tests, two sets of lights were provided, a green and a red light in the laboratory, and also a green and a red light in the cage where the subject could see them. The two green lights and the two red lights would, of course, be switched on and off in synchronism, and the lights in the cage would be of low intensity. Furthermore, the lights in the cage could either be allowed to operate, or be switched off permanently, as decided in consultation with the subject. Lights available to a subject could encourage conscious guessing, and so prevent the precognitive process from functioning. In the actual testing of subjects, often both ways were tried, but in most cases no substantial effect on the results was observed.

Whether a test is for telepathy, clairvoyance, or precognition, any push button operation can lead to either a hit or a miss. There are four possible outcomes following each push button operation as listed in Table 8.2.

Table 8.2

	Button Pressed	Telepathy: Light on at previous beep	Clairvoyance: Light on currently	Precognition: Light on at next beep	Outcome
1	Green	Green	Green	Green	Hit
2	Green	Red	Red	Red	Miss
3	Red	Red	Red	Red	Hit
4	Red	Green	Green	Green	Miss

Chapter 8 – Extrasensory Perception

Referring to Figure 8.2 once more, each push button operation delivered a voltage pulse to a logic circuit. As a subject may execute more than one push button operation between two consecutive beep signals, the circuit was designed to accept only the first push button signal during any one interval between two consecutive beeps, and ignore all subsequent ones. In the telepathy and clairvoyance modes, the circuit compared the push button signal with the light that was on during the previous beep, which it stored for the duration of all the interval, and recorded either a hit or a miss according to Table 8.2. In the precognition mode, the circuit stored the push button signal until after the onset of the next beep, and then compared the stored signal with the light that came on during the next beep, and recorded either a hit or a miss in accordance with Table 8.2.

The logic circuit had six output terminals, assigned to produce voltage pulses whenever the green or the red light came on, and also whenever a push button operation led to a hit or a miss. Each of these output terminals had a counter connected to it, and the count displayed on each counter was advanced by 1 count for each voltage pulse delivered to it. At the beginning of a test run all counters would, of course, be reset to zero. The six counters at any stage during a test run would then display the counts listed in Table 8.3.

Table 8.3

Counter No. 1:	The number of times the green light has come on
Counter No. 2:	The number of times the red light has come on
Counter No. 3:	The number of telepathy or clairvoyance hits obtained
Counter No. 4:	The number of telepathy or clairvoyance misses incurred
Counter No. 5:	The number of precognition hits obtained
Counter No. 6:	The number of precognition misses incurred

It was found that most subjects were happy with test runs involving 400 intervals, as demarked by 400 beeps, with around 7 seconds between consecutive beeps, so that a test run could be accommodated within one hour. Thus subjects were normally given 400 opportunities to respond, and typically responded 300 times, that is, made 300 decisions, each of which could be a hit or a miss.

It is to be noted that the test procedure was totally automatic, so that the experimenter needed only to reset all counters to zero, inform the subject via the intercom that the decision making by button pushing could start, and read the final counts off the counters when the test run had ended. Alternatively, if so desired, the counts could be recorded from time to time as the test run proceeded, so as to keep track of the subject's progress. In the case of telepathy tests, an agent needed to be present to observe the light coming on at the onset of each beep, and attempt to transmit mentally to the percipient either the colour of the light, or a previously agreed symbol associated with that colour.

It would not be unduly difficult to design an electronic circuit with five lights, having the same colour, but only one of which would be randomly selected to come on at the beginning of each interval, as indicated by a beep to the percipient. The lights, of course, could be observable by the percipient only in the case of precognition tests, but not in the case of telepathy and clairvoyance tests. The percipient would be provided with five push buttons for recording decisions. Furthermore, each light and each push button could be associated with one of the five ESP card symbols by prior agreement between all concerned, one possible scheme being depicted in Table 8.4.

Chapter 8 — Extrasensory Perception

Table 8.4

Square:	Light No. 1, Push Button No. 1
Circle:	Light No. 2, Push Button No. 2
Cross:	Light No. 3, Push Button No. 3
Star:	Light No. 4, Push Button No. 4
Wave:	Light No. 5, Push Button No. 5

If testing for telepathy, following each beep an agent would attempt to transmit mentally the ESP card symbol that was randomly selected by the oncoming light, and the percipient would push one of the five buttons, so as to indicate which symbol is being perceived, in accordance with the above scheme. Thus, for example, square transmitted, button No.1 pressed, would constitute a hit, while circle transmitted, button No.3 pressed, would incur a miss. A logic circuit and associated counters would then record the number of times each of the five lights came on, and the number of hits and misses resulting during a test run.

As a further example, if one is willing to work with four symbols instead of five symbols, two random noise voltage generators described in the foregoing may be operated in parallel, in conjunction with one clock, each random generator coming up with either a green or a red light for each beep. One may then adopt a scheme such as shown in Table 8.5.

Table 8.5

Light No. 1	Light No. 2	Symbol
Green	Green	Square
Green	Red	Circle
Red	Green	Cross
Red	Red	Star

The percipient would need to be supplied with four push buttons, one for each of the four symbols in Table 8.5.

Using this arrangement, continual automatic recording of the number of times each symbol came up, and the number of hits and misses obtained during a test run, could be arranged relatively easily. Deducing the probability of the outcome of the above five or four symbol test runs having come about by chance, would follow the method described earlier in this chapter in connection with the direct use of ESP cards.

The use of these five or four symbol schemes would minimise the role which clairvoyance may play in telepathy tests because actual physical cards would not be part of the test procedure, the symbols would only exist in the agent's mind. But, some may argue that it is still possible to obtain the information clairvoyantly, either from the electronic circuitry or from the agent's mind.

The five or four card schemes may also be adapted to clairvoyance and precognition tests by projecting the randomly selected symbol onto a screen, or causing it to light up, in the laboratory at the beginning of each interval as indicated by a beep. The process, including the projection or lighting up of the randomly selected symbols, may be fully automatic, and so obviate the need for any human agency during a test run.

Chapter 8 – Extrasensory Perception

During the 1980s and 1990s many extrasensory perception tests were run by the author and his associates, involving around 50 subjects, most of whom claimed to possess the ability to acquire information through extrasensory perception.

In the case of a new subject, normally three test runs were aimed at, with approximately a week elapsing between the test runs. If at least one of the three test runs was statistically significant, then it was proposed to the subject to continue up to ten test runs, or possibly beyond. On the other hand, if none of first three test runs were significant, then it was suggested to the subject, that while she or he may have psychic abilities, the available tests were not suitable to detect such abilities, and should perhaps be terminated. The tests would then continue only at the subject's insistence. However, most subjects would terminate the test series themselves right after the first test run, if they could not be assured that the result of the first test run was statistically significant. Some subjects were unwilling to go beyond the first test run, even if that run produced significant results.

Sceptics continually endeavour to refute the existence of paranormal phenomena, and the test results supporting such phenomena, by arguing that subjects have somehow acquired the information leading to the results by normal means. For this reason, precognition tests are particularly valuable, as it cannot be argued that knowledge of future events, which are entirely the outcome of random processes, could be acquired by normal means.

In what follows, the best two precognition test series results are presented in considerable detail. These were obtained with the cooperation of two subjects, namely: A.D. in 1983, and D.M. in 1993. The presentation of these two test series will then be followed by a less detailed description of other extrasensory perception tests conducted by the author.

The test series undertaken by D.M. in 1993 will be presented first, because this series was conducted exactly as described earlier in this chapter involving two lights, green and red, and two associated push buttons.

The electronic random generator and clock circuitry was adjusted to produce short sound beeps at 7 second intervals, which was the preferred interval by D.M. The duration of the beeps was arranged to be 1 second, and for the duration of any one beep either the green or the red light was turned on, as a result of random selection by the circuitry.

The task of D.M., inside the shielded cage, was to predict which of the two lights would come on at the next beep, by pressing one of the two push buttons marked green and red respectively. If the push button pressed matched the light at the next beep, the logic circuit recorded a hit by advancing the counter that counted hits by 1 count. If the button pressed did not match the light at the next beep, the logic circuit recorded a miss by advancing the counter that counted misses by 1 count. As mentioned earlier, in the case of more than one button operation between two consecutive beeps, the circuitry accepted only the first button operation. Counters were also assigned to count the number of times the green and the red lights came on. Following the resetting of all counters to zero, the test run would start at a point in time when the subject felt ready.

The results of this test series are detailed in Tables 8.7, 8.8, 8.9, and 8.10. The series was made up of 15 test runs. The number of intervals demarked by consecutive beeps was intended to be 400 per test run. However, departures from this figure were made at the request of the subject, as communicated to the experimenter via an intercom. Normally the counter readings were recorded after the completion of each batch of 20 intervals, so as to keep track of the subject's progress during the test run. Out of the 15 test runs the first one, run on 22/4/1993, yielded the best results, and its details are given in Table 8.7, where the horizontal lines give the results in 20 interval steps. The meanings of the symbols at the heads of the various columns in Table 8.7 are given in Table 8.6.

Table 8.6

A	=	Number of times the green light had come on
B	=	Number of times the red light had come on
C	=	Number of intervals each beginning with a beep ($C = A + B$)
X	=	Number of hits obtained
Y	=	Number of misses incurred
N	=	Number of decisions or attempts made ($N = X + Y$)
M	=	Mean ($M = N / 2$, as per Table 6.7, Chapter 6)
S	=	Standard deviation ($S = \sqrt{N/4}$, as per Table 6.7, Chapter 6)
Z	=	Normalised deviation [($X - 0.5 - M$) / S, as per Chapter 6]
P	=	Probability of the number of hits or more occurring by chance (from Table A6.4, Appendix 6.4)

While column C gives the number of opportunities the subject had for decision making, column N gives the number of attempts made by the subject. The figures in columns M, S, Z and P are calculated from the number of hits and misses in columns X and Y in accordance with Chapter 6, in particular Table 6.7, and Appendix 6.4, Table A6.4.

Columns A and B do not enter the calculations regarding the subject's performance, they serve only as a check on randomness, which requires that the green and the red lights should come on approximately the same number of times over a large enough number of intervals. As a check, at any stage of a test run, one may take the number of times the green or the red light came on, A or B whichever is larger, and calculate the probability for that number or higher occurring by chance in the total number of light operations ($A + B$). The probability figure so calculated would be expected to lie well above the significance probability level of 0.05, and thus indicate a chance result, and so randomness. For example in Table 8.7 let it be supposed that after 240 intervals, where $A = 124$, $B = 116$ and $C = 240$, the randomness is suspect. The probability of 124 green lights or more in 240 intervals occurring by chance is deduced as follows: $N = 240$, $M = N / 2 = 240 / 2 = 120$, $S = \sqrt{N/4} = \sqrt{240/4} \approx 7.75$, $Z = (X - 0.5 - M) / S = (124 - 0.5 - 120) / (7.75) \approx 0.45$. For this value of Z, Table A6.4, Appendix 6.4, yields $P \approx 0.33$, which is sufficiently larger than 0.05 to be considered a chance result, thereby confirming randomness.

The overall result of the test run after 420 intervals was 225 hits, and 173, misses out of 398 decisions, and the probability for this being a chance result is 0.0052 or 0.52%, as given at the bottom of column P in Table 8.7. Recalling that tests yielding a probability figure in the range of 0.05 to 0.01 are regarded statistically significant, while test results with a probability figure less than 0.01 are considered highly significant, it is seen that the test run in Table 8.7, with a probability figure of 0.0052, has yielded a highly significant result, strongly suggesting precognitive ability.

In Table 8.8, the intervals are divided into four ranges namely: 1 to 100, 101 to 200, 201 to 300, and 301 to 420, as listed in the first column marked I denoting the word interval.

Chapter 8 – Extrasensory Perception

Table 8.7
Precognition Test Run
Subject: D.M., Date: 22/4/1993

A Green	B Red	C A+B	X Hit	Y Miss	N X+Y	M N/2	S $\sqrt{N/4}$	Z $\dfrac{X-0.5-M}{S}$	P
9	11	20	11	8	19	9.5	2.18	0.46	0.32
18	22	40	23	15	38	19.0	3.08	1.14	0.13
28	32	60	36	22	58	29.0	3.81	1.71	0.044
39	41	80	43	34	77	38.5	4.39	0.91	0.18
49	51	100	55	42	97	48.5	4.92	1.22	0.11
61	59	120	69	48	117	58.5	5.41	1.85	0.032
72	68	140	81	56	137	68.5	5.85	2.05	0.020
81	79	160	94	63	157	78.5	6.26	2.40	0.0082
92	88	180	103	74	177	88.5	6.65	2.11	0.017
101	99	200	114	82	196	98.0	7.00	2.21	0.014
113	107	220	129	87	216	108.0	7.35	2.79	0.0026
124	116	240	140	95	235	117.5	7.66	2.87	0.0021
133	127	260	150	104	254	127.0	7.97	2.82	0.0024
144	136	280	159	113	272	136.0	8.25	2.73	0.0027
153	147	300	167	124	291	145.5	8.53	2.46	0.0069
162	158	320	175	134	309	154.5	8.79	2.28	0.011
173	167	340	184	144	328	164.0	9.06	2.15	0.016
184	176	360	195	152	347	173.5	9.31	2.26	0.012
193	187	380	206	160	366	183.0	9.57	2.35	0.0094
203	197	400	216	167	383	191.5	9.79	2.45	0.0071
212	208	420	225	173	398	199.0	9.97	2.56	0.0052

Table 8.8
Precognition Test Run
Subject: D.M., Date: 22/4/1993

I Intervals	A Green	B Red	C A+B	X Hit	Y Miss	N X+Y	M N/2	S $\sqrt{N/4}$	Z $\dfrac{X-0.5-M}{S}$	P
1-100	49	51	100	55	42	97	48.5	4.92	1.22	0.11
101-200	52	48	100	59	40	99	49.5	4.97	1.81	0.035
201-300	51	49	100	53	42	95	47.5	4.87	1.03	0.15
301-420	59	61	120	58	49	107	53.5	5.17	0.77	0.22

Table 8.9
Precognition Test Series
Subject: D.M., 1993 – Individual Test Runs

D Date	A Green	B Red	C A+B	X Hit	Y Miss	N X+Y	M N/2	S $\sqrt{N/4}$	Z $\frac{X-0.5-M}{S}$	P
22/4	212	208	420	225	173	398	199.0	9.97	2.56	0.0052
4/5	227	223	450	234	199	433	216.5	10.4	1.63	0.052
6/5	245	255	500	185	174	359	179.5	9.47	0.53	0.30
11/5	206	194	400	182	153	335	167.5	9.15	1.53	0.063
20/5	198	202	400	173	155	328	164.0	9.06	0.94	0.17
25/5	200	200	400	176	148	324	162.0	9.0	1.50	0.067
27/5	205	195	400	152	184	336	168.0	9.17	1.69	0.046*
1/6	196	204	400	159	149	308	154.0	8.77	0.51	0.31
3/6	228	232	460	215	186	401	200.5	10.0	1.40	0.081
8/6	201	199	400	177	160	337	168.5	9.18	0.87	0.19
10/6	214	211	425	204	170	374	187.0	9.67	1.71	0.044
15/6	218	214	432	211	180	391	195.5	9.89	1.52	0.064
17/6	197	203	400	169	173	342	171.0	9.25	0.16	0.44*
29/6	180	180	360	166	160	326	163.0	9.03	0.28	0.39
6/7	202	198	400	184	143	327	163.5	9.04	2.21	0.014

* Negative Results

Table 8.10
Precognition Test Series
Subject: D.M., 1993 – Running Totals

D Date	A Green	B Red	C A+B	X Hit	Y Miss	N X+Y	M N/2	S $\sqrt{N/4}$	Z $\frac{X-0.5-M}{S}$	P
22/4	212	208	420	225	173	398	199.0	9.97	2.56	0.0052
4/5	438	432	870	459	372	831	415.5	14.4	2.99	0.0014
6/5	686	684	1370	644	546	1190	595.0	17.2	2.82	0.0024
11/5	892	878	1770	826	699	1525	762.5	19.5	3.23	0.0006
20/5	1090	1080	2170	999	854	1853	926.5	21.5	3.35	0.0004
25/5	1290	1280	2570	1175	1002	2177	1088.5	23.3	3.69	0.0001
27/5	1495	1475	2970	1327	1186	2513	1256.5	25.1	2.79	0.0026
1/6	1691	1679	3370	1486	1335	2821	1410.5	26.6	2.82	0.0024
3/6	1919	1911	3830	1701	1521	3222	1611.0	28.4	3.15	0.0008
8/6	2120	2110	4230	1878	1681	3559	1779.5	29.8	3.29	0.0005
10/6	2334	2321	4655	2082	1851	3933	1966.5	31.4	3.66	0.0001
15/6	2552	2535	5087	2293	2031	4324	2162.0	32.9	3.97	0.00003
17/6	2749	2738	5487	2462	2204	4666	2333.0	34.2	3.76	0.0001
29/6	2929	2918	5847	2628	2364	4992	2496.0	35.3	3.73	0.0001
6/7	3131	3116	6247	2812	2507	5319	2659.5	36.5	4.16	0.00002

Inspection of Table 8.8 indicates that out of the four interval ranges, only the second, extending from 101 to 200, yielded significant results. This shows that, while the overall test run led to highly significant results, the subject's precognitive ability over the test run was far from being uniform, but rather it underwent considerable variation.

Table 8.9 lists the end results of the 15 test runs undertaken by D.M., on the dates in the first column labelled D. It will be seen from Table 8.9 that only the 1st test run (22/4) was highly significant with a probability figure of 0.0052. Further 3 test runs (27/5, 10/6, 6/7) were significant with probability figures in the range 0.05 to 0.01, however, one of these (27/5) was negative, the 0.046 figure in the P column being the probability of 184 misses or more, in 336 decisions. Another 5 test runs (4/5, 11/5, 25/5, 3/6, 15/6) were nearly significant with probability figures lying in the range 0.1 to 0.05, while the remaining 6 test runs (6/5, 20/5, 1/6, 8/6, 17/6, 29/6) with probabilities ranging between 0.5 to 0.1 should be regarded as chance results, including (17/6) which was negative also.

Table 8.10, gives the running totals of the test runs listed in Table 8.9, which means that any line in Table 8.10 gives the overall results of all test runs up to, and including, the date appearing in the date column. It is seen that, the probabilities for the running totals get steadily smaller, in spite of some reversals, and finish up with a probability smaller than 0.00002 for the overall result of the 15 test runs. This is less than 1 in 50,000. At this probability figure, the precognitive ability of subject D.M. could hardly be questioned.

The large variation of the probability figures over the 15 test runs is particularly notable. This, together with the variation seen in Table 8.8, indicates that the paranormal ability of the subject was far from being uniform, but that it underwent large variations from near chance results to highly significant results, and that it could only be detected reliably over a long series of test runs. In particular, the significant negative result (27/5) constituted a major retrograde step. If this test run did not take place, the overall probability figure would be around 1 in 1,000,000 that is, one in a million. However, the overall results cannot be selective, but must include all test runs, positive or negative, as is the case in Table 8.10.

Now let the test series be considered which was undertaken by subject A.D. during 1983. Here too, the electronic random generator and clock circuitry was adjusted to deliver sound beeps of 1 second duration, at 7 second intervals, to A.D. inside the shielded cage. An interval of 7 seconds was the preferred choice by A.D., like by most subjects.

However, in this case only a single light was provided, which for the duration of any given beep, was either turned on, or left off, as a result of random selection by the electronic circuitry. Further, A.D. was given one push button only, the task having been to predict whether the light would come on at the next beep, by pressing the button before the beep only if A.D. felt that the light would eventuate. If, following a push button operation the light did come on, the logic circuit recorded a hit by advancing the counter assigned to counting hits by 1 count, but if after a push button operation the light did not come on, the logic circuit recorded a miss by advancing the counter assigned to counting misses 1 count. As in all tests, in the case of more than one push button operation between two consecutive beeps, the circuitry accepted the first button operation only. Counters were also assigned to count the number of beeps associated with the light coming on, and the number of beeps with the light remaining off. Of course, prior to test runs, all counters were reset to zero. The test run would then commence at a point in time chosen by the subject.

Chapter 8 – Extrasensory Perception

Since only the "on" states of the light were predicted, but not the "off" states, the probabilities of a hit, or a miss, following a push button operation were not necessarily equal to 0.5 or 50% each, but rather at any stage of a test run, the probability of a hit would equal the fraction of the beeps with the light on, and the probability of a miss would equal the fraction of the beeps with the light off. Thus:

$$\text{Probability of a hit} = \frac{(\text{number of times the light has come on})}{(\text{number of intervals})}$$

$$\text{Probability of a miss} = \frac{(\text{number of times the light has stayed off})}{(\text{number of intervals})}$$

So, this is a situation covered by Table 6.9 in Chapter 6, which applies to the cases where following a single attempt the probabilities of the two possible outcomes are not equal.

The results of the test series undertaken by A.D. are presented in Tables 8.12, 8.13, 8.14, and 8.15. There were 10 test runs in the series. Here too, normally 400 intervals per test run were aimed for, but test runs were extended, or terminated, if so requested by A.D. via the intercom. Also, counter readings were recorded at the end of each 20 intervals, so as to keep track of the subject's progress during the test run. Out of the 10 test runs, the one undertaken on 16/10/1983 was the most significant. Detailed results of this run appear in Table 8.12, where the horizontal lines give the results in 20 interval steps. The meanings of the symbols at the heads of the various columns in Table 8.12 are given in Table 8.11.

Table 8.11

A	=	Number of times the light had come on
B	=	Number of times the light had stayed off
C	=	Number of intervals each beginning with a beep ($C = A + B$)
X	=	Number of hits obtained
Y	=	Number of misses incurred
N	=	Number of decisions or attempts made ($N = X + Y$)
p	=	Probability of a hit (A / C)
q	=	Probability of a miss (B / C)
M	=	Mean [$M = (N) \times (p)$, as per Table 6.9, Chapter 6]
S	=	Standard deviation [$S = \sqrt{(N) \times (p) \times (q)}$, as per Table 6.9]
Z	=	Normalised deviation [$(X - 0.5 - M) / S$, as per Chapter 6]
P	=	Probability of the number of hits or more occurring by chance (from Table A6.4, Appendix 6.4)

While C is the number of occasions the subject had for making decisions, N is the number of decisions actually made. The figures in columns M, S, Z, and P were calculated in accordance with Chapter 6, Table 6.9, and Appendix 6.4, Table A6.4.

Here again, it is essential that the light-on and the light-off intervals are randomly selected, in which case the numbers A and B should be nearly equal throughout the test run.

Chapter 8 — Extrasensory Perception

To check this, one needs to take the number of "on" periods, or "off" periods, A or B, whichever is greater, and find the probability for that number or higher, occurring by chance in the corresponding number of intervals $(A + B)$. The randomness requirement is met if the probability figure so deduced is substantially above the significance level of 0.05. In Table 8.12 the bottom line with $A = 218$ and $B = 232$ seems to be the most suspect. Proceeding as before: $N = 450$, $M = N/2 = 225$, $S = \sqrt{N/4} = \sqrt{450/4} \approx 10.6$, $Z = (B - 0.5 - M) / S = (232 - 0.5 - 225) / (10.6) \approx 0.61$. For this value of Z, Appendix 6.4, Table A6.4 yields $P \approx 0.27$, which is sufficiently larger than 0.05 to indicate a chance result, and so randomness.

The bottom line in Table 8.12 gives the end result of the test run on 16/10/1983 as 163 hits out of 247 decisions. The probability of 163 hits or more, in 247 attempts occurring by chance, as given by the bottom figure in the P column, is less than 10^{-7}, or less than 1 in 10 million, which is a very strong indication of precognitive ability being responsible.

In Table 8.13, the 450 intervals are split into five ranges, namely: 1 to 100, 101 to 200, 201 to 300, 301 to 400, and 401 to 450, as listed in the first column denoted I, which stands for the word: interval. It is seen that the interval ranges 1 to 100 and 201 to 300 yielded no significant results, while the ranges 101 to 200, 301 to 400, and 401 to 450 led to highly significant results. This indicates that the precognitive ability of A.D., as was also found for D.M., was not uniform through the test run, but rather chance performance and highly significant performance alternated. Yet, in spite of such variations, the overall test run result at a probability of less than 1 in 10 million is exceptionally significant.

Table 8.14 lists the overall results of the 10 test runs undertaken by A.D. in 1983, the dates of the individual test runs being listed in the first column marked D.

When looking at A.D.'s results in Table 8.14, and recalling that test runs with probability figures between 0.05 and 0.01 are statistically significant, while those with probabilities smaller than 0.01 are highly significant, one finds that 3 test runs (28/3, 1/4, 16/10) were highly significant with probability figures less than 0.01, and 1 test run (30/10) was significant with a probability figure of 0.044. Another test run (15/3) with probability falling in the range 0.1 to 0.05 was close to significance, while the remaining 5 test runs (1/3, 8/3, 22/3, 9/10, 23/10) with probability figures in the range 0.5 to 0.1 should be regarded as having yielded chance results, including (9/10) which was in fact negative. As already stated, the test run (16/10), considered in detail above, yielded the best result at a probability figure smaller than 10^{-7}, that is, less than 1 in 10 million.

The running totals of the 10 test runs in Table 8.14 are given in Table 8.15, where every line gives the overall test results up to and including the date in that line. It is seen that significance was reached by the end of the 3rd test run (15/3). The running totals became highly significant by the end of the 5th test run (28/3), and remained highly significant thereafter. By the end of the 8th test run (16/10), the running total probability fell below 10^{-7}, and the overall result of the test series also yielded a probability figure below 10^{-7} = 0.0000001, that is, less than 1 in 10 million. The individual test run (16/10), which produced a probability figure smaller than 10^{-7} by itself, is more significant than the rest of the 9 test runs combined. If this test run were omitted from the series, the overall result of the remaining 9 test runs would still be highly significant at a probability of $\approx 1.3 \times 10^{-4}$.

Chapter 8 – Extrasensory Perception

Table 8.12
Precognition Test Run
Subject: A.D., Date: 16/10/1983

A On	B Off	C A+B	X Hit	Y Miss	N X+Y	p A/C	q B/C	M Np	S $\sqrt{Npq}$	Z $\dfrac{X-0.5-M}{S}$	P
11	9	20	8	3	11	0.550	0.450	6.05	1.65	0.88	0.19
21	19	40	14	8	22	0.525	0.475	11.6	2.34	0.81	0.21
30	30	60	21	14	35	0.500	0.500	17.5	2.96	1.01	0.16
41	39	80	28	16	44	0.513	0.487	22.5	3.32	1.48	0.069
51	49	100	34	21	55	0.510	0.490	28.1	3.71	1.46	0.072
59	61	120	39	25	64	0.492	0.508	31.5	4.00	1.75	0.040
68	72	140	48	28	76	0.486	0.514	36.9	4.36	2.43	0.0075
79	81	160	58	32	90	0.494	0.506	44.5	4.74	2.74	0.0031
88	92	180	65	38	103	0.489	0.511	50.4	5.07	2.78	0.0027
99	101	200	72	41	113	0.495	0.505	55.9	5.31	2.94	0.0016
108	112	220	78	44	122	0.491	0.509	59.9	5.52	3.19	0.0007
117	123	240	83	49	132	0.488	0.512	64.4	5.74	3.15	0.0008
128	132	260	88	55	143	0.492	0.508	70.4	5.98	2.86	0.0021
137	143	280	97	59	156	0.489	0.511	76.3	6.24	3.24	0.0006
147	153	300	103	65	168	0.490	0.510	82.3	6.48	3.12	0.0009
156	164	320	109	71	180	0.488	0.512	87.8	6.71	3.08	0.0010
165	175	340	116	74	190	0.485	0.515	92.2	6.89	3.38	0.0003
176	184	360	124	76	200	0.489	0.511	97.8	7.07	3.64	0.0002
185	195	380	136	78	214	0.487	0.513	104.2	7.31	4.28	$< 10^{-4}$
194	206	400	143	82	225	0.485	0.515	109.1	7.50	4.45	$< 10^{-5}$
203	217	420	151	84	235	0.483	0.517	113.5	7.66	4.83	$< 10^{-6}$
218	232	450	163	84	247	0.484	0.516	119.5	7.85	5.48	$< 10^{-7}$

Table 8.13
Precognition Test Run
Subject: A.D., Date: 16/10/1983

I Interval	A On	B Off	C A+B	X Hit	Y Miss	N X+Y	p A/C	q B/C	M Np	S $\sqrt{Npq}$	Z $\dfrac{X-0.5-M}{S}$	P
1-100	51	49	100	34	21	55	0.510	0.490	28.1	3.71	1.46	0.072
101-200	48	52	100	39	19	58	0.480	0.520	27.8	3.80	2.82	0.0024
201-300	48	52	100	30	25	55	0.480	0.520	26.4	3.71	0.84	0.20
301-400	47	53	100	40	17	57	0.470	0.530	26.8	3.77	3.37	0.0003
401-450	24	26	50	20	2	22	0.480	0.520	10.6	2.34	3.80	0.0001

Chapter 8 — Extrasensory Perception

Table 8.14
Precognition Test Series
Subject: A.D., 1983
Individual Test Runs

D Date	A On	B Off	C A+B	X Hit	Y Miss	N X+Y	p A/C	q B/C	M Np	S $\sqrt{Npq}$	Z $\dfrac{X-0.5-M}{S}$	P
1/3	190	178	368	112	88	200	0.516	0.484	103.2	7.07	1.17	0.12
8/3	204	196	400	144	123	267	0.510	0.490	136.2	8.17	0.89	0.19
15/3	166	155	321	103	77	180	0.517	0.483	93.1	6.70	1.40	0.081
22/3	165	154	319	95	85	180	0.517	0.483	93.1	6.70	0.21	0.42
28/3	181	187	368	117	83	200	0.492	0.508	98.4	7.07	2.56	0.0052
1/4	212	197	409	135	75	210	0.518	0.482	108.8	7.24	3.55	0.0002
9/10	189	181	370	112	110	222	0.511	0.489	113.4	7.45	0.12	0.45*
16/10	218	232	450	163	84	247	0.484	0.516	119.5	7.85	5.48	$< 10^{-7}$
23/10	139	134	273	97	103	200	0.509	0.491	98.2	7.07	0.61	0.27
30/10	228	222	450	129	99	228	0.507	0.493	115.6	7.55	1.71	0.044

* Negative Result: Probability of 110 misses in 222 decisions.

Table 8.15
Precognition Test Series
Subject: A.D., 1983
Running Totals

D Date	A On	B Off	C A+B	X Hit	Y Miss	N X+Y	p A/C	q B/C	M Np	S $\sqrt{Npq}$	Z $\dfrac{X-0.5-M}{S}$	P
1/3	190	178	368	112	88	200	0.516	0.484	103.2	7.07	1.17	0.12
8/3	394	374	768	256	211	467	0.513	0.487	239.6	10.8	1.47	0.071
15/3	560	529	1089	359	288	647	0.514	0.486	332.6	12.7	2.04	0.021
22/3	725	683	1408	454	373	827	0.515	0.485	425.9	14.4	1.92	0.028
28/3	906	870	1776	571	456	1027	0.510	0.490	523.8	16.0	2.92	0.0018
1/4	1118	1067	2185	706	531	1237	0.512	0.488	633.3	17.6	4.10	0.00002
9/10	1307	1248	2555	818	641	1459	0.512	0.488	747.0	19.1	3.69	0.0001
16/10	1525	1480	3005	981	725	1706	0.507	0.493	864.9	20.6	5.61	$< 10^{-7}$
23/10	1664	1614	3278	1078	828	1906	0.508	0.492	968.2	21.8	5.01	$< 10^{-6}$
30/10	1892	1836	3728	1207	927	2134	0.508	0.492	1084.1	23.1	5.30	$< 10^{-7}$

Tables 8.13 and 8.14 show once more that paranormal abilities may undergo very large variations within a test run, or from one test run to another, as shown by the probability figures in Table 8.13 ranging from 0.2 to 0.0001, and in Table 8.14 from 0.45 down to below 10^{-7}. The conclusion is that paranormal abilities, even in the best of psychics, do not operate at all times, and can be detected only over an extended period involving a relatively large number of test runs. The overall results achieved by A.D. leave little room for doubting A.D.'s precognitive abilities.

In 1995, two precognition test series were conducted with subject R.D. These two series showed that rearranging the experimental procedure, in light of discussion between the experimenter and the subject, can lead to results which otherwise would have been missed.

The first test series was conducted exactly the same way as the test series with subject D.M. described above. It involved two lights, a green and a red, one of which was turned on as a result of random selection, for 1 second, at the beginning of each 7 second interval. The task of R.D. was to predict which light would come on next, by pressing the appropriate push button before the light eventuated, out of two buttons marked green and red.

The test series was terminated after 5 test runs because only 1 of the test runs yielded significant results, and even that was negative. The individual test run results, and also the overall test series result, are summarised in Table 8.16 below.

Table 8.16

Date	25/7	7/8	14/8	22/8	29/8	Overall
Number of decisions	406	394	385	331	268	1784
Number of "hits"	205	202	175	163	131	876
Number of "misses"	201	192	210	168	137	908
Probability (fraction)	0.44	0.33	0.042*	0.41*	0.38*	0.23*
Probability (percentage)	44	33	4.2*	41*	38*	23*

Negative results are marked by asterisks in Table 8.16. It will be noticed that the first 2 test runs (25/7 and 7/8) yielded positive results, more than half of the decisions being hits, while the remaining 3 test runs (14/8, 22/8 and 29/8) yielded negative results, less than half of the decisions being hits. The overall result was negative and not significant.

While discussing the possible causes of the foregoing non-significant results with R.D., he expressed the view that he felt certain about possessing psychic abilities, and that perhaps the reason for the non-significant results lay with the experimental procedure. In particular, being presented with an opportunity for decision making at regular intervals put pressure on R.D. to respond, even though it was understood that he did not have to respond during each and every interval.

It was then decided to modify the experimental setup in Figure 8.2 from continuous operation, to one which could be described as "self-actuated" operation. In the modified arrangement, the random generator and electronic clock circuits were operated the same way as before. The clock circuit was arranged to examine the random generator noise voltage at regular intervals, typically every 5 seconds. If the clock circuit found that the random generator noise voltage was positive at the beginning of an interval, it delivered a constant positive voltage to the logic circuit for the rest of that interval, which would be referred to as an "on" or "high" state. If, on the other hand, the clock circuit found that the random generator noise voltage was negative at the beginning of an interval, it delivered zero voltage to the logic circuit for the rest of that interval, which would be described as an "off" or "low" state.

Since at any instant, and so at the beginning of any interval, the random generator noise voltage being positive or negative was the result of a random process, the voltage "on" and the voltage "off" intervals, delivered to the logic circuit, were randomly interspersed. Also, since at any instant, positive or negative random generator noise voltages were equally likely, the numbers of "on" and "off" intervals, over an extended period of time, were expected to be very nearly equal, even though for each particular interval the "on" or the "off" states were randomly selected.

The subject was given one push button, which he could press at any instant of his choosing. Each push button operation actuated a timing circuit, such that a definite period after the button operation, say 10 seconds after, the timing circuit delivered a voltage pulse to the logic circuit, typically of 1 second duration. If at the instant of the onset of this delayed pulse, the logic circuit was receiving an "on" state voltage from the clock circuit, the logic circuit recorded a "hit", by advancing the counter assigned to counting hits by 1 count. If, on the other hand, at the instant of the onset of the delayed pulse, the logic circuit was receiving an "off" state voltage from the clock circuit, the logic circuit recorded a "miss", by advancing the counter assigned to counting misses by 1 count.

The timing circuit was so designed, that during the period elapsing between a push button operation, and the subsequent delivery of a delayed pulse to the logic circuit, the timing circuit ignored any other push button operation.

In order for the circuit to function as a precognition test circuit, it was essential that the timing circuit delay period, following a push button operation, exceeded the duration of the "on" and "off" state intervals. This ensured that at least one random change of state could take place between the instants of the push button operation and the delivery of the delayed pulse, so that the subject's prediction did apply to a future state, which came into being after the push button was pressed. Selecting 5 seconds for the duration of the "on" and "off" intervals, and 10 seconds for the pulse delay following a push button operation, satisfied this requirement, and it was found convenient by the subject as well.

As a matter of convenience, short sound beeps were also provided to coincide with the delayed pulses, to mark the instants when "hits" or "misses" were being recorded, and a light was also arranged to come on for the duration of the beep when a "hit" was being recorded. The beeps were audible to both the experimenter and the subject, while the light could be made available either to the experimenter only, or to both the experimenter and the subject at the subject's option.

In summary, the subject was essentially predicting that if he pushed the button at a particular instant, then 10 seconds after that instant an "on" state would prevail, and that the light would come on. A beep 10 seconds after the push button operation would tell the subject that his prediction was being evaluated, and a light, if provided, would inform the subject whether the prediction was a hit.

Chapter 8 – Extrasensory Perception

The test runs utilised four counters. Two counters were assigned to counting the numbers of "hits" and "misses". Another two counters were used for counting the numbers of "on" and "off" intervals. Each test run was then evaluated the same way as was done in Table 8.14 for subject A.D. In particular the probability of a "hit" or a "miss" was calculated from the number of "on" and "off" intervals as was done in Table 8.14.

A series of 6 test runs was conducted with subject R.D. as outlined above. Test runs were terminated when R.D. reported, via the intercom, of being tired or drowsy, and requested that the test run be discontinued. The results of the 6 test runs, and the overall result, are summarised in Table 8.17.

Table 8.17

Date	5/9	12/9	10/10	17/10	24/10	31/10	Overall
Number of intervals	250	250	200	200	600	600	2100
Number of "on" intervals	122	126	97	103	290	294	1032
Number of "off" intervals	128	124	103	97	310	306	1068
Probability of a "hit"	0.488	0.504	0.485	0.515	0.483	0.49	0.491
Probability of a "miss"	0.512	0.496	0.515	0.485	0.517	0.51	0.509
Number of decisions	94	91	48	79	167	140	619
Number of "hits"	51	47	20	46	90	80	334
Number of "misses"	43	44	28	33	77	60	285
Probability (fraction)	0.17	0.45	0.20*	0.14	0.087	0.033	0.0087
Probability (percentage)	17	45	20*	14	8.7	3.3	0.87

When consulting Table 8.17, it appears that the first 4 test runs (5/9, 12/9, 10/10, and 17/10) yielded chance, or near chance, results. In fact, as indicated by asterisks, test run (10/10) yielded a negative result. However, the last 2 test runs (24/10 and 31/10) led to much better results, in particular the last test run (31/10) being significant at a probability of 0.033 or 3.3%, showed a considerable improvement. The overall combined result of the 6 test runs is highly significant at a probability of 0.0087 or 0.87%.

It appears from Table 8.17, as if the subject needed the first four test runs to accustom to the new experimental procedure, before he could achieve results suggestive of precognitive abilities in the last two test runs. The overall highly significant result at a probability of 0.0087 or 0.87%, represents a great improvement over the results in Table 8.16. This suggests that it may well be worthwhile to try different experimental procedures in consultation with the test subjects.

As stated earlier, precognition tests were done in preference to clairvoyance and telepathy tests, because with precognition tests the suspicion that the subject acquired the information inadvertently, by normal means, could not arise.

However, even though a test was arranged to be a precognition test, the circuit in Figure 8.1 worked simultaneously in both the precognition and clairvoyance modes, with six counters, which were counting the "green light" or "on" intervals, the "red light" or "off" intervals, and also the "precognitive hits", the "precognitive misses", the "clairvoyant hits", and the "clairvoyant misses".

It was considered that even though a subject was asked to undergo a precognition test, and predict future states of the lights, yet she or he may have been responding in the clairvoyant

Chapter 8 – Extrasensory Perception

mode to the present state of the lights. Of course, for a valid clairvoyance test, the lights could not be available to the subject in the cage in the clairvoyant mode.

If the test was to be for precognition only, then lights could be made available to the subject, in which case the clairvoyance mode hits substantially exceeding the clairvoyance mode misses indicated that the subject did not function in the precognitive mode, but rather responded to the previously displayed state of the lights. This suggested that precognition tests with such a subject needed to be conducted with no lights available to the subject.

In testing for precognition, the question arose with each subject, if the subject performed better with the lights displayed or not, and then the decision would be made on that basis. In the cases, where the tests were conducted with no lights in the cage, so that both the precognition and the clairvoyance test results were available, it was found that, in general, subjects did not perform better in the clairvoyance mode than in the precognition mode.

Telepathy tests cannot be conducted as readily as precognition and clairvoyance tests, since testing for telepathy requires two subjects, who need to be compatible in the sense that one should be able to act as a sender or agent, while the other would have to be able to function as a receiver or percipient. Such a combination of subjects seems to be more difficult to find than single subjects for precognition or clairvoyance tests. Consequently, relatively few telepathy tests were run by the author, and most of those were found to yield chance results.

Perhaps, one telepathy test run merits mention. The test was conducted on 27/7/1993, and employed the four symbol ESP card method described in connection with Table 8.5, so that the card selection had been done by electronic random generators. The subjects were: agent D.M., and percipient M.K. The number of attempts made were 96, and the number of hits achieved was 32. Working as before: The probability of a hit is $1/4 = 0.25$, while the probability of a miss is $3/4 = 0.75$. One then has:

Mean $= 96 / 4 = 24$, Standard deviation $= \sqrt{96 \times 0.25 \times 0.75} \approx 4.24$,
Hence, the normalised deviation $= (32 - 0.5 - 24) / 4.24 \approx 1.77$.
From Table A6.4, Appendix 6.4, the probability for a normalised deviation of 1.77 is 0.038 or 3.8%. This is a moderately significant result.

The test run was also conducted with roles reversed: agent M.K., and percipient D.M., which yielded chance results only. The above significant result begged for expansion into a test series. Regrettably, M.K. could not make herself available for further participation.

The author had, at the time of writing, records of extrasensory perception test results, in addition to the ones described above, from a further 48 subjects. Out of these, 22 had undertaken multiple test runs, and 26 undertook a single test run only. Further, out of the 48 subjects, 34 were tested for precognition only, while the remaining 14 have undergone either combined precognition-clairvoyance tests, or telepathy tests.

Only 4 of these 48 subjects achieved significant results with probability below 0.05 or 5%. The results of another 6 subjects could be regarded as near to significance, with probabilities ranging up to 0.15 or 15%. The results of these 10 subjects are listed in Table 8.18, all of which were tests for precognition. In the subject's column, the letter X indicates that the subject gave a first name only. It is also stated whether the results were positive or negative. In extrasensory perception tests, only chance results are no results. Negative results may be thought of as being due to misunderstandings about the targets.

Table 8.18

Subject	Number of runs	Probability	Positive or Negative	Level of significance
J.K.	2	0.0072 (0.72%)	Positive	High
L.X.	1	0.0082 (0.82%)	Negative	High
D.S.	1	0.016 (1.6%)	Negative	Mid
I.G.	8	0.021 (2.1%)	Positive	Mid
P.B.	5	0.09 (9%)	Positive	Near
J.X.	8	0.11 (11%)	Positive	Near
K.X.	1	0.11 (11%)	Negative	Near
M.X.	1	0.13 (13%)	Positive	Near
N.B.	5	0.15 (15%)	Negative	Near
N.X.	2	0.15 (15%)	Negative	Near

The remaining 34 subjects produced results with the associated probabilities ranging from 0.16 or 16% upward. All these would have to be regarded as coming about by chance. The results of subject D.S., at a probability of 0.016 or 1.6%, were obtained following hypnotic suggestion. A similar run prior to the hypnotic suggestion resulted in a probability of 0.33 or 33%, negative. This is one of a few cases where hypnotic suggestion seemed to enhance extrasensory perception. If in Table 8.18, circumstances permitted conducting more test runs, then very probably the number of significant results would have been higher.

It has been stated earlier, that the randomness of the noise voltage generator would be expected to result in the green and red lights coming on nearly the same number of times, in a large enough number of intervals. While this is one criterion of randomness, it is not the only criterion. Recognisable patterns, in the way consecutive lights turn on, would also mean a lack of randomness. As a possible but unlikely example, the green and red lights could turn on in a way so that three consecutive greens were followed by three consecutive reds, with this pattern repeated indefinitely. While the green and red lights would come on an equal number of times, they would not be randomly interspersed. Anyone recognising the existence of such patterns could easily achieve highly significant results.

In order to test for the existence of such patterns, subjects were invited regularly to observe the lights visually, and try to obtain significant results in the precognition mode, by attempting to recognise patterns in the light sequences. No subject could ever achieve significant results this way, which testifies to the absence of this type of bias. Furthermore, if subjects could achieve significant results this way, then one would expect such results to be repeated over a number of test runs. No such repetition was ever observed.

When considering the results achieved by A.D., D.M., R.D., and others, the possibility of pattern recognition playing any role in achieving those results may be safely dismissed, not only because no invited subject could ever beat the random generator by attempting pattern recognition, but also since the large variations in significance within and between various test runs undertaken by individual subjects, including the above subjects, argues against it.

The precognition tests described in the foregoing, and the results obtained, illustrate some of the salient properties of extrasensory perception, that also apply to paranormal phenomena

Chapter 8 — Extrasensory Perception

in general. One such property is that such phenomena occur spontaneously, and are not normally repeatable at will. They can be observed and investigated when occurring by their own volition. This usually means a long series of experiments, of which only some may produce statistically significant results. The non-repeatability of the phenomena is one of the major reasons given for denying the existence of such phenomena. However, it is unreasonable to assert that events that are not repeatable at will do not exist at all, even though when occurring spontaneously, yield statistically highly significant test results, with all test results included.

Actually, extrasensory perception is often experienced by people in real life situations as "once in a while" events. When such experiences are described by individual observers, they are labelled "anecdotal" by orthodox science, and are dismissed either as coincidences or hallucinations. Single occurrences do not lend themselves to statistical evaluations.

Even though extrasensory perception experiences seem to be widespread in the community, they are difficult to demonstrate in the laboratory, under controlled conditions, involving artificial substitutes for real life situations. This may be at least partly due to the fact that extrasensory perception is essentially an unconscious activity, which cannot be produced reliably by conscious will, just as forgotten facts cannot always be called into consciousness by deliberate choice. Such facts may emerge into consciousness after a short or long delay, at times when not even expected. Successful laboratory tests for extrasensory perception appear to need cooperation from the unconscious mind, and such cooperation may, or may not, be forthcoming when conducting artificial laboratory tests.

Since extrasensory perception is essentially an unconscious activity, and relies on linkages between the unconscious minds of two or more individuals, telepathy in particular, the messages put out by the unconscious minds of the investigators, may have a profound effect on the performance of the test subjects. Negative thoughts entertained by the investigators, or anyone else connected with the tests, may totally inhibit extrasensory perception from taking place. This is one reason why sceptics usually get no results. Successful researchers must have a genuinely neutral mental attitude to the investigations, and a friendly attitude toward the subjects.

Results cannot be expected from testing a few subjects at random. Investigators must be prepared to test many subjects, possibly running into hundreds, and be prepared to carry out one or more long series of test runs with promising subjects, over extensive periods of time.

Information received via the senses usually involves waves. Visual information is delivered to the retina of the eyes by light waves that are electromagnetic waves travelling in electric and magnetic fields. Auditory information reaches the eardrums through sound waves travelling in air. By analogy, information received through extrasensory perception is also often thought of as waves propagating through a medium, sometimes called the "psi" field, a medium somewhat analogous to the ether through which electromagnetic waves were thought to travel during the late 1800s. However, such a field, or the waves in it, if they exist at all, are non-physical in the sense that they cannot be detected by currently existing physical instruments. In any case, the modus operandi would need to have extraordinary properties, to explain information acquisition about future events in the physical universe. More will be said about these matters in a later chapter.

Chapter 9
Psychokinesis

The term "psychokinesis" derives from the two words "psyche" and "kinesis", which are both of Greek origin, the first meaning the mind or soul, while the second refers to the study of movement or motion. Psychokinesis, in a narrow sense, denotes the ability of the mind to directly influence the motion of physical objects, but more generally it encompasses the ability of the mind to exert direct influence on physical processes of any kind. Orthodox science in its current state cannot explain such abilities of the mind, and consequently denies the existence of such abilities. It considers psychokinetic manifestations to be delusions, hallucinations, or outright fraud.

Psychokinesis is one of the three main branches of paranormal phenomena, the others being extrasensory perception and survival related phenomena. Psychokinetic phenomena include setting stationary physical objects into motion, influencing the motion of objects already moving, floatation of objects, deformation of the shape of physical objects, production of light and sound without reliance on physical causation, spontaneous ignition, interference with the functioning of mechanical, electrical, or electronic apparatus, unaccountable images on photographs, and more rarely dematerialisation and re-materialisation of physical objects and even of living organisms, all in contradiction to the currently known laws of physics.

The question automatically arises whether the reality of psychokinesis can be scientifically verified. The answer is that statistical verification can be obtained, and definitely exists. In Chapter 8, the statistical verification of extrasensory perception was described in some detail, via tossing coins and dice, cutting shuffled packs of cards, and electronic means.

Coin tossing methods can also be applied to obtain statistical verification for psychokinesis. Let a coin be tossed 200 times, preferably by a push button operated mechanical catapult, causing it to spin in the air before landing on a horizontal surface. If the coin has uniform density and near perfect even edges, so that the coin, and also the rest of the procedure, is free of "bias", then the most likely outcome, in 200 tosses, is 100 heads and 100 tails.

In practice, it is likely that a departure from this result will be observed, in fact, calculations, such as described in Chapter 6, show that the probability for obtaining a number of heads lying in the range of 95 to 105, and including both these figures, is 56%. If one keeps obtaining a number of heads within this range in successive batches of 200 tosses, it can be reasonably assumed that the coin, and the tossing procedure, is free of bias.

Now let a subject with suspected psychokinetic abilities be present, but so situated that any physical interference with the coin tossing procedure is totally excluded, and ask the subject to try influencing the motion of the coin mentally, while spinning in the air, so as to produce heads in preference to tails. Of course, it is most unlikely that anyone could produce 200 heads in 200 tosses, but it could happen that a subject would come up with 120 heads in 200 tosses. Probability calculations dealt with in Chapters 6 and 8, show that the probability of getting 120 heads or more, in 200 tosses by chance, is 0.0029 or 0.29%. As also stated in Chapters 6 and 8, if in any orthodox scientific test, the probability for a result having come about by chance is 0.05, namely 5%, or less, that result is considered "significant", chance is called into question, and a causative factor is suspected. Also, if the probability for a result having occurred by chance is 0.01, namely 1%, or less, the result is labelled "highly significant", chance is rejected, and some causative factor is assumed.

Chapter 9 – Psychokinesis

The result of the above coin tossing test, with a probability factor of 0.0029 or 0.29%, is thus highly significant, the suspected causative factor being the subject's psychokinetic ability, which should be considered as statistically indicated.

In practice one might arrange 10 test runs, typically one week apart, each with 200 tosses or more. One might then find that the psychokinetic ability of the subject varies from test run to test run, but if the overall result is highly significant, the psychokinetic ability should be considered as verified, doing otherwise would be inconsistent, and even dishonest.

Tests for psychokinetic abilities may also be based on throwing dice. A die, or a number of dice, would be enclosed in a transparent rectangular box, which upon pressing a push button would be turned over by a mechanism a number of times, and then stop with its bottom side horizontal, and the die or dice resting on it. The box being transparent, the number of spots uppermost could easily be read. Of course, all physical interference with the box would have to be totally excluded, other than pushing the button to initiate each throw.

However, before a die may be used for a psychokinesis test, control runs would need to be performed, to verify the absence of bias in both the die and the throwing procedure. In the absence of bias, a single throw of a die may result in one of six equally probable outcomes, corresponding to any one of the six sides of the die facing upward, that is, any number of spots between 1 and 6 coming topmost. In a single throw, the probability of a particular number of spots landing topmost is 1 in 6, or 1/6 = 0.1667, or 16.67%. Thus if a die is thrown 180 times, then in the absence of bias, one would expect each number of spots to come uppermost in 1/6 of the 180 throws, that is in 30 throws.

In practice, some departures from this expected result are likely, but a statistical calculation will indicate if the observed departures are attributable to chance, and consequently the die and the throwing technique may be regarded unbiased. For instance, let it be supposed that the outcome of a control run of 180 throws of a single die is as shown in Table 9.1.

Table 9.1

Number of spots	1	2	3	4	5	6
Number of times uppermost:	28	31	27	32	29	33

The largest departures from the chance expectation of each number of spots coming topmost 30 times, are 33 six spots and 27 three spots. One could proceed as in Chapter 6, using the normal probability curve, and find the probability of obtaining 33 six spots or more, in 180 throws, as is done in Table 9.2, leading to a normalised deviation $Z = 0.5$.

Consulting Appendix 6.4, Table A6.4, gives the corresponding probability as $0.30845 \approx 0.31$. Since this figure is well above the significance level of 0.05, the result is attributable to chance. It is obvious that similar calculations for the other number of spots in Table 9.1 would also yield chance results, and so the absence of bias may be considered as confirmed.

The calculation of probability from the normal probability curve, as described in Chapter 6, is only one of a number of possible ways of evaluating probability. In cases where a single action may result in more than two different outcomes, and where individual probabilities of these outcomes may be equal or unequal, another method of statistical calculation, known as the "chi-square" method, may be more useful. The throwing of dice is a specific example within the category of such cases, where a single throw of a die may result in 1 of 6

148   Chapter 9 – Psychokinesis

equally probable outcomes, namely any one of the six possible numbers of spots coming uppermost, the probabilities of these 6 outcomes in this case being equal to 1/6 each.

Table 9.2

The number of six spots	$X = 33$ or more
The number of throws	$N = 180$
The probability of a six spot in one throw	$p = 1/6$
The probability of any other than a six spot in one throw	$q = 5/6$
The mean	$M = (N) \times (p) = (180) \times (1/6) = 30$
The standard deviation	$S = \sqrt{(N) \times (p) \times (q)} = \sqrt{(180) \times (1/6) \times (5/6)} = \sqrt{25} = 5$
The normalised deviation	$Z = (X - 0.5 - M) / S = (33 - 0.5 - 30) / 5 = 2.5 / 5 = 0.5$

In what follows, the numbers in Table 9.1 are used to illustrate how one may employ the chi-square method, to show that the results in Table 9.1 have come about by chance. The procedure is laid out in Table 9.3, which applies to 180 throws, and where the meaning of the various terms is as follows: "Number of spots" stands for the faces of the die and the number of spots on them. "Actual frequency" means the number of times each face came uppermost in the given number of throws, that is, in 180 throws in this case. "Expected frequency" is the number of times each face would be expected to come uppermost from probability considerations in the given number of throws, namely 180 / 6 = 30 in this case. "Deviation" is the difference between the actual and expected frequencies, and may be positive or negative. "Deviation squared" is the deviation multiplied by itself, and is always positive. "Ratio" is the deviation squared divided by the expected frequency.

Table 9.3
(Number of throws = 180)

Number of Spots	1	2	3	4	5	6
Actual frequency	28	31	27	32	29	33
Expected frequency	30	30	30	30	30	30
Deviation = Actual – Expected	–2	+1	–3	+2	–1	+3
Deviation squared	4	1	9	4	1	9
Ratio = (Deviation squared) / (Expected frequency)	4/30	1/30	9/30	4/30	1/30	9/30

The chi-square is the sum of the ratios, and is denoted X^2. Rounded to three figures it is:

$$X^2 = \frac{4}{30} + \frac{1}{30} + \frac{9}{30} + \frac{4}{30} + \frac{1}{30} + \frac{9}{30} = \frac{28}{30} = 0.933$$

Clearly, if all numbers of spots came up 30 times as expected, then all the deviations would be zero, and one would also have the chi-square $X^2 = 0$, which would indicate an ideal chance result. Before one can ascertain whether the figures in Table 9.1 are chance results, one needs to determine the so called "degrees of freedom", which means the number of values in a set of values that can be freely chosen before the rest is determined. In the case of Table 9.1, one may choose any five numbers in the bottom line, which then determines

Chapter 9 – Psychokinesis

the sixth number, because the six numbers must add up to 180. Thus taking the first five numbers, and adding them yields 28+31+27+32+29 = 147, and so the sixth number must be 180 – 147 = 33. This then means that there are five degrees of freedom. Often the degrees of freedom equal the number of possible outcomes of a single action less one, in this case 6 – 1 = 5. The term degrees of freedom is often denoted by the short: *DF*.

One may now consult Appendix 9.1, Table A9.1. Having 5 degrees of freedom, one must enter the line starting with the number 5 in the *DF* column. It is seen that $X^2 = 0.933$ is less than the first entry in that line, namely 1.15, which in turn corresponds to a probability of 0.95 in the top line. So, the probability corresponding to $X^2 = 0.933$ must be larger than 0.95. Thus, the probability of the outcome in Table 9.1 having occurred by chance is larger than 0.95, which is far above the significance level of 0.05. Consequently, the result in Table 9.1 is a chance result, and the absence of bias may be safely assumed.

In general, the larger the chi-square figure is for a given number of degrees of freedom, the smaller is the probability of the result having come about by chance. It will also be noted, that the two methods of probability calculations dealt with in the foregoing, lead to different results. This is so because different questions are being asked. The first figure, namely 0.30854 or 0.31 approximately, is the probability of 33 six spots or more, in 180 throws, which indicates a chance outcome. The second figure, namely 0.95 approximately, is the probability of the sum total of all deviations from the expected frequencies, and is also indicative of a chance outcome. When considering the large difference between the two figures, it must be borne in mind that the upper limit to the first figure is 0.5 corresponding to 30 six spots or more, out of 180 throws, whereas the upper limit to the second figure is 1.0 corresponding to all faces of the die coming up exactly 30 times in 180 throws, which would yield a chi-square figure equal to zero.

In the foregoing, the procedure for using the chi-square statistical method was illustrated. The underlying theory is not dealt with in these pages, interested readers may find that information in books dealing with probability and statistics.

Now let a subject be tested for psychokinetic abilities, by the die throwing technique, employing a single die. As described above, the die would be enclosed in a rectangular transparent box, which would be turned over by a mechanism a few times in response to the experimenter pushing a button, and then come to rest with the die resting on its horizontal bottom face. The subject, seated some distance from the box, or perhaps in a nearby room, would be invited to try to influence the fall of the die, aiming for six spots uppermost each time. Let it be supposed that the outcome of 180 throws is as given in Table 9.4.

Table 9.4

Number of Spots	1	2	3	4	5	6
Number of times Uppermost	35	23	20	27	39	43

Proceeding as before, the normal curve can be used to find the probability of obtaining 43 six spots or more, in 180 throws, as done in Table 9.5. The normalised deviation is found to be $Z = 2.5$, for which Appendix 6.4, Table A6.4, gives the probability as $P \approx 0.0062$.

Since this figure is less than 0.01 or 1%, the result is statistically highly significant, and would suggest psychokinetic ability being responsible.

Chapter 9 – Psychokinesis

Table 9.5

The number of six spots	$X = 43$ or more
The number of throws	$N = 180$
The probability of a six spot in one throw	$p = 1/6$
The probability of any other than a six spot in one throw	$q = 5/6$
The mean	$M = (N) \times (p) = (180) \times (1/6) = 30$
The standard deviation	$S = \sqrt{(N) \times (p) \times (q)} = \sqrt{(180) \times (1/6) \times (5/6)} = \sqrt{25} = 5$
The normalised deviation	$Z = (X - 0.5 - M) / S = (43 - 0.5 - 30) / 5 = 12.5 / 5 = 2.5$

Alternatively, one may rely on the chi-square statistical method, which leads to Table 9.6.

Table 9.6
(Number of throws = 180)

Number of spots	1	2	3	4	5	6
Actual frequency	35	23	20	27	39	43
Expected frequency	30	30	30	30	30	30
Deviation = Actual – Expected	+5	–7	–10	–3	+9	+13
Deviation squared	25	49	100	9	81	169
Ratio = (Deviation squared) / (Expected frequency)	25/30	49/30	100/30	9/30	81/30	169/30

Hence, the chi-square, rounded to three figures, is:

$$X^2 = \frac{25}{30} + \frac{49}{30} + \frac{100}{30} + \frac{9}{30} + \frac{81}{30} + \frac{169}{30} = \frac{433}{30} = 14.4$$

For the same reason as for Table 9.3, the number of degrees of freedom is 5. Consulting Appendix 9.1, Table A9.1, the line applicable to five degrees of freedom ($DF = 5$) shows that $X^2 = 14.4$ comes between 12.8 and 15.1.

Thus, the probability lies between 0.025 and 0.01. One may work out the probability corresponding to $X^2 = 14.4$ by proportion, leading to $P \approx 0.015$. However, it may be sufficient to state that the probability of the above result having come about by chance is smaller than 0.025 or 2.5%, which is a statistically significant result.

Once more it will be noted, that the two methods of probability calculations lead to different results, namely 0.0062 and 0.015 respectively. This is because, as explained earlier, different questions are being asked. The first figure is the probability of 43 six spots or more, in 180 throws. The second figure is the probability of the sum total of all the deviations from the expected frequencies. Thus, both results are statistically significant, and so the likelihood of psychokinesis being responsible is indicated.

Many tests aiming at verifying the reality of psychokinesis by means of coin tossing and die throwing have been carried out during the 20th century. In particular, Joseph and Louisa Rhine, who pioneered extrasensory perception tests by means of coins, dice and cards, also reported significant psychokinesis test results relying on coin and die throwing techniques in the 1930s, and their work has been replicated by many other investigators since.

Results were obtained by many other means, which is not surprising, since the variety of physical processes that may be subject to psychokinetic influence is nearly limitless. A few examples are: influencing balls rolling down an incline, bubbles rising in a liquid, rotation of sensitive wheels, and reliance on piezoelectric crystals which when physically deformed, or compressed, produce electrical voltage differences between points on their surfaces.

The author's own work in the late 1990s involved experimental setups built around a sensitive rotating wheel, called the "Egely Wheel", and also a piezoelectric crystal, both of which eventually yielded statistically significant results.

The Egely wheel is a very light, thin, metallic disk, having a diameter of 6.5 centimetres, with 72 cogs around its perimeter, and so pivoted that it can rotate in a horizontal plane around its centre. It is found in general, that it is much easier to psychokinetically influence the motion of an object which is already moving, than to set a stationary object into motion. Consequently, an experimental procedure was devised, whereby the wheel was set into motion by the experimenter using an impulse start mechanism, and then the task was to ascertain if, under the psychokinetic influence of a test subject, the wheel could be made to rotate longer and further before stopping, than it would otherwise do by itself.

This required an impulse start mechanism, and also facilities for measuring the total wheel movement before coming to rest after having been impulse started.

The overall experimental setup is depicted in Figure 9.1.

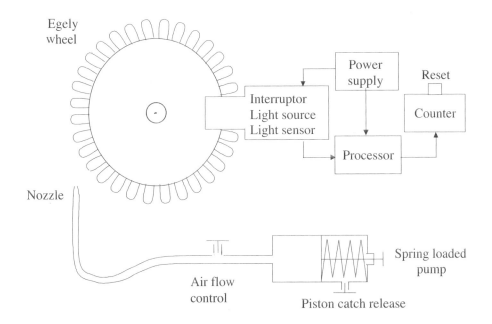

Figure 9.1

Figure 9.1 shows the top view of the wheel. An air pump served as the impulse start mechanism. The piston of the pump could be pushed to the right against the force exerted by a compressed spiral spring, to a position where the piston would be held by a catch mechanism. Upon releasing the catch by actuating the push button of the catch mechanism, the piston would be pushed to the left by the spring, completing its motion within a fraction of a second. The pump would thus deliver a puff of air, via a flexible hose and a nozzle, in a direction tangential to the edge of the wheel, but perpendicular to the cogs of the wheel. This would set the wheel in a rotary motion. The speed of the rotation of the wheel would be highest just after the application of the air-puff, subsequent to which the speed of the wheel would gradually diminish. The volume and the speed of the air delivered to the edge of the wheel, and so the applied impulse, could be controlled by means of an airflow control valve. This was set so that the wheel, after having been impulse started, would typically come to a stop in less than 50 seconds, after making close to one revolution. Furthermore, the shape of the nozzle, its position relative to the wheel, and the volume and speed of the air delivered, all had to be carefully adjusted so as to ensure a smooth start of the wheel, free of any wobble. This was found to be essential for achieving good results.

The cogs of the rotating wheel were arranged to pass between the jaws of an "interruptor", with its bottom and top jaws being located below and above the cogs of the wheel. A power supply activated a light source in the bottom jaw of the interruptor, which produced a light beam that was directed toward a light sensor mounted in the top jaw. Depending on the position of the wheel as it revolved, the light beam could either pass between two adjacent cogs and reach the light sensor, or alternatively, it could be blocked by an intervening cog from reaching the sensor. Whenever the light beam passing between two adjacent cogs could reach the sensor, a voltage generated by the sensor was delivered to an electronic processor, and whenever a cog between the light source and the sensor blocked light from reaching the sensor, the voltage delivered to the processor would be nearly zero.

Subsequent to the passage of each cog between the jaws of the interruptor, the light reaching the sensor caused the processor to produce a fixed magnitude, fixed duration output voltage pulse, typically 10 volts in magnitude and of 0.01 second duration. These pulses were counted by an electronic counter. The counter would need to be reset to zero, prior to each impulse start of the wheel.

Whenever the wheel came to a stop, or nearly so, it was possible for a cog to hover in a position where it only partly blocked the light from reaching the sensor. This could have resulted in sending many consecutive on and off voltage signals to the processor, each producing a pulse and a count, without the wheel actually moving by 1 cog. To prevent such false counts, the processor had to be so designed that once it had produced a pulse, and sent it to the counter, it could not produce another pulse until after the sensor voltage had fallen back to near zero, indicating that a cog has definitely passed between the light source and the light sensor.

When using the wheel in psychokinesis tests, it had to be free of any extraneous mechanical influences. As even the smallest air current could affect the wheel's motion, it was found necessary to enclose the wheel, together with the air delivery nozzle and the interruptor, into a transparent plastic box, with small holes just large enough for passing into the box the air delivery hose to the nozzle, and the electrical leads to the interruptor. Also, in order to exclude any other possible mechanical interference, the box with the wheel in it was placed

Chapter 9 – Psychokinesis

on a shelf bolted to the solid brick wall of the laboratory, the wall itself resting on concrete foundations. All other parts of the experimental setup, namely the pump, the processor, and the counter were placed on an adjacent bench, at which the experimenter would be seated.

A control run involved impulse starting the wheel at exactly 1 minute intervals, with the counter having been reset to zero just before each impulse start. The counter readings were then recorded at 10 second intervals after starting, that is at 10, 20, 30, 40, and 50 seconds after the start. The counter would again be reset to zero just before the next start, which would take place 60 seconds after the previous start.

An active run would be conducted exactly the same way as a control run, except that the subject to be tested for psychokinetic ability would be seated in the laboratory, at a distance of 1 to 4 metres from the wheel, in a position enabling the subject to see the wheel, but not physically interfere with it, as confirmed by continual observation by the experimenter.

An experimental test run would consist of 2 active runs and 2 control runs. Each active run, and each control run, involved 10 impulse starts of the wheel at 1 minute intervals, and 5 counter readings at 10 second intervals, after each impulse start. Each such run would thus take 10 minutes to complete, and yield 50 counter readings. Normally, a rest period of 5 minutes would be allowed between the 2 active runs. The control runs were conducted usually 1 hour before to the subject's arrival at the laboratory, and 1 hour after the subject had left. This had been done, because experience indicated that the subject's psychokinetic influence on the wheel could not be turned off at will, in fact, such influence tended to prevail while the subject was on the premises, even though she or he consciously may have wished to terminate that influence. It was also found that the subject's influence on the wheel can operate while she or he was either under way to the laboratory before the active runs, or on the way from the laboratory after the active runs. Placing the control runs about 1 hour before, and 1 hour after, the active runs minimised this problem.

It was also observed, that the mental state of the experimenter conducting the experiment occasionally had a noticeable influence on the wheel's motion. Disturbing or worrying thoughts entering the experimenter's mind tended to cause the counter readings to rise. So, the experimenter had to learn to suppress such thoughts, and replace them with thoughts of a neutral nature, such as contemplating aspects of the furniture in the laboratory.

It was found that, through appropriate impulse control, the wheel could almost always be arranged to stop moving close to but within 50 seconds after the impulse start. Thus, the counter reading at 50 seconds normally represented the total number of cogs the wheel had moved following an impulse start. A complete test run would yield 40 such "total readings", 20 from the 2 active runs, and another 20 from the 2 control runs.

It was also surmised, that the psychokinetic agency would tend to prolong the motion, rather than speed the wheel up, and so its effect was more likely to show up toward the end of the wheel's movement, rather than shortly after the start of the motion. It was therefore decided to take "incremental readings" as well, which were the number cogs moved either between the 20 and 50 second marks, or the 10 and 50 second marks. Thus, an overall test run yielded 80 readings in all, namely:

20 total active readings,	20 total control readings,
20 incremental active readings,	20 incremental control readings.

Chapter 9 – Psychokinesis

The question was then, if the 20 total active readings were significantly higher than the 20 total control readings, and also if the 20 incremental active readings were significantly higher than the 20 incremental control readings.

Thus, the task was to decide statistically, if one set of readings was significantly higher than another set of readings. In such cases, another statistical method, called the "student's t" method, is particularly useful. This involves calculating a quantity called the student's t parameter, that is denoted by the letter t. In general the larger is the calculated t value, the smaller is the probability of any difference between the two sets of readings having come about by chance, or putting it differently, the more likely it is that the two sets of readings differ owing to some underlying causative factor. Thus, in the rotating wheel tests for psychokinesis, one would expect the active readings to be significantly higher than the control readings, if the psychokinetic ability of the subject has successfully made the wheel move considerably further than it otherwise would.

The essential quantities involved in the student's t statistical calculations are:
1. The number of readings in each active run and each control run, (denoted N)
2. The mean of the readings in each active run and each control run, (denoted M)
3. The variance of the readings in each active run and each control run, (denoted S^2)

If two sets of readings were significantly different, one would expect the difference between their means to be large, and at the same time the variances of the sets to be small, so as to reduce any overlap between the sets. Also, the larger the number of readings is in the sets, the more certain one could feel that the difference between their means is not due to chance.

The necessary calculations are simpler if the number of readings in the two sets are equal, which has been deliberately arranged by making the number of active readings equal the number of control readings. In view of the foregoing, it is perhaps not surprising to find that the student's t parameter is given by:

$$t = (\text{mean of set 1} - \text{mean of set 2}) \times \sqrt{\frac{(\text{number of readings in one set}) - (1)}{(\text{variance of set 1}) + (\text{variance of set 2})}}$$

Here again, as in the case of the chi-square statistics, the probability corresponding to any given t value depends on the number of degrees of freedom, which in this case is given by:

Degrees of Freedom: $DF = (\text{total number of readings in the two sets}) - (2)$

Knowing the student's t value, and the degrees of freedom DF, one may find the corresponding probability from the student's t tables in Appendix 9.2, Table A9.2.

Now let an artificial example of two sets of readings be considered as shown in Table 9.7, where the means and the variances were deduced as described in Chapter 6, and illustrated by the example in Table 6.6, Chapter 6.

With reference to Table 9.7, the student's t parameter from the above expression, and the values in Table 9.7, rounded to three figures, is:

$$t = (5-4) \times \sqrt{\frac{(4-1)}{(5)+(5)}} = (1) \times \sqrt{\frac{3}{10}} = 0.548$$

Chapter 9 – Psychokinesis

Table 9.7

Quantities involved	Set 1	Set 2
Actual readings	2, 4, 6, 8	1, 3, 5, 7
Number of readings	4	4
Mean of readings	(2+4+6+8) / 4 = 5	(1+3+5+7) / 4 = 4
Deviations from mean	−3, −1, +1, +3	−3, −1, +1, +3
Squares of deviations	9, 1, 1, 9	9, 1, 1, 9
Variance of readings	(9+1+1+9) / 4 = 5	(9+1+1+9) / 4 = 5

The number of degrees of freedom is: $DF = (4 + 4) - (2) = 6$.

Consulting the student's t tables in Appendix 9.2, Table A9.2, one finds in the line for $DF = 6$, that $t = 0.27$ corresponds to a probability of 0.4, while $t = 0.72$ corresponds to a probability of 0.25. The required probability for $t = 0.548$ above, lies between these two values, and could be worked out by proportion. However, it is obvious by inspection, that the probability is larger than 0.25, and so it is well above the significance level of 0.05. Consequently, the two sets of readings are sufficiently similar to have come from two tests that were not influenced by different causative factors.

Now let a second example be considered as shown in Table 9.8.

Table 9.8

Quantities involved	Set 1	Set 2
Actual readings	5, 6, 7, 8	1, 2, 3, 4
Number of readings	4	4
Mean of readings	(5+6+7+8) / 4 = 6.5	(1+2+3+4) / 4 = 2.5
Deviations from mean	−1.5, −0.5, +0.5, +1.5	−1.5, −0.5, +0.5, +1.5
Squares of deviations	2.25, 0.25, 0.25, 2.25	2.25, 0.25, 0.25, 2.25
Variance of readings	(2.25+025+0.25+2.25) / 4 = 1.25	(2.25+0.25+0.25+2.25) / 4 = 1.25

The student's t from the above expression, and the values in Table 9.8, to four figures, is:

$$t = (6.5 - 2.5) \times \sqrt{\frac{(4-1)}{(1.25) + (1.25)}} = (4) \times \sqrt{\frac{3}{2.5}} = 4.382$$

Here also the degrees of freedom $DF = 6$. From Appendix 9.2, Table A9.2, with $DF = 6$ one finds that $t = 4.32$ corresponds to a probability of 0.0025, while $t = 5.21$ corresponds to a probability of 0.001. Since $t = 4.382$ is between above two t values, the probability corresponding to $t = 4.382$ lies between 0.0025 and 0.001. The figures suggest that it is only slightly below 0.0025. The probability is thus smaller than 0.01, below which results are normally regarded highly significant. Consequently, there is a highly significant difference between the two sets of readings, and so they are likely to have come from experiments, the results of which were brought about by different causative factors.

In the foregoing, the application of the student's t statistical method for finding if one set of values was higher than another set of values by a statistically significant amount was illustrated by means of two artificial examples. The underlying theory is not treated in these pages, interested readers are referred to books on probability and statistics.

In 1998, subject A.D. had undertaken a rotating wheel psychokinesis test series of 10 test runs. The tests were conducted as described in the foregoing, with the subject seated approximately 1 metre from the wheel, on a high stool, so that she could see the wheel by looking down at it obliquely. During the active runs A.D. was kept under observation, she sat quite motionless, and any physical interference with the wheel during all test runs, be it active or control runs, was totally excluded.

The test run undertaken on 26/10/98 was the most significant, and its results are given in Table 9.10. The first column lists the instants at which readings were taken, namely 10, 20, 30, 40, and 50 seconds after the wheel was impulse started. The second and subsequent columns of numbers, list the number of cogs the wheel had moved during the minute designated at the top of those columns, as read from the counter at the instants listed in the first column. The readings at 50 seconds are the total readings, while the bottom figures in the columns are the number of cogs moved between the 20 and 50 second marks, and equal the differences of the counter readings at 50 and 20 seconds. These differences are termed the incremental readings. The meaning of the various symbols appearing in Table 9.10 are listed in Table 9.9.

Table 9.9

$M \& S^2$	=	Mean and variance of 10 total readings
$\Delta M \& \Delta S^2$	=	Mean and variance of 10 incremental readings
$M_A \& S^2_A$	=	Mean and variance of 20 total active readings
$M_C \& S^2_C$	=	Mean and variance of 20 total control readings
$\Delta M_A \& \Delta S^2_A$	=	Mean and variance of 20 incremental active readings
$\Delta M_C \& \Delta S^2_C$	=	Mean and variance of 20 incremental control readings
$t \& P$	=	student's t and probability for total readings
$\Delta t \& \Delta P$	=	student's t and probability for incremental readings
$N_A \& N_C$	=	Number of total active and total control readings
$\Delta N_A \& \Delta N_C$	=	Number of incremental active and incremental control readings

With reference to Table 9.10, using the formula established in the foregoing for calculating the student's t parameter, one gets the rounded figures:

$$t = (73.55 - 60.00) \times \sqrt{\frac{20 - 1}{26.85 + 16.50}} = 8.97$$

$$\Delta t = (8.75 - 2.85) \times \sqrt{\frac{20 - 1}{1.59 + 0.43}} = 18.09$$

The corresponding degrees of freedom are: the total number of active readings plus the total number of control readings less two, that is, $DF = 20 + 20 - 2 = 38$. Since $DF = 38$ is not listed in Appendix 9.2, Table A9.2, one needs to rely on the nearest value, $DF = 40$. However, it is found that the probabilities corresponding to the above t, Δt, and DF values are so small, that they fall outside the range of Table A9.2, in Appendix 9.2.

Chapter 9 – Psychokinesis

When meeting student's t values falling outside the range of Table A9.2, in Appendix 9.2, one can estimate the corresponding probabilities P from the normal probability curve, that is, Table A6.4 in Appendix 6.4. This is feasible because for any given probability value, and large enough number of degrees of freedom, the student's t value, as given by Table A9.2, approaches the normalised deviation, or Z value, as given by Table A6.4. For example, Table A6.4 for $Z = 1.96$, gives $P = 0.025$, while Table A9.2 for infinite degrees of freedom, $DF = \infty$, and $t = 1.96$, also gives $P = 0.025$. The two figures for t and Z are not equal in general, and may differ considerably when the degrees of freedom are small, or the values of t are large. Furthermore, as was found earlier in Chapter 6, the normal curve yields only approximations to the probabilities obtainable from Pascal's triangle, or the binomial theorem. Nevertheless, taking $t \approx Z$ may yield a close enough estimate for the probability P, when the student's t value falls outside Table A9.2.

Subject to these approximations, the above calculated values of t and Δt yield from Table A6.4: $t \approx Z = 8.97 \approx 9$, $P \approx 10^{-19}$, and $\Delta t \approx Z = 18.09 \approx 18$, $\Delta P \approx 10^{-72}$.

In view of these very low probability figures, and the uncertainties in deducing them, probabilities in the rest of this chapter will be presented as follows. Probabilities ascertainable from the student's t table, Appendix 9.2, Table A9.2, will be given to the nearest single figure. Probabilities not ascertainable from the student's t table will be estimated from the normal probability curve, Table A6.4, Appendix 6.4, based on the assumption that $t \approx Z$, and given either to the nearest single figure, or the nearest order of magnitude. But for $t \approx Z = 6$ or higher, the probability is $P \approx 10^{-9}$, or 1 in 1000 million, or smaller, in which case the probability will be given as $P \approx 0$ (nearly zero).

Tables 9.11 and 9.12 summarise the results of 10 test runs undertaken by A.D. in 1998. The first column in the tables lists the dates of the test runs, and the meaning of the symbols at the heads of the remaining columns have been listed in Table 9.9. The symbol Σ in the bottom lines of the two tables, stands for the combined result of the 10 test runs. While the overall result of the 10 test runs could be worked out the same way as the results of the individual test runs, formulae exist which enable the overall result to be deduced from the individual test run results in a less laborious way. The formulae are given in Appendix 9.3.

As seen from Table 9.11, the total motion results of 2 test runs (17/8 and 31/8) were not significant, those of 2 further test runs (24/8 and 28/9) were significant at a probability $P = 0.03$, while the results of the remaining 6 test runs (7/9, 12/10, 19/10, 26/10, 9/11, and 16/11) were highly significant. The combined result of the 10 total motion test runs was also highly significant with $t = 9.63$, $DF = 398$, and $P \approx 0$.

As was anticipated, the incremental motion results as given in Table 9.12 were better. Only 1 test run (17/8) was not significant, while the result of another test run (24/8) was significant at a probability $\Delta P = 0.02$. The results of the remaining 8 test runs (31/8, 7/9, 28/9, 12/10, 19/10, 26/10, 9/11 and 16/11) were highly significant, as was the combined result of the 10 incremental motion test runs at $\Delta t = 16.36$, $DF = 398$, $\Delta P \approx 0$.

When the rotating wheel test setup was being developed, prior to the first test run with subject A.D., it was noted that the experimenter's mental state occasionally appeared to cause anomalous wheel movement. It was also noted that such anomalous behaviour could be minimised, or avoided, most of the time, by the experimenter trying to maintain a calm and peaceful mental disposition.

Table 9.10
Psychokinesis Test Run by Rotating Wheel, Subject: A.D., 26/10/98

Pre-Control Run, 1.00 p.m. to 1.10 p.m.

Sec \ Min	1	2	3	4	5	6	7	8	9	10	
10	43	43	44	43	39	51	46	45	47	42	$M = 59.60$
20	56	54	57	55	51	65	59	59	61	53	$S^2 = 19.44$
30	58	57	59	58	52	69	62	62	63	56	
40	58	57	59	58	52	69	62	62	63	56	$\Delta M = 2.60$
50	58	57	59	58	52	69	62	62	63	56	$\Delta S^2 = 0.64$
50-20	2	3	2	3	1	4	3	3	2	3	

Active Run, 2.10 p.m. to 2.20 p.m.

Sec \ Min	1	2	3	4	5	6	7	8	9	10	
10	51	42	48	51	42	50	49	57	47	50	$M = 73.70$
20	68	55	64	68	57	65	65	76	61	66	$S^2 = 39.61$
30	74	59	69	74	62	71	71	82	67	72	
40	77	61	71	76	65	73	73	85	69	74	$\Delta M = 9.20$
50	79	63	71	77	66	74	74	86	70	77	$\Delta S^2 = 1.36$
50-20	11	8	7	9	9	9	9	10	9	11	

Active Run, 2.25 p.m. to 2.35 p.m.

Sec \ Min	1	2	3	4	5	6	7	8	9	10	
10	47	47	47	48	49	48	48	52	51	54	$M = 73.40$
20	60	61	63	65	66	63	64	69	69	71	$S^2 = 14.04$
30	66	67	69	70	71	68	70	75	75	77	
40	68	69	70	71	73	70	72	78	78	79	$\Delta M = 8.30$
50	69	70	70	72	73	70	74	78	79	79	$\Delta S^2 = 1.41$
50-20	9	9	7	7	7	7	10	9	10	8	

Post-Control Run, 3.35 p.m. to 3.45 p.m.

Sec \ Min	1	2	3	4	5	6	7	8	9	10	
10	42	50	44	41	46	47	41	48	47	43	$M = 60.40$
20	54	64	56	53	58	60	52	61	59	56	$S^2 = 13.24$
30	57	67	59	56	62	63	55	64	62	59	
40	57	67	59	56	62	63	55	64	62	59	$\Delta M = 3.10$
50	57	67	59	56	62	63	55	64	62	59	$\Delta S^2 = 0.09$
50-20	3	3	3	3	4	3	3	3	3	3	

$N_A = 20$ $M_A = 73.55$ $S_A^2 = 26.85$ $\Delta N_A = 20$ $\Delta M_A = 8.75$ $\Delta S_A^2 = 1.59$

$N_C = 20$ $M_C = 60.00$ $S_C^2 = 16.50$ $\Delta N_C = 20$ $\Delta M_C = 2.85$ $\Delta S_C^2 = 0.43$

$t = 8.97$ $P \approx 0$ $\Delta t = 18.09$ $\Delta P \approx 0$

Chapter 9 – Psychokinesis

Table 9.11
Psychokinesis Test Runs by Rotating Wheel, 1998
Subject: A.D., 1 metre from wheel, Total motion

	ACTIVE			CONTROL			PROBABILITY	
Date	N_A	M_A	S_A^2	N_C	M_C	S_C^2	t	P
17/8	20	61.95	73.75	20	62.45	39.05	-0.21	> 0.1
24/8	20	63.40	35.94	20	60.20	18.86	1.88	0.03
31/8	20	60.95	26.25	20	58.80	39.76	1.15	> 0.1
7/9	20	68.55	48.85	20	61.65	29.13	3.41	0.0008
28/9	20	65.25	35.39	20	62.30	9.81	1.91	0.03
12/10	20	73.80	53.96	20	60.60	32.94	6.17	≈ 0
19/10	20	65.55	44.35	20	59.80	13.86	3.29	0.001
26/10	20	73.55	26.85	20	60.00	16.50	8.97	≈ 0
9/11	20	67.90	39.39	20	60.75	23.49	3.93	0.0002
16/11	20	71.30	20.01	20	62.60	17.84	6.16	≈ 0
Σ	200	67.22	59.53	200	60.92	25.61	9.63	≈ 0

Table 9.12
Psychokinesis Test Runs by Rotating Wheel, 1998
Subject: A.D., 1 metre from wheel, Incremental motion

	ACTIVE			CONTROL			PROBABILITY	
Date	ΔN_A	ΔM_A	ΔS_A^2	ΔN_C	ΔM_C	ΔS_C^2	Δt	ΔP
17/8	20	4.10	0.69	20	3.90	0.89	0.69	> 0.1
24/8	20	4.85	8.53	20	3.35	1.83	2.03	0.02
31/8	20	4.15	0.43	20	3.15	1.33	2.30	0.01
7/9	20	4.80	1.66	20	2.15	0.63	7.63	≈ 0
28/9	20	5.55	0.95	20	3.45	0.45	7.74	≈ 0
12/10	20	10.10	1.39	20	3.15	0.53	21.86	≈ 0
19/10	20	6.80	1.26	20	3.50	0.45	11.00	≈ 0
26/10	20	8.75	1.59	20	2.85	0.43	18.09	≈ 0
9/11	20	5.45	1.35	20	3.10	0.99	6.70	≈ 0
16/11	20	7.00	1.00	20	3.20	1.56	10.35	≈ 0
Σ	200	6.16	5.50	200	3.18	1.10	16.36	≈ 0

Table 9.13
Psychokinesis Control Runs by Rotating Wheel, 1998
No subject, Experimenter only, Total motion

Date	ACTIVE			CONTROL			PROBABILITY	
	N_A	M_A	S_A^2	N_C	M_C	S_C^2	t	P
18/8	20	61.95	18.05	20	62.05	44.25	-0.06	>0.1
25/8	20	60.05	5.65	20	61.00	17.10	-0.87	>0.1
1/9	20	62.30	23.11	20	60.25	16.09	1.25	0.1
8/9	20	59.50	12.85	20	61.50	17.95	-1.65	0.05
29/9	20	61.40	28.94	20	61.95	13.45	-0.37	>0.1
13/10	20	61.85	19.13	20	61.15	39.13	0.40	>0.1
20/10	20	60.05	18.25	20	60.30	63.91	-0.12	>0.1
27/10	20	61.60	16.94	20	60.35	17.33	0.93	>0.1
10/11	20	62.50	28.75	20	61.25	41.49	0.65	>0.1
17/11	20	62.65	30.03	20	62.30	18.21	0.22	>0.1
Σ	200	61.39	21.31	200	61.21	29.40	0.36	>0.1

Table 9.14
Psychokinesis Control Runs by Rotating Wheel, 1998
No Subject, Experimenter only, Incremental motion

Date	ACTIVE			CONTROL			PROBABILITY	
	ΔN_A	ΔM_A	ΔS_A^2	ΔN_C	ΔM_C	ΔS_C^2	Δt	ΔP
18/8	20	3.20	0.46	20	3.10	0.59	0.43	>0.1
25/8	20	3.65	0.53	20	3.95	0.55	-1.26	0.1
1/9	20	4.20	0.96	20	3.40	0.74	2.67	0.006
8/9	20	3.65	1.03	20	3.70	0.51	-0.18	>0.1
29/9	20	3.60	0.64	20	3.80	0.36	-0.87	>0.1
13/10	20	4.15	0.33	20	3.35	0.93	2.91	0.003
20/10	20	3.80	0.46	20	3.95	0.95	-0.55	>0.1
27/10	20	3.25	0.69	20	3.30	0.71	-0.18	>0.1
10/11	20	3.95	0.65	20	3.20	0.56	3.04	0.002
17/11	20	3.50	0.45	20	3.60	0.54	-0.22	>0.1
Σ	200	3.70	0.72	200	3.54	0.73	1.87	0.03

Chapter 9 – Psychokinesis

Nevertheless, when carrying out test runs with subjects, the possibility could not be ignored that the experimenter's own mental states could have contributed to the results obtained.

Because of this, it was decided to repeat each test run conducted with subject A.D., the next day, at the same time, and exactly the same way, as was done with A.D., but with A.D. absent and, not having been informed, consciously unaware of the repeat test run being done. The 10 "no-subject" control runs led to the results summarised in Tables 9.13 and 9.14. It will be noted that only 1 total motion test run (8/9) produced significant results, while the remaining 9 total motion test runs, and also the combined total of the 10 test runs, led to chance results. In comparison, 3 incremental motion test runs (1/9, 13/10, and 10/11) yielded highly significant results, the remaining 7 incremental motion test runs led to chance results, and the combined incremental result of the 10 test runs at $\Delta t = 1.87$, $DF = 398$, and probability $\Delta P = 0.03$ or 3% was only moderately significant.

This implies that the experimenter's mind, at times, may exhibit unconscious psychokinetic activity. However, there is a very great difference in the level of significance between the results obtained with the subject A.D. present, and with A.D. absent, as indicated by comparison of Tables 9.11 and 9.12 on the one hand, with Tables 9.13 and 9.14 on the other hand. This suggests that the experimenter's contribution to the results achieved by subject A.D. was very small, if any.

The results achieved by A.D. indicate that her psychokinetic abilities are hardly disputable. The student's t values, and associated probabilities, imply that psychokinesis having taken place is very close to certainty.

In 1999, subject D.M. had undertaken two rotating wheel psychokinesis test series, each consisting of 10 test runs. The first test series was conducted the same way as described in the foregoing, and implemented with subject A.D. in 1998. Subject D.M. was seated 1 metre from the wheel, and was able to view the wheel by looking obliquely down at it.

The second test series differed from the first in one important respect, the difference being that D.M. was seated at a distance of 4 metres from the wheel. During the first test run of the second series, subject D.M. could not see the wheel itself, but was able to monitor the wheel's motion by being able to observe the counter displaying the number of cogs moved by the wheel at any given point in time. Subject D.M. found this frustrating, and felt that seeing the wheel was essential for her. So, for the remaining 9 test runs in the second series, a mirror was fixed above the wheel at an angle of 45 degrees, so that D.M. seated 4 metres away could observe the wheel, and its motion, in the mirror. This arrangement was found to be acceptable to D.M.

Also, there was another difference between the tests undertaken by A.D. and D.M., as in the case of D.M. the incremental motion was taken from 10 to 50 seconds after each impulse start, and not from 20 to 50 seconds as was the case with A.D. This change was made so as to explore if it had a substantial effect on the incremental motion test results.

The most highly significant test run in the first series was the last run on 26/4/99. The results of this test run are given in Table 9.15. The meaning of the various symbols in Table 9.15 is as listed in Table 9.9, and the layouts of Table 9.15 and Table 9.10 are the same, so that columns and rows fulfil the same role in both.

With reference to Table 9.15, the formula for calculating the student's t parameter, when applied to the values in Table 9.15, yields the following rounded figures:

$$t = (70.95 - 61.70) \times \sqrt{\frac{20-1}{12.85+15.01}} = 7.64$$

$$\Delta t = (21.90 - 16.70) \times \sqrt{\frac{20-1}{2.09+1.81}} = 11.48$$

The relevant degrees of freedom equal the total number of active readings plus the total number of control readings less two, that is, $DF = 20 + 20 - 2 = 38$. As $DF = 38$ is not listed in Appendix 9.2, Table A9.2, one needs to rely on the nearest listed value, namely $DF = 40$. When consulting Table A9.2, here again one finds that for the above values of t, Δt, and DF, the corresponding probability figures fall outside the listed range of values in Table A9.2. In view of the previous discussion on this matter, the associated probabilities were estimated from the normal probability curve, Table A6.4, assuming that $t \approx Z$, which leads to: $t \approx Z = 7.64$, $P \approx 10^{-14} \approx 0$, and $\Delta t \approx Z = 11.48$, $\Delta P \approx 10^{-28} \approx 0$.

Tables 9.16, 9.17, 9.18, and 9.19 summarise the results achieved by D.M. in the two test series undertaken by her. The first column in each table lists the dates of the various test runs, while the meanings of the symbols at the heads of the remaining columns are as listed in Table 9.9.

Tables 9.16 and 9.17 give the total motion and incremental motion results respectively, of the 10 test runs, obtained by D.M. when seated 1 metre from the wheel. Inspection of these tables shows that except 3 total motion test runs (8/2, 15/2, and 22/2), all other total and incremental motion test runs yielded highly significant results. The combined result of the 10 test runs was also highly significant, for both the total motion and the incremental motion case, with $t = 8.58$, $DF = 398$, $P \approx 0$, and $\Delta t = 15.28$, $DF = 398$, $\Delta P \approx 0$.

Tables 9.18 and 9.19 give the total motion and incremental motion results of D.M., when seated 4 metres from the wheel. In this test series only 3 total motion test runs (24/5, 1/7, and 13/7) yielded highly significant results, 1 test run (10/8) was significant at a probability $P = 0.05$, and the remaining 6 test runs (19/4, 10/5, 31/5, 8/6, 6/7, and 20/7) yielded chance results. However, the combined total motion result of the 10 test runs was still highly significant at $t = 3.30$, $DF = 398$, $P = 0.0005$. The incremental results were considerably better, 5 test runs (24/5, 8/6, 1/7, 13/7, and 10/8) yielded highly significant results, 2 test runs (6/7 and 20/7) were significant, and only 3 test runs (19/4, 10/5, and 31/5) led to chance results. The combined incremental motion result of the 10 test runs was also highly significant with $\Delta t = 9.98$, $DF = 398$, $\Delta P \approx 0$.

It may be well worthwhile to compare all the foregoing rotating wheel psychokinesis test series results, as listed in Table 9.20.

It is noted that with A.D. and D.M. seated 1 metre from the wheel, both results are very good, with A.D. ahead of D.M. by a small margin. The results achieved by D.M. at a distance of 1 metre are considerably better than the results obtained by D.M. at a distance of 4 metres. This, however, may or may not be a distance related effect, as at times good results were obtained, with subjects separated from the wheel by several intervening rooms.

Chapter 9 – Psychokinesis

Table 9.15
Psychokinesis Test Run by Rotating Wheel, Subject: D.M., 26/4/99

Pre-Control Run, 8.00 p.m. to 8.10 p.m.

Sec \ Min	1	2	3	4	5	6	7	8	9	10	
10	48	42	44	46	45	46	42	46	42	42	$M = 61.3$
20	62	55	57	60	59	60	55	60	55	55	$S^2 = 6.81$
30	65	57	60	63	63	63	58	64	59	59	
40	65	58	60	64	63	63	58	64	59	59	$\Delta M = 17.0$
50	65	58	60	64	63	63	58	64	59	59	$\Delta S^2 = 0.60$
50-10	17	16	16	18	18	17	16	18	17	17	

Active Run, 9.10 p.m. to 9.20 p.m.

Sec \ Min	1	2	3	4	5	6	7	8	9	10	
10	46	47	54	48	51	46	51	52	45	50	$M = 70.6$
20	59	60	71	63	67	61	68	69	61	65	$S^2 = 18.64$
30	64	66	77	68	72	66	73	74	66	70	
40	64	67	78	69	73	67	74	76	67	71	$\Delta M = 21.6$
50	64	67	78	69	73	67	74	76	67	71	$\Delta S^2 = 3.04$
50-10	18	20	24	21	22	21	23	24	22	21	

Active Run, 9.25 p.m. to 9.35 p.m.

Sec \ Min	1	2	3	4	5	6	7	8	9	10	
10	47	52	47	51	49	48	50	48	48	51	$M = 71.3$
20	62	69	62	67	64	63	67	64	63	68	$S^2 = 6.81$
30	67	74	67	73	69	68	72	69	68	73	
40	68	76	68	74	71	69	73	70	69	74	$\Delta M = 22.2$
50	68	76	69	74	71	69	73	70	69	74	$\Delta S^2 = 0.96$
50-10	21	24	22	23	22	21	23	22	21	23	

Post-Control Run, 10.35 p.m. to 10.45 p.m.

Sec \ Min	1	2	3	4	5	6	7	8	9	10	
10	40	45	44	43	49	50	49	42	47	48	$M = 62.1$
20	51	57	56	55	64	65	61	54	60	62	$S^2 = 22.89$
30	54	61	59	58	68	69	65	57	64	66	
40	54	61	59	58	68	69	65	57	64	66	$\Delta M = 16.4$
50	54	61	59	58	68	69	65	57	64	66	$\Delta S^2 = 2.84$
50-10	14	16	15	15	19	19	16	15	17	18	

$N_A = 20$ $M_A = 70.95$ $S_A^2 = 12.85$ $\Delta N_A = 20$ $\Delta M_A = 21.90$ $\Delta S_A^2 = 2.09$

$N_C = 20$ $M_C = 61.70$ $S_C^2 = 15.01$ $\Delta N_C = 20$ $\Delta M_C = 16.70$ $\Delta S_C^2 = 1.81$

$t = 7.64$ $P \approx 0$ $\Delta t = 11.48$ $\Delta P \approx 0$

Table 9.16
Psychokinesis Test Runs by Rotating Wheel, 1999
Subject: D.M., 1 metre from wheel, Total motion

Date	ACTIVE			CONTROL			PROBABILITY	
	N_A	M_A	S_A^2	N_C	M_C	S_C^2	t	P
25/1	20	66.10	10.79	20	62.05	20.85	3.14	0.002
½	20	65.80	22.06	20	62.35	12.43	2.56	0.008
8/2	20	62.35	13.13	20	61.40	16.04	0.77	> 0.1
15/2	20	63.35	17.03	20	61.55	6.15	1.63	0.06
22/2	20	61.50	9.75	20	61.25	6.99	0.27	> 0.1
1/3	20	64.35	11.83	20	61.45	8.85	2.78	0.004
8/3	20	66.45	23.65	20	62.00	10.70	3.31	0.001
29/3	20	65.30	15.21	20	61.95	20.15	2.46	0.01
12/4	20	68.15	22.43	20	61.95	14.85	4.43	0.00003
26/4	20	70.95	12.85	20	61.70	15.01	7.64	≈ 0
Σ	200	65.43	22.87	200	61.77	13.31	8.58	≈ 0

Table 9.17
Psychokinesis Test Runs by Rotating Wheel, 1999
Subject: D.M., 1 metre from wheel, Incremental motion

Date	ACTIVE			CONTROL			PROBABILITY	
	ΔN_A	ΔM_A	ΔS_A^2	ΔN_C	ΔM_C	ΔS_C^2	Δt	ΔP
25/1	20	17.30	1.31	20	15.25	3.19	4.21	0.00005
½	20	18.60	3.54	20	15.90	1.79	5.10	≈ 10^{-7}
8/2	20	17.05	1.35	20	15.45	2.45	3.58	0.0005
15/2	20	18.15	2.13	20	16.10	0.79	5.23	≈ 10^{-6}
22/2	20	17.55	1.35	20	16.40	0.84	3.39	0.0008
1/3	20	19.10	2.09	20	16.05	1.05	7.50	≈ 0
8/3	20	19.20	2.86	20	16.25	1.99	5.84	≈ 10^{-8}
29/3	20	20.15	2.73	20	17.05	2.05	6.18	≈ 0
12/4	20	21.20	3.36	20	16.70	2.41	8.17	≈ 0
26/4	20	21.90	2.09	20	16.70	1.81	11.48	≈ 0
Σ	200	19.02	4.71	200	16.19	2.12	15.28	≈ 0

Table 9.18
Psychokinesis Test Runs by Rotating Wheel, 1999
Subject: D.M., 4 metres from wheel, Total motion

Date	ACTIVE			CONTROL			PROBABILITY	
	N_A	M_A	S_A^2	N_C	M_C	S_C^2	t	P
19/4	20	59.7	8.01	20	61.15	12.23	-1.40	0.1
10/5	20	61.10	18.29	20	60.70	15.21	0.30	>0.1
24/5	20	63.90	10.59	20	61.00	15.60	2.47	0.009
31/5	20	60.95	27.75	20	62.15	18.13	-0.77	>0.1
8/6	20	62.85	22.93	20	60.75	22.19	1.36	0.1
1/7	20	65.95	20.35	20	61.35	14.03	3.42	0.0008
6/7	20	59.90	26.59	20	60.65	20.83	-0.47	>0.1
13/7	20	66.15	27.73	20	61.30	12.91	3.32	0.001
20/7	20	62.40	20.64	20	61.05	16.55	0.96	>0.1
10/8	20	64.00	25.30	20	61.55	16.45	1.65	0.05
Σ	200	62.69	25.63	200	61.17	16.60	3.30	0.0005

Table 9.19
Psychokinesis Test Runs by Rotating Wheel, 1999
Subject: D.M., 4 metres from wheel, Incremental motion

Date	ACTIVE			CONTROL			PROBABILITY	
	ΔN_A	ΔM_A	ΔS_A^2	ΔN_C	ΔM_C	ΔS_C^2	Δt	ΔP
19/4	20	16.10	1.39	20	16.25	1.39	-0.39	>0.1
10/5	20	16.35	2.33	20	15.90	1.29	1.03	>0.1
24/5	20	19.60	1.94	20	16.50	1.85	6.94	≈0
31/5	20	17.35	3.83	20	16.50	2.35	1.49	0.07
8/6	20	18.95	3.15	20	16.60	2.54	4.29	0.00004
1/7	20	19.55	3.65	20	15.50	1.35	7.89	≈0
6/7	20	17.65	4.63	20	16.50	2.35	1.90	0.03
13/7	20	19.90	4.29	20	16.20	1.76	6.56	≈0
20/7	20	17.10	3.79	20	15.95	1.55	2.17	0.02
10/8	20	18.65	3.93	20	16.60	1.74	3.75	0.0003
Σ	200	18.12	5.04	200	16.25	1.94	9.98	≈0

Chapter 9 – Psychokinesis

Further, at times high readings were obtained when a subject was on way to, or from, the laboratory at a distance of several kilometres. The better performance at 1 metre could perhaps be due to the subject feeling that a direct view of the wheel was essential to her.

Table 9.20

Test Run	DF	t	P	Δt	ΔP
A.D. 1 metre from wheel	398	9.63	≈ 0	16.36	≈ 0
D.M. 1 metre from wheel	398	8.58	≈ 0	15.28	≈ 0
D.M. 4 metres from wheel	398	3.30	0.0005	9.98	≈ 0
Experimenter G.K. only	398	0.36	> 0.1	1.87	0.03

The results obtained from experimenter G.K., in the absence of any subject, are attributable to chance for the total motion, and are barely significant for the incremental motion. These results with only G.K. present, are very valuable in confirming that the highly significant results obtained by subjects A.D. and D.M. were indeed achieved by the subjects, and are not attributable to some overlooked extraneous factors.

A number of unsuccessful attempts were made during the 1980s to obtain significant psychokinesis test results, that involved subjects aiming to influence a piezoelectric crystal psychokinetically. The apparatus used in these tests was redesigned in the late 1990s, mainly by including integration into the setup, that led to good results in the year 2000.

The experimental setup is depicted in Figure 9.2. The sensor consisted of a piezoelectric crystal, primarily designed to serve as a pickup for a record player. A stylus, originally serving to transfer vibrations from a rotating phonographic disk to the crystal, was arranged to be in light contact with the free end of a thin, highly flexible metallic cantilever strip, which was mechanically fixed at its other end. Any slight mechanical interference with the cantilever would thus be transferred to the crystal via the stylus. The crystal in turn would produce a minute voltage between its output terminals.

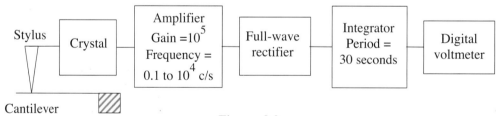

Figure 9.2

This voltage was then amplified by means of an electronic amplifier, having a gain close to $100{,}000 = 10^5$, and a frequency ranging from 0.1 to $10{,}000 = 10^4$ cycles per second (c/s). This meant that a voltage produced by the crystal at any instant of time would cause a voltage to appear at the amplifier output terminals, which was 100,000 times as large as the voltage produced by the crystal. However, this would only work for voltages alternating between positive and negative values a number of times per second within the above frequency range, extending from 0.1 to 10,000 cycles per second. Moving outside this frequency range at either end would cause the amplifier output voltage to fall gradually to

Chapter 9 – Psychokinesis

zero. The amplifier was powered from a direct voltage source, in the form of a battery consisting of four 1.5 volt dry cells. The output voltage from the amplifier served as input voltage to a "full-wave rectifier", which is an electronic circuit that changes negative voltages to positive voltages of the same magnitude, while leaving positive voltages unchanged. Thus the output voltage of the rectifier was a voltage varying with time, but which could have positive values only.

With the help of suitable electronic circuitry, one could measure the rectifier output voltage at short time intervals, and for each time interval obtain a rectangular area with a base equal to the length of the time interval, and a height equal to the corresponding rectifier output voltage. If the time intervals were short enough, so that the rectifier output voltage could change very little within any one time interval, then the sum of all such areas over a given time period would be designated the "voltage-time area", or the "integral", of the rectifier output voltage over that time period. Furthermore, the average rectifier output voltage over that period would equal the above integral divided by the length of the time period.

An electronic integrator circuit carries out the above summation process automatically, and also precisely, since it works on the principle that the time intervals are infinitesimally short and correspondingly many. The integrator in Figure 9.2 was designed to produce a short audible beep every 30 seconds, and following the onset of each beep, to produce a steady output voltage, that equalled the integral of the rectifier output voltage over the previous 30 second integration period preceding the onset of the beep. So, the integrator output voltage, as displayed on the voltmeter in Figure 9.2 between any two beeps, equalled the integral of the rectifier output voltage between the former two beeps. Consecutive integrator output voltages were thus measures of the very small voltages produced by the crystal due to either mechanical interference with the crystal, or due to internally generated noise voltages within the crystal and associated electronic circuitry. In view of the above, the integrator output voltage displayed on the digital voltmeter was updated at the onset of each beep.

The experimental setup was found to be very sensitive to extraneous influences, in particular any magnetic fields originating from electrical appliances and associated electrical wiring. Consequently, it was necessary to place the crystal and the amplifier in a totally enclosed and earthed metallic box, which in turn was placed inside a shielded cage. The amplifier output voltage was then conveyed from inside the box and the cage by a shielded cable to the rectifier, the integrator, and the voltmeter situated in the laboratory, which was separated from the room accommodating the cage by a 10 centimetre thick brick wall.

Experimental test runs were conducted the same way as was the case with the rotating wheel psychokinesis tests. A test run consisted of 1 pre-control run, 2 active runs, and 1 post-control run, each such run involving 20 consecutive integrator readings at 30 second intervals, over a 10 minute period. The 2 active runs had a few minutes break between them. During the active runs, the subject was seated in the laboratory in an armchair facing the brick wall, with the cage and the box containing the crystal and the amplifier beyond that wall, and attempted to mentally influence the setup so as to increase the readings. The experimenter also seated in the laboratory, recorded the integrator output readings from the voltmeter, and was thus in a position to keep the subject under observation.

The pre-control run was conducted approximately 1 hour before the subject's arrival, and the post-control run about 1 hour after the subject's departure. As with the rotating wheel

Chapter 9 – Psychokinesis

tests, this was found to be a good compromise, in view of the fact that the readings could be affected once the subject was on the premises, or on the way to, or from, the laboratory.

Subject A.D. had undertaken 10 crystal psychokinesis test runs, as described above, the results of which are summarised in Table 9.21. As before, the first column lists the dates of the test runs, and the symbols at the heads of the remaining columns have meanings as listed in Table 9.9. The symbol Σ indicates the combined result of the 10 test runs.

As an example, one of the experimental test runs was conducted on 3/5/2000. For this test run, from Table 9.21, the average of the 40 active integrator output voltage readings was: $M_A = 5.40969$ volts, with a variance $S^2_A = 0.00020$, while the average of the 40 control integrator output voltage readings was: $M_C = 5.39972$ volts, with variance $S^2_C = 0.00024$. The amplifier gain was not exactly 10^5, but was so set as to yield integrator output voltages of the order of 5 volts, about half way within the integrator working voltage range. As in previous tests, here too it was arranged that: $N_A = N_C = N$, but with $N = 40$.

Hence the corresponding rounded student's t parameter is:

$$t = (M_A - M_C) \times \sqrt{\frac{N-1}{S^2_A + S^2_C}} = (5.40969 - 5.39972) \times \sqrt{\frac{40-1}{0.00020 + 0.00024}} = 2.97$$

The associated degrees of freedom are 40 active readings plus 40 control readings less 2, that is, $DF = 40 + 40 - 2 = 78$, which is not listed in Appendix 9.2, Table A9.2. However, Table A9.2 shows that $DF = 40$ and $t = 2.97$ correspond to a probability $P = 0.0025$, and so the probability corresponding to $DF = 78$ and $t = 2.97$ must be smaller than 0.0025. Thus, the above is a highly significant result. It will be noted that the above calculations involve 5 decimal places. This had been done to secure sufficient non-zero figures for all variances. Consulting Table 9.21, it is seen that 3 test runs (16/2, 8/3 and 10/5) with probabilities $P > 0.05$ were not statistically significant, 1 test run (22/3) with probability $P = 0.04$ was significant, while the remaining 6 test runs (9/2, 1/3, 15/3, 12/4, 3/5, and 23/5) with probabilities $P < 0.01$ were highly significant. Of these, 2 test runs (9/2 and 12/4) yielded probabilities $P < 10^{-6}$, that is smaller than 1 in 1,000,000 or less than one in a million. The overall result of the 10 test runs was also highly significant with a probability $P < 10^{-6}$, namely smaller than 1 in 1,000,000 or one in a million.

Each experimental run listed in Table 9.21 was repeated the following day, at the same time, exactly the same way, the only difference being that A.D. was absent, and not having been informed, was consciously unaware of the proceedings. The results of this control test series are presented in Table 9.22. It is seen that only 1 test run (17/2) was significant, with probability $P = 0.03$, another test run (10/2) narrowly missed being significant at $P = 0.06$, while the remaining 8 test runs with probabilities $P > 0.1$ must all be regarded as having yielded chance results. The overall result of the 10 control test runs, at a probability $P = 0.32$, was also a chance result.

The results of the control test series in Table 9.22 thus help to confirm that the results obtained by A.D., as listed in Table 9.21, were not the outcome of some overlooked normal causative factors, but that they were in all probability the outcome of purely mental activity, that is psychokinetic activity, on the part of subject A.D.

Chapter 9 – Psychokinesis

Table 9.21
Crystal Psychokinesis Test Runs, Subject: A.D., 2000

Date	ACTIVE			CONTROL			PROBABILITY	
	N_A	M_A	S_A^2	N_C	M_C	S_C^2	t	P
9/2	40	5.42926	0.00207	40	5.35119	0.00265	7.10	≈ 0
16/2	40	5.34581	0.00099	40	5.33533	0.00159	1.29	≈ 0.1
1/3	40	5.37414	0.00191	40	5.35022	0.00104	2.75	0.004
8/3	40	5.41650	0.01318	40	5.39314	0.00237	1.17	> 0.1
15/3	40	5.36826	0.00047	40	5.34138	0.00113	4.20	$\approx 10^{-5}$
22/3	40	5.35217	0.00240	40	5.33774	0.00011	1.80	0.04
12/4	40	5.40612	0.00101	40	5.37279	0.00071	5.02	$< 10^{-6}$
3/5	40	5.40969	0.00020	40	5.39972	0.00024	2.97	0.002
10/5	40	5.30105	0.01611	40	5.31014	0.01742	-0.31	> 0.1
23/5	40	5.36645	0.00053	40	5.34586	0.00111	3.18	0.001
Σ	400	5.37695	0.00526	400	5.35375	0.00351	4.94	$< 10^{-6}$

Table 9.22
Crystal Psychokinesis Control Runs, No Subject, Experimenter only, 2000

Date	ACTIVE			CONTROL			PROBABILITY	
	N_A	M_A	S_A^2	N_C	M_C	S_C^2	t	P
10/2	40	5.36141	0.00068	40	5.35102	0.00103	1.57	0.06
17/2	40	5.37455	0.00025	40	5.38179	0.00033	-1.88	0.03
2/3	40	5.38276	0.00567	40	5.37941	0.00405	0.21	> 0.1
9/3	40	5.40111	0.01298	40	5.37067	0.01558	1.12	> 0.1
16/3	40	5.37233	0.00044	40	5.36986	0.00137	0.36	> 0.1
23/3	40	5.36362	0.00147	40	5.37631	0.00206	-1.33	0.1
13/4	40	5.32252	0.00305	40	5.32866	0.00311	-0.49	> 0.1
4/5	40	5.34800	0.00018	40	5.34946	0.00022	-0.46	> 0.1
11/5	40	5.34214	0.00734	40	5.34254	0.00862	-0.02	> 0.1
24/5	40	5.35418	0.00022	40	5.35264	0.00018	0.48	> 0.1
Σ	400	5.36226	0.00367	400	5.36024	0.00394	0.46	0.32

Chapter 9 – Psychokinesis

This conclusion is further strengthened by the fact that both A.D. and D.M. have achieved highly significant results, suggestive of psychokinesis, also by a very different procedure, namely the previously described rotating wheel test.

The psychokinesis test results achieved by the subjects A.D. and D.M., as presented in the foregoing, are the best results, but not the only significant results obtained by the author. A number of other subjects have undertaken the rotating wheel test. Unfortunately, most of these subjects volunteered for one test run only, even though in some cases the results suggested an extension to a test series worthwhile. The results of three subjects, who achieved statistically significant results, are given in Table 9.23 below. All three were single test runs with 20 active readings, 20 control readings, and 38 degrees of freedom.

Table 9.23

Subject	Total t	Incremental Δt	Total P	Incremental ΔP
C.M.	2.52	5.36	≈ 0.01	$\approx 10^{-5}$
I.G.	1.2	2.74	≈ 0.1	≈ 0.005
V.D.	0.23	2.53	≈ 0.4	≈ 0.01

It was stated earlier, that the rotating wheel setup was so adjusted that the wheel would usually come to rest within 50 seconds, after having been impulse started. While this was almost always the case, in a few exceptional instances, subject A.D., and also some others, were able to keep the wheel moving, following an impulse start, for 3 minutes or longer. However, as such prolonged wheel motions occurred rarely and unexpectedly, they did not lend themselves to statistical evaluation. Nevertheless, such prolonged wheel movements are also highly suggestive of psychokinesis taking place.

It may also be informative to compare the rotating wheel psychokinesis test results achieved by subjects A.D. and D.M., with the precognition test results obtained by the same two subjects as presented in Chapter 8.

It will be noted that the rotating wheel psychokinetic test results are considerably better than the precognition test results, as indicated by much lower probability figures. The tests conducted with subjects A.D. and D.M., and a number of other subjects, indicate that, in general, obtaining significant psychokinesis results by means of the rotating wheel test is easier, than obtaining significant extrasensory perception results. In fact, there are subjects who can achieve moderately significant results in rotating wheel psychokinesis tests, and yet are unable to reach significance, at the $P = 0.05$ probability level, in extrasensory perception tests. This does not seem to apply to piezoelectric crystal psychokinesis tests. The results achieved by A.D. in extrasensory perception tests, and crystal psychokinesis tests, yielded approximately the same level of significance.

Whether the psychokinesis test procedure involved the rotating wheel, or the piezoelectric crystal, one would expect higher variances during active runs than during control runs. Inspection of the overall results in Tables 9.11, 9.12, 9.16, 9.17, 9.18, 9.19, and 9.21 shows this to be the case. However, inspection of Table 9.22, containing piezoelectric crystal test results obtained in the absence of a test subject, indicates very large fluctuations in variance, ranging from 0.0018 to 0.01558, differing by a factor of $0.01558 / 0.00018 \approx 86$. This indicates that the crystal test is subject to highly variable extraneous influences.

Such influences may be due to magnetic storms interfering with the earth's magnetic field, or perhaps cosmic ray showers reaching the earth from outer space. Such fluctuations may lead to lower significance levels in test results than what would otherwise be obtained, but do not invalidate the results actually obtained.

The above described laboratory tests for psychokinesis were designed for detecting minute psychokinetic effects. In some real life situations, involving psychics who may be described as physical mediums, or in the case of claimed haunted locations and poltergeist outbreaks, psychokinetic effects may take place on a massive scale. Such macro-psychokinetic effects are also considered to originate from the unconscious minds of agents, who are not consciously aware of their involvement. However, such macro-manifestations do not easily lend themselves to scientific investigations, and are readily dismissed as the products of fertile imaginations.

Also, in view of the above test results, cases of outstanding performance in such activities as ball games and sports shooting may to some extent involve the unconscious psychokinetic guidance of balls and bullets, while such are in motion.

As for the nature of the modus operandi, measurable physical force fields, such as electric and magnetic fields, have not been found to play a role in psychokinesis. In fact, test procedures are normally designed to exclude the possibility of the involvement of such fields. However, in the known physical universe, both energy and information are often transmitted by means of waves, such as sound waves in air, or electromagnetic waves in electric and magnetic fields. Analogously, in psychokinesis the involvement of as yet unknown hypothetical fields, at times referred to as "psi" fields, is often suspected. The interaction between such fields and matter, if such fields exist, may occur at, or possibly below, the subatomic level.

Chapter 10
Bioelectric Phenomena – Biofeedback

Living organisms are built of fundamental units called cells. The biological cell is the smallest entity that possesses life, in the sense that it absorbs nutrients, grows, excretes unwanted waste, and reproduces itself. It does so by one cell dividing and developing into two cells, which then lead separate existences. Cell reproduction is facilitated by the nucleic acid molecule (DNA), which is embedded in the nucleus of the cell, and carries genetic information. The nucleic acid molecule can split into two identical molecules, leading to the creation of two nuclei, and the division of the cell into two identical cells.

The simplest organisms consist of single cells, such as algae and bacteria. Although viruses can also reproduce within host cells, it is disputable if viruses are living organisms. The shapes of the cells vary, the simplest shapes are globular or cylindrical. A typical cell size would be around 10 microns, (a micron equals one-thousandth of a millimetre), and so visible only under a microscope. Yet, cells are very large compared with their constituent molecules, that are made up mostly from atoms of carbon, hydrogen, oxygen, and nitrogen. A typical cell may contain around 10^{15} atoms, and the human body would contain a comparable number of cells.

While there are many different types of cells in the human body, cells of particular interest are nerve cells, also called neurones, brain cells, sensory receptor cells, and muscle cells. Information acquired through the senses of sight, hearing, smell, taste, and touch are picked up by the sensory cells, and are then conveyed to the brain cells for interpretation via the nerve cells. Likewise, instructions from the brain for muscular action are conveyed from the brain cells to the muscle cells via nerve cells as well. More generally, nerve cells are the conveyors of all kinds of information throughout the human body. A typical nerve cell consists of a number of constituents, as shown in Figure 10.1.

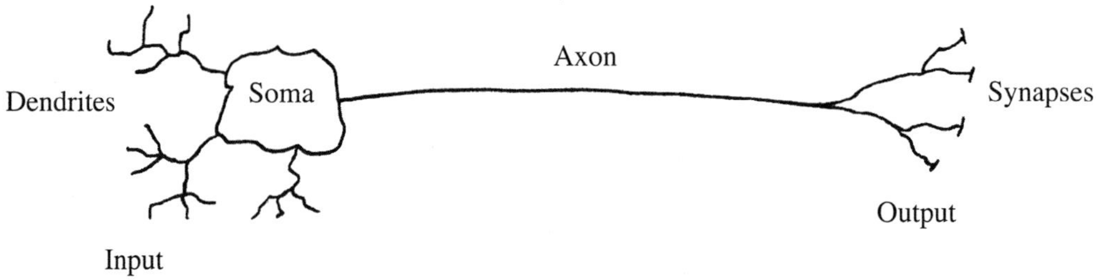

Figure 10.1

Nerve cells have an elongated shape with definite input and output ends. Near the input end is situated the main cell body, called the soma, measuring up to 30 microns in diameter. The soma receives input signals via a number of thin, tentacle-like, input elements, called dendrites, which are up to 2 millimetres long. Also, issuing from the soma is a cylindrical transmission element, called the axon, which has a diameter typically ranging up to 20 microns, and a length varying from 50 microns upward into the centimetre range, and in some cases reaching a metre or more. The axon is often embedded into a protective sheath, called the myelin sheath, but this is not always the case. Furthermore, the axon at its output end, also branches into a number of tentacle-like output elements.

Chapter 10 – Bioelectric Phenomena – Biofeedback

Each nerve cell has its input dendrites connected to the outputs of a number of preceding nerve cells, and each nerve cell has its outputs connected to the input dendrites of a number of follow-up nerve cells. These connections are called the synapses. Within each synapse, the input to output connection has a membrane, referred to as the synaptic membrane, interposed between the pre and postsynaptic regions. While the synapses are shared by the input and output elements, they are shown at the output end in Figure 10.1.

The functioning of nerve cells is rather complex, it involves both electrical and chemical processes, which probably are not yet fully understood. The following is a simplified description of the essentials of nerve cell operation.

The nerve cells carry information in the form of electrical impulses, called action potentials, which are not conveyed by electrons, as they would be in metallic conductors, but rely on conduction by ions. The sources of these ions are the chlorides of sodium, potassium, and calcium, which are always present in body fluids. Upon dissociation, these produce positive ions of sodium, potassium and calcium, and negative ions of chlorine. Due to such ions, when the nerve cell is in its resting or inoperative state, there is a potential difference across the axon walls, the inside being negative relative to the outside by about 100 millivolts. Likewise, there also is a potential difference across the synaptic membranes.

Any inputs to a nerve cell from preceding nerve cells, cause chemical neurotransmitter compounds to be released into the synaptic joints, which are accompanied by an increase in the permeability of the synaptic membranes to ions. The resulting ion diffusion through the synaptic membrane causes a reduction in the potential difference across the membrane. If a sufficient number of synapses of a nerve cell are so activated, then the soma causes the permeability of the axon wall to ions, near the soma end, to be increased. The resulting ion diffusion then results in the potential difference across the axon wall, at the soma end of the axon, to reverse from about 100 millivolts negative to about 80 millivolts positive (inside relative to outside). This voltage reversal is called the action potential, which then travels along the axon at a finite speed toward the output end of the axon, much the same way as waves propagate in a medium. A typical speed of propagation of the action potential along the axon is around 30 millimetres per millisecond, the speed depending primarily on the axon diameter, but also on other factors. When the action potential reaches the output end of the axon, it may contribute to the activation of the synapses of follow-up nerve cells.

Synaptic joints are unidirectional, they can pass activation only from presynaptic nerve cells to postsynaptic cells, but not the opposite way, which is essential for the proper functioning of the nervous system. Transmission across the synaptic joints is aided by nerve stimulants, and hindered by analgesics and relaxants. Further, consciousness altering drugs also affect the functioning of the synaptic transmission.

The signals carried by nerve cells, do not travel along a single chain of end to end connected nerve cells. Many such chains are arranged in parallel bundles, in which numerous chain to chain cross connections exist. These ensure that even if some nerve cells were out of action, the signal could travel from one point to another along many alternative routes.

The outputs of sensory receptor cells are similar to those of nerve cells, but their inputs are different. For instance the input elements of the cells in the retina of the eye respond to light, the sensory cells in the ear are stimulated by vibrations in the air, while sensory cells associated with touch, smell, and taste, likewise possess specialised input elements.

Brain cells are similar to nerve cells, with many interconnections, which facilitate the interpretation of incoming signals, decision making, and the production of outgoing signals to various parts of the body, such as the muscles in particular.

Muscle cells, also referred to as muscle fibres, vary in length from a few millimetres to several centimetres, and are 10 to 100 microns thick. They are also arranged in bundles, and have the ability to contract, or shorten, in response to action potentials delivered to them by nerve cells. Action potentials delivered to muscle fibres spread over the fibres at a speed of several millimetres per millisecond, a process in which calcium ions play a role.

So, it is seen that electrical impulses, in the form of action potentials, are a significant factor in the operation of the human body. It is therefore not surprising to find that if one attaches conducting metallic electrodes to the skin at various locations on the surface of the body, small potential differences (voltages) appear between such electrodes. Such voltages can be a helpful source of information about the functioning of the human body. The electrodes used are usually made of pure silver, often coated with silver chloride, which is not essential but is found to enhance reliability. The electrodes typically have about 1 square centimetre area, but may be larger or smaller. Good electrical contact with the skin is very important, that is achieved by thorough cleaning of the skin, possibly by sandpapering to remove dead tissue, and then by cleaning with alcohol, followed by the application of an electrically conducting paste between the electrode and the skin. Indeed, without applying a conducting paste between the skin and the electrode, useful measurements could be difficult to make. The electrodes can be held in place either by means of flexible bandage, or by adhesive tape.

The measurement of a potential difference between two points on the surface of the body normally involves the use of three electrodes, two electrodes attached to the two active sites between which the potential difference is to be measured, and a third electrode attached to a reference site. Using three electrodes is necessitated by the fact that bioelectric potential differences may be as low as a few microvolts, a microvolt being equal to one-millionth of a volt. The successful measurement of such low voltages requires the use of high gain "instrumentation amplifiers", capable of amplification by a factor up to a million, that is, 10^6. Such amplifiers have three input terminals, two active input terminals and a reference input terminal. The amplifier has the property that if an input voltage is applied between one active input terminal and the reference input terminal, and another input voltage is applied between the other active input terminal and the reference input terminal, then the amplifier amplifies only the difference between these two input voltages.

This is a very useful property, since the two active electrodes often pick up voltages from stray magnetic and electric fields, which can be large enough to swamp the biological voltage difference between the two active electrodes. However, these stray voltages at the two active electrodes would normally be equal, with the difference between them zero, and so would be ignored by the amplifier. This then enables the measurement of small biological voltage differences between the active electrodes, even in the presence of stray fields that often are very difficult to exclude. Earthing the reference electrode usually further aids this process.

The current chapter deals with the question whether correlations exist between bioelectric activities in the brain, heart, muscles, or the skin on the one hand; and psychic abilities, such as extrasensory perception and psychokinesis on the other hand. The question is also raised

Chapter 10 – Bioelectric Phenomena – Biofeedback

whether feeding some of the bioelectric activities of the body of a subject back to that subject in the form of light, sound, magnetic field, or electric field could possibly induce or enhance psychic abilities.

Brain Waves

The electrical activities of the brain cells cause small voltages to appear between any two points on the scalp, or between any one point on the scalp and one of the earlobes. These voltages vary with time, they go through successive positive and negative peak values. Because of the periodic variations of these voltages with time, they are called brain waves. A plot of these waves on paper is called an electroencephalogram, or EEG for short.

Typical brain wave amplitudes, that is maximum deviations from the average level, are of the order of 10 microvolts, and brain wave frequencies, namely the number of positive or negative peaks occurring in one second, typically range from 1 to 50 peaks per second.

In view of the foregoing discussion, brain wave voltages may be picked up by two active electrodes attached either to two positions on the scalp, or alternatively to one position on the scalp, the second position being an earlobe. The reference electrode would be attached to a neutral position, which could be the centre of the forehead, or the underside of the chin. The two active electrodes would then be connected to the two active input terminals of an instrumentation amplifier, while the reference electrode would be connected to the reference input terminal of that amplifier.

As far as possible active positions on the scalp go, there are 21 arbitrarily chosen, but generally agreed, positions on the scalp. Of these, 5 are on the centre line running from the top of the nose, through the centre of the scalp, to the middle of the back of the neck. There are 8 positions on both the left side and the right side of this line, making 21 active positions in all. Each of these positions is assigned a symbol. In the investigations described here, only 4 of these positions were used, namely the positions labelled O_1 and O_2 being on the left and right side respectively on the back of the head called the occipital region, and the positions labelled F_3 and F_4 being on the left and right side respectively on the top of the head in what is considered the frontal region of the scalp.

Two active electrodes connected to positions on the opposite sides of the centre line, such as O_1 and O_2, or F_3 and F_4, are called bipolar connections, while one active electrode connected to one position on the scalp, whereas the other connected to an earlobe, or to the skin in front of the ear, is called a monopolar connection. In the author's investigations, all brain wave measurements were made with monopolar connections.

The subject was placed in a double walled metal cage, seated in a comfortable armchair, with electrodes attached to 6 positions on the head: O_1, O_2, F_3, F_4, the ear, and a reference position which was either the forehead or the chin. The 6 electrodes were then connected to shielded leads, which conveyed the signals from the subject in the cage, to a four-channel amplifier and associated instruments in the laboratory situated in an adjacent room. The overall setup employed in these investigations is illustrated in Figure 10.2.

In Figure 10.2, arrows indicate the directions of signal flow. Not all blocks in Figure 10.2 would need to be operational at all times. The function of the various blocks will be described as the discussion proceeds.

The O_1, O_2, F_3, and F_4 electrodes were connected to one of the active input terminals of each of the four amplifier channels, while the earlobe electrode was connected to the other active input terminal of each of the four amplifier channels. The reference electrode was then connected to the common reference input terminal.

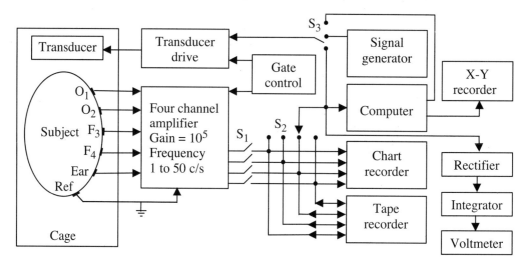

Figure 10.2

The amplifier gain is the factor by which the amplifier output voltage exceeds the difference between the two active amplifier input voltages, or simply the differential amplifier input voltage, that is:

(amplifier output voltage) = (amplifier gain) x (differential amplifier input voltage)

It was found that in most cases an amplifier gain equal to $100,000 = 10^5$ was a sufficient and convenient round figure to work with. Also, the amplifier frequency range needed to be 1 to 50 cycles per second (c/s), to handle all brain wave frequencies of interest.

The four amplifier output voltages would be applied to four channels of a chart recorder, and also to four channels of an instrumentation tape recorder operated in the record mode, by closing all four poles of switch S_1. Also, any one of the amplifier output voltages could be selected by means of switch S_2, and applied to a full-wave rectifier – integrator – digital voltmeter chain, and also to a computer.

The chart recorder provided a visual display of the brain waves emerging from the amplifier channels, enabling to see if the amplified brain wave magnitudes were appropriate. If not, small adjustments could be applied to the amplifier gains. However the four amplifier gains were always kept equal, and noted, so that the actual brain wave magnitudes could always be deduced at a later stage. The chart recorder displays also indicated if any of the brain waves were affected by troublesome noise voltages called artefacts, which could result from poor electrode contacts. If so, these would have to be put right before proceeding.

The analysis of the brain wave from one of the amplifier channels, as selected by switch S_2, could be carried out on line, that is done straight away as the experiment proceeded. The analysis of all four brain waves could be completed only after the experiment. This

Chapter 10 – Bioelectric Phenomena – Biofeedback

involved opening all four contacts of switch S_1, and then recovering the recorded brain waves from the tape recorder operated in the replay mode. All four brain waves could then be analysed, one at a time, as selected by switch S_2.

Whether the analysis was on line, or from tape recordings, two main features of brain waves were of importance, namely their magnitudes and frequencies. Such information could be obtained either by means of a relatively simple electronic circuitry, or through computer calculations. Both were done, so that the two results so obtained could be compared.

With reference to Figure 10.2, one way of obtaining information about the magnitude of brainwaves involved the rectification and integration of the amplifier output voltages. The full-wave rectifier converted the negative values of the amplifier output voltages to positive values of the same magnitude, and left the positive values unaltered. So, the rectifier output voltage, while varying with time, was always positive. This voltage then served as input voltage to an integrator. As described in Chapter 9, in connection with Figure 9.2, the integrator produced short beeps at regular preset intervals, and during the integration period between any two beeps it displayed a constant voltage on a digital voltmeter, which was proportional to the average value of the rectifier output voltage between the previous two beeps. Integrators often fulfil two functions, namely they integrate and amplify at the same time, and so the integrator output voltage between any two beeps, in terms of the amplifier gain, the integrator gain, and the integration period, was given by:

(voltmeter reading in volts)

$$= \left(\begin{array}{c} \text{full-wave rectified average} \\ \text{brain wave in volts} \end{array} \right) \times \left(\begin{array}{c} \text{amplifier} \\ \text{gain} \end{array} \right) \times \left(\begin{array}{c} \text{integrator} \\ \text{gain} \end{array} \right) \times \left(\begin{array}{c} \text{integration period} \\ \text{in seconds} \end{array} \right)$$

from which:

(full-wave rectified average brain wave magnitude in volts)

$$= \frac{(\text{voltmeter reading in volts})}{(\text{amplifier gain}) \times (\text{integrator gain}) \times (\text{integration period in seconds})}$$

At each beep, the integrator was automatically reset to zero, subsequent to which the integration started anew. Integrators, as all electronic circuits, can handle output voltages up to some definite maximum value, typically 10 volts, which must not be exceeded. This could be complied with, by adjusting the integrator gain and integration period accordingly. The integration period would normally be chosen in the range 10 to 30 seconds, and then the integrator gain set so as to yield an integrator output voltage of around 5 volts. These settings were maintained unaltered during any given experiment. Typically, full-wave rectified average brain wave magnitudes would be of the order of 10 microvolts.

The other important information about brain waves is their frequency. A way of deducing numerical values for frequency would be by electronically converting either the positive brain wave peaks, or the positive to negative brain wave crossovers, into narrow pulses, and then electronically count these pulses over set periods. The average frequency for a period would then equal the count divided by the length of the period in seconds. The average frequencies so obtained as peaks per second, or crossovers per second, would not only vary from one period to the next, but the peaks per second values would normally be higher than the crossovers per second values, as peaks are not necessarily followed by crossovers. Such variations show that brain waves do not have a single frequency, but are the sum of a large number of single frequency "sine waves" having differing amplitudes, frequencies, and relative positions of their peaks. The fact that complex waves are the sum of component sine waves was touched on in Chapter 3. In particular, Figure 3.4 shows a wave with two peaks for each crossover.

A computer may be programmed to provide information about both the magnitudes and the component frequencies of brain waves by using "Fast Fourier Transform" (FFT) methods, which yield the brain wave amplitudes associated with the various frequency components. Such information is referred to as a brain wave spectrum.

In the work recounted here, computer analysis involved the sampling of the brain waves, that is, reading the brain wave voltage values together with their signs, positive or negative as the case may be, at regular time intervals, over a selected sampling time period. A total of 512 samples were taken over a period of 4 seconds. Then, 256 amplitudes were calculated, associated with 256 frequency subranges, each 0.25 cycles per second wide, extending from zero frequency to 256 x 0.25 = 64 cycles per second. It should be noted that the calculated amplitudes did not apply at discrete frequencies, but rather were average amplitudes applicable over finite frequency subranges, each 0.25 cycles per second wide.

When using a computer for the determination of spectra in this manner, it is essential that the input voltage to the computer contains next to no frequencies beyond the programmed computer spectral range, that is, 64 cycles per second in this case. Otherwise the computed spectrum could contain false frequency components, referred to as "aliasing" errors. This is the main reason why the amplifier was arranged to work up to around 50 cycles per second only. This does not affect the analysis adversely, as brain waves are not normally regarded to contain frequency components of interest beyond 50 cycles per second.

At the lower frequency end of the spectrum, the amplifier and the computer could work down to zero frequency. But, since often the highest magnitude component of a bioelectric voltage signal is the steady, or zero frequency component, the computer could come up with the maximum amplitude occurring at zero frequency, and it could display finite frequency components to an objectionably small scale. To avoid this, the amplifier was designed to work down to a frequency of around 1 cycle per second, but not down to zero frequency.

The advisability of limiting the amplifier frequency range at both ends of the spectrum holds for most bioelectric voltage signals and not to brain waves only. However, the frequency boundaries are not sharp, and the fall in amplifier gain at the boundaries is always gradual.

The computer was programmed to start sampling in response to pressing an assigned key, but only after the input voltage to the computer first exceeded 0.4 of a volt, which was approximately 5% of the computer's input voltage range. This was arranged, so that the computer would not mistake small noise voltages, always present in circuits, for brain wave signals. Upon completing the sampling, the computer displayed the sampled brain wave of 4 second duration on its screen for inspection. At this stage, if the sampled brain wave was found to have been affected by artefacts, it could be rejected by pressing another assigned key. If accepted, then upon pressing a third assigned key, the spectrum would be calculated and displayed on the screen. The display essentially consisted of 256 rectangles, the base of each representing a frequency subrange 0.25 cycles per second wide, and the height representing the corresponding amplitude. The highest amplitude was always displayed by a rectangle of the same height, as high as the screen could conveniently accommodate, with

Chapter 10 – Bioelectric Phenomena – Biofeedback

the heights of the other rectangles correctly scaled relative to it. Also depicted on the screen were an arbitrarily chosen vertical numerical amplitude scale, and a horizontal frequency scale giving correct numerical frequency values in cycles per second. Further, displayed on the screen were the numerical value of the frequency at which the maximum amplitude occurred, and the numerical values of the maximum amplitude and the average of the 256 amplitudes on the above arbitrary scale. The screen also displayed the average value of the magnitudes of the 512 samples taken, on yet another arbitrary scale. This last item should equal a constant factor times the full-wave rectified average value of the amplified brain wave input voltage to the computer during the 4 second sampling period.

The arbitrary amplitude scale displayed on the computer screen would need to be calibrated. This could be done by applying a single frequency pure sine wave to the computer input, having exactly 1 volt amplitude, and a frequency within the 1 to 50 cycles per second frequency range, and at the middle of a subrange. Proceeding this way, the spectrum displayed on the screen would consist of a single rectangle, 250 arbitrary units high. So, the arbitrary computer scale was 250 arbitrary units per volt of amplitude.

After examination of the brain wave spectrum on the screen, it could be either rejected, or retained in the computer memory by pressing the appropriate assigned key. In either case, a second spectrum could be obtained, examined, and either rejected, or added to the previous spectrum, by pressing the appropriate assigned key. In the latter case, the computer would add corresponding amplitudes in the two spectra, and then work out the average for each of the 256 amplitudes. Any number of spectra could be added and averaged this way, and the averaged spectrum displayed on the screen, together with its associated numerical values.

It was also possible to press the appropriate key any number of times in quick succession, in which case the computer would be taking 512 samples over successive 4 second periods as many times as the key was pressed, but with a 1 second rest period interposed between the successive 4 second sampling periods. Following each rest period, sampling would start only after a voltage of 0.4 volt was first detected. The computer then would average the spectra, and also average the magnitudes of all samples taken, corresponding to the above number of key operations. Upon completion of the calculations, the computer would display on its screen the averaged spectrum, together with all the associated numerical values, as described above.

The computer had two output terminals. At one of these, the previously sampled brain wave would be reproduced, or echoed, starting 1 second after a 4 second sampling period was concluded, and ending 5 seconds after the conclusion of that sampling period. This meant that during any 4 second period, while the brain wave was sampled, the previously sampled brain wave was echoed at the above said output terminal. This time delayed, echoed brain wave was provided for feedback purposes to be described later on.

The second computer output terminal served for outputting the 256 calculated amplitudes of a single or averaged spectrum, over 256 successive equal time intervals. This enabled drawing the spectrum on a sheet of paper. The second computer output terminal would be connected to an x-y recorder, or x-y plotter, working on the same principle as a chart recorder. Drawing or plotting the spectrum by the x-y plotter on a sheet of paper, required entering into the computer the desired overall output plotting time, usually chosen as 100 seconds, and entering an output voltage scale factor as explained below. The plotting would then be initiated by pressing the assigned keys on the plotter and the computer.

Chapter 10 – Bioelectric Phenomena – Biofeedback

Whenever the computer displayed an averaged spectrum, it also gave updated values for the averaged maximum amplitude, the frequency at which that maximum amplitude occurred, together with the overall average of all spectral amplitudes, and the overall average of the magnitudes of all time samples taken. This then enabled the computer output to the x-y recorder to be scaled, so that all spectra were drawn to the same microvolt per centimetre brain wave amplitude scale, and also to the same cycles per second per centimetre frequency scale. From the foregoing discussion, it follows that for any frequency step in the spectrum:

(amplitude on the arbitrary computer scale)
= (brain wave amplitude) x (amplifier gain) x (250)

Experience indicated that the maximum amplitude in brain wave spectra rarely exceeded 20 microvolts (20×10^{-6} volts). So it was decided to let this be the maximum value on all the brain wave spectrum x-y plots drawn on paper. The corresponding maximum amplitude on the arbitrary computer scale would be:

$$(20 \times 10^{-6}) \times (\text{amplifier gain}) \times (250)$$

Thus, if the x-y plots were to display all spectral amplitudes to the above chosen scale, then the computer output voltage to the x-y plotter would have to be scaled down by a scale factor equal to the actual maximum spectral amplitude on the arbitrary computer scale, divided by the maximum amplitude on the arbitrary computer scale corresponding to a brain wave amplitude of 20 microvolts. Thus:

$$(\text{output voltage scale factor}) = \frac{(\text{actual maximum amplitude on the arbitrary computer scale})}{(20 \times 10^{-6}) \times (\text{amplifier gain}) \times (250)}$$

With this output voltage scale factor applied, brain wave amplitudes on the x-y plots would be given correctly, with the maximum on the scale corresponding to 20 microvolts.

This factor had to be entered into the computer, together with the desired plotting time, and the key assigned to initiating the outputting to the plotter pressed just after the plotter had been started. The brain wave amplitudes on the resulting x-y plots were then depicted with a vertical scale: 20 centimetres = 20 microvolts, and horizontal scale: 20 centimetres = 64 cycles per second. The spectra depicted in Tables 10.4, 10.5, 10.6, and 10.7 have been obtained this way, except that they were reduced to suit the size of the pages in the book.

The frequencies present in brain wave spectra are usually divided into five frequency ranges, and designated by Greek letters as illustrated in Table 10.1.

Table 10.1

Designation	δ	θ	α	β	γ
Range (cycles/second)	1-3	4-7	8-13	14-25	Over 25

While much could be said about these ranges, a brief summary would be as follows:
- δ waves: normally present in deep sleep only,
- θ waves: characteristic of drowsiness or light sleep,
- α waves: accompany a relaxed state, more so with eyes closed,
- β waves: usually prevail in alert wakefulness,
- γ waves: associated with active mental involvement in a task.

Chapter 10 – Bioelectric Phenomena – Biofeedback

There is no definite relation between the computer calculated average spectral amplitude, and the full-wave rectified average magnitude of brain waves. This is because the relative positions of the peaks of various frequency components in the brain wave vary with time. The full-wave rectified average is a better guide to the overall magnitude of the brain wave, while the computer calculated spectral amplitudes are a guide to the relative importance of the various frequency components, and in particular to the dominant frequencies.

Discussion of the brain wave spectra actually obtained from various subjects, such as those given in Tables 10.4 to 10.7, will be undertaken toward the end of the current chapter.

Returning to Figure 10.2, the rest of the circuit served the purpose of providing the subject with either stimulation, or feedback information about her or his brainwaves. This could be done by employing stimulation or feedback signals in the form of light, sound, magnetic or electric field. It was hoped that psychic abilities may perhaps be enhanced this way.

In all cases of stimulation, the source of the stimulation was a signal generator, connected through switch S_3 to the transducer drive circuit, which was energising a transducer inside the cage. The signal generator was normally set to provide pure sine wave output voltages, usually at 2, 5, and 10 cycles per second, which were considered to be typical δ, θ, and α brain wave frequencies. For feedback, the output of one of the brain wave amplifier channels was connected to the transducer drive, by switches S_2 and S_3.

For stimulation by light, the subject was seated in the cage with the electrodes connected as before, facing the transducer, which in this case was either an incandescent lamp, or a neon lamp. The transducer drive circuit, driven by the signal generator, was so designed that either of the two lights could be operated in one of two alternative modes.

The first mode involved the light intensity varying about a mean level, so that positive deviations from the mean corresponded to an increase in light intensity, while negative deviations from the mean caused the light intensity to diminish. In this mode of operation the light intensity would never become zero. In the second mode, the light intensity variation was biased relative to the negative peak, so that at the negative peak of the signal generator voltage the light intensity was zero, while at the positive peak the light intensity was maximum. In this mode of operation the light intensity would assume zero level once in each cycle. In both modes, the mean light intensity was determined by the transducer drive circuit settings, while the maximum light intensity deviations, and the frequency of the variation, were determined by the signal generator settings. The choices of the type of lamp, and the mode of operation, were selected in consultation with the subject.

For stimulation by sound, a loud speaker facing the subject acted as the transducer. It was possible to vary one of two attributes of the sound. One was the loudness or intensity, variation of which is called amplitude modulation, while the other was variation of pitch or frequency, which is referred to as frequency modulation. Here again the transducer drive circuit was designed for two alternative modes of operation. The first mode involved variation of either the loudness, or the pitch, about a mean level, while in the second mode, variation of the loudness took place upward from the barely audible. Variation of the pitch in the second mode was not feasible. In either mode, the mean levels of loudness or pitch were determined by the transducer drive circuit settings, while the limits of their variation would be determined by the signal generator settings. The choice of loudness, or pitch, and the mode of operation were decided in consultation with the subject.

While light and sound stimulation could be applied simultaneously with the brain wave monitoring, magnetic and electric field stimulation could not. This was so because with the magnetic or electric field applied, the electrodes on the subject's scalp picked up voltages from the field far exceeding the brain wave voltages, in fact, by such large margins, that the brain wave amplifiers would have been driven far beyond their operating voltage ranges.

The problem was overcome by the gate control circuit in Figure 10.2. This circuit ensured that whenever the magnetic or electric field was applied, the brain wave signal was blocked inside the brain wave amplifier at an intermediate signal level, and vice versa. The gate control circuit worked on the basis of a 10 second cycle, as illustrated in Table 10.2.

Table 10.2

Time (sec)	0 to 4	4 to 5	5 to 9	9 to 10
Brain wave	Passed	Blocked	Blocked	Blocked
Field	Blocked	Blocked	Passed	Blocked

Let it be recalled that the computer was programmed to sample the amplified brain wave voltage for 4 seconds following the pressing of the appropriate key, the sampling starting after the key operation at an instant when the amplified brain wave voltage first reached 0.4 of a volt. Recall also that in response to pressing the same key any number of times in quick succession, the 4 second sampling process would be repeated as many times as the key was pressed, but with a 1 second rest period inserted between the 4 second sampling periods, sampling starting after each rest period only when 0.4 volt was first detected. It follows that during consecutive 10 second periods, brain waves would be monitored for 4 seconds with the magnetic or electric field blocked, and then after a 1 second delay the magnetic or electric field signal was passed to the transducer drive circuit for 4 seconds with the brain wave voltage inside the brain wave amplifier blocked. After a further 1 second delay the process would be repeated a number of times depending on the number of key operations. So, 4 seconds of brain wave monitoring and recording were interleaved with 4 seconds of field stimulation, along with a 1 second break between the two. The delay preceding the brain wave monitoring could be slightly longer than 1 second because the computer having to wait for the amplifier output voltage to reach 0.4 of a volt.

Stimulation by magnetic field involved the use of a flat coil as transducer. The coil was wound with 1000 turns, and had an inner diameter of 35 centimetres. Stimulation was normally applied with the subject in the cage, either seated in an armchair, or lying on a bed, with the head inside the coil, and supported so as to avoid the head resting on any electrode attached to it. The coil was able to carry a steady current of 1 ampere continuously without overheating. With 1 ampere current flowing, the magnetic field at the centre of the coil was approximately 3 milliteslas, as could be ascertained either by calculation or by measurement. Near the inner edges of the coil the field was considerably higher. The coil was driven from a suitable transducer drive amplifier with an alternating current, the peak value and frequency of which were determined by the signal generator settings. An alternating current having a peak value of 1.5 amperes could be passed continuously into the coil, or even a larger current if the operation was intermittent such as described above.

For the purposes of stimulation by electric field, the transducer consisted of two flat metallic plates. The plates were electrically insulated, each plate had an area 40 centimetre square, and the plates were fixed parallel to each other 40 centimetres apart. The subject in the

Chapter 10 – Bioelectric Phenomena – Biofeedback

cage would once more be either seated in an armchair, or lying on a bed, with the head between the plates in such a way as to avoid the head resting on electrodes attached to it.

The transducer drive consisted of a high voltage transformer and an amplifier. The plates were connected to the transformer's high voltage secondary (output) winding terminals, and the transformer's low voltage primary (input) winding was driven from the same transducer amplifier that was used for supplying current to the above mentioned coil. The voltage ratio of the transformer was 70, that is, its output voltage to the plates was designed to be 70 times its input voltage coming from the transducer amplifier.

Transformers can operate over a range of frequencies. However, since the allowable peak magnetic field in the transformer core is fixed by its design, the maximum voltage handling capability of the transformer falls as the operating frequency is reduced, and so does the maximum available electric field between the plates connected to it. The figures applicable to the transformer used for providing the electric field are listed in Table 10.3.

Table 10.3

Frequency (cycles per second)	Peak secondary Voltage (volts)	Peak electric field (volts per metre)
10	4000	10,000
5	2000	5000
2	800	2000

The figures in Table 10.3 give the available maximum peak values of the field, that could be expected near the centre of the plates, with lesser fields near the edges. The peak value of the field and the frequency of its variation, were once more determined by the signal generator settings.

The brain waves of a subject may be fed back to her or him by means of light, sound, magnetic field, or electric field. This can be done by connecting the transducer drive circuit in Figure 10.2, to one of the outputs of the four-channel amplifier, by means of switches S_2 and S_3. Only one of the four brain wave signals could be fed back at any one time. The transducer outputs could not be expected to be exactly proportional to the brain wave voltages, because of nonlinearities in the transducers and in the transducer drive circuits.

Feedback by means of light and sound could be applied in "real time", that is the brain wave could be fed back continuously as soon as it was picked up, subject only to a minute delay present in all electronic circuitry. However, in view of the foregoing discussion, feedback via magnetic or electric fields could not be applied in real time, since the voltages picked by the electrodes from the field would have swamped the brain wave voltages.

As it was mentioned earlier, the computer stored the last 4 second long sampled brain wave in its memory, and then echoed back that sampled brainwave at one of its output terminals, starting 1 second after the conclusion of the sampling, and finishing 5 seconds after the conclusion of the sampling. The echoed brain wave could be applied as input to the transducer drive via switch S_3. Thus with the aid of the gate control circuit, during any 10 second period, the brain wave was sampled into the computer memory during a 4 second sampling period, and then after a 1 second delay, it was echoed into the transducer drive during the following 4 second period. Sampling would start again after a 1 second delay.

The computer key initiating sampling could be pressed any number of times in quick succession, and then the above cycle of 4 second sampling, and 4 second echoing, with the interposed 1 second delays, would be repeated automatically a number of times depending on the number of key operations, as was the case with stimulation.

After pressing the sampling key a number of times in quick succession, the computer would calculate the overall average spectrum, and then signal by means of a beep when the spectrum was ready for inspection and plotting. The effects of stimulation and feedback, as suggested by the brain wave spectra obtained from various subjects under such conditions, will be considered as part of a general discussion of the results later on in this chapter.

Muscle Tension

The electrical activities of muscle fibres, and the nerve cells activating them, also produce detectable potential differences (voltages) on the overlying skin surfaces. These may be picked up by electrodes attached to the skin over the muscles, much the same way as brain waves are monitored. Muscle tension voltages, like brain wave voltages, vary with time in a wave like manner, and go through successive positive and negative peak values. A plot of muscle tension voltages on paper is called an electromyogram, briefly denoted EMG.

In order to monitor muscle tension, electrodes may be placed on the skin over any muscle in the body, but if possible correlations between muscle tension and mental activities are of interest, then suitable electrode positions would be the forehead, the chin, and the back of the neck. All muscle tension data presented in this chapter were obtained by means of electrodes attached to the forehead. Of the two active electrodes, one was fixed above each eye, approximately 2.5 centimetres above the eyebrows, and a reference electrode was put either above the nose, halfway between the electrodes above the eyes, or under the chin. Cleaning the skin, and the application of conductive electrode paste, was done as for brain wave electrodes, and the electrodes were held in position by adhesive tape. The two active electrodes were then connected to the two active input terminals of an amplifier channel, while the reference electrode was connected to the reference input terminal of that amplifier channel. Earthing the reference input terminal normally yielded better signal quality. The amplifier channel was similar to those used for brain wave monitoring. The amplifier was situated in the laboratory, and the connections from the electrodes attached to the subject in the cage, to the amplifier in the laboratory, were by means of shielded leads. In view of the discussion on brain wave electrode placements, the above connections were, in fact, bipolar.

The determination of the magnitudes and frequencies of muscle tension voltages was carried out exactly the same way as for brain waves, with one significant difference. Examination of muscle tension spectra indicated that the useful frequency components of muscle tension voltages cover a wider frequency range, 10 or more times wider than was the case for brain waves. Consequently, some of the quantities entering into the computer program designed for calculating brain wave spectra, had to be modified for computing muscle tension spectra. The required changes were as follows. The number of equally spaced samples taken was 1024 over a sampling period of 1 second. The number amplitudes calculated was 512, each applying to a frequency subrange of 1 cycle per second, so that the overall frequency range covered was 512 x 1 = 512 cycles per second. Under these conditions, the arbitrary amplitude scale for the spectra displayed on the computer screen was modified to 500 arbitrary units equalling 1 volt sine wave voltage amplitude.

Chapter 10 – Bioelectric Phenomena – Biofeedback

The relevant parts of the circuit diagram in Figure 10.2 apply with one notable exception, namely that the frequency range of the amplifier channel needed to be suitably altered for muscle tension voltages. As muscle tension voltage frequencies were monitored up to 512 cycles per second, the upper frequency limit of the amplifier had to be set close to 500 cycles per second. Also, in order to avoid near zero frequencies dominating the spectrum, the lower frequency limit of the amplifier was increased to around 10 cycles per second.

All other statements made in connection with brain waves, also apply to muscle tension. Attempts were made to find correlation between muscle tension voltage magnitudes and their frequencies on the one hand, and mental states on the other hand, for a number of subjects. The results of these attempts will be considered later in this chapter. However, the effects of stimulation, or feedback, on muscle tension were not investigated.

Heart Rate

By far the largest potential differences (voltages) that can be picked up by electrodes fixed to the skin, result from the functioning of the heart. A graph displaying the variation of these heart-related voltages with time is called an electrocardiogram, or ECG for short.

It would be expected, that the largest heart voltage signals could be obtained by attaching electrodes to the chest close to the heart. However, good quality heart signal voltages may be obtained by electrodes fixed to the arms and legs. In this latter case, one each of the two active electrodes would be attached to the left and right lower arm respectively, and the reference electrode would usually be fixed to the lower left leg. Here again, the skin was cleaned, conducting electrode paste was applied, and then the electrodes were held in place either by bandage or adhesive tape. With reference to Figure 10.3, the subject with the electrodes attached was placed in the cage, and the active electrodes were then connected to the active inputs, and the reference electrode to the reference input, of an amplifier channel in the laboratory, via shielded leads. As heart signal voltages are relatively large, of the millivolt range, an amplifier gain of the order of 1000 (10^3) would normally be sufficient, and a frequency range of 0.1 to 50 cycles per second would be adequate. The amplifier output voltage was then applied to the rest of the circuit via the switch S as shown in Figure 10.3, which could facilitate analysis either in real time, or at a later stage.

The time varying voltage associated with the functioning of the heart has a relatively sharp peak in each heart cycle, called the QRS complex. The differentiator in Figure 10.3 had the property that its output voltage was proportional to the slope, or the steepness, of the time-varying input voltage to it, and in this case produced an even sharper output pulse than the QRS complex normally would do by itself. The differentiator had a further advantage, namely ignoring any slow drift in the steady component of the heart signal voltage, which at times could reach objectionable levels.

The task of the pulse shaper in Figure 10.3 was to convert these sharper pulses produced by the differentiator into narrow, short duration, rectangular voltage pulses, suitable for feeding into either a counter or a computer. The counter would then count the number of pulses over set intervals, and at the end of each interval, displayed the updated result in pulses per minute. This equalled the number of heart beats per minute, which is often called simply as the heart rate.

However, using a computer, one can obtain in addition to heart rate readings, information about how steady the heartbeat is. To do this, the computer was programmed to measure the time elapsing between the leading edges of any two successive rectangular heart beat pulses, that is, the period of each individual heart cycle in seconds. Then, dividing 60 seconds by each heart cycle period in seconds, gave the heart rate applicable to each individual heart cycle in beats per minute. If, for example a heart cycle period were found to be 0.850 of a second, then the corresponding heart rate, to three figures is 60 / 0.850 = 70.6 beats per minute. Likewise, a heart cycle period of 0.860 seconds would correspond to 60 / 0.860 = 69.8 beats per minute. Over a minute the computer would accumulate typically around 70 such beats per minute readings and, if so programmed, it would calculate both the mean and the standard deviation of these readings. (The average or the mean, and the standard deviation, associated with a set of readings was considered in Chapter 6.) A larger value for the standard deviation would be indicative of a more irregular heartbeat.

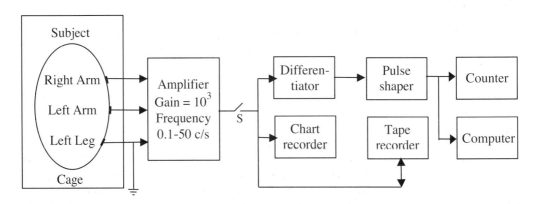

Figure 10.3

The computer in Figure 10.3 was programmed this way, and on receiving the rectangular pulses from the differentiator and pulse shaper, it calculated the mean heart rate, and also the standard deviation, and displayed updated values of both at set regular intervals.

As shown in Figure 10.3, the heart signal voltage was normally recorded on a chart recorder channel serving as a visual monitor, and also on a tape recorder channel from which it could be replayed, with switch S open, for analysis at a later time or date. As with brain waves, heart signals could not be monitored in the presence of strong enough electric or magnetic fields, as the voltages picked up by the electrodes from the field would swamp the heart signals.

Respiration

Respiration refers to breathing, that is the regular inhaling and expelling of air, normally via the nose. Three attributes of respiration could convey useful information, namely the magnitude, the frequency, and the standard deviation, which relate to the depth, the rate, and the regularity of breathing respectively. One way of obtaining estimates of these variables is by means of a "thermistor", that is a heat sensitive electronic device. If the temperature of the air surrounding a thermistor increases, its electrical resistance falls, and vice versa.

A thermistor was fixed in position under one nostril of a subject, by means of adhesive tape. The temperature of the air flowing past the thermistor upon breathing in would normally be cooler, than the temperature of the air coming from the lungs and passing the thermistor when breathing out. Consequently the resistance of the thermistor would undergo a periodic variation.

As indicated in Figure 10.4, the subject with the thermistor attached was situated in the cage. The leads from the thermistor were passed into the laboratory, and connected to an electronic circuit designed to convert resistance variation into voltage variation.

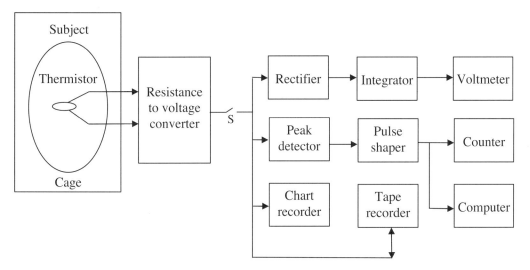

Figure 10.4

With switch S closed, this voltage could be passed to the rest of the circuit for real time analysis. The average magnitude of the respiration, over a set time period, was obtained by means of a full-wave rectifier – integrator – digital voltmeter chain, the same way as described above in the case of brain wave monitoring. The frequency of the respiration was determined with the help of a peak detector which, together with a pulse shaper, produced narrow rectangular voltage pulses, one for each detected positive peak of the resistance to voltage converter output voltage. A positive peak is detected when the voltage reaches a positive maximum value followed by a prescribed amount of drop in voltage level.

Alternatively, one could detect positive to negative voltage crossovers, instead of positive peaks. However, while small reversals of airflow, as in shallow breathing, would produce peaks, they would not necessarily produce cross overs, which would normally accompany deep breathing only. It was felt, that counting all air flow reversals, large or small, were the more appropriate indicators of respiration frequency, which was the reason for the choice of a peak detector in this case.

The pulses emerging from the pulse shaper were then counted over set time intervals, giving updated breaths per minute readings following each interval. The pulses were also fed into the computer, which dealt with them as with pulses obtained from heart signals, and yielded updated breaths per minute readings and standard deviation readings after each interval.

The voltage emerging from the resistance to voltage converter was also applied to one channel of a chart recorder for visual monitoring, and one channel of a tape recorder, from where it could be played back with switch S open, for analysis at a later time or date.

Skin Potential and Skin Conductance

As stated before, potential differences (voltages) can be picked up between two electrodes fixed to about any two positions on the skin. However, skin potential is usually obtained from specific positions, often from a pair of electrodes, one of which is attached to one side of the palm, and the other to the palm side of the lower arm. All skin potential values given in this chapter were obtained this way.

The voltage of the palm relative to the arm is normally negative, and is of the order of tens of millivolts. This voltage exhibits a slow drift with time as a rule, and may occasionally assume small positive values. This slowly drifting voltage is called the "skin potential level" or SPL, for short. On top of the skin potential level, there normally is superposed a much smaller, but more rapid periodic variation, with amplitudes in the microvolt range, which is referred to as the "skin potential response", or briefly SPR.

When a voltage is applied to a conductor, such as a length of metallic wire, an electric current results in the wire. The ratio of the current in amperes, divided by the voltage in volts, is called "conductance", and is measured in units named "siemens". If a voltage of 10 volts is applied, and a current of 0.01 ampere results, then the conductance of the wire is 0.01 / 10 = 0.001 siemens, which also equals 1 millisiemens, or 1000 microsiemens. One may apply a voltage, usually less than 1 volt, between two electrodes attached to the skin at two locations, measure the current, and deduce the conductance as above. The measured conductance would be made up of three components, the conductance of the skin under each of the two electrodes, and the conductance of the underlying tissue between the electrode locations. The contribution of the latter would normally be negligible, and so the overall conductance would very nearly be due to the skin surface conductance. Skin conductance depends on the electrode area. If the electrode areas are 1 square centimetre, then one is measuring the conductance of two 1 square centimetre skin areas in series.

The two electrodes are often attached to the centre digits of two adjacent fingers, usually the forefinger and the middle finger, on the underside, or palm side, of the fingers. The skin conductance measured this way is a slowly drifting positive quantity in the millisiemens range, and is called the "skin conductance level" or SCL for short. The slowly drifting skin conductance level has a much smaller more rapid periodic variation superposed on it, having amplitudes in the microsiemens range. This more rapid variation is called the "skin conductance response", or briefly SCR. All skin conductance values given in this chapter were obtained from two fingers as described above.

In view of the foregoing discussion, the measurement of bioelectric quantities normally requires two active electrodes and a reference electrode. In line with the above, for the measurement of skin potential, the two active electrodes were attached to one side of the palm and the palm side of the forearm, while for skin conductance measurements, the two active electrodes were attached to the middle digits of the fore and middle fingers on the underside, or palm side. A single reference electrode serving both, skin potential and skin conductance measurements, was then fixed to the lower part of one leg. All five electrodes were located on the same side of the body.

Chapter 10 – Bioelectric Phenomena – Biofeedback

Prior to attaching of the electrodes, the skin was cleaned, either by gentle sandpapering followed by wiping clean with alcohol soaked cotton wool, or by washing with water and soap followed by rinsing and drying. Electrode cream was then applied, and the electrodes were fixed in place either by bandage or adhesive tape. It should be noted that the effective electrode area would always be larger than the electrode surface, due to the electrode cream spreading past the edges of the electrodes. Also, since measured values, especially of skin conductance, depended on the method of skin preparation, consistency in this respect was an important consideration.

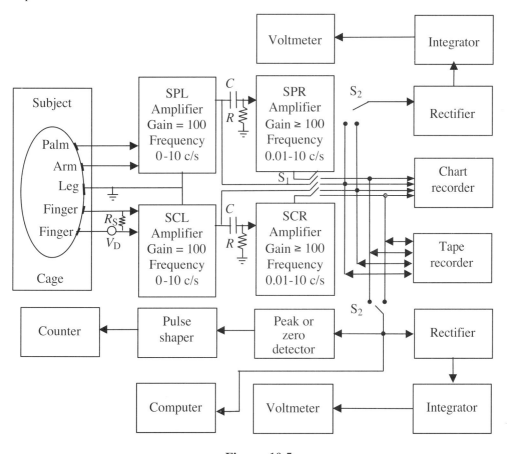

Figure 10.5

With the subject inside the cage, the five electrodes were connected by means of shielded leads to the SPL and SCL amplifiers in the laboratory as shown in Figure 10.5. The reference electrode was normally earthed, as that usually led to improved signal quality.

The circuit arrangement was designed for monitoring and analysing the four quantities introduced above, namely SPL, SPR, SCL and SCR. The task of separating the SPR component from the SPL, and also the SCR component from the SCL, was implemented by the resistance-capacitance circuits marked R and C in Figure 10.5. These circuits prevented the steady components, and also the very low frequency components, of the SPL

Chapter 10 – Bioelectric Phenomena – Biofeedback

and SCL from passing to the SPR and SCR amplifiers, so that only the higher frequency SPR and SCR components could reach those amplifiers. This ensured that the output voltages of the four amplifiers were proportional to the SPL, SPR, SCL, and SCR components respectively. The frequency boundaries of the SPR and SCR components at the low frequency end were determined by the R and C values in accordance with:

(frequency boundary)
$= 1 / [(6.28) \times (\text{resistance } R \text{ in ohms}) \times (\text{capacitance } C \text{ in farads})]$

For example, if the resistance $R = 1$ megohm $= 10^6$ ohms, and the capacitance $C = 10$ microfarads $= 10 \times 10^{-6}$ farads, then:

(frequency boundary)
$= 1 / [(6.28) \times (1 \times 10^6) \times (10 \times 10^{-6})] \approx 0.016$ of a cycle per second.

The frequency boundary resulting from the above simple R-C circuit is not sharp, but is rather gradual, which is not objectionable, and could even be considered beneficial.

The most suitable amplifier gains were found to be around 100 for all four amplifiers SPL, SPR, SCL, and SCR. However, in some cases, the gains of the individual amplifiers had to be suitably altered. Since the SPL is amplified by the SPL amplifier only, one has:

$$(\text{SPL in volts}) = \frac{(\text{SPL amplifier output voltage in volts})}{(\text{Gain of the SPL amplifier})}$$

The R-C circuit affects the SPR amplifier frequency range only, but not its gain. So, the SPR component of the SPL is amplified by both the SPL and SPR amplifiers, and thus:

$$(\text{SPR in volts}) = \frac{(\text{SPR amplifier output voltage in volts})}{(\text{Gain of the SPL amplifier}) \times (\text{Gain of the SPR amplifier})}$$

If both amplifier gains were made equal to 100, then the SPL and SPR values per volt of the SPL and SPR amplifier output voltages would be: SPL $= 1 / 100 = 0.01$ volt $= 10$ millivolts, while SPR $= 1 / (100 \times 100) = 0.0001$ volt $= 100$ microvolts.

Before skin conductance could be measured, it had to be first converted into a suitable input voltage to the SCL amplifier. To do this, a voltage V_D was applied to the two finger electrodes via a series resistance $R_S = 500$ ohms, as shown in Figure 10.5. The voltage V_D had to be kept less than 1 volt, in order to prevent a persistent unidirectional drift in the SCL. (This was arranged by connecting a silicon diode in series with another 500 ohm resistance across a 1.5 volt dry cell, which then resulted in a constant voltage across the diode: $V_D = 0.765$ volt. The voltage V_D remained constant even if the dry cell voltage dropped due to the current drain on it. In Figure 10.5 only the diode voltage V_D is shown, but not the dry cell and the resistance in series with it.) The voltage V_D caused a current to flow through the resistance R_S, and also through the skin and underlying tissue between the finger electrodes. In view of the foregoing discussion, the skin conductance (in siemens) equals the current (in amperes) divided by the voltage between the electrodes (in volts).

Now let another quantity be introduced, namely the skin resistance, that (in ohms) equals the voltage between the electrodes (in volts), divided by the resulting current (in amperes). The skin conductance and the skin resistance are thus the "reciprocals" of each other.

Chapter 10 – Bioelectric Phenomena – Biofeedback

Once more with reference to Figure 10.5, the skin resistance between the finger electrodes was found to be always large compared with the series resistance R_S, which therefore could be neglected in comparison with the skin resistance. Thus, one may write with little error:

(current in amperes)
= (voltage V_D in volts) / (skin resistance in ohms)
= (voltage V_D in volts) x (skin conductance in siemens)

Hence, in Figure 10.5:

(SCL amplifier input voltage in volts)
= (current in amperes) x (resistance R_S in ohms)
= $\begin{pmatrix}\text{voltage } V_D \\ \text{in volts}\end{pmatrix}$ x $\begin{pmatrix}\text{skin conductance} \\ \text{in siemens}\end{pmatrix}$ x $\begin{pmatrix}\text{resistance } R_S \\ \text{in ohms}\end{pmatrix}$

In the above, the skin conductance is essentially the skin conductance level (SCL). Thus:

(SCL amplifier output voltage in volts)
= (SCL amplifier input voltage in volts) x (SCL amplifier gain)
= $\begin{pmatrix}\text{voltage } V_D \\ \text{in volts}\end{pmatrix}$ x $\begin{pmatrix}\text{SCL} \\ \text{in siemens}\end{pmatrix}$ x $\begin{pmatrix}\text{resistance } R_S \\ \text{in ohms}\end{pmatrix}$ x $\begin{pmatrix}\text{SCL amplifier} \\ \text{gain}\end{pmatrix}$

and hence:

(SCL in siemens)
= $\dfrac{(\text{SCL amplifier output voltage in volts})}{\begin{pmatrix}\text{voltage } V_D \\ \text{in volts}\end{pmatrix} \text{ x } \begin{pmatrix}\text{resistance } R_S \\ \text{in ohms}\end{pmatrix} \text{ x } \begin{pmatrix}\text{SCL amplifier} \\ \text{gain}\end{pmatrix}}$

If the SCL amplifier gain were made equal to 100, then the SCL value, per volt of the SCL amplifier output voltage, would correspond to:

SCL = 1 / [(0.765) x (500) x (100)] ≈ 0.000026 siemens = 26 microsiemens.

Recalling that the R-C circuit affects the SCR amplifier frequency range only, but not its gain, and also that the SCR component of the SCL amplifier input voltage is amplified by both the SCL and SCR amplifiers, one has:

(SCR amplifier output voltage in volts)
= (SCR component of SCL input voltage) x (SCL amplifier gain) x (SCR amplifier gain)
= $\begin{pmatrix}\text{voltage } V_D \\ \text{in volts}\end{pmatrix}$ x $\begin{pmatrix}\text{SCR} \\ \text{in siemens}\end{pmatrix}$ x $\begin{pmatrix}\text{resistance } R_S \\ \text{in ohms}\end{pmatrix}$ x $\begin{pmatrix}\text{SCL amplifier} \\ \text{gain}\end{pmatrix}$ x $\begin{pmatrix}\text{SCR amplifier} \\ \text{gain}\end{pmatrix}$

and so:

(SCR in siemens)
= $\dfrac{(\text{SCR amplifier output voltage in volts})}{\begin{pmatrix}\text{voltage } V_D \\ \text{in volts}\end{pmatrix} \text{ x } \begin{pmatrix}\text{resistance } R_S \\ \text{in ohms}\end{pmatrix} \text{ x } \begin{pmatrix}\text{SCL amplifier} \\ \text{gain}\end{pmatrix} \text{ x } \begin{pmatrix}\text{SCR amplifier} \\ \text{gain}\end{pmatrix}}$

If both gains equal 100, then the SCR value, per volt of the SCR amplifier output, is:

SCR = 1 / [(0.765) x (500) x (100) x (100)] ≈ 0.00000026 siemens = 0.26 microsiemens.

Chapter 10 – Bioelectric Phenomena – Biofeedback

The evaluation of skin potentials and skin conductances by means of the circuit in Figure 10.5 proceeded as follows. With all four contacts of switch S_1 closed, the four quantities: SPL, SPR, SCL, and SCR were displayed on four channels of the chart recorder for inspection, and were also recorded on four channels of the tape recorder. Using switch S_2, either the SPL and SPR on the one hand, or the SCL and SCR on the other hand, could be selected for analysis, one at a time.

The determination of the level and response magnitudes, averaged over successive time intervals, typically 10 seconds or more, was done by means of two full-wave rectifier – integrator – digital voltmeter chains. As described before, the integrator produced a short beep at the end of each interval, and then displayed the integrator output voltage applicable to the integration period between the previous two beeps, on a voltmeter. From this the average integrator input voltage, equalling the average SPL, SPR, SCL, or SCR amplifier output voltage over the integration period, could be deduced as:

(average integrator input voltage in volts)
= (average SPL, SPR, SCL, or SCR amplifier output voltage in volts)
$$= \frac{(\text{integrator output voltage in volts})}{(\text{integrator gain}) \times (\text{integration period in seconds})}$$

Combining this last expression, with the foregoing expressions for SPL, SPR, SCL, and SCR yields the average values of the SPL, SPR, SCL, and SCR respectively.

For example, if the integrator gain equals 0.1, the integration period equals 10 seconds, and both the SCL and SCR amplifier gains equal 100, then average SCR in siemens, per volt of integrator output voltage, would be:
(average SCR in siemens) = 1 / [(0.1) x (10) x (0.765) x (500) x (100) x (100)]
≈ 0.00000026 siemens = 0.26 microsiemens.

The determining of the response frequencies was done by both: a peak and a zero crossover detector, followed by a pulse shaper and a counter. Counts were obtained over successive periods of 1 minute or longer, which upon division by the number of minutes in the count period yielded the frequencies in peaks per minute, and zero crossovers per minute.

In addition to the above, the spectra of the SPR or SCR could be obtained by means of the computer, one at a time, the same way was done for brain waves, but suitably modified for SPR and SCR. These have frequencies of interest ranging to about 5 cycles per second, that is around 10 times lower than the brain wave frequency range. The modifications involved taking 512 evenly spaced samples over a period of 64 seconds, and then calculating 256 amplitudes for 256 frequency steps, each 0.0156 cycle per second wide, covering a frequency range from zero to 256 x 0.0156 ≈ 4 cycles per second. The rest of the relevant procedures and calculations were exactly the same as described for brain waves earlier. In particular, the arbitrary computer amplitude scale still was, as for brain waves, 250 arbitrary scale units, per 1 volt amplitude of the SPR and SCR amplifier output voltages, together with the facility for averaging a large number of individual spectra.

The foregoing described essentially the on line analysis of either SPL and SPR, or SCL and SCR, one at a time. However, with switch S_1 open, all four could be replayed from the tape recorder, and analysed individually at a later time or date. Any results of these investigations are given and discussed further on in the current chapter.

Chapter 10 – Bioelectric Phenomena – Biofeedback

It could be appropriate at this stage to mention, that in addition to bioelectric variables, physical variables were also often monitored and recorded. The physical variables included possible interference with low intensity light beams, small variations in temperature, and disturbances in magnetic, electric, and gravitational fields. Such physical variables were of particular interest with two types of subjects. The first of these were trance mediums, claiming that discarnate entities were verbally communicating through them, while they themselves were unconscious and unaware of communications taking place. The second were subjects claiming to be able to undergo out of body experiences, an altered state in which the subject claims to experience a total separation of consciousness from the body, so that she or he is able to view her or his own body, and also any activity taking place around the body, from an outside vantage point.

In the first case, a discarnate entity is claimed to associate itself with, or enter, the physical body of the subject, and in the second case a discarnate aspect of the subject is claimed to leave the physical body of the subject. It was considered that such discarnate entities, if they existed at all, could possibly interfere with physical variables in the vicinity of the subject's body.

The detection of possible interference with weak light beams entailed the same physical setup that was used in the aura investigations described in Chapter 4. Briefly a very low intensity light beam, at wavelengths ranging from the ultraviolet, through the visible, to the infrared, was passed from a monochromator into the cage, and aligned to fall on the window of a photomultiplier. A mesh sreen placed between the subject and the beam served to obviate the possibility of any physical interference with the beam by the subject, be it inadvertent or otherwise.

The photomultiplier output, conveyed to the laboratory, was either photon counted, or was integrated, or both, over successive 30 second periods or longer. Under these conditions, any small change in the photon count, or the integrated output, could possibly have been considered as indicative of discarnate interference with the light beam.

Subjects believing to perceive the proximity of discarnate entities, frequently report feeling extreme coldness. In order to check if such a feeling was physically real, the probe of an electronic thermometer was located near to the subject, but separated from the subject by the above mentioned screen mesh, so as to avoid the possibility of any physical interference. The thermometer was not designed to give exact absolute temperature readings, but rather it was able to detect changes in temperature of the order of 0.01 of a degree Celsius reliably. This was achieved by making the thermometer output voltage proportional to temperature changes from the prevailing ambient temperature level, for instance by selecting a 0.1 volt change in output voltage, correspond to 0.01 degree temperature change. The thermometer output voltage was continuously monitored, by chart and tape recorders, so that it could be examined for unexpected changes in temperature, either on line, or later.

The possibility of small disturbances in magnetic and electric fields were investigated by placing the previously described 1000 turn coil, and parallel plates, in the cage near the subject, but separated from the subject by the above-said mesh, and then connecting them to high gain amplifiers in the laboratory. These amplifiers were designed to handle alternating voltages over a wide frequency range, so that they would respond only to changes in the prevailing fields. The amplifier output voltages were full-wave rectified, then integrated typically over 30 second periods or longer, and displayed on digital voltmeters at the end of each period. It will be noted that these circuits were not designed to make absolute measurements, but were designed to be very sensitive to small changes in magnetic and electric fields.

Finally, it was attempted to detect small disturbances in the earth's gravitational field by using a pendulum, essentially a small weight suspended by means of a length of thin fibre. Light from a source was allowed to reach a light sensor through a small hole, marginally smaller in diameter than that of the suspending fibre, and fixed so that with the pendulum swinging, the fibre interrupted the light twice in each pendulum period, producing a voltage pulse each time. These pulses were then passed from the cage to a counter in the laboratory, which was set up to count the 1 microsecond periods of a 1,000,000 cycles per second square wave, from a high frequency stability square wave generator, between any two consecutive pendulum pulses. The resulting count gave the time for one half of the pendulum's period in microseconds. As shown in Appendix 6.1, the period of a pendulum of given length varies inversely with the square root of the gravitational acceleration. Theoretically, at a pendulum period designed to be 1 second, a change in the pendulum's period could be detected with an accuracy up to 1 in 500,000. The small weight was made of iron, so that it could be pulled to one side by an electromagnet, in order to initiate a swing by pushing a button in the laboratory. The pendulum was enclosed in a sealed box, mounted on a solid base so as to exclude extraneous non-gravitational influences, and placed near the subject in the cage, but separated from the subject by the above-said mesh screen.

In general, variables were available in two forms: firstly as time varying voltages, which could be displayed on a chart recorder, and also recorded on tape, and secondly as digital readouts on voltmeters or counters, which were updated typically, but not necessarily, at 10 to 30 second intervals. The digital readouts were more accurate, but needed to be written down at regular intervals, while the chart and tape recordings were less accurate, but yielded a continuous record of the whole experiment, without the need for regular attention.

The question arises as to how many variables could be dealt with within one experiment. This was primarily determined by the fact that a maximum of 8 channels were available on both the chart recorder and the tape recorder. Usually, one of three options was adopted. <u>Option 1</u> - Brain Waves: 4 channels; muscle tension, heart, respiration and intercom: 1 channel each. <u>Option 2</u> - Brain waves: 2 channels time shared; heart, respiration, intercom, photomultiplier, and temperature: 1 channel each; electric and magnetic field: 1 channel time shared. <u>Option 3</u> - SPL, SPR, SCL, SCR and intercom: 1 channel each; 3 channels free, or used as desired.

When investigating possible effects of magnetic or electric fields on bioelectric variables, and on states of consciousness, one also needs to consider claims made by some people to be able to feel the presence of magnetic and electric fields, to be able to tell if those fields were on or off at particular instants of time, and even to see fields around current carrying conductors or electrically charged bodies.

Such claims were investigated by combining the extrasensory perception test circuit in Chapter 8, Figure 8.2, with part of the circuit in Figure 10.2, as shown in Figure 10.6.

With reference to Figure 10.6, the clock produced evenly spaced short audible beeps, typically seven seconds apart, which was the preference of most subjects. Between any two consecutive beeps, the field (magnetic or electric) was either turned on, or switched off, as randomly determined by the random generator and the clock circuitry, the same way as was done with the lights in Figure 8.2. The voltages that were turning the lights on or off in Figure 8.2 were also applied to electronic switches in Figure 10.6, which randomly either allowed, or blocked, signal passage from the signal generator through the amplifier.

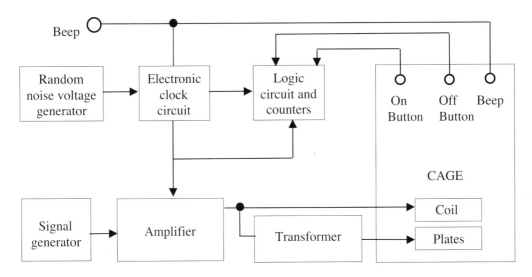

Figure 10.6

The subject was either seated in an armchair, or was lying on a bed, in the cage, with her or his head inside the coil, or between the plates, and was asked to press one of two buttons between any two consecutive beeps, the "on" button if the subject felt that the field was on, and the "off" button when no field was perceived. As in Figure 8.2, in the case of more than one button operation between any two beeps, the circuit accepted only the first one.

The direction of the field was alternating at preset frequencies. The subjects were tested at three frequencies: 2, 5, and 10 cycles per second, these being considered as typical δ, θ, and α brain wave frequencies respectively. For each frequency, tests were carried out at three field magnitudes corresponding to 0.5, 1.0, and 1.5 amperes peak current in the coil, or in the primary winding of the transformer driving the plates.

The tests were done exactly the same way as clairvoyance tests, the logic circuit in Figure 10.6 counting hits and misses. The field was considered as detected, if the probability for the results to have come about by chance was below $P = 0.05$.

As a further variant, tests were carried out in order to ascertain whether stimulation by light, sound, magnetic field, or electric field at δ, θ, or α frequencies, could be used to enhance extrasensory perception abilities in some subjects. This needed the extrasensory perception test circuit in Figure 8.2, to be operated in parallel with the relevant parts of Figure 10.2.

Results of the tests involving the detection of magnetic or electric fields, and the effects of stimulation by light, sound, and magnetic or electric fields, at brain wave frequencies, on extrasensory perception test results, will be discussed toward the end of the current chapter.

Chapter 10 – Bioelectric Phenomena – Biofeedback

Results

The examination of bioelectric variables in conjunction with paranormal phenomena aims at investigating possible correlations between these two areas of study. Doing so could aid the understanding of paranormal phenomena, and possibly facilitate the inducement or the enhancement of paranormal abilities in suitable subjects.

One question arising is if bioelectric variables significantly differ in psychic individuals demonstrating paranormal abilities, from those met in the general population. Another question is if some bioelectric variables differ in the same psychic subject in normal states of consciousness, as compared with altered states of consciousness.

Normal states of consciousness would include normal wakeful states in which speech or conversation may take place, also mentally active states involving problem solving without speech such as mentally adding up numbers, and relaxed states associated with no physical activity, minimal mental activity, and no speaking.

Altered states of consciousness would be considered to prevail when a subject exhibits extrasensory perception or psychokinetic activities, also when a subject is in a trance, that could be mediumistic, or hypnotic, or when dreaming takes place during sleep.

A test involving the monitoring and recording of bioelectric variables during altered states of consciousness would be preceded and followed by such recordings in normal states of consciousness, so that a comparison of the bioelectric variables in the normal and altered states could be made. Some altered states would involve speech, such as a clairvoyant subject reporting visions, or a trance medium conveying messages from apparent secondary personalities. As speaking loudly may affect bioelectric variables, recordings were usually made both with and without speech, in both normal and altered states. In the investigations outlined in the foregoing, an intercom was always employed, so that the experimenter in the laboratory could hear speech from the subject and other sounds originating from the cage, but the subject could not hear proceedings in the laboratory, except when the experimenter activated a microphone so as to communicate with the subject via the intercom. All speech by the subject, or the experimenter, and other sounds originating from the cage, were always recorded on one of the tape recorder channels. The intercom connections are not shown in Figures 10.2 to 10.6, in order to minimise possible adverse effects on clarity.

Tables 10.4, 10.5, 10.6, and 10.7 are brain wave spectra of subjects G.B., P.B., A.D., A.B., M.S., M.B., I.G., and R.D., as shown either at the head of the tables, or on the individual spectral plots. The spectra give the brain wave amplitudes in microvolts, for frequency values within the frequency range from near zero to 50 cycles per second. Most of the spectral plots are averaged spectra, coming from a relatively large number of four-second sampling periods, in some cases approaching 100 such periods. The symbols O_1, O_2, F_3, and F_4 refer to the position of one of the active electrodes on the scalp, the position of the second active electrode, in each pair of active electrodes, having been one of the ear lobes.

The letter "S" signifies "speech", the spectra marked by suffix S having been calculated from sampled brain waves monitored while the subject was in a normal state of consciousness, and speaking. The subject was usually asked to count aloud from 1 to 10, and keep repeating the same, until requested to stop.

Chapter 10 – Bioelectric Phenomena – Biofeedback

The letter "M" stands for "mental" activity in a quiet, normal state, the spectra marked by suffix M having been obtained from brain waves monitored while the subject, in a normal state, was engaged in a mental task. The subject was usually asked to mentally add up numbers ranging randomly from 1 to 5, as presented via the intercom, until asked for the final answer. It was made clear to the subject that making mistakes did not matter, only an attempt to add the numbers correctly was asked for.

The letter "R" indicates "relaxed" normal states without speech, the spectra marked by suffix R coming from brain waves recorded after the subject had been asked to relax. It was suggested that the subject relax all muscles as far as possible, and perhaps try to limit mental activity to visualising pleasing objects, or peaceful scenes.

The letters "AQ" stand for "altered quiet", the spectra marked by suffices AQ obtained from brain waves while the subject was in a quiet, no speech, transitional state between a relaxed state and an altered state.

The letters "ES" and "EQ" represent "entity speaking" and "entity quiet" respectively. The word "entity" refers to a secondary personality seeming to emerge from the subject when in a trance state. When the subject spoke in such a state, a different personality seemed to come forward, whose character, voice, and manner of speech, appeared to be very different from those of the subject while in a normal state. On returning to the normal state, the subject claimed to have been unconscious and unaware of an entity having emerged and spoken through her or him. Some people believe that at least some of these entities are manifestations of discarnate beings, or deceased persons, often referred to as "discarnate entities". Spectra marked by the suffices ES were obtained with an entity speaking while the EEG was being sampled, and the spectra marked by the suffices EQ were obtained from EEG sampling during quiet periods occurring between speech segments by a given entity. The separation of speech and no speech periods, for the purpose of analysis, could normally be achieved only when replaying brain wave recordings from tape.

The letter "C" stands for "clairvoyance", the spectra marked by suffix C having been obtained from brain waves while the subject was perceiving clairvoyant visions, in a quiet, no speech, but apparently altered state of consciousness. Any verbal reporting of visions by the subject took place after the subject had returned to a normal state of consciousness.

The letter "C", and the spectra marked by suffix C, could also signify spectra obtained from brain waves while the subject was undertaking a clairvoyance test run.

The letters "WF" and "NF" imply "with feedback" and "no feedback" respectively. Spectra marked by the suffices WF were obtained from brain waves, while those brain waves were fed back to the subject in the form of light, sound, electric field, or magnetic field, as described in connection with Figure 10.2. Spectra marked by suffix NF came from brain waves just before, of just after, feedback was applied. The subject was quiet during such tests, and reported her or his visions only after returning to a normal state.

The letter "P" stands for "precognition", the spectra marked by suffix P having been obtained from brain waves while the subject was undergoing a precognition test run.

The letter "K" signifies "psychokinesis", the spectra marked by suffix K having been calculated from brain waves while the subject was attempting to produce psychokinetic effects during a test run for psychokinesis.

Chapter 10 – Bioelectric Phenomena – Biofeedback

The letter "O" indicates "out of body experience", an altered state where the subject claims to perceive her or his consciousness located outside of the body, and claims being able to view her or his own body from an outside vantage point. The spectra marked by suffix O were obtained from the brain waves of a subject while claiming to undergo such an experience.

The letters "PH" stand for "precognition - hypnotic trance", the spectra marked by the suffices PH coming from brain waves while the subject was attempting a precognition test, following hypnotic suggestion.

The letter "N" indicates a "post-normal" state, spectra marked by suffix N having been obtained from brain waves after the subject returned to a normal state of consciousness, at the end of an altered state experiment.

Before proceeding with any discussion of brain wave spectra obtained from a number of subjects, it may be helpful to recall Table 10.1, where brain wave frequencies were divided into five ranges labelled by five Greek letters, each of which has been assigned a frequency range in cycles per second as follows: δ (1-3), θ (4-7), α (8-13), β (14-25) and γ (over 25). It may also be helpful to refer to the centre of these ranges as dominant frequencies within the ranges, so that the dominant δ, θ, α, and β frequencies, to convenient round figures, would be 2, 5, 10, and 20 cycles per second respectively.

Table 10.4 lists some of the brain wave spectra obtained from subject G.B. This subject exhibited the attributes of a trance medium, that is, a psychic person apparently capable of delivering messages from sources other than her or his own conscious mind, without being consciously aware of the proceedings. The source of the messages could be secondary personalities in the medium's own unconscious mind, or the unconscious minds of others via telepathy, or as some believe, discarnate entities surviving physical death. Subject G.B. was the only trance medium who volunteered for participation in the author's experiments.

As Table 10.4 shows, the dominant frequencies in G.B.'s brain wave spectra in normal states depended on the activities undertaken by her. When she spoke (O_{1S}, O_{2S}, F_{3S}, F_{4S}) the dominant frequencies were in the δ region. If performing a mental task without speaking (O_{1M}, O_{2M}, F_{3M}, F_{4M}) the δ frequencies were reduced, while the θ and α frequencies increased to a level comparable to the δ frequencies. However, when moving to the quiet relaxed state (O_{1R}, O_{2R}, F_{3R}, F_{4R}) both the δ and θ frequencies fell to relatively low levels, and the α frequencies became dominant.

On entering a quiet altered state, but prior to the appearance of entities, the α frequencies still dominated, but the δ frequencies reappeared. With entities coming through and speaking (O_{1ES}, F_{4ES}) the dominant frequency peaks were once more δ, that could have been due to speech. However, with the entity present but quiet, no speech, the occipital region (back of the head) spectrum (O_{1EQ}) had a dominant α peak, and the frontal region spectrum (F_{4EQ}) was dominated by a δ peak, but with a smaller α peak still present.

In summary, it appeared that in normal states, the dominant brain wave frequencies shifted from δ through θ to α as the subject moved from speech through mental activity to a quiet relaxed state.

Chapter 10 – Bioelectric Phenomena – Biofeedback

In the altered states, δ frequencies still dominated when the subject was speaking, but secondary α peaks also appeared. When the subject fell silent in the altered state, the δ peaks were reduced, while the α peaks became more prominent. The spectra also suggest that α frequencies were more pronounced in the occipital region (back of the head) than in the frontal region.

Table 10.5 shows brain wave spectra obtained from subject P.B., a subject who could be best described as a clairvoyant, claiming to experience visions of past, present, or future events, while retaining consciousness.

In the normal state, spectra associated with speech (O_{1S}, O_{2S}, F_{3S}, F_{4S}) exhibited dominant δ peaks, accompanied by smaller but substantial α peaks. Normal state spectra obtained during quiet mental activity or relaxation (O_{1M}, O_{2M}, F_{3M}, F_{4M}, O_{1R}, O_{2R}, F_{3R}, F_{4R}) were rather similar, with δ peaks absent or much reduced, and α peaks dominating. This suggests that in this subject's brain waves there was little or no difference between quiet mental activity and quiet relaxation.

In altered states, while the subject had clairvoyant visions (O_{1C}, O_{2C}, F_{3C}, F_{4C}), the δ peaks very nearly vanished, and very sharp, dominant α peaks were produced. These α peaks appear to have been further enhanced by feeding back to the subject her own brain waves in the form of an electric field, as indicated by the spectrum with feedback (O_{2WF}) peaking around 20% above the spectrum with no feedback applied (O_{2NF}).

Other means of feedback: light, sound, and magnetic field were also tried with subject P.B., but were found to be either less effective, or not effective at all.

Table 10.6 depicts brain wave spectra of subject A.D., a clairvoyant who has participated in many extrasensory perception and psychokinesis tests conducted by the author. Her highly significant precognition and psychokinesis test results were presented in Chapter 8 and Chapter 9 respectively. The altered states spectra in Table 10.6 were obtained during such test runs.

It will be noted that in general A.D.'s brain wave spectra were substantially different from G.B.'s spectra and P.B.'s spectra shown in Tables 10.4 and 10.5. In the normal state, all of A.D.'s spectra were similar, regardless of whether taken during speech (O_{1S}, O_{2S}, F_{3S}, F_{4S}), quiet mental activity (O_{1M}, O_{2M}, F_{3M}, F_{4M}), or relaxation (O_{1R}, O_{2R}, F_{3R}, F_{4R}).

Some of A.D.'s altered states spectra exhibited notable departures from the normal state spectra. Especially spectrum (O_{2P}) associated with precognition, and spectra (O_{1K}, F_{4K}) associated with psychokinesis, showed a significant increase of β and γ frequencies in the 20 to 30 cycles per second region, which appeared to have been unique to subject A.D.

Table 10.7 presents brain wave spectra from a number of different subjects, as indicated by their initials on their spectral plots. Subject A.B. was the only one who claimed to be able to undergo out of body experiences. The normal state spectra of A.B. (O_{1S}, F_{4S}, O_{1M}, F_{4M}) were very similar, all exhibited dominant δ peaks. This indicated that dominant δ peaks could be associated with both speech, and quiet mental activity.

The altered state spectra, associated with the subject's perceived experience of being out of body, showed a shift toward higher frequencies. The occipital region spectrum (O_{1O})

exhibited a sharp α peak, while the frontal region spectrum (F_{4O}) displayed dominant θ frequencies, with a somewhat smaller α peak.

Normal state spectra obtained from subject M.S., speech (O_{1S}) and quiet mental activity (O_{1M}) both yielded wide frequency distributions, while relaxation (O_{1R}) was characterised by a rather unexpected sharp α peak.

Subject M.B.'s spectra were all normal state, speech (O_{2S}), quiet mental activity (O_{2M}), and relaxation (O_{2R}). All three were very similar with a wide frequency distribution.

Subject I.G. undertook precognition tests with and without hypnotic suggestion. In the normal relaxed state (F_{3R}) no dominant peaks appeared. Attempting precognition without hypnotic suggestion (F_{3P}) resulted in a small α peak, while attempting the same following hypnotic suggestion (F_{3PH}) appears to have resulted in a considerably increased α peak. Whereas hypnotic suggestion did not substantially improve the overall precognition test results, which were only bordering on significance, it appears to have been responsible for an increased α peak.

Subject R.D. was also undertaking precognition test runs while brain waves were being monitored. The precognition test spectrum (F_{3P}) showed a small α peak, but the normal state spectra before the test (F_{3R}) and after the test (F_{3N}) produced no such peaks. The precognition test results were better than chance, but mostly not significant, with the exception of R.D.'s unique "self-actuated" tests, which did produce significant results.

It has been known for some time that specific mental faculties appear to be handled in particular areas of the brain. For example various regions of the brain have been identified where sensory inputs resulting from sight, hearing, smell, touch, and taste are processed. However, considerable overlaps also seem to exist.

It has also been suggested that the left and right sides of the brain play different roles. The left side of the brain is associated with intellectual abilities, such as language skills, numerical and scientific skills, and reasoning in general. On the other hand, the right side of the brain is responsible for artistic abilities, imagination, and intuition.

This would suggest, that spectra obtained while a subject was engaged in some mental task (adding numbers) should show a higher brain wave activity on the left side of the scalp (O_1 and F_3), as compared with the right side (O_2 and F_4). On the other hand, when a subject is in an altered state (for instance attempting extrasensory perception) the right side spectra (O_2 and F_4) may be expected to show higher activity, than the left side spectra (O_1 and F_3).

Higher brain wave activity could be expected to show up in the spectra as higher amplitudes on the average, or more precisely, as larger areas under the spectral curves. There appears to be some evidence for this in the spectral plots. For example in Table 10.4, the left side quiet mental activity spectra (O_{1M} and F_{3M}) appear to display marginally higher activity than the right side spectra (O_{2M} and F_{4M}). On the other hand, in Table 10.5, the left side clairvoyance spectra (O_{1C} and F_{3C}) seem to show marginally lower activity than the right side spectra (O_{2C} and F_{4C}). Precise differences could be obtained either from computer averaged amplitudes, or from full-wave rectified and averaged magnitudes, however, the differences were so marginal that pursuing them did not appear to be worthwhile.

Table 10.4
Brain Wave Spectra, Subject G.B.

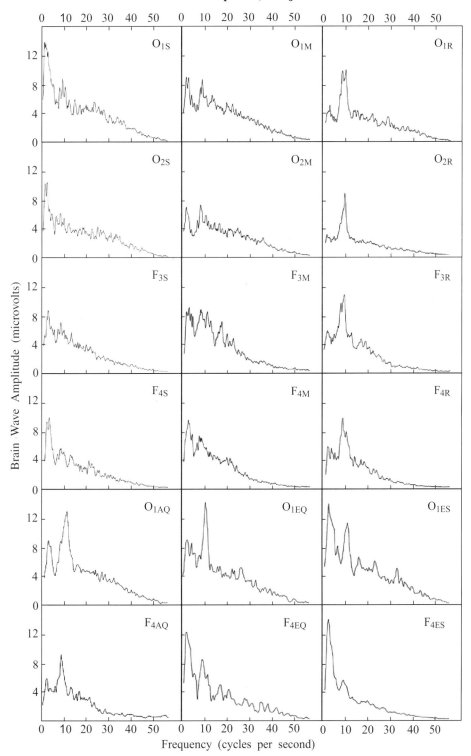

Table 10.5
Brain Wave Spectra, Subject P.B.

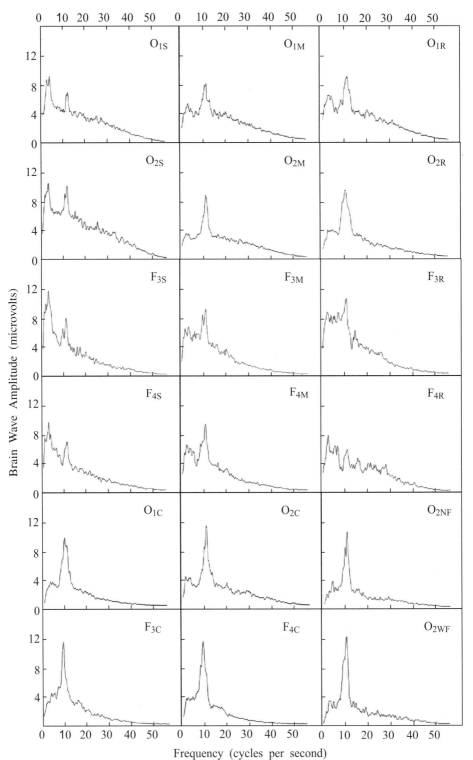

Table 10.6
Brain Wave Spectra, Subject A.D.

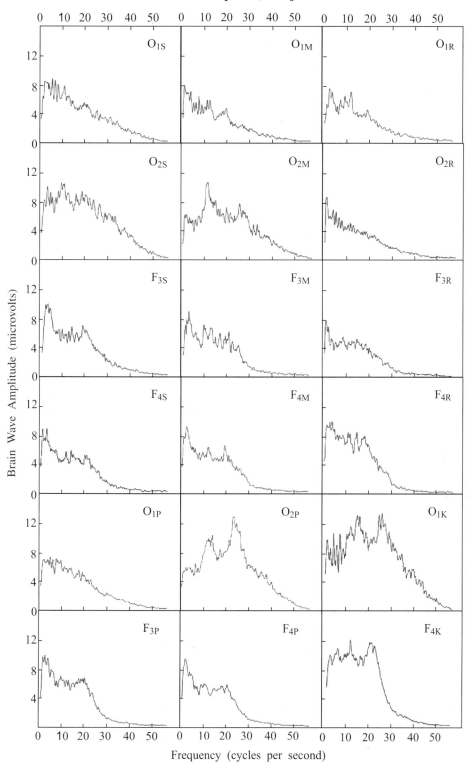

Frequency (cycles per second)

Brain Wave Amplitude (microvolts)

Table 10.7
Brain Wave Spectra, Subjects as Indicated

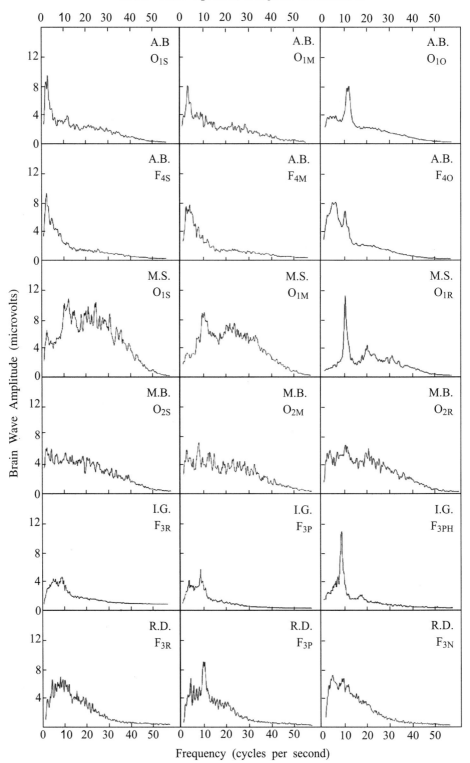

Chapter 10 – Biolectric Phenomena – Biofeedback

Table 10.8 gives muscle tension spectra for four subjects: G.B., P.B., A.D., and J.K. as indicated by initials on the individual spectral plots. The muscle tension voltages were obtained from the forehead, in the bipolar mode, as described earlier. The meanings of the letters: S, M, R, EQ, C, P, and N are the same as for the brain wave spectra before. The spectra were drawn to the correct frequency scale, extending from 0 to 500 cycles per second. However, the muscle tension amplitudes were not drawn to scale. Rather, the maximum height of each curve representing the maximum amplitude, together with the frequency at which the maximum amplitude occurred, is given numerically in the top right corner for each spectral plot. Thus, S(12.1-26) stands for a maximum amplitude of 12.1 microvolts, occurring at a frequency of 26 cycles per second, with the subject speaking.

When examining the spectra, it appears that for each subject, the amplitudes in general, and the maximum amplitude in particular, fell as one proceeded from speech (S), through quiet mental activity (M), and relaxation (R), to altered states: entity quiet (EQ), clairvoyance (C), and precognition (P). This suggests that a reduction in muscle tension could possibly correlate with an enhancement of paranormal abilities.

However, it also appears that muscle tension levels vary greatly amongst subjects. The muscle tension magnitudes were by far the highest for subject G.B., they were intermediate for subjects P.B. and A.D., and the lowest for subject J.K. The variations in muscle tension magnitudes from subject to subject appeared to be greater, than such variation with the state of consciousness in the same subject. In particular, the rather unexpected graph A.D., P(6.0-4), could have been the result of psychokinetic interference produced by A.D.

The bar graphs in Table 10.9 give five variables, namely: the heart rates in beats per minute, the standard deviations of the heart rates, respiration magnitudes in arbitrary units, respiration rates in peaks per minute, and the standard deviations of the respiration rates. These five variables are given for four subjects, namely: G.B., P.B., A.D., and A.B. as indicated on the graphs. Once more, the symbols: S, M, R, ES, EQ, C, NF, WF, P, O, and N have the same meaning as for brain waves.

When looking at subject G.B.'s results in normal states, it appears that as the experiment proceeded from speech (S), through quiet mental activity (M), to relaxation (R), some of the biological variables, namely heart rates, respiration magnitudes, and respiration rates tended to fall. In the altered states, column four (ES), and column five (EQ), came from more active entities, exhibiting higher heart and respiration rates, as compared with column six (ES), and column seven (EQ), that were obtained from less active entities, and perhaps expectably exhibiting lower heart and respiration rates. It also appears that standard deviations were higher in the case of more active entities, indicating more variable rates.

Subject P.B.'s results were more irregular. Notably, electric field feedback (WF), resulted in rather high heart rates, and exceptionally high respiration rates and associated standard deviations, indicating greatly increased magnitudes and irregularities of respiration rates.

Subject A.D.'s results were also rather irregular, however, it could be said that precognition (P) tended to be associated with higher and more variable heart rates, while respiration appeared to be highest in the normal relaxed state in all three of its aspects: magnitude, rate, and variability.

Subject A.B. showed a steady fall of heart rate as the tests proceeded from normal states (S), (M), and (R) into altered states, namely an out of body experience (O), while the variability of the heart rate was higher in the relaxed states (R), than in the altered states (O). Respiration of subject A.B. appeared to be too irregular for drawing any conclusions.

The bar graphs shown in Table 10.10 give skin conductance and skin potential values for two subjects G.B. and P.B. The skin conductance level (SCL) and skin conductance response (SCR) magnitudes are given in microsiemens. The skin potential level (SPL) and the skin potential response (SPR) magnitudes are given in millivolts. Response frequencies (for both SCR and SPR) are given as peaks per minute, and also as zero crossovers per minute. The meanings of the letters S, M, R, ES, EQ, C, and N here too are the same as for brain waves.

Skin conductances and skin potentials were not monitored and recorded simultaneously with the previously considered variables, namely brain waves, muscle tension, heart rate, or respiration, for lack of a sufficient number of recording channels. Consequently, the results in Table 10.10 cannot be correlated with the results in the previous tables.

It appears that both the magnitude and the frequency values of SCL, SCR, SPL, and SPR tend to be marginally higher in the altered states than in the normal states. In particular, the normal relaxed state (R) appears to have yielded the lowest values in most cases.

Computer calculated SCR and SPR spectra were determined in relatively few cases only, which appeared to be insufficient for drawing conclusions. Examination of these spectra seemed to indicate, that they did not offer significant additional information over and above the response magnitudes and response frequencies in terms of peaks and zero crossovers per minute, as presented in Table 10.10. Consequently, it was decided not to include such spectra amongst the results presented in this chapter.

When correlations between states of consciousness and the foregoing bioelectric variables is considered overall, then based on the above results, correlations appear to be moderate, with perhaps skin conductance and skin potential showing the least correlation. However, two observations may merit notice. Firstly, some subjects claiming or displaying extrasensory perception abilities, exhibited prominent α frequency peaks at around 10 cycles per second. In particular, subject P.B. produced exceptionally sharp α peaks while claiming to experience clairvoyant visions, that were further enhanced by feedback (Table 10.5 – O_{2NF}, O_{2WF}). Secondly, subject A.D. produced brain wave spectra extending far into the β and even the γ regions up to 30 cycles per second and beyond, especially during precognition and psychokinesis test runs (Table 10.6 – O_{2P}, O_{1K}, F_{4K}).

A considerable number of experiments were designed to look for physical disturbances in the vicinity of subjects claiming to undergo paranormal experiences. Such events included, amongst others, a trance medium in an ostensibly unconscious state conveying messages from purported discarnate beings, a clairvoyant in a conscious state claiming the ability to "see" and communicate with discarnate beings, and a subject claiming to undergo an out of body experience. Such experiments, typically lasted two hours or more, and involved the monitoring various physical variables. These included attempts to detect interference with low intensity light beams, unexpected sudden temperature variations, and disturbances in magnetic, electric, and gravitational fields. None of the tests involving physical variables yielded definite results. Although the test procedures were highly sensitive, with perhaps the exception of the gravity tests, any variations in these physical quantities could have occurred at such low levels, so as to be beyond the sensitivity of the test procedures.

Table 10.8
Muscle Tension Spectra, Subjects as Indicated

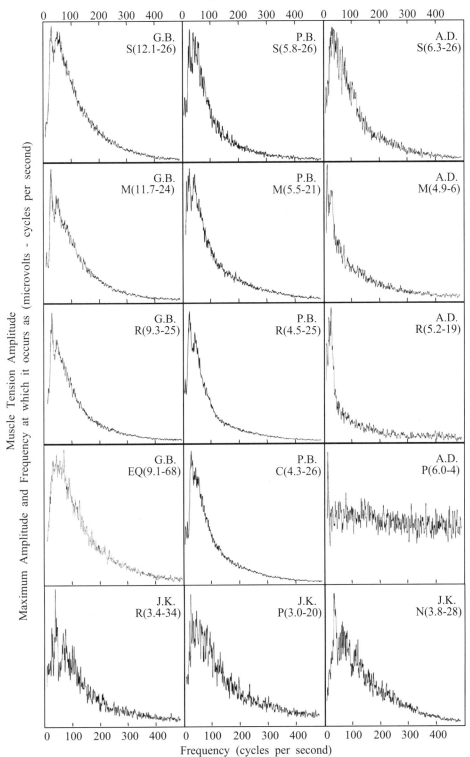

Table 10.9
Heart Rate and Respiration Graphs, Subjects as Indicated

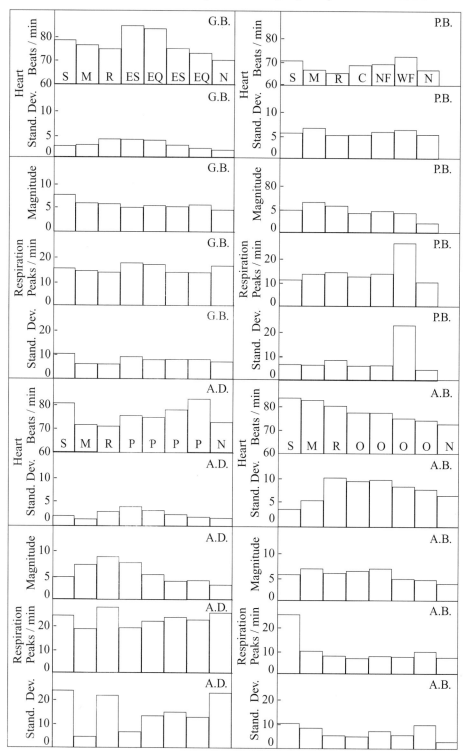

Table 10.10
Skin Conductance and Skin Potential Graphs, Subjects as Indicated

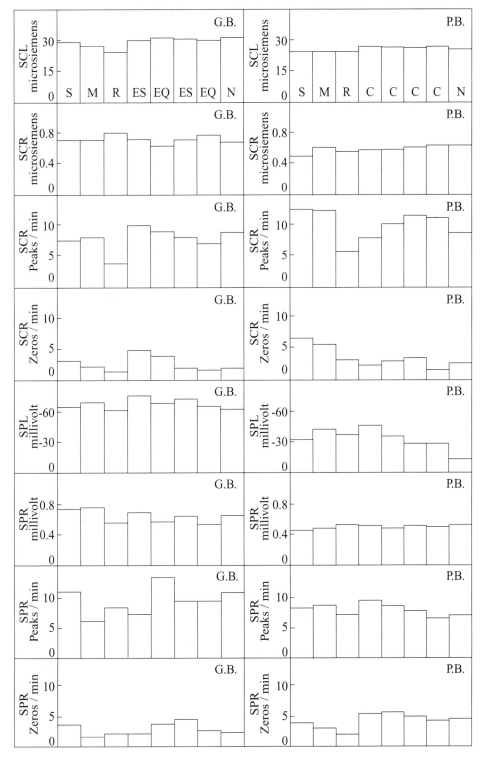

Chapter 10 – Bioelectric Phenomena – Biofeedback

The application of stimulation or feedback by means of light, sound, magnetic field, and electric field entailed four objectives. Firstly, to investigate whether the subjects had felt anything at all, and if so what were their subjective sensations. Secondly, to examine if stimulation or feedback had any effect on the bioelectric variables themselves and in particular if it affected brain waves. Thirdly, to determine if paranormal abilities could be enhanced by stimulation or feedback. Fourthly, to examine if some subjects could reliably detect the presence of magnetic or electric fields.

The possibility that the application of stimulation or feedback could have adverse effects on subjects was given serious consideration. No subject was ever asked to undergo an experiment, before the author tried it on himself, at maximum intensity, and for periods of around ten times as long as a subject would be exposed in the course of an experiment. For example, in tests involving magnetic or electric fields, a subject would be exposed to these fields at various field strengths for approximately half an hour. The author, on a number of occasions, exposed himself to the maximum available field strengths, both magnetic and electric, for periods of around eight hours, which entailed both overnight sleep and wakeful states before and after sleep. The author did not notice any adverse effects on himself, and experienced no sensations whatever. However, a number of subjects reported sensations when undergoing stimulation or feedback by light, sound, magnetic field, or electric field. Normally stimulation was found to be more effective than feedback, and in what follows the term stimulation may imply both.

The first objective of stimulation or feedback was probing the sensations as reported by subjects. Most subjects found sound stimulation, or neon light stimulation, disagreeable, especially in the θ frequency region, while α and δ frequencies were better tolerated. Stimulation by incandescent lamp drew a neutral response, and occasionally was described as pleasant. This may be due to the fact that incandescent lamp filament temperatures, and associated light intensities, follow electric current variations less rapidly.

Stimulation or feedback by means of magnetic or electric fields, resulted in more definite responses. Two subjects reacted negatively, especially toward the end of the experiments, suggesting that the feeling of discomfort was cumulative. Comments made by the various subjects, subsequent to electric and magnetic field stimulation were as follows:

Comments by G.B., after stimulation involving θ and δ frequencies, were: "feeling pleasant at first, but then getting increasingly edgy, nervous, dizzy, tired, developing headache, numbness, eyes closing and feeling sleepy, loss of control, vibrations across the skin". However, G.B.'s comments following α frequency stimulation were: "pleasant, floating sensations, visions of being at home, and passing through a solid door".

Comments by P.B., following θ and δ frequency stimulation, were: "feeling heavy and pushed down, heaviness in head, loss of ability to tune into clairvoyant visions". However, at α frequencies P.B. reported: "floating sensations, feet feeling as if rising from bed, feeling of being off the bed, although aware that this was a sensation only".

Comments by M.B., irrespective of frequency: "feeling of coldness but not unpleasant, feeling sleepy".

Comments by M.S., irrespective of frequency: "comfortable, nice, tingly all over, seeing light flashes" while situated in total darkness.

Chapter 10 – Bioelectric Phenomena – Biofeedback

Some of these remarks suggest partial out of body sensations, but not a definite out of body experience. A number of other subjects made similar remarks, but the above is a good representative sample of comments.

The second objective of stimulation or feedback was investigating its effects on biological variables. The effects on three variables, namely on brain waves, heart rate, and respiration rate were readily comparable, since these variables were often monitored together within the same experiment. In general, it was found that when stimulation was first applied, it tended to have a substantial effect on the above variables, but the effect wore off within a minute or so, and thereafter the overall effect was small, or disappeared all together.

In the case of subjects G.B. and P.B., magnetic field stimulation tended to reduce all three: the brain wave magnitude, the heart rate, and the respiration rate, by up to 10%. A notable exception was that in some cases magnetic field stimulation at α frequencies resulted in an increase of the α components of the brain waves by about 10%.

In the case of subject M.B., the sudden application of light stimulation at α frequencies caused an initial doubling of the α component of the brain wave, accompanied by a reduction of the δ component, with the θ and β components barely affected. However, the effect wore off in a minute or so. No such initial reaction was observed upon the sudden application of θ or δ frequency light stimulation.

The bioelectric variables of subject M.S. showed little or no response to stimulation. While a number of other subjects were also examined for correlations such as above, their results were very similar, so that the foregoing may be regarded as a good representative sample. Possible correlations between stimulation and skin potential, skin conductance, muscle tension, heart rate, and respiration, were not examined.

The third objective was examining the effects of stimulation or feedback on paranormal abilities. Subject M.S. had undertaken three clairvoyance test runs. The first, with no field applied, led to chance results at a probability $P = 0.47$ or 47%. The second, with electric field stimulation, resulted in $P = 0.38$ or 38%, which was a improvement but was still a chance result. The third, with magnetic field stimulation gave $P = 0.038$ or 3.8%, which was statistically significant. These results suggested that M.S.'s extrasensory perception abilities could possibly be induced or enhanced by magnetic field stimulation. To settle the issue would have needed more tests with M.S., but there was no opportunity for doing so.

Although at least 10 other subjects were tested for extrasensory perception with various types of stimulation applied, none of them showed substantial improvement in extrasensory perception test results. Some psychokinesis tests were also run with stimulation applied, again with no significant improvement in results. Thus, the conclusion appeared to be that paranormal abilities were not readily induced, or enhanced, by the methods of stimulation or feedback as described in the foregoing.

The fourth objective of stimulation was questioning whether some subjects could reliably detect the presence of magnetic or electric fields. This was examined using the test setup described before, and depicted in Figure 10.6. Out of some 10 subjects tested, three displayed such an ability to varying degrees. Two subjects achieved significant results in electric field detection, namely C.B. at a probability $P = 0.04$ or 4%, and M.S. at $P = 0.015$ or 1.5%. Three subjects came up with significant results in magnetic field detection, namely R.D. at $P = 0.05$ or 5%, C.B. at $P = 0.02$ or 2%, and M.S. at $P \approx 10^{-17}$. The last result came from the normal probability curve for 269 hits out of 373 attempts.

The ability of subject M.S. to detect the presence of magnetic fields is not just probable, but appears to border on certainty. These results were obtained at 1 ampere peak current in the coil. With 0.5 ampere peak current in the coil M.S. produced chance results. Thus, the ability to detect the field seemed to operate only over a threshold level of field intensity. One is tempted to consider that M.S. achieved the above result by some unidentified extraordinary biological ability. If that were the case, M.S. was the only one to have done so. In particular, while subjects G.B. and P.B. reported discomfort after having been exposed to magnetic and electric fields for some time, of the order of half an hour, their field detection tests yielded chance results. Thus they could not identify the presence, or absence, of the fields at particular instants of time, and their feeling of discomfort bridged over the actual on and off periods.

It could also be instructive to recall that in Chapter 4, subject M.S. was the only one who demonstrated an ability to see far into the infrared region, once again provided that the light intensity exceeded a certain threshold level. It appears that some people possess sensory abilities well beyond that of the average for the population.

Commenting on the foregoing chapter overall, the extensive and yet limited range of investigations undertaken by the author, and his associates, suggests that while some correlations between biological variables and paranormal abilities seem to exist, however, any apparent correlations lack consistency. One case suggesting correlation is the frequent coincidence between extrasensory perception and sharp α peaks in the brain wave spectra. Another case appears to be a correlation between psychokinesis and the extension of brain wave spectra far into the β and even the γ regions. In general, the foregoing findings suggest that biological variables vary more from subject to subject, than from normal states of consciousness to altered states of consciousness in the same subject.

Chapter 11
Survival Related Phenomena

Humans believed from time immemorial, that an aspect of their being survives the death of the physical body. The immortality of the "soul" is a fundamental tenet of most religions, past and present. Some tribes had such firm beliefs in post-mortem existence, that they physically tied up the dead prior to burial to prevent their return. Others have provided elaborate instructions for the guidance of the departed, of which the Egyptian and Tibetan Books of the Dead are examples.

Of course, to believe is not to prove, but one must bear in mind that to disbelieve is not to disprove either. In this spirit, scientific research has been seeking answers to the enigma of survival beyond bodily death for over a hundred years.

The term survival, as a paranormal phenomenon, is inherently bound up with the mind-body duality principle. According to this principle the mind on the one hand, and the brain and the body on the other hand, are separate entities that during the lifetime of the physical body function together in a complementary manner. This complementary interaction between the mind and the brain in the control of the body, could be regarded as somewhat analogous to the relation between software and hardware in computers.

Some survival related phenomena suggest that the mind is capable of existing and operating outside the physical body, independently of the brain. This contradicts orthodox scientific views according to which the mind, including such of its manifestations as consciousness, memory, and reasoning ability, are all attributes of the brain, and consequently the mind, and its above manifestations, cease to exist upon the death of the physical body.

On the contrary, the mind-body duality principle, in assigning to the mind the possibility of separate existence from the body, leads to the survival hypothesis, which advocates the purported ability of the mind to survive the death of the physical body.

Before going further let it be recalled that, as stated in Chapter 7, unlike extrasensory perception and psychokinesis, the reality of survival cannot be statistically verified. However, there exists a large body of accumulated evidence, which suggests that survival cannot be dismissed out of hand, and must be considered as a possible explanation for the various kinds of survival related phenomena.

The following is a brief survey of various phenomena suggestive of the survival hypothesis. These include:

- Exteriorisation of Consciousness,
- Apparitions,
- Mediumistic Messages,
- Poltergeist Phenomena,
- Near Death Experiences,
- Deathbed Observations,
- Apparent Past Life Memories.

Exteriorisation of Consciousness

As many case histories indicate, under certain conditions some individuals undergo an experience of perceiving the environment from a location outside their physical bodies. This suggests that consciousness may detach itself from the physical body, and may exist outside, often far removed from the body. A commonly used term describing this type of phenomenon is "out of body experience".

Predisposing factors are: extreme tiredness, prolonged fasting, severe illness or injury, anaesthesia, and hallucinogenic drugs. When consciousness is exteriorised, the physical body is often claimed to be observed from a well-defined outside vantage point.

As it appears from the reports of subjects, who claim to have had an out of body experience, the vehicle of the exteriorised consciousness may assume various forms. It can appear as an immaterial human form matching the physical body in every detail, or it may assume an ill-defined form resembling a ball of light, or it may not be any discernible spatial entity at all.

Most subjects claiming to experience exteriorisation, report that while out of body they can observe the physical environment, but cannot physically interact with it.

Clairvoyance, unlike the exteriorisation of consciousness, could be considered an expansion of awareness to regions beyond the reach of the senses, but still centring in the body. Both clairvoyance and exteriorisation are altered states of consciousness, and there are indications that subjects may experience one, or the other, or a whole continuum of states in-between.

All these states can be tested for by asking subjects to identify targets on a double blind basis. The statistical evaluation of such tests has established the existence of these phenomena to a high degree of probability. However, when it comes to distinguishing between exteriorisation and clairvoyance, one is largely dependent on the description by the subject of her or his experiences.

In one attempt aimed at differentiating between these two phenomena, an optical device was constructed at the American Society for Psychical Research, which enabled a range of images to be assembled optically from various components by a prism system. The images were observable only from a particular position in front of the device. It was hypothesised, that only the exteriorised consciousness projected to that position would be able to identify the whole image, clairvoyant vision could recognise only the components. To obviate recognition by telepathic means from the experimenter's mind, the images were assembled by a random event generator, and were not known to anyone prior to the subject's exteriorisation attempt, and the subject's report. These experiments supported the out of body hypothesis to a moderate degree of significance. Nevertheless, target identification having taken place by extrasensory perception could not be fully ruled out.

Attempts to detect exteriorisation may involve three kinds of detectors, namely: human, animal, and instrumental.

Human detectors are in essence psychics with clairvoyant ability, who are seemingly able to perceive the out of body aspect. However, human detectors are not reliable insomuch that they are often unable to localise position or ascertain time, and may pick up a faraway subject clairvoyantly when the latter is not undergoing any out of body experience at all.

Chapter 11 – Survival Related Phenomena

Animals are often observed to be responsive to paranormal phenomena. In experiments carried out at the Psychical Research Foundation in North Carolina in the 1970s, attempts of exteriorisation were made to the location of a subject's pet animal, coupled with monitoring the behaviour of the animal during exteriorisation attempts, and also in the absence of such attempts. These experiments have yielded moderately significant results.

Based on the consideration, that the out of body aspect may interact with physical variables, exteriorisation attempts were made to instrument locations, designed to detect minute variations in certain physical quantities. These included temperature, gravitational field, magnetic and electric fields, permittivity and permeability, absorptivity and reflectivity with respect to low intensity light rays covering a wide wavelength spectrum. However, an occasional significant response could be attributed to psychokinetic effects operative over a distance, rather than exteriorisation to the instrument location.

Definite correlations between exteriorisation attempts and bioelectric variables appear to be difficult to establish. Most such variables, including brain waves, muscle tension, eye movement, heart rate, respiration, skin conductance, and skin potential appear to remain largely unaffected. The author failed to secure statistical significance during such attempts.

Investigations are greatly dependent on the availability of subjects, capable of undergoing exteriorisation by arbitrary choice. Since such subjects are relatively few, efforts have been made to learn to induce exteriorisation at will. The techniques tried included sensory deprivation aimed to exclude outside influences, relaxation to reduce body awareness, suitable suggestions, audio-visual stimuli such as viewing a rotating spiral, or modulated light, also modulated sound, or music specially composed for the purpose, exposure to time-varying electric and magnetic fields, or any combination of these. While such techniques have at times appeared to have induced experiences suggestive of exteriorisation, it is questionable if any such attempts ever led to a definite out of body experience.

Biofeedback techniques have also been employed, but since definite relationships between exteriorisation and bioelectric variables do not seem to exist, there is insufficient indication as to the type of biofeedback that may prove successful, if any. Hypnotic suggestions alone were not found to be effective. While some subjects had the impression of being out of their bodies, they failed to identify targets to a statistically significant level.

Investigations by the author and his associates, as described in Chapter 10, into possible correlations between states of consciousness in general and the out of body experience in particular on the one hand, and physical and bioelectric variables including biofeedback on the other hand, have not led to statistically significant conclusions.

Based on case histories, anaesthesia and hallucinogenic drugs appear to be rather promising, however, investigations in this direction are severely limited by legal restrictions.

In order to establish exteriorisation as a phenomenon in its own right, as distinct from clairvoyance, it would be necessary to show the existence of its spatiotemporal nature, namely that the exteriorised consciousness, or its vehicle, may be temporarily localised in a discrete region of space outside the physical body. Succeeding in this task would have important implications for the survival hypothesis, since if consciousness could be shown to be able to exist outside the physical body, and function independently of the body, then it may be expected to be able to survive physical death.

In summary, it may be said that the detection and distinguishing of exteriorisation, or out of body experience, from clairvoyant phenomena, is fraught with difficulties. Nonetheless, the large number of reported experiences, and in particular the many common features of these reports, offer substantial circumstantial evidence for the ability of the mind to exist outside the body. This in turn, is strongly suggestive of the possible survival of the mind beyond physical death.

Apparitions

The age-old belief, that an aspect of human beings and also of animals survives physical death, was prompted by the occasional ostensible observation of immaterial human and animal forms, generally referred to as "ghosts" or "apparitions", the latter term being the preferred usage by investigators.

Toward the end of the 19th century, two research societies were established, namely the Society for Psychical Research in England in 1882, and the American Society for Psychical Research in 1885. These societies were founded by individuals trained in the sciences, with the scientific examination of survival related phenomena amongst their prior objectives. One of their particular concerns was if apparitions could be considered as indicative of survival. Three early members of the Society for the Psychical Research, namely: Edmund Gurney, Frederic Myers, and Frank Podmore published their findings in 1886 in a book titled "Phantasms of the Living".

It was noted that few people claimed the ability to "see" apparitions. In reported "haunted" locations, in a group of observers simultaneously present, only one might claim to see an apparition, although occasionally a number of observers reported having similar impressions at the same time. The experience was rarely repeated, and so it was not readily verifiable.

It also became apparent that most reported apparitions were those of people dying, and appeared close to the time of death, the aim seemingly being to inform interested parties of the impending death. It was realised that the phenomenon was similar to telepathy, in that it involved the extrasensory transfer of information from an agent whose apparition was seen, to a percipient to whom the apparition appeared. In fact, an important attribute looked for in apparitional phenomena became whether transfer of verifiable information took place, in which case the occurrence was labelled veridical.

It was also realised, that in most cases it could not be clearly established if at the time when the apparition was perceived, the agent was still alive, or if the agent was already dead. However, as investigations progressed, it became clear that apparitions of living agents were perceived much more often, than the apparitions of the dead.

In the information transfer from agent to percipient, it was originally assumed that the agent was the active player, while the percipient fulfilled a passive role only. This assumption turned out to be erroneous, as it was found that on occasions, when a number of observers were in a position to perceive the same apparition, there were discrepancies in their descriptions. Some saw nothing, while those reporting seeing the apparition gave differing descriptions of its appearance. Such discrepancies led G.N.M. Tyrell, in his book titled "Apparitions" published in 1943, to the conclusion that the percipient's mental processes contributed to what was reported as perceived by the percipient. In fact, it seemed that the agent's mental processes may have acted only as a trigger, which then caused the mental processes of the percipient to formulate what was reported as seen by the percipient.

The question arises how it may be possible for a percipient to experience vision without objective causation, and in particular to see an apparition, which has no physical existence. A possible modus operandi may follow from the consideration of normal vision. Vision depends on the formation of an image of a physical object on the retina of the eye, from where optical nerve signals convey the information to the occipital region of the brain for interpretation. Only after such interpretation has taken place, can one become consciously aware of the object being seen. A likely causative factor in perceiving apparitions is an extrasensory signal or message, picked up by the unconscious mind, which then causes nerve signals to be generated and delivered to the occipital region of the brain, where these signals are interpreted as signals arriving from the retina would normally be interpreted. This way the percipient could undergo visual experiences without any objective causation. Such experiences may be termed "hallucinations", which are not just imagination, but may well be the result of induced neural processes in the brain.

Much the same way, it seems possible to hear, smell, taste, and to feel being touched, in response to extrasensory signals or messages, picked up by the unconscious mind, and appropriate nerve signals delivered to the relevant parts of the brain, without any physical causative factors being involved.

It may be helpful to recall, as discussed in Chapter 8, that information acquired through extrasensory perception, in the large majority of cases, may be described as intuitive, that is, the information simply crossing from the unconscious mind into consciousness, so that the percipient suddenly knows, much the same way as forgotten information is recalled. Alternatively, the extrasensory information acquisition may occur in the sleep state, in the form of a realistic dream. However, in a relatively small number of cases, the information transfer from the unconscious to the conscious is aided by hallucinatory experiences.

The hallucinatory experiences of percipients may conveniently be divided into three categories: firstly "visual", that is apparitions with or without delivering voice messages, secondly "auditory", entailing only voice messages or other noises, and thirdly "sensuous", comprising of experiences involving the remaining senses, that is: smell, taste, touch, and also emotions, feelings, or ideas, to the exclusion of any visual or auditory experiences.

Based on the extensive work done at the Duke University Parapsychology Laboratory, and elsewhere, it appears that approximately 10% of all extrasensory perception cases entail hallucinations. Of these, around 30% are visual, 50% auditory, and 20% sensuous.

The large majority of visual experiences, around 80%, involve the percipients seeing the apparitions of incarnate agents, who are physically alive, or in the process of dying, and only about 20% involve the apparitions of discarnate agents, who are already dead.

Study of the apparitions of incarnate agents indicates that the phenomenon could be initiated either by the agent, or by the percipient. In some cases, an agent has a wish to communicate with a percipient, to whom the apparition of the agent appears, and may, but not necessarily does, deliver a veridical message, without the agent being consciously aware of this taking place. In other cases, the percipient has a desire to obtain some information from the agent, with the same result as above, and once more without the agent's conscious knowledge. In fact, occasionally an agent was found to be engaged in some totally unrelated conscious activity, at the time when her or his apparition was seen by a percipient. In both of the above cases, the appearance of the apparition seems to serve the purpose of aiding the communication between the percipient and the agent. While most of the cases involve the apparitions of living agents, apparitions of discarnate agents cannot be ignored. In these cases the source of the apparition could still be the unconscious mind of a living agent, who had known the deceased, the apparition of whom is seen by the percipient. Alternatively, the process could possibly take place through retrocognition. Nonetheless, discarnate agents being directly responsible cannot be dismissed with certainty.

A special case of hallucinatory experiences is met in "haunted houses". Haunted premises appear to act as focal points for extrasensory signals or messages, most probably originating and directed from the unconscious minds of incarnate agents, who experienced significant events which have occurred in the haunted house sometime in the past. Such events may have involved past residents in the house, who have since died. Anyone, who is sensitive to such extrasensory messages, may pick up those messages upon entering or staying in the haunted house, and unconsciously create hallucinatory experiences which may be visual, auditory, or sensuous, that is olfactory, somatic, and so on. This way, a sensitive individual entering a haunted house may see apparitions of the living or the dead, hear voices or inarticulate noises, experience bad smells, and feel cold or pain. Here again, while the source of the experiences is likely to be a living agent, the possibility of discarnate agents being responsible should be taken into consideration, and not dismissed altogether.

Such experiences would not be physically detectable by instruments, unless either the agent, or the percipient, or both jointly, produce psychokinetic effects at the same time. One example of such effects is "spirit photography", where attempts by the percipient to photograph an apparition can result in psychokinetic interference with the camera, leading to "spirit photos". These are often little more than blurred patches, but can also be meaningful images. Likewise, attempts to record paranormal sounds or voices on tape, may result in psychokinetically produced, distorted but recognisable voice fragments.

In conclusion, apparitions seem to be primarily products of the unconscious mind of the living. In the relatively small number of cases apparently involving discarnate agents, the information could possibly still be acquired through extrasensory perception from the unconscious mind of a living agent, or the collective unconscious, and then the percipient would unconsciously hallucinate the discarnate agent into a visual impression, for the purpose of conveying a message to the percipient's conscious mind. But, as stated above, the existence of discarnate agents cannot be definitely ruled out, and so apparitions are at least suggestive of the existence of surviving minds beyond bodily death.

Before leaving the subject of apparitions, it may be appropriate here to draw attention to the similarities between apparitions and the human aura. As the work described in Chapter 4 failed to show that the aura is of physical origin, it appears that people who report "seeing" auras are picking up extrasensory messages from the minds of the subjects whose auras are seen, and that the viewer's mental processes construct the aura as a visual impression, the same way as is the case with apparitions. The ultimate result of seeing the aura is an enhanced telepathic information transfer from the subject to the viewer.

Chapter 11 – Survival Related Phenomena

Mediumistic Messages

Modern spiritualism, as it is known in our time, had its beginnings around 1850. Since the late 1800s, spiritualism has been the subject of extensive scientific investigations. Before considering these investigations, a brief review of spiritualistic principles may be helpful. According to these principles, some aspects of the human personality survive the death of the physical body, and "pass over" to a disembodied or discarnate state of existence.

Spiritualists hold that the human being consists of three aspects, namely the "body", the "soul", and the "spirit". Following the death of the body, the soul and the spirit survive, the soul being the immaterial equivalent of the physical body, whose role is to act as a vehicle for the spirit. If such a vehicle exists, investigators would prefer to call it a "mind body".

Under favourable conditions, the "passed over" can manifest through gifted psychics who possess special abilities enabling them to act as "mediums" of communication, also called as "channelers", functioning as message bearers between the incarnate and the discarnate.

Mediums may be one of two kinds, namely "mental" and "physical". The process of communication through a mental medium is claimed to involve up to four entities:

- The "communicator" is the discarnate entity from whom the message originates.
- The "control" is a discarnate entity passing the message to a mental medium.
- The "mental medium" is the incarnate individual verbally delivering the message.
- The "sitter" is the incarnate individual to whom the message is delivered.

It is thought that some communicators may develop the ability of passing messages directly through the medium, in which case no control would be needed.

Mental mediums appear to function in different ways.

The "clairvoyant medium" claims to see and hear the discarnate.

The "automatist" claims that part of her or his body is controlled by discarnate agency, such as the hands in automatic writing, or the vocal cords in automatic speaking.

The "trance medium" appears to have her or his body fully taken over and controlled by a discarnate entity. Such a medium usually claims to be totally unaware of the proceedings.

Physical mediums are referred to as such, because through their psychokinetic abilities they can produce message bearing physical manifestations, for example voice messages not originating from any identifiable physical source, that may convey meaningful information ostensibly from a discarnate source.

Mediumistic messages were first investigated, relying on scientific methodology, toward the end of the 19th century, by members of the then newly established psychical research societies in England and America, and such investigations were continued over the past hundred years by many others.

The usual explanations, such as fraud, coincidence, hypnosis, and multiple personalities on part of the medium, were all closely examined. In the end, spiritualism was often found to convey highly accurate messages, inexplicable in terms of any generally recognised principles, and so seemed to support the survival hypothesis.

Particularly impressive were the so-called "cross correspondences", a term referring to the acquisition of complex information through a number of different mediums, in disjointed, meaningless segments, which only when assembled yielded a meaningful whole, apparently originating from a particular communicator.

However, as the number of investigated cases grew, it was found that at times ostensibly discarnate communicators were, in fact, physically alive at the time of the communication. Furthermore, they were consciously absorbed in some activity, and totally unaware of their unconscious mind being the source of the communication taking place. The medium was likewise ignorant of the fact that the communication came from an incarnate source. Such cases suggest that the unconscious mind of the living may assume the role of a discarnate communicator, without the knowledge of the conscious mind. This type of phenomenon casts doubt on the survival value of mediumistic communications.

The very existence of extrasensory perception makes the origins of mediumistic message questionable as well. If the mind is capable of acquiring information from other minds without any reliance on the senses, and it is also able to acquire information relating to past, present, and future events, then the contents of all unconscious minds, at times referred to as the collective unconscious, could be expected to be a collection of all information there is, past, present, and future. This reservoir of information could possibly be the source of mediumistic communications. However, securing the correct information would require a selectivity of enormous magnitude, which could prove less probable than survival itself.

Poltergeist Manifestations

Poltergeist activities are essentially psychokinetic phenomena, and were already considered in Chapter 9 on psychokinesis. These phenomena are included here primarily for the sake of completeness.

The word poltergeist is of German origin, often translated as "noisy spirit", but perhaps "rampant spirit" would be a more appropriate translation.

The phenomenon includes various kinds of physical disturbances without any detectable objective causes. The most frequent occurrences involve the movements of physical objects, which may be soft or violent, and at times may involve very heavy articles. Less frequently, sound effects are observed such as knocks or raps, and also noises resembling explosions. Sound effects accompanying the movement of objects are often inconsistent. For example, the soft landing of a light object may be accompanied by a very loud crashing sound. On record are also flashes of light, spontaneous ignition, and apparent dematerialisation and re-materialisation of physical objects. The disturbances at a given location are of relatively short duration as a rule, of the order of a few months. Recorded outbreaks go back at least as far as a thousand years.

During the latter half of the 20th century, the phenomenon has undergone extensive study. As a result, it now appears that the disturbances centre around incarnate agents, frequently adolescents, or young adults, with psychological problems. The agent is not consciously aware of his or her involvement as a rule. So, one seems to deal with unconscious cases of psychokinesis that appear to be unpredictably repetitive. The phenomenon was accordingly coined "recurrent spontaneous psychokinesis". It is notable that the manifestations are

Chapter 11 — Survival Related Phenomena

very similar to those produced in the vicinity of "physical mediums", the poltergeist agent seemingly acting as a temporary physical medium.

As a result of work done by William Roll at the Psychical Research Foundation in North Carolina, and by other investigators, certain regularities have emerged.

The number of events appears to fall off exponentially with the distance from the agent. Affected objects tend to follow arcs with the agent approximately at the centre. Objects further away from the agent move longer distances than those closer, as points would on a rotating beam pivoted at the agent's location. There is a tendency for objects and areas to be repeatedly affected, referred to as "object focussing" and "area focussing" respectively.

The involvement of discarnate agents was originally assumed. Some people still consider that poltergeist phenomena may involve discarnate agents, acting in association with the unconscious mind of the living agent. However, since the only indications for this are the observed phenomena that could fully originate from the unconscious mind of the incarnate agent, most of the investigators nowadays consider this to be the case. Thus, poltergeist manifestations may be regarded as rather questionable support for the survival hypothesis.

Near Death Experiences

It has been often reported that individuals, who are revived after being "clinically dead" for a short period as a result of illness, surgery, or accident, often describe a state of discarnate existence. This normally involves passing through a "tunnel" into a "brilliant light". Occasionally they report meeting discarnate beings, that is, beings who are physically dead at the time. Upon revival they often report having returned with reluctance only, because of some unfinished task in the physical realm. Again, extrasensory messages causing neural brain activity could be an explanation, but these seem possible only if clinical death is not synonymous with brain death. The fact that upon revival not all clinically dead recall such an experience, does not rule out near death experiences being supportive of the survival hypothesis. Total disbelief by the revived clinically dead may act as an inhibitory factor.

Deathbed Observations

Some people, when close to death, make utterances suggestive of post mortem existence, and in particular claim to see apparitions. A particular study carried out by the American Society for Psychical Research involved 1708 medical personnel, physicians and nurses, 1004 in the United States, and 704 in India. Detailed interview schedules were produced for 877 cases, which were then computer evaluated.

The object of the study was to ascertain whether these phenomena are in general attributable to confused hallucinations, conditioned by such factors as desires, expectations, inner conflicts, cultural and religious upbringing, emotional and mental preoccupation preceding the death, and medical factors known to affect mentality.

However, numerous cases were found where patients coming from widely different cultural and religious backgrounds, and whose minds were unimpaired and clear to the end, reported seeing visions, which were free of this world's concerns, and also of religious next world expectations, and yet strongly suggestive of the survival hypothesis.

In particular, it was found that in about 80% of the cases where the subject died within ten minutes of seeing an apparition, the latter did come, as reported by the subject, for the definite purpose of taking her or him away to another state of existence. This cannot be attributed to a desire to die, since in a number of cases the subject was observed to be rather unwilling to being taken away into an unfamiliar and questionable state of existence.

Such observations suggest that people when close to death, not only exhibit a gradually increasing loss of awareness of physical reality, but that they also exhibit a heightened sensitivity to extrasensory signals or messages which may be of discarnate origin. Thus, it appears that some cases of deathbed observations are indicative of existence beyond death.

Deathbed observations are also suggestive of exteriorisation occurring at the time of dying. An early researcher, Duncan McDougall, claimed that a weight loss of the order of grams took place at the time of death. This appears to tie in with claims by some subjects, that when undergoing an out of body experience, they perceive a slight gravitational drag. If these claims were to be true, they would entail important implications for the universe, which will be considered in the next chapter.

Apparent Past Life Memories

Some people recall memories that are incompatible with their present lives. Such memories seem to support the age-old idea of reincarnation. The term reincarnation is normally interpreted to mean an aspect of the human personality, after physical death, re-entering into a newly born physical body of an infant. Reincarnation appears in ancient Egyptian and Greek writings, Plato in particular, also in some early Christian esoteric writings, and is firmly accepted by many eastern religions.

Recent investigations fall into two categories, namely: the critical examination of case histories, and hypnotic regression techniques.

During the latter half of the 20th century, considerable investigations were carried out on case histories by Ian Stevenson and his associates at the University of Virginia. It was suggested that three kinds of cases should be distinguished, namely those of the "adult", the "suppressed child", and the "permitted child".

In the typical adult case, the subject has dreams with contents which cannot be reconciled with the experiences of her or his present life. They depict an earlier time in history, and if the subject follows these up with systematic search for a corresponding historical setting, further memories may emerge. Eventually, the subject may have the feeling that she or he lived in that period before. However, since past life memories are mixed with present life experiences, adult cases have questionable value for the investigator.

A child, on the other hand, may suddenly start giving vivid descriptions of previous experiences, totally incompatible with the child's present life, as soon as the child is able to express herself or himself. The child's very first words may be the names of people not belonging to the child's present family. If confused parents actively discourage these manifestations, the result is a case of a suppressed child. By the time the case becomes available to investigations, it may have limited value, owing to the interaction of past life memories with present life experiences.

Chapter 11 – Survival Related Phenomena

In the case of a permitted child, the parents allow free expression, and may even encourage it. If such a case is brought to the attention of researchers at an early stage, valuable work may be done. All the memories of the child would be carefully recorded, and then a search undertaken for the people and places the child is recalling.

In a number of cases matching people and places have been located and identified, to a degree well beyond expectable chance coincidences.

Hypnotic regression techniques led some psychologists and psychiatrists to consider reincarnation seriously, when occasionally patients were found troubled by memories seemingly originating from previous lives. The question arises, as to what extent such cases may be attributed to multiple personalities, or genuine past life memories filtering through.

A hypnotic regression investigation needs to be guided by both technical and ethical considerations. The subject must be carefully chosen, to be able to undergo deep trance states, and to tolerate ambiguity and confusion. Care must be taken to leave any repressed memories from the present life to remain so. The subject should never be allowed to linger over unpleasant experiences, but should be induced to move backwards or forwards along the time track, so as to view such experiences from a distance. Of course, leading questions must be totally avoided, as such would result in false fantasies. There is always the danger of inducing secondary or multiple personalities, having traits similar to those emerging during regression. To minimise this, the subject must always be taken back to the present slowly, never suddenly.

The following case may serve as an example. In 1973 the Medical Committee of the Toronto Society for Psychical Research undertook a hypnotic regression investigation. A carefully chosen subject had undergone 100 hours of sessions over a period of a year, followed by monitoring for possible ill effects for another year. This particular investigation yielded six identifiable apparent past personalities, the earliest one dating back to the times of Ancient Egypt.

However, in some hypnotic regression cases, personalities may emerge that are eventually identified to be those of some other currently living incarnate individuals. So, information extracted from the unconscious mind of a living agent, can appear as a past life memory of a subject under hypnotic regression. Nevertheless, careful analysis should enable the investigators to distinguish between the two, to a fair degree of certainty.

While past life memories are real, their origin is questionable. Once again, as with mediumistic messages, the source of these memories can possibly be the unconscious minds of incarnate individuals, or the collective unconscious, from where such memories could be extracted through the mechanism of extrasensory perception. Yet, a large number of cases remain suggestive of reincarnation, and so supportive of the survival hypothesis.

During the past century, much discussion has taken place questioning as to what extent personality or character is inherited from parents genetically, or is acquired via nurturing by parents and society. Lately it has been claimed that to a significant extent, character is not attributable to either, but appears to be a result of random selection. This suggests that personality and character may well come from three sources, firstly inherited genetically, secondly acquired through nurturing, and thirdly coming from past life experiences.

In particular, exceptional aptitudes at a very young age in the arts and sciences, or a high level of moral development displayed in early childhood, especially if such is not exhibited by the child's parents or the child's environment, may possibly originate from past life experiences. In general, it appears that for most people one lifetime is totally inadequate for achieving a high level of moral development, pointing to the possibility of reincarnation serving an essential role in the moral progress of the individual.

In conclusion, let it be reiterated that while survival related phenomena do not lend themselves to precise statistical evaluation, the possible validity of the survival hypothesis is based on the careful examination of many meticulously observed, well documented, and systematically analysed case histories. When a large number of case histories are examined meticulously, and are found to have persistently recurring common characteristics, one no longer relies on anecdotal information accepted blindly, but deals with objectively accumulated scientific evidence. Such evidence suggests that the survival hypothesis cannot be dismissed with certainty, even though extrasensory perception and psychokinesis may often offer feasible alternative explanations. Rather, the sum total of the evidence is highly suggestive of survival beyond bodily death being a reality.

Chapter 12
Parallel Universes

In the early 1900s communications by radio and telepathy were both new concepts. It was rather expectable that explanations for telepathy would be sought in terms of information transmission by means of electromagnetic waves. It was thought that the agent's brain acted as a radio transmitter, and the percipient's brain functioned as a radio receiver.

Sheet metal, especially if earthed, can act as a shield against electromagnetic waves. This suggests that an obvious way to test whether telepathic information transfer took place by means of electromagnetic waves, was to place a percipient inside a solid walled metallic cage, with an agent situated outside the cage, and examine if telepathic messages from the agent could get through to the percipient in the cage, at a statistically significant level.

The Soviet Union, founded on the principles of Marxist materialistic philosophy, which totally rejected the existence of anything beyond the physical, would tolerate investigations into telepathy only on the basis that it could be explained in physical terms. It is therefore not surprising that pioneering work along such lines took place in the Soviet Union, in the early 1930s, at a university in St. Petersburg, then called Leningrad, by a researcher named Leonid Vasiliev and his associates.

A thick walled metal cage was constructed with all seams welded, except the bottom. The cage was then lowered onto a metal base, the bottom edges of the cage fitting into mercury filled grooves in the base, and so forming an all around complete metallic seal. Agents then attempted to pass telepathic messages from outside the cage, to percipients inside the cage. Subsequently, the experiments were repeated exactly the same way, except that the metal cage was replaced by a wooden box.

Not only did the messages pass through the metallic walls of the cage, as clearly indicated by statistically significant results, but also there was no statistically significant difference between the results obtained with the metal cage and the wooden box. Thus, this indicated that metallic shielding did not present an obstacle to the passage of telepathic messages, and so argued against electromagnetic waves being the message carriers.

However, the walls of metal cages are not necessarily able to totally block electromagnetic waves from passing through. In fact, electromagnetic waves penetrate into solid metal, but the intensity, or what is the same the amplitude, of the waves diminishes with the depth of penetration. The attenuation of the waves at a given depth of penetration increases with the frequency of the waves, and also with the conductivity and permeability of the metal. The conductivity is a measure of the metal's ability to pass electric currents, and the permeability is a measure of the metal's ability of being magnetised when exposed to magnetic fields. As a result of the interplay of these attributes, iron is a more effective shielding material than, for example, aluminium or copper. One might consider the shielding to be effective, if the amplitude of the electromagnetic wave passing through the shield is 1% of that entering it. If the frequency of the waves is 1,000,000 cycles per second, then the thickness of the iron shielding, having typical values for conductivity and permeability, which attenuates the amplitude of the wave down to 1%, works out to 0.07 millimetre. But, if the frequency of the waves is electric power mains frequency, typically 50 cycles per second, then using the same iron material, attenuation to 1% requires 10 millimetres thick iron shielding.

It follows that, the effective shielding out of electromagnetic waves is feasible at higher frequencies only. This has forced the proponents of electromagnetic wave transmission for telepathy to consider lower frequencies. However, one then runs into another difficulty.

The effective transmission of electromagnetic waves at lower frequencies requires very large transmitting and receiving antennas, up to kilometres in length. So, those adhering to explanations of telepathy in terms of electromagnetic waves proposed that the human brain perhaps can act as a "folded" antenna, equivalent to linear antennas in the kilometre range.

The foregoing discussion has been included here to illustrate where attempts to explain paranormal phenomena in terms of the current state of scientific knowledge may lead, simply because of unwillingness on the part of orthodox science to accept that telepathy may exist in spite of the fact that its modus operandi cannot be explained in terms of the prevailing state of scientific knowledge.

While, historically speaking, telepathy may have been the first to emerge, it was soon followed by clairvoyance and precognition, that is extrasensory information acquisition relating to objects and events, be it present, past, or future, the existence of which was indicated by numerous statistically significant test results. Thus, the question arose if electromagnetic waves could possibly account for extrasensory information acquisition about physical objects, and also about events be it past, present, or future.

The conclusion appears to be that accounting for extrasensory perception in terms of electromagnetic waves, or in terms of any other currently known physical principles is untenable, and that one deals with phenomena apparently lying outside the four-dimensional space-time continuum, which constitutes the physical universe as it is currently understood.

It has also been attempted, to explain psychokinetic phenomena in purely physical terms. Explanations often rely on bioelectricity and biomagnetism, that is, biologically produced electric and magnetic fields. Biologically produced electric fields could exert forces on objects that bear induced electrical charges, much the same way as physically produced electric fields do. Likewise, biologically created magnetic fields could produce forces of attraction on objects containing magnetisable materials.

However, such biologically produced electric or magnetic fields would also be blocked, or at least reduced, through appropriate interposed shielding. Many psychokinesis experiments were carried out, with the objects of the experiment placed inside well-shielded enclosures. An example is the author's piezoelectric crystal experiment described in Chapter 9. Such experiments indicate that psychokinetic effects cannot be blocked through shielding of any kind. Thus, psychokinesis seems to be unexplainable in biological terms.

It could be that some types of psychokinesis involve interference by the mind with the gravitational field in that the object is situated. If this were the case, then one would expect shielding to be ineffective, since gravitational fields appear to pass through all physical barriers. In fact, if the mind were capable of suitably modulating the gravitational field at the location of a subject, who in turn would respond to such variation in the field, then telepathy could also be explainable this way. However, such abilities of the mind, whether alone or in conjunction with the brain, would still amount to psychokinetic interaction with physical processes, and as such would still constitute paranormal phenomena.

Chapter 12 – Parallel Universes

It would seem from the foregoing discussion that paranormal phenomena, in particular both extrasensory perception and psychokinesis, operate outside the currently known physical universe. This then suggests, that there may exist either a "non-physical" extension to the currently recognised four-dimensional space-time physical universe, or there could exist a "non-physical universe", or even several "non-physical universes", in parallel with the currently known physical universe. These universes would be expected to interpenetrate, but not normally interact with each other. In what follows, the existence of at least one non-physical parallel universe will be assumed, and referred to as "the non-physical universe".

It may now be opportune at this stage to recall the dual nature of the mind, the conscious and unconscious minds prevailing as distinguishable entities, and operating in a somewhat complementary way. Furthermore, as stated previously, paranormal phenomena cannot be produced by conscious will as a rule, but such phenomena usually result from the random activities of the unconscious mind. At the same time, paranormal phenomena do not fit into the physical universe, but rather appear to operate via the parallel non-physical universe.

These considerations suggest the conclusion that the conscious mind is an entity that enables operation in, and interaction with, the physical universe, while the unconscious mind is capable of functioning in, and interacting with, the non-physical universe.

Telepathy would then entail the extrasensory transfer of information between the conscious minds of individuals in the physical universe, say from the conscious mind of person A to the conscious mind of person B. The path followed by such information transfer appears to be from the conscious mind of A to the unconscious mind of A, then from the unconscious mind of A, via a non-physical link in the non-physical universe, to the unconscious mind of B, and finally from the unconscious mind of B to the conscious mind of B.

It appears that all unconscious minds can exchange information by the above mechanism, through non-physical links connecting them in the non-physical universe. The sum total of all unconscious minds so linked may be referred to as the "collective unconscious".

It also appears that the collective unconscious in the non-physical universe contains all information there is, about objects and events in the physical universe, be it past, present, or future. This implies that time, as experienced in the physical universe, does not apply in the non-physical universe. Information acquisition via clairvoyance, precognition, or retrocognition, is then a matter of an ability of extracting information from the collective unconscious in the non-physical universe, and its transfer to the conscious mind. Psychics are people possessing such abilities. The extent of such abilities may vary in the same psychic from time to time, and of course varies greatly from one psychic to another.

One may be tempted to consider that information transmission in the non-physical universe takes place by some kind of waves, as it happens in the physical universe by means of sound waves or electromagnetic waves. This idea would appear to be supported by the fact that, as discussed in Chapter 3, electromagnetic waves do not require a medium for their propagation. Nevertheless, electromagnetic waves are physically detectable, travel at finite speed, and require finite time to cover a given distance.

This begs the question, whether extrasensory message transfer between minds, likewise needs finite time. A finite time requirement for telepathic information transmission has not been found to exist. In any case, the question would have to be asked, how a finite time requirement could apply to information transfer from the future to the present in the physical universe, as it occurs in the case of precognition. The existence of time in the non-physical universe does not seem to lend itself to meaningful discussion within the prevailing state of science as applicable to the physical universe.

A rather simplistic hypothetical attempt to depict the relation between the physical and non-physical universes is suggested in Figure 12.1. For simplicity, the three dimensions of physical space have been merged into one dimension, which could be thought of as the displacement from the origin, with its direction specified or unspecified. Time then can be shown as a second dimension. This way the physical universe can be depicted as the top plane in Figure 12.1, while the bottom plane then represents the non-physical universe.

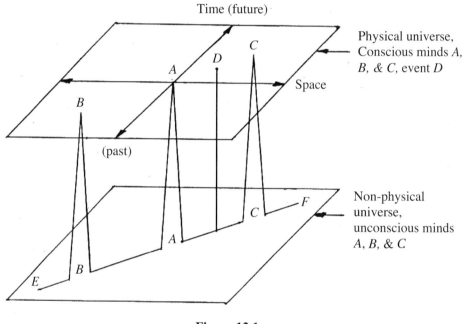

Figure 12.1

Conscious mind A in the present, may obtain information from conscious minds B and C, relating to past, present, or future events in the physical universe, from anywhere in the physical universe, via an unconscious link EF in the non-physical universe. Likewise conscious mind A in the present, may acquire information about an object or an event, past, present, or future, from anywhere in the physical universe, via unconscious links in the non-physical universe. In Figure 12.1, point D refers to a future event, and the information ostensibly comes from the collective unconscious, along the non-physical link EF.

As psychokinesis is essentially an interaction between mind and matter, an insight into psychokinetic phenomena may be facilitated by an understanding of the structure of matter. It may thus be helpful at this point to recall Chapter 2, and in particular the discussion on the atomic structure of matter. An atom model, based on a nucleus surrounded by orbiting particles, was proposed early in the 20th century. By the 1930s, it was generally accepted that atoms were built of three fundamental subatomic particles, namely the proton carrying a positive electrical charge, the neutron possessing zero electrical charge, and the electron carrying a negative electrical charge, which was equal in magnitude to that of the proton. It appeared that the atomic nucleus consisted of a number of protons and neutrons, which was orbited by as many electrons as there were protons in the nucleus. So, in any atom the total positive charge equalled the total negative charge, and thus the atom was electrically neutral.

It was also found that, as unlike charges attract each other, the negative electrons were kept in orbits around the positive nucleus by the electric force of attraction between them, much the same way as the planets are kept in orbits around the sun by the gravitational force of. attraction. Further, it was found that the masses of the proton and the neutron were nearly equal, and both were some 1820 times heavier than the electron.

Also, since the positively charged protons repel each other, it would seem that an atomic nucleus containing a number of protons should not be possible. However, if the distance between protons is reduced below a critical value, the electrical repulsive forces appear to be overridden by strong nuclear attractive forces, which enable protons and neutrons to be combined into a stable atomic nucleus.

As discussed in Chapter 2, the early investigations into atomic structure indicated that the positive nuclei are confined to a small region at the centre of the atoms, and that the sizes of the atoms essentially equal the diameters of the outermost orbits carrying electrons. This in turn suggests that the sizes of the subatomic constituents are small compared with the sizes of the atoms. Consequently the atom, and matter built up of atoms, including solid matter, is expected to be largely empty space, with the subatomic particles occupying only a small fraction of this space. Yet charged subatomic particles, such as protons or electrons, cannot readily penetrate this space, because of the electrical repulsive forces exerted on them by charged subatomic particles within the atoms. Penetration by charged particles is possible only if they have high kinetic energy, and approach the atoms at high speed.

On the other hand, electrically neutral particles, such as the neutrons, can readily penetrate into atoms, or solid matter, because they are not subject to electrical repulsive forces. The penetration of an atom by neutrons is a process similar to the penetration of the solar system by meteorites and comets, with the relatively small gravitational effects on them ignored.

In a number of cases, involving poltergeist outbreaks or physical mediums, it was claimed that solid objects contained inside a box were observed to have passed through the solid wall of the box to the outside. Now solids, liquids, and gases, and even electrically charged subatomic particles, are confined to remain inside a solid walled enclosure because the subatomic particles of the atoms and molecules, making up the walls of the enclosure, and also the contents of the enclosure, carry electrical charges.

Any attempt by the atoms or molecules of the contents of the enclosure to penetrate the solid walls of the enclosure would be opposed by electrical forces of repulsion between like charges, that is between the atomic nuclei in the contents and the walls of the enclosure, and also between the orbiting electrons in the contents and the walls of the enclosure.

As stated above, in atoms the number of positively charged protons in the nucleus always equals the number of negatively charged electrons orbiting the nucleus, so that the overall charge of the atom is zero, that is, the atom is electrically neutral, provided that the atom has not lost or gained electrons through the process of ionisation.

Suppose now that the unconscious mind had the ability to psychokinetically dismantle the atoms of the contents in an enclosure, and combine each nuclear proton with an orbital electron into an electrically neutral particle, essentially a neutron, then these neutral particles could easily pass through the walls of the enclosure. Further, if the unconscious mind were capable to perform the reverse process outside the enclosure, then this would amount to passing the contents through the solid walls of the enclosure, thus resulting in the apparent dematerialisation of the contents inside the enclosure, and their re-materialisation outside the enclosure. The term "apparent" was used since conversion into a stream of neutrons would not strictly amount to dematerialisation, as neutrons are physically existing particles.

As mentioned in previous chapters, dematerialisation and re-materialisation of physical objects, and also of organisms, even human beings, have been reported from time to time by a considerable number of observers, some of whom would have to be regarded as reliable. Such observations have been made during poltergeist activities, and also in the presence of physical mediums. While there is no proof for dematerialisation and re-materialisation ever having definitely taken place, the possibility that such phenomena may exist should not be dismissed out of hand.

If dematerialisation and re-materialisation does take place, then it is more likely that matter is dismantled into much smaller entities than protons, neutrons, or electrons, possibly into neutrino-like entities, having zero electrical charge and zero, or near zero, mass. Neutrinos, as mentioned before in Chapter 2, have no electrical charge, and their mass, if any, is either equal to, or less than, that of an electron. While neutrinos are not considered constituents of atoms, there is some evidence that radioactive decomposition of matter leads to neutrinos indirectly. Radioactivity may result in the emission of free neutrons, which appear to decay into protons, electrons, and neutrinos, on the average in about 1000 seconds.

It is not suggested here that dematerialisation results in neutrinos, but rather that it may lead to neutrino-like entities having no electrical charge, and also either no mass, or very small mass. Such entities could easily pass through solid walls of any enclosure just as actual neutrinos would. Reassembly of these entities outside the enclosure would then amount to re-materialisation. In so far as such constituent entities are not detectable by any physical means, they could be regarded as non-physical, and situated outside the physical universe.

The constituent subatomic particles of the atoms, for some time following their discovery, were considered fundamental, indivisible, and the only constituents of matter. However, as investigations progressed, involving the collisions between atoms and subatomic particles accelerated in magnetic fields to very high speeds, hundreds of additional particles, akin to the above three, came to be discovered and identified. Most of these additional particles were found to be unstable, and consequently possess temporary existence only.

Further, recent investigations suggest that the heavier subatomic particles, such as the proton and the neutron, are not fundamental, but are composed of yet smaller constituent entities called "quarks", which are essentially mathematical concepts. It may eventually turn out that the electron is not fundamental either, but that it is also further divisible into smaller constituents. Thus, as advancing knowledge allows ever-finer subdivision of matter, matter seems to virtually disappear, and dissolve into little more than mathematical concepts.

If a physical object, or a living organism, were to dematerialise, followed by subsequent re-materialisation, it would seem to temporarily disappear from the physical universe. The protons, neutrons and electrons would appear to be dismantled into constituent entities that no longer possess physical existence, and so they are situated outside the four-dimensional continuum constituting the physical universe. Furthermore, as re-materialisation amounts to reassembly in the same form as the object or organism existed prior to dematerialisation, a "blue print" of the object or organism would have to exist outside the physical universe, that would enable the exact reproduction of the object or organism upon re-materialisation.

One could devise experiments, run along similar lines as the psychokinesis tests described in Chapter 9, a subject being given the task to attempt mentally to reduce the weight of a physical object, which was placed in a well-shielded environment, while the weight of the object was monitored with microgram accuracy. Any weight loss during active periods, in comparison to control periods, could possibly be indicative of levitation, that is, it could be the result of interference with the gravitational field in which the object was situated. However, it could also be indicative of partial dematerialisation on a minute scale.

If it were true that matter, and ultimately its currently recognised smallest constituents, the proton, neutron, and electron, could be broken down further, by psychokinetic activities or otherwise, into entities which are no longer physically detectable, then it may be possible that these entities could act as building blocks for a non-physical, or a parallel, universe. These non-physical building blocks could be held together by non-physical forces to form larger composite entities, much the same way as protons, neutrons, and electrons are held together by nuclear and electrical forces in the physical universe, thereby forming larger composite physical and biological entities. The contents of the non-physical universe, including these larger composite entities, could then interpenetrate with physical and biological matter in the physical universe, without producing detectable physical effects.

The composite entities in the non-physical universe could be inanimate, or possibly animate carrying consciousness and intelligence. The human mind, both conscious and unconscious, and its vehicle if it needed any, could be just some of these composite entities in the non-physical universe.

It may be helpful at this stage to draw attention to an as yet unresolved discrepancy existing between the two major theories of physics, namely the theory of relativity and the quantum theory. On the one hand, the theory of relativity appears to explain satisfactorily large scale effects in the physical universe involving the galaxies and the intergalactic space, while on the other hand, quantum mechanics successfully accounts for the structure of the atoms, and subatomic phenomena in general.

However, attempts to unify these two theories into a single comprehensive theory appear to lead to inconsistencies. While no attempt can be made here to consider the complex mathematical nature of these inconsistencies, it may be of great significance, that some of the many attempts to unify the two theories, and also attempts to gain insight into the origins of the physical universe, have led to the consideration of the existence of multidimensional continua, involving 10 dimensions or more, in parallel with the physical universe.

Chapter 12 – Parallel Universes

An insight as to how extra dimensions could play a role in paranormal phenomena may be gained from the following simple hypothetical example. Let it be supposed that conscious biological entities could exist in two-dimensional space, namely a plane, with time being a third dimension. Any communication between such entities, taking place outside the plane, that is, in a third dimension of space perpendicular to the plane, would appear extrasensory to such entities. Likewise, any transfer of a two-dimensional object between two points in the plane, but outside the plane in a third dimension of space, that is, in a direction perpendicular to the plane, would appear to such entities as dematerialisation at one point, and re-materialisation at another point in the plane.

While a multidimensional continuum, extending beyond the familiar four-dimensional space-time continuum of the currently known physical universe, is hard to visualise, it can be readily handled mathematically.

Whether a realm exists in the form of a parallel universe, constructed from non-physical building blocks, or such a realm takes the form of a multidimensional hyperspace extending beyond the known physical universe, or indeed, whether its existence rests on a combination of both, or any other unknown principles, such a non-physical universe can account for all the paranormal phenomena that are claimed to have been observed, or experienced.

Extrasensory perception, as already discussed in the foregoing, may possibly be explainable as information exchange between the conscious and unconscious minds, coupled with information transmission between unconscious minds via links in the non-physical universe.

Psychokinesis appears to be an interaction between the unconscious mind of an agent and matter, or a physical or biological process. It entails the appearance of physical forces and physical energy in the physical universe, which are not traceable to a physical origin. The unconscious mind is unlikely to be the source of these forces and energy, but rather it is likely to act as a catalyst, facilitating the transfer of energy from the non-physical universe to the physical universe.

As stated earlier, extrasensory perception and psychokinesis may operate in conjunction with each other, the conscious mind being directed to the information acquired through extrasensory perception, by the unconscious mind causing physical manifestations.

Dematerialisation is the disassembly of matter, including material objects, or biological organisms, into physically undetectable constituents, that could be constituents of subatomic particles, namely: the proton, the neutron, and the electron.

Re-materialisation is the reassembly of such non-physical constituents into the original material objects, or biological organisms. Reassembly at a different physical location would amount to teleportation.

It may be appropriate at this point, to mention the numerous claims by many people of encountering "unidentifiable flying objects". Some people believe such objects to be of extraterrestrial origin. Others reject this possibility on the grounds that the interstellar space is so large, that even when travelling at the speed of light, it would take 100,000 years to cross the galaxy, and some two million years, to reach earth from the closest neighbouring galaxy. Therefore, it is argued, that such travel would be time-wise unfeasible.

Chapter 12 – Parallel Universes

However, it has been reported a number of times, that attempts by military aircraft to approach such objects led to the objects suddenly vanishing. There have also been many reports of such objects suddenly disappearing from radar screens. Such reports suggest, that unidentified flying objects, if they exist, perhaps can dematerialise at one location, and rematerialise at a different location, and so may be capable of travelling over vast distances via teleportation, which might not require any time at all.

Also, at times, out of a number of potential observers, some see such an unidentified flying object, and others do not, much the same way as is the case with the viewing of apparitions. This suggests that extrasensory perception phenomena may also be involved, which further hinders rational considerations.

Exteriorisation, or out of body experience, seemingly entails the mind, both conscious and unconscious, operating in the non-physical universe, resulting in consciousness functioning outside the physical body. A non-physical link between the mind and the brain is likely to be maintained, that may play a role in sustaining the physiological functioning of the body.

Death would be the final break between the brain and the mind. Following death, the mind is out of body, and functions as a discarnate entity in the non-physical universe. However, it may be the case that the mind, in the non-physical universe, still possesses an immaterial vehicle, which is sometimes referred to as the "mind body".

Reincarnation refers to the proposition of a discarnate mind establishing a new link with the brain of a newly created human being, presumably sometime after conception and before birth. If reincarnation is a reality, then it appears that at least part, if not all, of the contents of the unconscious mind is preserved, however, the new human being is apparently created with a blank conscious mind. Consideration should also be given to the proposition that reincarnation may not be limited to the confines of planet earth, but could possibly operate over a wider region of space.

Further, while on the subjects of exteriorisation and death, this may be the place to recall two statements made earlier. One is the claim by some people undergoing exteriorisation, that while out of body, they had experienced a slight gravitational pull. The other is a claim made by an early researcher that there is a small weight loss occurring at death. These observations suggest that, while electrical forces would not seem to operate in the non-physical universe, gravitational forces perhaps do.

It has been claimed in orthodox scientific circles, that the physical universe behaves as if it had far more mass distributed in it, than what is readily detectable. This extra mass has been referred to as the "dark matter". It could be worthwhile to bear in mind that, the above claims suggest the possibility of what was alluded to in the foregoing, namely that the non-physical or parallel universe could be, partly or fully, responsible for the dark matter.

It could also merit consideration that if extraterrestrial entities, or discarnate entities, or both exist, then they may from time to time interfere, either physically or psychokinetically, with developments on planet earth. Thus, while evolution is likely to operate most of the time, it may not be responsible for all developments on earth. An example of outside intervention could be the relatively sudden appearance of modern Homo sapiens on earth, arguably some 30,000 years ago.

Chapter 12 – Parallel Universes

It may be appropriate to conclude this chapter with some remarks on miracles. It would not be surprising, that some paranormal phenomena should appear miraculous to cursory observers. However, most miracles, as reported or described, are identifiable as one of the paranormal phenomena discussed in the foregoing, or a combination of a number of such phenomena. The miracles attributed to Christ in the New Testament may serve as examples.

It is not claimed here that such miracles have indisputably taken place, but nevertheless they would be identifiable as paranormal events. Thus, the prediction of the destruction of Jerusalem could have been a case of precognition. The walking on water would have been levitation. The virgin birth could have resulted from psychokinetic action originating from a discarnate source, while the resurrection may have been psychokinetic restoration of the body and reinstallation of the mind. Christ's going to heaven could have been stage managed for the benefit of the disciples, as levitation up to the clouds, followed by dematerialisation of the body, and the transfer of the mind to the non-physical universe. Of course, for Christ to perform paranormal phenomena on such a scale, would have required an extraordinary level of paranormal abilities. Judging by the New Testament, Christ also exhibited an extraordinary level of moral development.

The statement by Christ to his disciples, saying that in "his father's house there were many mansions", was obviously metaphorical. If Christ said, that his father's house was situated in a parallel universe, the disciples would have been hard put to know what he meant.

As mentioned in the foregoing, the theory of relativity and the quantum theory are not yet convincingly reconcilable. Attempts are being made continually to unify all theories into a "grand unified theory", that would explain all physical phenomena, whether on cosmic or subatomic scales, without any contradictions.

The relatively recent "big bang" theory claims that the physical universe came into being suddenly, virtually out of nothing some twelve thousand million years ago in the form of highly condensed matter and energy, and expanded ever since to its current state. This theory would be more tenable if the physical universe were considered as having emerged from a pre-existing non-physical universe. This would still leave the question about the origin of the non-physical universe, or universes, unanswered.

However, no theory will ever be complete, or unified, unless it can successfully account for all the paranormal phenomena as well.

Chapter 13
Epilogue – Moral Issues

When dealing with the paranormal, and in particular with survival related phenomena, the question arises if there is a reason for life. More precisely, what may be the reason for being born, and going through a lifetime of limited length, inevitably leading to the death of the physical body? Further, what could be the purpose of a professed existence beyond physical death as a discarnate entity, and a purported possibility of reincarnation, that is, the re-entry from a discarnate existence into a new physical body through the process of rebirth?

An explanation offering itself almost self-evidently, is that the aim of life would have to be a continual development and improvement of one's personality in at least two main respects, namely intellectually and morally. Out of these two the second, that is moral advancement, would appear to be far more important than the first, namely improvements in one's intellectual capabilities.

A requisite for intellectual progression is an attribute called intelligence, which normally means an ability to learn and understand, including the ability to apply what has been learnt and understood to new situations, so as to facilitate the solution of hitherto unsolved problems. Tests can be devised which enable intelligence to be quantified, so that the level of intelligence of different individuals can be quantitatively evaluated and compared.

On the contrary, the level of an individual's moral development, which alternatively could be referred to as an individual's level of maturity, cannot be quantified or measured, mainly because no self-evident moral code exists, and consequently as to what is morally right, or morally wrong, is largely a matter of opinion.

However, many believe in the existence of a God, who is thought to have laid down an absolute moral code, and communicated that code to humans through "prophets", who claimed to have had the special ability of receiving such communications from God. If this were so, then all prophetic insights should have led to the same moral code, which is demonstrably not the case, as any impartial examiner of prophetic messages would have to admit. It is likely that some prophets were honest, who genuinely acquired ideas about right and wrong through extrasensory perception, probably from the collective unconscious, and then put their own interpretation on the information so acquired, which they then claimed to have been inspired by God. Putting it more bluntly, whether prophets were honest, or otherwise, they were likely to have put words in the mouth of God. It is very probable that most "holy books" have come about this way.

One could approximate a valid set of moral values, by comparing the various moral codes put forward by as many diverse religions as practicable, and look for concurrences and inconsistencies. While such a comparison will not be undertaken here, one attempt of establishing a set of values of general validity will be offered for consideration. A starting point could be based on the "seven deadly sins" put forth by Thomas Aquinas as follows:

Avarice:	greed, primarily for money and power,
Pride:	overhigh opinion of oneself, haughtiness, arrogance,
Envy:	discontent, or ill will, over another's advantages,
Anger:	hostile feeling because of opposition or injury,
Gluttony:	eating more than necessary for sustenance,

Lust: uncontrolled or excessive sexual desire,
Sloth: disinclination to work, laziness.

It was attempted to list the seven sins in order of severity, avarice or greed having been regarded the worst. It is realised that such an order is subjective, and could be regarded by some as a matter of opinion. None of the above "sins" have a sharp dividing line between right and wrong. For example it may not be clear at what stage the pursuance of the fundamental human rights, namely the rights to life, liberty, and property, may become avarice, pride, or envy, and when eating for sustenance, and physical love, become gluttony and lust respectively. While none of the seven sins can be regarded as particularly grievous, they appear to be the root causes of most other moral failings, ranging from the moderate to the extreme.

There is also the problem that intelligence and maturity do not go hand in hand. In fact, a high level of intelligence often results in its possessor aiming for and succeeding in gaining advantages at the expense of others, and thereby transgressing into the domains of the seven sins. Only the attainment of a sufficient degree of maturity would enable one to counteract moral failures that advanced levels of intelligence could otherwise facilitate. In fact, much of the adversity plaguing physical existence derives from scientific progress, produced by human intelligence, operating unrestrained by a commensurate moral advancement.

The question arises if living well past the currently prevailing physical lifespan, or perhaps living forever, would enable the attainment of moral perfection. The answer to this question seems to be a definite "No". It is quite apparent that the rate of moral progress of many individuals falls off with age. Much of one's character appears to be laid in early childhood, some even claim that the first five years of physical life are the most critical. Indeed, most people retain habits acquired from their parents and others, in early childhood, throughout their life. Nevertheless, it also appears to be true that some reassessment and realignment does take place during the adolescent years, or later, which may lead to an improvement in moral values, or the opposite. Not only does the rate of moral development tend to slow down with advancing age, but in many cases it may come to a complete standstill. These considerations suggest that a steady moral advancement could only be facilitated through the process of dying and rebirth, which is a strong argument for the ostensible existence of reincarnation, and for reincarnation fulfilling a necessary role.

Another question arising is, that if there is a discarnate existence after physical death, can moral progress be brought to a level of perfection in such a discarnate state, and if so why should it be helpful to go through cycles of death and rebirth. In attempting to answer this question, one would need to gain some information about the possible mode of existence in an ostensible, parallel, non-physical universe of the discarnate. Some information may be gleaned from mediumistic messages, and also from the behaviour of apparitions, assuming that at least some of these are of discarnate origin. Some information may also emerge from out of body and near death experiences, and also from deathbed observations.

Putting all such information together suggests that there is no sudden change in moral status upon dying, and that the character of the discarnate after physical death is much the same as what it was before dying. While there seems to be no "judgement, fire, and brimstone", or assignment to a "heaven" or "hell", there appears to be an opportunity for the discarnate to review and assess any improvements or failings, that may have taken place during the prior physical existence. It also seems to be the case that the discarnate is relatively free of constraints, and is not bullied about by "authorities", the same way as it is continually perpetrated in the physical realm by politically organised states, and their agencies.

However, the discarnate may well find that acceptance into higher morally advanced circles is not forthcoming, and that the best way of continuing moral progression is to be reborn into the physical world, that is, into the physical universe, and have another go. Having made such a decision, there may well be a waiting list for available places.

As it has been claimed in the foregoing, religions differ on moral issues, and there is no undisputed and unique moral code in existence. Attempts have been made to deduce comprehensive moral codes from fundamental guiding principles. For example the basic principle of Christianity is "love thy neighbour as thyself", even if he or she is hostile, and reciprocates with animosity. While this principle is very meritorious, it does not lead to a sufficiently all-encompassing moral code.

A better fundamental principle may well be: "abstain from all actions that may cause harm, or suffering, to any being that is capable of experiencing suffering as a result". Putting it differently, any action that may cause physical or mental suffering to any other being is immoral. An extensive list of immoral behaviour is deducible from this fundamental principle, and from the principles implied by the seven sins, to an almost endless number of situations. What follows is an attempt to deduce a brief moral code from these principles.

Positions of power attract immature individuals, since such positions not only provide those individuals with opportunities to exercise power over others, but also enable them to create wealth for themselves in the process. It is immoral to covet positions of power over others, such as within the legislative, executive, or judiciary bodies of the state, and particularly so if such positions of power carry remuneration. Coveted power is exercised for its own sake, and is almost always abused. However, administrative positions may be accepted upon request from those who would be subjects to that administration, and at such levels of remuneration, if any, as those affected by that administration approve. It is also immoral for an individual to share in the exercise of the state's power, by seeking positions that lend themselves to the abuse of power in the state's enforcement and bureaucratic agencies.

It is immoral for the seekers of power to institute slanted or rigged elections. Morally acceptable elections could only be based on genuine proportional representation, not subject to a lower limit of votes that a group or party must attain before it can gain representation in a legislature, except when the number of votes obtained is insufficient for securing even a single place in the legislature. However, even if genuine proportional representation did exist, morality would require that all important decisions be made by the whole population at periodic referenda, which could deal with a number of issues at the same time. Provisions should also exist to enable citizens initiating referenda. But, successful functioning of direct decision making would require the existence of genuine free speech and a truthful media.

It is immoral for any group of individuals, whether the wielders of the powers of a state, or the majority of the population of a state, to deprive any other group, such as an ethnic or religious minority, of independent existence within justly drawn boundaries, provided that the desire for independence by that group is based on a genuine free vote. It is also immoral to hinder such a genuine free vote from taking place. In areas of mixed population, a border could be regarded just, if it had approximately equal minorities on either side. During the 20th century, following two world wars, grossly unfair peace treaties created unjust borders and many ethnic minorities. In the course of the century, most of these minorities were subjected to ethnic cleansing, including the denial of equal opportunities, the right to practice minority language and religion, and even brutal torture, and outright murder.

It is immoral for states to initiate war. Only genuine wars of independence, or self defence, or wars aiming to liberate unjustifiably occupied territories, are morally excusable.

Individuals born on the territory of a state owe no allegiance to that state. It is not the duty of individuals to serve the state, but rather it is the duty of the state to serve all individuals inhabiting its territory. It is immoral for the state to exercise power for its own sake. It is the state's duty to provide equal freedom and equal justice for all, free of any legal costs.

It is immoral for a group of individuals, or a state, to create victimless offences and crimes. Any action can be regarded an offence or a crime, only if it entails real individual victims. A group as a whole cannot be a victim, only its individual members can be victims. Consequently, it is immoral to create offences or crimes, aiming to protect the "common good", a term which usually hides the vested interests of the few. It is immoral to turn any action into an offence or a crime, on grounds that there is a finite chance of accidental harm to an acting individual, or a second party. A list of victimless offences and crimes, created by states is so extensive, that enumerating such a list here is not feasible. The death penalty is murder by the state, and as such it is utterly immoral, no matter what the alleged guilt is.

It is immoral for the state to brainwash the majority into acceptance of victimless offences and crimes, and then persecute the minority for noncompliance. It is the moral duty of the state to serve, but not to rule.

It is immoral for the state to force any individual into servitude. As a specific example, it is immoral on the part of a state to institute conscription for any reason, military or otherwise. Refusal to comply with conscription is a victimless offence. If a group, when unjustifiably attacked, cannot defend itself by relying on volunteers only, should not expect to survive.

While voluntary association for any morally acceptable purpose is a fundamental human right, it is immoral for the state to coerce or allow associations, such as industrial or professional unions, to enforce compulsory membership.

Taxation is a grey area that may serve as another example for the questionable use of state power. It is arguably immoral to impose compulsory taxation, since that amounts to seizing rightful property by force. Services rendered by the state should be based on the user pay principle, at genuinely just rates. Taxation, if any, for justifiable purposes, such as essential social security, should be indirect. Charity ought to be fostered as a highly moral activity.

It is immoral in work environments to covet leading positions in order to gain power over others, or to gain increased remuneration. Such positions should be filled by invitation only, and with the approval of those affected.

It is immoral for private individuals, or private corporations, such as privately owned banks, to create money out of nothing in the form of interest bearing loans, as is the case with fractional reserve banking. Money may be morally created only by publicly owned organisations, such as genuine national banks, and either issued free, or as loans at a level of interest covering administrative costs only. The amount of money so created from time to time should go to support morally justifiable causes, and should be just sufficient for the unhindered functioning of the economy, with minimal inflation. The primary cause of inflation is greed. It is also immoral to facilitate private ownership of natural monopolies.

It is immoral for businesses and corporations to operate at excessive profit levels. While businesses must break even after paying non-exploitative and morally acceptable levels of wages and salaries, a morally justifiable profit margin over the break even point is around 20%. Morality would require employees to be the sole shareholders of their corporations.

Unemployment should be obviated through work sharing. It is immoral to insist on a larger share of work opportunities than what is available through equitable distribution.

It is immoral to strive for unearned income, such as obtained through speculation in stocks, shares, real estate, currency markets, or gambling. Earned income includes salaries and wages at morally justifiable levels. Business profits can also be regarded as earned income at morally acceptable levels, as stated above. It is also morally permissible to lend or invest savings from earned income, yielding interest, dividends or rent, not exceeding more than about 2% yearly above the inflation rate. In particular, the lending of money at compound interest amounts to usury, and as such it is immoral. Overall income becomes immoral if it approaches or passes certain limits, arguably around ten times the average earnings.

It is immoral to deny equal consideration on basis of sex, race, ethnicity or belief.

Heterosexual or homosexual relationships between genuinely consenting parties involve no victims, and as such are amoral activities. However, it is immoral for partners in a relationship, whether sanctioned by state, church, or otherwise, to break up while a child resulting from that relationship is underage, and is not ready to lead an independent life. Furthermore, it is the moral duty of the partners to create an amicable environment for the children in their care. It is immoral for parents to subject their children to body mutilations, such as male or female circumcision, or body piercing of any kind. Such may be undertaken by individuals by their own volition after coming of age. It may be arguable if abortion is immoral right from conception, but it is certainly immoral once a brain and nervous system has formed, and reincarnation may have taken place.

It is immoral to abandon parents in their old age, and offload them to institutions for the aged, whether private or state run. It is a moral obligation to care for parents until they die.

It is immoral to issue, covet, or accept titles or prizes of any kind, be it issued by the state, church, or academia. Postgraduate work is commendable if undertaken for its innate worth, and not for title, prestige, or future financial gain. Bearing a title amounts to declaring: "I am more than you, and I am entitled to more than you", which entails both pride and greed.

It is immoral to engage in competitive sports, which produce winners and losers, and in particular for money. It is also immoral to support such activities by attendance. Sports undertaken for exercise only are amoral activities.

Intolerance results from being unduly critical of the mistakes or failings of others, while conveniently overlooking one's own moral shortcomings. Intolerance is a highly immoral trait, ranking close to the worst amongst the seven sins.

As it was stated earlier, a fundamental principle enabling the identification of an immoral act is, whether the act causes harm to any being that is capable of suffering. It is hardly disputable that animals possessing brains and nervous systems can experience suffering.

Animals in this category are the vertebrates such as mammals, birds, and fish, and also some soft bodied animals. All such animals possess varying degrees of consciousness, and are referred to as sentient. The degree of sentience of insects is questionable.

It follows from the above principle, that it is immoral to raise sentient animals for food and eat them, or to raise and kill such animals for any other purposes, such as toiletries, clothing, and medicaments. It also follows that, it is immoral to hunt or fish for any reason, but especially so if it constitutes killing for pleasure. Further, it is immoral to experiment on sentient animals for any purpose, including medical purposes, no matter what the claimed benefits could be, true or false. Much animal experimentation is undertaken for personal gain, namely: money, title, or prestige. If animal populations are to be controlled for human benefit, then fertility control could possibly be the only morally acceptable option.

It is a fact that humankind has evolved to be totally vegetarian, as have some of the closest relatives of humans amongst the animals, namely the anthropoid apes, some of which are totally vegetarian. Humans have not evolved to be omnivores, even though most humans have adopted such a diet for disputable reasons.

Foods of plant origin contain all the necessary nutrients for humans, including all essential and nonessential components of proteins, called amino acids. Some plants, rye for instance, yield amino acids in a proportion closer to that found in human milk, which nature intended as ideal food for the human newborn, than the proportion found in most protein sources of animal origin. The amino acid contents of some food items, coming from both animal and plant sources, are given in Appendix 13.1. The figures in Appendix 13.1 clearly refute the claimed superiority of animal protein over plant protein. Further, from the health point of view, an excessive protein intake of any kind may be harmful, as can be the saturated fatty acids often present in animal food sources. In fact, eating animals is one of the main causative factors leading to a host of degenerative diseases in humans. Saying otherwise amounts to lies promulgated by vested interests.

Claims have been made, that some experiments point to the possibility of plants possessing a degree of consciousness. Some plants seemed to react to hostile thoughts emanating from human experimenters, as indicated by changes in bioelectric variables, such as galvanic skin response. These were monitored by electrodes attached to plants, and analysed much the same way, as would be done with human subjects. It has been suggested that such experiments indicated plant consciousness, and therefore no essential difference in the morality of eating, or otherwise harming, plants and animals.

Attempts to repeat such experiments have failed. However, it is true that plant physiology can be influenced psychokinetically, just as all processes, inanimate or animate, can be. It is likely that what had been mistaken for plant consciousness and plant reaction to threatening thoughts by human experimenters were, in fact, produced psychokinetically by the experimenters' unconscious minds. In any case, it is generally accepted that "in body" consciousness, unlike "out of body consciousness", necessitates a brain and a nervous system, which plants do not possess.

Chapter 13 – Epilogue – Moral Issues

So how is humankind to live on barren land with sparse vegetation, or in the arctic regions? The answer is that humans should either live only in places where food of plant origin is readily producible, or if humans have to live in areas where plants cannot be cultivated, then plant based food should be transported to their place of habitation.

Defenders of an animal based diet often point to nature, animals eating each other, with humans situated at the top of the food chain. However, it should be borne in mind that nature evolved without moral guidance, and makes no moral decisions. Perhaps, humans have been deliberately planted into such an environment, so that they can make moral progress by rising above nature via deliberate choice. Moral progress can only be made as a result of free choice, but not through enforcement. "Holy books" giving instructions as to which animals are permissible to eat, and how they should be killed, disseminate false religious doctrines. In general, the imposition of any doctrine is an immoral act.

Humans are morally entitled to a comfortable existence that the earth can provide sustainably for its current population, and more. Unsatisfied needs result from immoral and greatly unequitable distribution of goods, governed by greed. However, it is also immoral to waste the earth's resources. Recycling is morally preferable to the use of fresh resources.

Much could be done to aid moral progress, during the critical formative years of the young, by parents and educational institutions. Unfortunately, the state hinders moral progress in many ways, not least by entrusting state run education to a morally deficient bureaucracy, corrupting the young during their important formative years. Consequently, most parents, having been through state run institutions, are in no position to pass on moral values to their children, and so corruption becomes self-perpetuating. The aim seems to be the production of a compliant population incapable of challenging the state, and the hidden interests lurking behind it. Some better off parents, aware of the problems, send their children to private institutions, in the hope that their children would be exposed to a modicum of moral values.

Moral progress is also greatly hindered due to most of the media being in the hands of morally bankrupt monopolies, continually disseminating disinformation about rights and wrongs, in the interests of the often unelected few. At times the media is state controlled, at other times the media exercises controlling influence over the state, or collusion may prevail between the two. Be that as it may, the outcome is the stifling of moral progress in the interests of a few.

In particular, the state causes great harm to the moral progress of humankind by confusing illegal issues with immoral issues. By creating a myriad of victimless offences and crimes, the state makes countless actions illegal which are in no way immoral, and at the same time condones many actions as legal which are utterly immoral, such as animal exploitation for whatever purpose, just to name one of the many. This makes distinguishing between moral and immoral acts difficult for the majority of humankind.

Ultimately, the question remains if there is a God who has laid down an absolute moral code. In the foregoing it was argued, that there exists substantial circumstantial evidence for the survival of the mind into a parallel universe. It was also said, that such survival does not appear to be accompanied by a sudden alteration in the level of moral development of the surviving minds. If so, then the parallel universe is inhabited by many discarnate beings, with a wide range of moral advancement. It may well be possible that amongst those at the highest levels of moral advancement, there is a chief fulfilling the role of God.

However, it is clear that while these highly developed beings could exert wide-ranging influence on the physically alive through the various paranormal phenomena, they do not normally exercise such influence. They allow free will, and thereby they also allow all the evil besetting the physical universe to prevail.

The possible reason for this, as already suggested above, may be that free will is essential if moral progress is to take place. If free choice were not allowed, but rather morally correct behaviour were imposed, then moral progression of the individual could not take place. Good, or morally correct behaviour, can exist only as the outcome of free choice.

Nevertheless, on rare occasions, these highly developed discarnate beings appear to exert influences via extrasensory perception, and psychokinetic action. If that happens, miracles appear to take place, which are normally attributed to God, or to some of God's associates.

It also appears possible that discarnate beings of low moral development occasionally exert adverse influences through paranormal activities that would be considered by some as the works of evil spirits, or the devil.

Notwithstanding any such possibilities, the ultimate aim of existence remains a relentless moral progression through all the influences, be it beneficial or detrimental, incarnate or discarnate, by the exercise of free choice. It may well be, that moral perfection can only be approximated through a series of reincarnations, followed by the eventual permanent transfer to a non-physical, parallel universe, when the requisite moral development has been achieved. It could also be that, as those with a sufficient level of moral advancement leave the physical universe permanently, others come in at the bottom end of the moral scale. If so, the physical universe could not be expected to progress morally as a whole, but would remain morally static at a relatively low level.

Further, it could well be, that a number of parallel universes exist, serving as habitats for discarnate beings having reached varied levels of moral development, roughly analogous to the religious ideas of "heaven, purgatory, and hell". This, however does not appear to be essential, since it is likely that discarnate beings at various stages of moral development could be accommodated in a single parallel universe, without interfering with each other in ways as it happens in the physical universe.

Finally, it could be that there is no survival into any parallel universe at all. While many consider that passing over into a morally more perfect parallel universe, or passing into non-existence, are both far preferable to existence in the physical, some consider that non-existence is preferable to survival into any kind of parallel universe. However, survival is likely, because without it there would be no purpose to physical existence.

In conclusion, there can be little doubt that moral advancement is the primary aim of existence in the physical and possibly beyond, which necessitates the existence of a moral code. The code derived from the basic principle of causing no harm to any being that is capable of suffering as a result of such harm, and the principles of the seven sins, may appear self-evident to a few, and unfathomable to many. It is not suggested that refusal to adopt such a code would lead to dire consequences. However, for many it may mean that only through a number of lifetimes could a level of moral perfection be reached, that could well be an essential qualification for acceptance into the company of God.

Appendices

Appendices to Chapter 2

Appendix 2.1 – Some Basic Rules of Arithmetic and Algebra

While it was attempted to limit quantitative arguments in the body of the book to arithmetic only, the appendices rely on algebra to various degrees. A brief summary of some basic rules of arithmetic and algebra are given below.

Let a and b represent two numbers, say $a = 2$ and $b = 3$, then:

$a + b = 2 + 3 = 5, \quad b + a = 3 + 2 = 5$
$b - a = 3 - 2 = 1, \quad a - b = 2 - 3 = -1$
$(a) \times (b) = ab = 2 \times 3 = 6, \quad (b) \times (a) = ba = 3 \times 2 = 6$
$(a) / (b) = a/b = 2/3 = 0.667, \quad (b) / (a) = b/a = 3/2 = 1.5$
$(b) \times (b) = b^2 = 3 \times 3 = 3^2 = 9$
$(a) \times (a) \times (a) = a^3 = 2 \times 2 \times 2 = 2^3 = 8$

$$\frac{1}{(b) \times (b)} = \frac{1}{b^2} = b^{-2} = \frac{1}{3 \times 3} = \frac{1}{3^2} = 3^{-2} = \frac{1}{9}$$

$$\frac{1}{(a) \times (a) \times (a)} = \frac{1}{a^3} = a^{-3} = \frac{1}{2 \times 2 \times 2} = \frac{1}{2^3} = 2^{-3} = \frac{1}{8}$$

Also if: $(b) \times (b) = b^2 = d = 3 \times 3 = 3^2 = 9$

then: $\sqrt{d} = \sqrt{b^2} = b = \sqrt{9} = \sqrt{3^2} = \sqrt{3 \times 3} = 3$

where: $\sqrt{9}$ is read as the square root of 9.

The square of a number is the number multiplied by itself. The square root of a number is another number, which when multiplied by itself leads back to the original number.

Likewise if: $(a) \times (a) \times (a) = a^3 = c = 2 \times 2 \times 2 = 2^3 = 8$

then: $\sqrt[3]{c} = \sqrt[3]{a^3} = a = \sqrt[3]{8} = \sqrt[3]{2^3} = \sqrt[3]{2 \times 2 \times 2} = 2$

where: $\sqrt[3]{8}$ is read as the cube root of 8.

An alternative notation is:
$\sqrt{d} = d^{1/2}$ and $\sqrt[3]{c} = c^{1/3}$
$\frac{1}{\sqrt{d}} = d^{-1/2}$ and $\frac{1}{\sqrt[3]{c}} = c^{-1/3}$

Again: $(a) \times (a) \times (a) \times (b) \times (b) = (a^3) \times (b^2) = a^3 b^2$
$= 2^3 \times 3^2 = (2 \times 2 \times 2) \times (3 \times 3) = 8 \times 9 = 72$

Further if: $a = 2, \quad b = 3, \quad c = 4, \quad \text{and} \quad d = 5, \quad \text{then:}$

Appendices to Chapter 2

$$\left(\frac{a}{b}\right) \times \left(\frac{c}{d}\right) = \left(\frac{a}{b}\right)\left(\frac{c}{d}\right) = \frac{ac}{bd} = \left(\frac{2}{3}\right) \times \left(\frac{4}{5}\right) = \frac{2 \times 4}{3 \times 5} = \frac{8}{15}$$

$$\left(\frac{a}{b}\right) / \left(\frac{c}{d}\right) = \left(\frac{a}{b}\right)\left(\frac{d}{c}\right) = \frac{ad}{bc} = \left(\frac{2}{3}\right) / \left(\frac{4}{5}\right) = \left(\frac{2}{3}\right) \times \left(\frac{5}{4}\right) = \frac{2 \times 5}{3 \times 4} = \frac{10}{12}$$

Also: (a) x (b) = ab = (2) x (3) = 2 x 3 = 6,   (a) x (–b) = – ab = (2) x (–3) = – 6
(– a) x (– b) = ab = (–2) x (–3) = 6,   (– a) x (b) = – ab = (–2) x (3) = – 6
(b) / (a) = b/a = (3) / (2) = 3 / 2 = 1.5,   (b) / (– a) = – b/a = (3) / (–2) –3 / 2 = –1.5
(– b) / (– a) = b/a = (–3) / (–2) = 1.5,   (– b) / (a) = – b/a = (–3) / (2) = –3 / 2 = –1.5

Equations may be manipulated by applying the same operation to both sides, thus:

If: $a + b = c$,   then: $a + b + d = c + d$,   and: $a + b - d = c - d$
$(a + b) \times (d) = (c) \times (d)$,   or: $(a + b) d = cd$
$(a + b) / (d) = (c) / (d)$,   or: $(a + b) / d = c / d$
$(a + b)^2 = c^2$,   and: $\sqrt{a+b} = \sqrt{c}$

Again if: $a + b = c$,   then: $a + b - b = c - b$,   or: $a = c - b$
$a - b = d$,   then: $a - b + b = d + b$,   or: $a = d + b$
$ab = c$,   then: $ab / b = c / b$,   or: $a = c / b$
$a / b = d$,   then: $(a / b) b = db$,   or: $a = db$

Note that $\frac{a}{b}$ is often written as a / b. Both signify division of a by b.

In the above four lines, brackets are used only in expressions such as $(a / b) b = db$, where they are essential. In the book brackets are used extensively, regardless of whether they are essential or not. This was done in the hope that doing so would enhance readability. In rare cases the appendices also contain geometry, trigonometry and, differential-integral calculus.

In particular, the principle of similar triangles is employed on a few occasions.

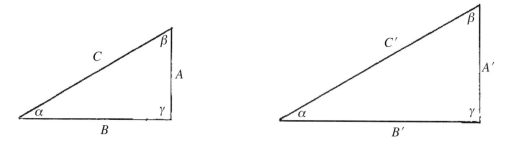

Figure A2.1–1

Referring to Figure A2.1–1 two triangles are similar if their corresponding angles α, β, and γ are equal, in which case their respective sides are proportional: $A / A' = B / B' = C / C'$. While in Figure A2.1–1 the angle γ is a right angle (90°), the above principles apply even if none of the angles of a triangle is a right angle. The derivation of important results in science often relies on the similarity of triangles.

Appendix 2.2 – Summary of Physical Quantities and their Units

A <u>scalar quantity</u> has magnitude only. A <u>vector quantity</u> has both magnitude and direction.

MECHANICAL QUANTITIES - UNITS

The units of three mechanical quantities can be chosen freely. These are the units of length, mass, and time. The rest of the mechanical units then follow from these via scientific laws.

Length or Displacement, alternative name: Distance
Vector, Symbol: l, Unit: metre, abbreviated: m.
Displacement is the linear (straight line) distance covered in moving from one point to another point. It has both magnitude and direction. Its magnitude is often called length.

Mass
Scalar, Symbol: m, Unit: kilogram, abbreviated: kg.
Mass refers to the quantity of matter, and is not synonymous with weight. The mass of a quantity of matter is the same everywhere, but its weight is gravity dependent. The mass of 1 litre of water is 1 kilogram, and while its weight on the earth's surface is 1 kilogram also, yet on the surface of the moon it weighs approximately 1/6 of a kilogram only.

Time
Scalar, Symbol: t, Unit: second, abbreviated: s.

Area
Vector, Symbol: a or A, Unit: square metre, abbreviated: m^2.
Area is a vector because it has both magnitude and also orientation in space.

Volume
Scalar, Symbol: v or V, Unit: cubic metre, abbreviated: m^3, ($1\ m^3$ = 1000 litres).

Velocity
Vector, Symbol: v or u, Unit: metre per second, abbreviated: m/s.
Velocity is the distance covered by a moving object per second, and it has both magnitude and direction. The magnitude of the velocity is often called speed. If an object moves 1 metre in a given direction in 1 second, then its speed is 1 metre per second. In general:
   (speed in metres per second)
= (distance moved in metres) / (time during which motion takes place in seconds)
Algebraically: $v = l/t$

Acceleration
Vector, Symbol: a in general, g for gravitational acceleration. Unit: metres per second per second, or more briefly: metres per second squared, abbreviated: m/s^2. Acceleration is a change in velocity when the velocity varies with time, either in magnitude, or in direction, or both. It has both magnitude and direction. The direction of the acceleration may be the same as, or different from, the direction of the velocity. If the velocity changes by 1 metre per second in each second, the acceleration is 1 metre per second squared. In general:
   (acceleration in metres per second squared)
= (change in velocity in metres per second) / (time in which change occurs in seconds)
Algebraically: $a = v/t = l/t^2$

Force

Vector, Symbol: F, Unit: newton, abbreviated: N.

Force is the agency that causes a mass to move and accelerate, provided that the mass is not restrained and is free to move. Force has both magnitude and direction. If a mass is acted on by a force, and it is free to move in the direction of that force, it is accelerated in that direction, but not necessarily in the direction of its velocity. The magnitude of the force equals the mass multiplied by the magnitude of the acceleration. If a 1 kilogram mass is accelerated at 1 metre per second squared, the force acting on it is 1 newton. In general:

(force in newtons)
= (mass in kilograms) x (acceleration in metres per second squared)
Algebraically: $F = ma$

A readily observed force at the earth's surface is the force of gravity. It causes a free falling mass to accelerate at 9.807 metres per second squared, that is $g = 9.807 \approx 9.81$ m/s^2. As an example, the gravitational force at the earth's surface on a 3 kg mass is (3) x (9.81) = 29.43 newtons, and is directed vertically downward. (Note: $g \approx 9.81$ is a rounded figure).

Work and Energy

Scalar, Symbol: W, Unit: joule, abbreviated: J.

Work is done, or energy is expended or gained, when force is applied, or force is overcome, in moving a mass over a given distance. The magnitude of the work, or energy, equals the force multiplied by the distance moved in the direction of the force. If the applied force is 1 newton, and the distance moved in the direction of the force is 1 metre, then the work done is 1 joule. In general:

(work in joules)
= (force in newtons) x (distance moved in direction of force in metres)
Algebraically: $W = Fl$

When the force is due to gravitation acting on a mass at the surface of the earth, one has:

(gravitational force in newtons)
= (mass in kilograms) x (gravitational acceleration = 9.81 metres per second squared)
Algebraically: $F = mg$

If the mass is raised a given distance vertically, and air resistance to the motion is negligible:
(work done in joules) = (gravitational force in newtons) x (distance raised in metres)
Algebraically: $W = Fl = mgl$

This work also equals the "potential energy" gained by the mass raised. Let the mass be allowed to fall from its raised position, starting with zero speed, over a period of t seconds. Then, if the air resistance to the fall is negligible, one has after t seconds have elapsed:

(speed) = (gravitational acceleration) x (time), or $v = gt$
(average speed over t seconds) = (speed at t seconds) / 2, or $v/2 = gt/2$
(distance moved in t seconds) = (average speed) x (time), or $vt/2 = gt^2/2$
(force at any instant) = (mass) x (gravitational acceleration), or $F = mg$
(energy gained during t seconds) = (force) x (distance fallen), or $W = mg^2t^2/2$
But, since $gt = v$, and $g^2t^2 = v^2$, one has $W = mv^2/2$
This equals the "kinetic energy" of the falling mass at t seconds, when its speed is $v = gt$.

Appendices to Chapter 2

In general any mass m, moving with velocity v, has kinetic energy given by:

(kinetic energy in joules)
= (mass in kilograms) x (speed in metres per second) x (speed in metres per second) / 2
= (mass in kilograms) x (speed in metres per second)^2 / 2

Algebraically: $W = mv^2/2$

If the mass is allowed to fall on top of a pile, the kinetic energy at impact is converted into work done, by driving the pile some distance into the ground against the resisting force offered by the ground.

Returning to the previous example, the gravitational force acting on a 3 kg mass is:
(force) = (mass) x (acceleration) = mg = (3) x (9.81) = 29.43 newtons.
The work done by raising the 3 kg mass through 2 metres, at negligible air resistance, is:
(work) = (force) x (distance) = $F l$ = (29.43) x (2) = 58.86 joules.

This equals the potential energy gained by the mass. If the mass is allowed to fall 2 metres back to its original position, its 58.86 joules of potential energy will be converted into the same amount of kinetic energy, if air resistance to the fall is negligible. So, one must have:

(kinetic energy) = (mass) x (speed)^2 / 2, or $W = mv^2/2$ = 58.86 joules.

Thus, if $m = 3$ kilograms, then from the above equation, the speed after falling through 2 metres must be $v = \sqrt{2W/m} = \sqrt{(2) \times (58.86)/(3)}$ = 6.264 metres per second.

Power

Scalar, Symbol: P, Unit: watt, abbreviated: W.
Power is the rate at which work is done, or energy is expended or gained, expressed in joules per second. If 1 joule work is done in each second, then the power is 1 watt. In general:
(power in watts) = (work done in joules) / (time in which work is done in seconds).
Algebraically: $P = W/t$

Thus, in the above example, if the 3 kilogram mass is raised by 2 metres in each second, then 58.86 joules of work is done per second, and the power developed is 58.86 watts.

Pressure

Scalar, Symbol: p, Unit: newton per square metre or pascal, abbreviated: N/m^2, or P.
Pressure normally arises from force exerted by a liquid, or a gas, on the walls of the containing vessel, per unit area of the walls of the vessel. Forces causing pressure are perpendicular to the walls on which they act. The pressure equals the force acting on a wall of a vessel divided by the area of the wall. Thus if 1 newton force is exerted on 1 square metre area, the pressure is 1 newton per square metre, or 1 pascal. In general:
(pressure in pascals) = (force in newtons) / (area on which force acts in square metres)
Algebraically: $p = F/A$

Temperature

Scalar, Symbol: T, Unit: degrees Celsius or degrees absolute, abbreviated: $^{\circ}$C or $^{\circ}$K.
Temperature is a measure of the vibrations of atoms, or molecules, in matter. Arbitrarily, the temperature at which ice melts, and water boils, were chosen as 0°C and 100° C respectively. These correspond to 273° K and 373° K respectively.

ELECTRICAL QUANTITIES - UNITS

One electrical unit may be chosen arbitrarily, which could be the unit of any of the three quantities: charge, current, or voltage. Then, the remaining electrical units follow from the chosen electrical unit and the foregoing mechanical units, via scientific laws. In what follows, the unit of voltage is chosen arbitrarily.

Voltage, alternative names: Electromotive Force, or Potential Difference

Scalar, Symbol: v or V, Unit: volt, abbreviated: V.

The electromotive force is the agency which in electric cells, or batteries, causes the positive and the negative charges to separate, and to be driven to the positive and the negative terminals of the cell, or battery, through chemical processes. The electromotive force is also responsible for driving the positive and the negative charges to the opposite ends of a conductor, when the conductor is moving in a magnetic field.

As a first approximation, the unit of voltage could be chosen as the voltage developed by a particular electric cell, called the "Weston standard cell". However, for historical reasons, in terms of the currently accepted value of the volt, the Weston standard cell develops a voltage equal to 1.0183 volts.

Electric Field

Vector, Symbol: E, Unit: volt per metre, abbreviated: V/m.

An electric field exists wherever an electrically charged body is acted on by a force due to the charge carried by that body. The magnitude of the field is proportional to the magnitude of the force, and the direction of the field is the same as the direction of the force acting on a positively charged body. As a specific example, if two parallel metallic plates are connected to the positive and the negative terminals of a battery, then an electric field is set up between the plates. If the edges of the plates are long compared with the distance between the plates, then the magnitude of the electric field between the plates, well away from the edges, equals the voltage applied to the plates in volts, divided by the distance between the plates in metres, and is expressed in units of volts per metre. If the parallel plates are 1 metre apart, and the applied voltage between them is 1 volt, then the electric field produced between the plates is 1 volt per metre. For parallel plates in general:

(electric field in volts per metre)
= (voltage applied to plates in volts) / (distance between the plates in metres)

Algebraically: $E = V / l$

A body carrying a positive electric charge, situated between the plates well away from the edges, is subject to a force having a direction perpendicular to both plates and directed from the positive to the negative plate, which by definition is the direction of the electric field.

Electric Charge

Scalar, Symbol: Q, Unit: coulomb, abbreviated: C.

An electrically charged body situated in an electric field is acted on by a force. It is found in general that, the magnitude of the force is proportional to the magnitude of the charge multiplied by the magnitude of the electric field. If the charge is positive, the direction of the force is the same as the direction of the electric field. If the charge is negative, then the direction of the force is opposite to that of the field. A charged body has 1 coulomb charge on it, if it is acted on by a force of 1 newton, in an electric field of 1 volt per metre .

The following holds in general:

(electric charge in coulombs)
= (force acting on charged body in newtons) / (electric field in volts per metre).
Algebraically: $Q = F/E$

Electric Current

Scalar, Symbol: i or I, Unit: ampere, abbreviated: A.
An electric current is a continuous flow of electric charge in a conductor, such as a length of metallic wire, connected between the positive and negative terminals of a battery. The flow is directed from the positive battery terminal through the conductor to the negative terminal. Such a charge flow, or electric current, may be measured as the amount of charge flowing across any cross sectional area of the conductor per second. The electric current equals 1 ampere if 1 coulomb charge flows past any cross section in 1 second. In general:

(electric current in amperes)
= (charge flowing past a cross section in coulombs) / (time of charge flow in seconds)
Algebraically: $I = Q/t$

Resistance

Scalar, Symbol: R, Unit: ohm, abbreviated: Ω.
The resistance of a conductor, such as a length of metallic wire, equals the voltage applied between its ends, divided by the resulting electric current in the conductor. If a conductor is so chosen, that a voltage of 1 volt applied between its ends results in a current of 1 ampere flowing through it, then the resistance of the conductor is 1 ohm. In general:

(resistance of conductor, or a length of wire, in ohms)
= (voltage between the ends of the conductor in volts) / (resulting current in amperes)
Algebraically: $R = V/I$

Electrical Energy

Scalar, Symbol: W, Unit: joule, abbreviated: J
The relation between electric charge and electric field is analogous to that between mass and gravitational field. Thus, if an electrically charged body is moved in opposition to the force acting on it due to an electric field, work is done, and potential energy is gained, that equals the force multiplied by the distance moved. If a body carrying 1 coulomb charge, is moved a distance of 1 metre, in a 1 volt per metre electric field, in opposition to the 1 newton force acting on it, the work done, and the potential energy gained, is 1 joule. In general:

(work done in joules) = (potential energy gained in joules)
= (charge in coulombs) x (electric field in volts per metre) x (distance moved in metres)
Algebraically: $W = QEl$

Now the product: (electric field in volts per metre) x (distance moved in metres), equals the voltage difference in volts through which the charge is moved, and so it is also true that:

(work done in joules) = (potential energy gained in joules)
= (charge in coulombs) x (voltage difference, in volts, through which charge is moved)
Algebraically: $W = QV$

If the force acting on a charged body is allowed to return it back to its original position, the work that was converted into potential energy becomes an equal amount of kinetic energy, provided that any frictional retarding forces opposing the motion are negligible.

Expressing all these algebraically: $W = QEl = QV = mv^2/2$ where $W, Q, E, l,$ and V stand for work done, electric charge on the body, electric field, distance moved, and the voltage difference through which the motion took place respectively, while m and v represent the mass, and speed of the charged body when it is back at its original position.

Electrical Power
Scalar, Symbol: P, Unit: watt, abbreviated: W.
Electrical power, as mechanical power, is work done, or energy expended or gained per second. If 1 joule of work is done in each second, then power is expended or gained at a rate of 1 watt. Thus, if a charge of 1 coulomb is moved through a voltage difference of 1 volt in each second, then work is done at a rate of 1 joule per second, or 1 watt. In general for any amount of charge moving through any given voltage difference per second:

(work done per second, in joules per second) = (power in watts)
= (voltage difference in volts) x (charge moving through the voltage difference in coulombs per second)

Algebraically: $P = VQ/t = W/t$

An electric current flowing in a conductor, or a length of metallic wire, with a voltage difference between its ends, amounts to a quantity of charge being moved through that voltage difference in each second, and so to a quantity of work done per second, which is tantamount to power being expended at a certain rate. If a conductor, with a voltage difference of 1 volt between its ends, carries an electric current of 1 ampere, that is, 1 coulomb charge is flowing through it in each second, then work is done at a rate of 1 joule per second, and the power expended is 1 watt. In general, if any conductor, with any given voltage difference between its ends, is carrying an electric current, that is, carrying an amount of charge per second, as determined by its resistance, then the following holds:

(work done per second, in joules per second) = (power in watts)
= (voltage difference in volts) x (charge flow in coulombs per second)
= (voltage difference in volts) x (electric current in amperes)
Algebraically: $P = VQ/t = VI$

This electrical power is consumed in overcoming the resistance of the conductor. The electrons, responsible for the current flow, collide with atoms in the conductor, and cause them to increase their vibrations, a process which manifests itself in the conductor heating up. Thus, electrical energy is being continually converted into heat energy.

Capacitance
Scalar, Symbol: C, Unit: farad, abbreviated: F.
Capacitance is the ability of a pair of parallel metallic plates, of any given area and any given distance apart, to store electric charge on the plates. If one plate is connected to the positive terminal of a battery, while the other plate is connected to the negative terminal, the plates acquire equal amounts of positive and negative charge respectively.

The amount of charge on the plates, for a given applied voltage, depends on the capacitance, determined by the area and the separation of the plates. If 1 volt applied across the plates results in 1 coulomb charge on each plate, then the capacitance is 1 farad. In general:
(capacitance in farads) = (charge on one plate in coulombs) / (voltage applied in volts)
Algebraically: $C = Q/V$

Appendices to Chapter 2

Magnetic Field

Vector, Symbol: B, Unit: tesla, abbreviated: T.

A magnetic field exists where a force is acting on a moving electrically charged body, or a conductor carrying an electrical current. The direction of the magnetic field is that direction, in which the north pole of a compass needle points. The magnitude of the force depends on the angle between the direction of the field, and the direction of the movement of the charge, or the direction of the current. As this angle increases from zero to 90 degrees, the force increases from zero to a maximum value. The direction of the force is perpendicular to both, the directions of the field, and of the charge movement or of the current. In the special case, when an observer sees the velocity of a positive charge directed horizontally to the right, or an electric current flowing in a straight conductor horizontally toward the right, situated in a magnetic field directed vertically downward, then the charge, or the current carrying conductor, is found to experience a force directed away from the observer, so that the directions of the force, the field, and the velocity or the current, are mutually perpendicular to each other. If in this specific case, the magnetic field is so chosen that 1 coulomb charge moving with a speed of 1 metre per second, or 1 ampere current in a conductor 1 metre long, experiences a force of 1 newton, then the magnitude of the magnetic field is 1 tesla.

In general, when the directions of the force, the field, and the velocity of the charge or the electric current, are mutually perpendicular, then in terms of magnitudes one has:

(force in newtons)
= (charge in coulombs) x (velocity in metres per second) x (magnetic field in teslas)
= (current in amperes) x (length of conductor in metres) x (magnetic field in teslas)

Algebraically: $F = QvB = IlB$

Magnetic Flux

Scalar, Symbol: Φ, Unit: weber, abbreviated: Wb.

A flat loop of wire situated in a uniform magnetic field that is perpendicular to the plane of the loop has a "magnetic flux" linked with it. The flux is given by the product of the area of the loop multiplied by the magnetic field. If the area of the loop is 1 square metre, and the magnetic field is 1 tesla, then the flux linked with the loop is 1 weber. In general:

(magnetic flux linked with a loop in webers)
= (area of the loop in square metres) x (magnitude of the magnetic field in teslas)

Algebraically: $\Phi = AB$

The loop may be replaced by a flat coil of n turns, in which case the magnetic flux linked with coil is increased by a factor of n, to $n\Phi$.

Inductance

Scalar, Symbol: L, Unit: henry, abbreviated: H.

A current passed into a coil sets up a magnetic field passing through the coil, and so causes a magnetic flux to be linked with the coil. The inductance of the coil equals the flux linked with the coil, divided by the current in the coil. Thus if 1 ampere current causes 1 weber flux to be linked with the coil, then the inductance of the coil is 1 henry. In general:

$$\text{(inductance in henrys)} = \frac{\text{(number of turns in the coil) x (flux passing through the coil in webers)}}{\text{(current in the coil in amperes)}}$$

Algebraically: $L = n\Phi / I$

The above algebraic expressions strictly apply at one point in space at one instant of time. However, they do apply over a finite region of space, if space variables, such as force fields, are uniform, namely constant in both magnitude and direction, over that region. They also apply over finite periods of time provided that time variables, for example acceleration, remain constant, in both magnitude and direction, over those periods. If these conditions are not satisfied, then algebraic calculations have to be replaced by differential-integral calculus. Calculus, and also trigonometry, occur in the Appendices only, on a very few occasions.

DRIVED UNITS

The units listed in the foregoing, often turn out to be very large or very small, in which case it is convenient to used derived units. Before listing some of these, a mathematical notation for large or small numbers, expressed as exponents of 10, that is 10^N or 10^{-N}, need to be considered. Some of these are:

$1000 = 10^3$, $1,000,000 = 10^6$, $1,000,000,000 = 10^9$ etc.
$1/1000 = 10^{-3}$, $1/1,000,000 = 10^{-6}$, $1/1,000,000,000 = 10^{-9}$ etc.

It will be noted that 10^N stands for a number consisting of the number 1 followed by N zeros, while 10^{-N} stands for a fraction, namely the number 1 divided by another number consisting of the number 1 followed by N zeros. Such numbers are at times referred to as "orders of magnitude".

The derived units are given names of Latin or Greek origin, as follows:

10^3 = kilo (k), thus 1000 metres = 10^3 metres = 1 kilometre = 1 km
10^6 = mega (M), thus 1,000,000 metres = 10^6 metres = 1 megametre = 1 Mm
10^9 = giga (G), thus 1,000,000,000 metres = 10^9 metres = 1 gigametre = 1 Gm
10^{-2} = centi (c), thus 1/100 metre = 10^{-2} metre = 1 centimetre = 1 cm
10^{-3} = milli (m), thus 1/1000 metre = 10^{-3} metre = 1 millimetre = 1 mm
10^{-6} = micro (μ), thus 1/1,000,000 metre = 10^{-6} metre = 1 micrometre = 1 μm
10^{-9} = nano (n), thus 1/1,000,000,000 metre = 10^{-9} metre = 1 nanometre = 1 nm
10^{-12} = pico (p), thus 1/1,000,000,000,000 metre = 10^{-12} metre = 1 picometre = 1 pm

For example:
2150 grams = 2.15 x 1000 grams = 2.15 x 10^3 grams = 2.15 kilograms = 2.15 kg,
0.000015 second = 15/1,000,000 second = 15 x 10^{-6} second = 15 microseconds = 15 μs.

In calculations, one must use the original set of consistent units listed in the previous pages, which include only one derived unit, namely the unit of mass, which was chosen to be the kilogram (kg). The unit gram, and the derived units, other than the kilogram, cannot be used in calculations, and may be used only in stating quantities in a more convenient way.

The symbols used to represent physical quantities and their units may be confusing, mainly because a symbol may have more than one meaning. For example the letter a can stand for either area or acceleration. The letter v can represent either volume, or velocity, or voltage. The meaning normally would be clear from the context.

Appendix 2.3 – The Thompson Experiment

With reference to Figure 2.6 in Chapter 2, let:
E = electric field (volts per metre)
B = magnetic field (teslas)
v = horizontal velocity of charged particles (metres per second)
l = length of horizontal plates (metres)
d = distance moved by spot from P_1 to P_2 (metres)
q = charge on a single particle (coulombs)
m = mass of a single particle (kilograms)

The force F_1 acting downward on a charged particle due to the electric field is:
(force) = (magnitude of charge) x (magnitude of electric field)
or $F_1 = qE$ (A2.3 – 1)

Force F_2 acting upward on a horizontally moving charged particle due to the magnetic field:
(force) = (magnitude of charge) x (horizontal speed) x (magnitude of magnetic field)
or $F_2 = qvB$ (A2.3 – 2)

If these two forces are arranged to be equal, the spot is not deflected, and one must have:
$F_1 = F_2$ or $qE = qvB$ and so the horizontal velocity must be: $v = E/B$ (A2.3 – 3)

When only the electric field is applied, the particle is subject to a downward acceleration:
(acceleration) = (force) / (mass)   or $a = qE/m$ (A2.3 – 4)
which applies while the particle moves between the plates of length l with horizontal velocity v. The time necessary for this passage is:
t = (distance moved) / (velocity)   or $t = l/v$ (A2.3 – 5)

The downward velocity when the particle first enters the space between the plates is zero, and reaches a maximum value when the particle leaves the space between the plates. The maximum downward velocity v_m from equations (A2.3 – 4) and (A2.3 – 5) is:
(maximum velocity) = (acceleration) x (time),   or $v_m = at = (qE/m)(l/v)$

The average downward velocity v_{av} is half of this: $v_{av} = (qE/m)(l/v)/2$ (A2.3 – 6)

The total downward deflection d equals the distance between P_1 and P_2:
(deflection) = (average downward velocity) x (time)
or $d = (qE/m)(l/v)^2/2$ (A2.3 – 7)

If E, l, $v = E/B$, and d are known, or measured, q/m may be calculated from equation (A2.3 – 7) as: $q/m = 2d(v/l)^2/E$ (A2.3 – 8)

As an example, suppose that an experiment involved the following quantities:
E = 1000 volts per metre, B = 0.0001 tesla, then $v = E/B = 10^7$ metres per second.
If in addition: l = 0.2 metre, d = 0.0352 metre, then $q/m = 2d(v/l)^2/E$
   or: $q/m = (2)(0.0352)(10^7/0.2)^2/(1000) = 1.76 \times 10^{11}$ coulombs per kilogram.

The above values were chosen for illustrative purposes only, and are not necessarily the values used in the original experiment. In particular at B = 0.0001 tesla, the magnetic field of the earth would need to be taken into consideration.

Appendix 2.4 – The Millikan Experiment

Let:
- r = radius of droplet (metres)
- ρ = density of the oil = 800 (kilograms per cubic metre)
- m = mass of the droplet (kilograms)
- g = gravitational acceleration = 9.81 (metres per second)
- Q = electric charge on droplet (coulombs)
- E = applied electric field (volts per metre)
- η = coefficient of viscosity of air at 20° Celsius
  = 1.72×10^{-5} (newton second per square metre)
- v = constant terminal velocity of fall of the droplet with no electric field applied (metres per second)
- π = 3.14

The volume of a droplet of radius r is $(4/3)\pi r^3$
The mass of the droplet is $m = (4/3)\pi r^3 \rho$ \hfill (A2.4 – 1)
When the electric field is so adjusted as to make the droplet hover:
(electric force) = (gravitational force)
or $QE = mg = (4/3)\pi r^3 \rho g$ \hfill (A2.4 – 2)

If, with the electric field turned off, the droplet falls with constant terminal velocity v, then:
(viscous retarding force) = (gravitational force)
or algebraically: $6\pi\eta r v = mg = (4/3)\pi r^3 \rho g$ \hfill (A2.4 – 3)

If v is measured, then the radius of the droplet is calculable from (A2.4 – 3) as:
$r = \sqrt{9\eta v / 2\rho g}$ \hfill (A2.4 – 4)

Knowing the radius r, the mass m of the droplet can be deduced from (A2.4 – 1). Then, knowing the mass m, and the electric field E, the charge Q can be found from (A2.4 – 2).

As a possible example, suppose that an electric field of 2000 volts per centimetre (200,000 volts per metre) made the droplet hover, and the constant terminal velocity of the falling droplet with the field turned off was found to be 10^{-4} metres per second.

Then, the radius from (A2.4 – 4) is:
$r = \sqrt{(9)(1.72 \times 10^{-5})(10^{-4}) / (2)(800)(9.81)} = 0.993 \times 10^{-6}$ metre.

Hence, the mass from (A2.4 – 1) is:
$m = (4/3)(3.14)(0.993 \times 10^{-6})^3 (800) = 3.28 \times 10^{-15}$ kilogram.

The charge from (A2.3 – 2) is now obtainable as:
$Q = mg/E = (3.28 \times 10^{-15})(9.81)/(2 \times 10^5) = 1.61 \times 10^{-19}$ coulomb.

The droplet could, of course, carry a number of electrons. If after repeating the experiment many times, the above charge is the smallest charge ever found, it must be the charge of one electron. The currently accepted value of the electronic charge is 1.602×10^{-19} coulomb.

Appendix 2.5 – Force on Electric Current in Magnetic Field

Let:
- l = length of the conducting wire (metres)
- a = sectional area of the wire (square metres)
- Q_C = charge density due to moving electrons in wire (coulombs per cubic metre)
- Q = charge due to moving electrons in l metres of wire (coulombs)
- v = average electron speed in wire (metres per second)
- I = electric current in wire (amperes)
- N_O = Avogadro's number = 6.03×10^{23} atoms per gram atom

Then: moving charge in a piece of wire l metres long = $Q = Q_C\, al$ \hfill (A2.5 – 1)
and: moving charge in a piece of wire v metres long = $Q_C\, av$ \hfill (A2.5 – 2)

Equation (A2.5 – 2) gives the charge passing through a cross section of the wire in 1 second, which is the electric current, and so: $I = Q_C\, av$ or: $Il = Q_C\, alv$

But by equation (A2.5-1): $Q_C\, al = Q$ so that: $Il = Qv$ \hfill (A2.5 – 3)

The task now is to calculate the charge Q due to moving electrons in a piece of wire, of sectional area a square metres, and l metres long. If the wire is made of copper, each atom has one loosely bound electron in its outermost shell, which may break away and move, each providing 1.602×10^{-19} coulomb to the overall moving charge. Now:

The atomic weight of copper = 63.5
Thus 63.5 grams of copper contains $N_O = 6.03 \times 10^{23}$ atoms
The number of atoms in 1 gram of copper = $(6.03 \times 10^{23})/(63.5) = 9.50 \times 10^{21}$
The number of atoms in 1 kilogram of copper = 9.50×10^{24}
The mass of 1 cubic metre of copper = 8.92×10^3 kilograms
Number of atoms in 1 cubic metre of copper = $(9.5 \times 10^{24}) \times (8.92 \times 10^3) = 0.847 \times 10^{29}$.
Since each copper atom provides one moving electron of charge 1.602×10^{-19} coulomb, the moving charge per cubic metre of copper is:
$Q_C = (0.847 \times 10^{29}) \times (1.602 \times 10^{-19}) = 1.36 \times 10^{10}$ coulombs.

If the wire has a sectional area of 1 square millimetre, and is 1 metre long, then:
a = 1 square millimetre = 10^{-6} square metre, l = 1 metre, and from (A2.5 – 1):
$Q = Q_C\, al = (1.36 \times 10^{10}) \times (10^{-6}) \times (1) = 1.36 \times 10^4$ coulombs.

Further, if the current in the wire, 1 metre long, having 1 square millimetre sectional area, is 1 ampere, that is $I = 1$, then from (A2.5 – 3):
$Qv = (1.36 \times 10^4) v = Il = (1) \times (1) = 1$

Hence, the average speed of the electrons in the wire is:
$v = Il/Q = 1/(1.36 \times 10^4) = 0.735 \times 10^{-4}$ metre per second, and of course:
$Qv = (1.36 \times 10^4) \times (0.735 \times 10^{-4}) = 1$, and also: $Il = (1) \times (1) = 1$

If the wire is situated in a magnetic field of 1 tesla, directed perpendicular to the wire, then the force F acting on the wire, perpendicular to both the wire and the field, is:
$F = IlB = (1) \times (1) \times (1) = 1$ newton,
$\quad = QvB = (1.36 \times 10^4) \times (0.735 \times 10^{-4}) \times (1) = 1$ newton.

Appendices to Chapter 3

Appendix 3.1 – Michelson - Morley Experiment

Referring to Figure 3.5, the light beam from the light source S is split into two beams by the semitransparent mirror M. The first of these two beams travels through mirror M to mirror M_1, which reflects it back to mirror M, from where part of it is reflected into telescope T. The path of the beam from mirror M to mirror M_1, and back to mirror M, is arranged to be parallel to the earth's motion in its path around the sun.

The second beam is reflected by the semitransparent mirror M to mirror M_2, that reflects it back to mirror M, through which part of it passes into telescope T. The path of the beam from mirror M to mirror M_2, and back to mirror M, is perpendicular to the earth's motion.

The telescope T enables any relative shift in the crests of the two beams to be determined.

Let:
v = orbital speed of earth = 3×10^4 metres per second
c = speed of light = 3×10^8 metres per second
λ = wavelength of light = 550 nanometres (5.5×10^{-7} metres)
f = frequency of light = c / λ
l = distance between M and M_1, also between M and M_2 = 11 metres.

The expected time t'_1 taken for the light to travel the distance l from M to M_1, with an expected speed $(c - v)$, equals the distance l divided by the speed, that is $t'_1 = l/(c-v)$. The expected time t'_2 for the light to travel the same distance back from mirror M_1 to mirror M, with an anticipated speed $(c + v)$, is $t'_2 = l/(c+v)$. The overall time for the return trip t_1, is the sum of these two, namely $t_1 = t'_1 + t'_2$, or:

$$t_1 = \frac{l}{c-v} + \frac{l}{c+v} = \frac{2lc}{c^2-v^2} = \frac{2l}{c}\left(1-\frac{v^2}{c^2}\right)^{-1} \approx \frac{2l}{c}\left(1+\frac{v^2}{c^2}\right) \qquad (A3.1-1)$$

where t_1 has been approximated by the first two terms of the binomial expansion for $(2l/c)(1-v^2/c^2)^{-1}$. The binomial expansion is given in Appendix 6.5.

The paths from M to M_2, and back from M_2 to M, are not quite perpendicular to the earth's orbital motion, but are slightly oblique due to the motion of the earth, as shown in Figure A3.1–1. This obliqueness is catered for automatically by the small amount of scattering of the light, which is always present.

With reference to Figure A3.1–1, if t' denotes the time for the one way trip from M to M_2, then the oblique path ct', the earth's movement vt', and the distance l between the mirrors M and M_2, must satisfy Pythagoras' theorem, that is: $(ct')^2 = (vt')^2 + l^2$

giving: $t' = \dfrac{l}{\sqrt{c^2-v^2}} = \dfrac{l}{c}\left(1-\dfrac{v^2}{c^2}\right)^{-1/2} \approx \dfrac{l}{c}\left(1+\dfrac{v^2}{2c^2}\right)$

where t' was also approximated by the first two terms of the binomial expansion for $(l/c)(1-v^2/c^2)^{-1/2}$.

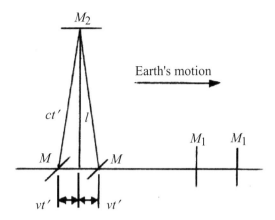

Figure A3.1–1

The time t_2 for the return trip from M to M_2 and back to M, is twice t':

$$t_2 = 2t' = \frac{2l}{c}\left(1 + \frac{v^2}{2c^2}\right) \qquad (A3.1-2)$$

The number of wavelengths associated with the time intervals t_1 and t_2, as given by equations (A3.1–1) and (A3.1–2), are equal to these time intervals multiplied by the frequency of the light f, and so equal ft_1 and ft_2 respectively. Hence the relative shift in the crests, in terms of wavelengths, is the difference of these:

$$ft_1 - ft_2 = f\left(\frac{2l}{c}\right)\left(1 + \frac{v^2}{c^2}\right) - f\left(\frac{2l}{c}\right)\left(1 + \frac{v^2}{2c^2}\right) = f\left(\frac{2l}{c}\right)\left(\frac{v^2}{2c^2}\right) \qquad (A3.1-3)$$

Since: $f = c/\lambda$, this further equals:

$$ft_1 - ft_2 = \left(\frac{c}{\lambda}\right)\left(\frac{2l}{c}\right)\left(\frac{v^2}{2c^2}\right) = \frac{lv^2}{\lambda c^2}$$

Substituting numerical values for l, λ, v, and c from above:

$$ft_1 - ft_2 = \frac{(11) \times (3 \times 10^4)^2}{(5.5 \times 10^{-7}) \times (3 \times 10^8)^2} = 0.2 \text{ of one wavelength.}$$

The accuracy of the procedure may be enhanced, and any error caused by slightly unequal distances between mirrors from M to M_1 and from M to M_2 cancelled out, by turning the setup consisting of the light source, the telescope, and the mirrors, through 90 degrees. The roles of the mirrors would then be interchanged, leading to an anticipated overall shift of $2 \times 0.2 = 0.4$ of a wavelength from the two orientations. So, if light waves propagated in an ether, the same way as sound waves propagate in air, the above shifts would be expected to occur between the crests of the waves returning from mirrors M_1 and M_2. As the experiment, and many of its repetitions, did not find any such shifts, it had to be concluded that an ether did not exist, and that the speed of the electromagnetic waves was constant, irrespective of the movement of the source and the observer.

Appendix 3.2 – The Special Theory of Relativity

THE LORENTZ TRANSFORMATION

Let two coordinate frames be considered as shown in Figure A3.2 – 1, namely $S(x, y, z, t)$ and $S'(x', y', z', t')$, moving relative to each other at some constant velocity v, in such a way that the x and x' axes are always in the same straight line, while the y and y' axes, and also the z and z' axes, remain in the same planes. Note that the universality of time is given up, the times t and t' in the two frames may be different, $t \neq t'$.

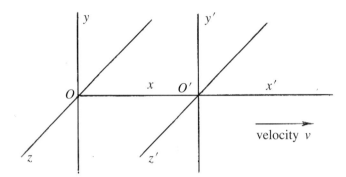

Figure A3.2 – 1

Let the two origins O and O' coincide initially at $t = t' = 0$, and then let S' move relative to S at a constant velocity v along the common x and x' axes. Then, the following relations must always hold:

$$y' = y \qquad (A3.2-1)$$
$$z' = z \qquad (A3.2-2)$$

If a light ray starts at $t = t' = 0$ from the coincident origins, and then travels in the positive x and x' directions at speed c, which has the same value in both frames, then the positions of the wave fronts in the two frames must satisfy:

$$x = ct \quad \text{or} \quad x - ct = 0 \qquad (A3.2-3)$$
$$x' = ct' \quad \text{or} \quad x' - ct' = 0 \qquad (A3.2-4)$$

Alternatively, if the light ray starts at $t = t' = 0$ from the coinciding origins, and then travels in the negative x and x' directions at a speed $-c$, which once more is the same in both frames, then one has for the positions of the two wave fronts:

$$x = -ct \quad \text{or} \quad x + ct = 0 \qquad (A3.2-5)$$
$$x' = -ct' \quad \text{or} \quad x' + ct' = 0 \qquad (A3.2-6)$$

Equations (A3.2 – 3) and (A3.2 – 4), and also equations (A3.2 – 5) and (A3.2 – 6), may be merged yielding:

$$(x' - ct') = \lambda(x - ct) = 0 \qquad (A3.2-7)$$
$$(x' + ct') = \mu(x + ct) = 0 \qquad (A3.2-8)$$

where λ and μ are two constants.

Adding equations (A3.2 – 7) and (A3.2 – 8), and then solving for x' gives:

$$x' = \left(\frac{\lambda + \mu}{2}\right) x - \left(\frac{\lambda - \mu}{2}\right) ct = \beta x - \alpha ct \tag{A3.2 – 9}$$

Subtracting equation (A3.2 – 8) from (A3.2 –7), and then solving for ct' gives:

$$ct' = \left(\frac{\lambda + \mu}{2}\right) ct - \left(\frac{\lambda - \mu}{2}\right) x = \beta ct - \alpha x \tag{A3.2 – 10}$$

where: $\beta = \dfrac{\lambda + \mu}{2}$ and $\alpha = \dfrac{\lambda - \mu}{2}$ are another two constants.

After the S' frame has moved some distance x relative to the S frame, the following must hold at the origin of the S' frame: $x' = 0$, $x = vt$.

Putting these into equation (A3.2 – 9) gives:

$$0 = \beta v t - \alpha ct \tag{A3.2 – 11}$$
or: $\quad \beta v = \alpha c \tag{A3.2 – 12}$

which upon substitution back into equations (A3.2 – 9) and (A3.2 – 10) yields:

$$x' = \beta x - \beta v t \tag{A3.2 – 13}$$
$$ct' = \beta ct - \frac{\beta v}{c} x \tag{A3.2 – 14}$$

Now, again let a ray of light start at $t = t' = 0$ from the joint origins and travel obliquely, then after t and t' seconds have elapsed, it must be true for the wave fronts that:

$$x^2 + y^2 + z^2 = c^2 t^2 \tag{A3.2 – 15}$$
$$x'^2 + y'^2 + z'^2 = c^2 t'^2 \tag{A3.7 – 16}$$

Let now equations (A3.2 – 1), (A3.2 – 2), (A3.2 – 13) and (A3.2 – 14) be substituted into equation (A3.2 – 16):

$$(\beta x - \beta v t)^2 + y^2 + z^2 = \left(\beta ct - \frac{\beta v}{c} x\right)^2$$

Expanding and collecting terms in x^2 and $c^2 t^2$ gives:

$$\left(\beta^2 - \frac{\beta^2 v^2}{c^2}\right) x^2 + y^2 + z^2 = \left(\beta^2 - \frac{\beta^2 v^2}{c^2}\right) c^2 t^2 \tag{A3.2 – 17}$$

Given that the same physical laws must apply in both frames, equation (A3.2 – 17) must be identical with equation (A3.2 – 15), and so one may equate the corresponding coefficients of x^2 and $c^2 t^2$ in the two equations, yielding:

$$\left(\beta^2 - \frac{\beta^2 v^2}{c^2}\right) = \beta^2 \left(1 - \frac{v^2}{c^2}\right) = 1$$

or $\quad \beta = 1 / \sqrt{1 - (v^2 / c^2)} \tag{A3.2 – 18}$

Thus, equations (A3.2 – 13) and (A3.2 – 14) may be written as:

$$x' = \beta(x - vt) \tag{A3.2 – 19}$$

$$t' = \beta\left(t - \frac{v}{c^2}x\right) \tag{A3.2 – 20}$$

where β is given by equation (A3.2 – 18).

Equations (A3.2 –19) and (A3.2 – 20) are the transformation equations which enable x' and t' to be calculated in terms of x and t.

The inverse relations are obtainable from equations (A3.2 – 19) and (A3.2 – 20) as below:

$$\beta x = x' + \beta vt \tag{A3.2 – 21}$$

$$\beta t = t' + \beta \frac{v}{c^2}x \tag{A3.2 – 22}$$

Substituting (A3.2 – 22) into (A3.2 – 21) and solving for x gives:

$$x = \beta(x' + vt') \tag{A3.2 – 23}$$

Likewise, substituting (A3.2 – 21) into (A3.2 – 22) and solving for t yields:

$$t = \beta\left(t' + \frac{v}{c^2}x'\right) \tag{A3.2 – 24}$$

Equations (A3.2 – 23) and (A3.2 – 24) are the inverse transformation equations enabling x and t to be calculated in terms of x' and t'.

Note that β is always larger than unity, but it approaches unity as v approaches zero. On the other hand β approaches infinity as v approaches the speed of light c.

Values of v and β for some values of v/c are as follows:

v/c	0	0.1	0.3	0.5	0.7	0.9	0.99	0.999
v	0	0.3×10^8	0.9×10^8	1.5×10^8	2.1×10^8	2.7×10^8	2.97×10^8	2.997×10^8
β	1	1.005	1.048	1.155	1.400	2.294	7.092	22.371

EFFECT OF RELATIVITY ON LENGTH AND TIME

With reference to the coordinate frames S and S' in Figure A3.2 – 1, consider a straight rod to be situated in the S' frame, on the x' axis, with its ends at x_1' and x_2' respectively. Also, let the S' frame be moving relative to the S frame, with a constant velocity v, in the x direction as described above.

Then by equation (A3.2 – 19):

$$x_2' = \beta(x_2 - vt_2) \tag{A3.2 – 25}$$
$$x_1' = \beta(x_1 - vt_1) \tag{A3.2 – 26}$$

so that:

$$x_2' - x_1' = \beta[(x_2 - x_1) - v(t_2 - t_1)] \tag{A3.2 – 27}$$

If x_2 and x_1 are measured in the S frame at the same instant so that $t_2 = t_1$, or $t_2 - t_1 = 0$, then from equation (A3.2 – 27) above:

$$x_2 - x_1 = (x_2' - x_1')/\beta \qquad (A3.2 - 28)$$

Since β is larger than unity, the rod viewed from the S frame must appear shorter than what it is in the S' frame.

As an example, a 1 metre long stationary rod, in the line of the x' axis in the S' frame, which is moving relative to the S frame in the x direction with a speed $v = 0.9c$, would appear to an observer in the S frame to be $1/2.294 = 0.436$ metre long. It is to be noted that the inverse transformation equations cannot be used in this case, since they do not allow x_2 and x_1 to be calculated at the same instant $t_2 = t_1$ in the S frame.

It should also be noted that the apparent contraction observed from the S frame takes place only in the x direction, which is the direction of the motion of the S' frame, but that no contraction occurs perpendicular to that motion. This follows from equations (A3.2 – 1) and (A3.2 – 2), namely $y' = y$ and $z' = z$.

Now, let a clock be situated in the S' frame, stationary at some point x_1' on the x' axis, and let time pass from t_1' to t_2' in the S' frame, while that frame is moving relative to the S frame in the direction of the x axis with a velocity v. The corresponding instants of time in the S frame are:

$$t_2 = \beta \left(t_2' + \frac{v}{c^2} x_1' \right) \qquad (A3.2 - 29)$$

$$t_1 = \beta \left(t_1' + \frac{v}{c^2} x_1' \right) \qquad (A3.2 - 30)$$

Hence: $t_2 - t_1 = \beta (t_2' - t_1')$ \qquad (A3.2 – 31)

Once again, since β is greater than unity, any period of time in the S' frame, when observed from the S frame, appears to be longer. In other words clocks in the S' frame, when viewed from the S frame, appear to run slower.

Thus, if $v = 0.9c$, and the second hand of a clock in the S' frame, as viewed from the S frame, appears to have made one full revolution indicating that 60 seconds have elapsed in the S' frame, the corresponding passage of time in the S frame would be $2.294 \times 60 = 137.6$ seconds.

It is notable that the shortening of rods, and slowing of clocks, situated in the S' frame, as viewed from the S frame, do not depend on whether the S' frame is moving away from the S frame, or toward the S frame, as the above results do not depend on the sign of v.

Again, an observer stationary in the S' frame, could consider that the S frame is moving with respect to the S' frame, and would observe from the S' frame stationary rods in the S frame to shorten, and clocks at fixed positions in the S frame to run slow.

Two specific cases may merit consideration.

Case 1: Let two events take place in the S' frame at the same location ($x_2' = x_1'$), that is ($x_2' - x_1') = 0$, but at different instants ($t_2' \neq t_1'$). From equation (A3.2 – 23) one has:

$$x_2 - x_1 = \beta(x_2' - x_1') + \beta v(t_2' - t_1') = \beta v(t_2' - t_1') \tag{A3.2 – 32}$$

Hence, it follows that $x_2 \neq x_1$, and so an S frame observer would see the two events to take place at different locations.

Case 2: Let two events take place in the S' frame at the same instant ($t_2' = t_1'$), that is ($t_2' - t_1') = 0$, but at different locations ($x_2' \neq x_1'$). These could be two synchronised clocks in the S' frame at different locations. Then from equation (A3.2 – 24) one has:

$$t_2 - t_1 = \beta(t_2' - t_1') + \frac{\beta v}{c^2}(x_2' - x_1') = \frac{\beta v}{c^2}(x_2' - x_1') \tag{A3.2 – 33}$$

Hence, it follows that $t_2 \neq t_1$, and so the two events in the S' frame, viewed from the S frame, would appear to have taken place at different times, or the two clocks synchronised in the S' frame would appear unsynchronised to an S frame observer. The clock further away from the S frame observer would appear to be further behind in time.

<u>VELOCITIES</u>

Let the $x, y, z,$ and the x', y', z' components of the velocities in the S and S' frames be:

$$u_x = \frac{dx}{dt}, \quad u_y = \frac{dy}{dt}, \quad u_z = \frac{dz}{dt}, \quad u_x' = \frac{dx'}{dt'}, \quad u_y' = \frac{dy'}{dt'}, \quad u_z' = \frac{dz'}{dt'}$$

Then, it follows from equations (A3.2 –1), (A3.2 – 2), (A3.2 – 19) and (A3.2 – 20) that:

$$dy' = dy \tag{A3.2 – 34}$$
$$dz' = dz \tag{A3.2 – 35}$$
$$dx' = \beta(dx - v\,dt) \tag{A3.2 – 36}$$
$$dt' = \beta\left(dt - \frac{v}{c^2}dx\right) \tag{A3.2 – 37}$$

which yield upon substitution:

$$u_x' = \frac{u_x - v}{1 - \frac{u_x v}{c^2}} \tag{A3.2 – 38} \qquad u_x = \frac{u_x' + v}{1 + \frac{u_x' v}{c^2}} \tag{A3.2–41}$$

$$u_y' = \frac{u_y}{\beta\left(1 - \frac{u_x v}{c^2}\right)} \tag{A3.2 – 39} \qquad u_y = \frac{u_y'}{\beta\left(1 + \frac{u_x' v}{c^2}\right)} \tag{A3.2 – 42}$$

$$u_z' = \frac{u_z}{\beta\left(1 - \frac{u_x v}{c^2}\right)} \tag{A3.2 – 40} \qquad u_z = \frac{u_z'}{\beta\left(1 + \frac{u_x' v}{c^2}\right)} \tag{A3.2 – 43}$$

Appendices to Chapter 3

EFFECT OF RELATIVITY ON MASS

An often-met physical quantity is the momentum of a moving body. Momentum is defined as the product of the mass of the body multiplied by the body's velocity. As velocity is a directed (vector) quantity, so is momentum, its direction being that of the associated velocity. Let the body's mass be denoted m, and let the body's velocity be designated u, having x, y, and z components:

$$u_x = dx/dt, \qquad u_y = dy/dt, \qquad u_z = dz/dt.$$

Then, the x, y, and z components of the momentum are:

$$m\,u_x = m\,dx/dt, \qquad m\,u_y = m\,dy/dt, \qquad m\,u_z = m\,dz/dt.$$

If two bodies of masses m_1 and m_2, originally travelling with velocities u_1 and u_2 respectively, collide with each other, then in general after collision the velocities of both bodies will change to some new values w_1 and w_2 respectively. It will be always found that the sum of the momenta of the two masses before and after the collision is the same, that is, no change in the sum of the momenta takes place. This is referred to as the principle of the conservation of momentum.

Momenta, as all directed quantities, can be added or subtracted algebraically, by adding and subtracting their respective x, y, and z components.

Let the x, y, and z components of the momenta of the two masses m_1 and m_2 before the collision be:

$$m_1 u_{x1}, \quad m_1 u_{y1}, \quad m_1 u_{z1} \qquad m_2 u_{x2}, \quad m_2 u_{y2}, \quad m_2 u_{z2}$$

and denote the corresponding values after the collision by:

$$m_1 w_{x1}, \quad m_1 w_{y1}, \quad m_1 w_{z1} \qquad m_2 w_{x2}, \quad m_2 w_{y2}, \quad m_2 w_{z2}$$

then the principle of conservation of momentum requires:

$$m_1 u_{x1} + m_2 u_{x2} = m_1 w_{x1} + m_2 w_{x2}$$
$$m_1 u_{y1} + m_2 u_{y2} = m_1 w_{y1} + m_2 w_{y2}$$
$$m_1 u_{z1} + m_2 u_{z2} = m_1 w_{z1} + m_2 w_{z2}$$

The above equations may be written in the alternative form:

$$(m_1 u_{x1} + m_2 u_{x2}) - (m_1 w_{x1} + m_2 w_{x2}) = 0 \qquad (A3.2-44)$$
$$(m_1 u_{y1} + m_2 u_{y2}) - (m_1 w_{y1} + m_2 w_{y2}) = 0 \qquad (A3.2-45)$$
$$(m_1 u_{z1} + m_2 u_{z2}) - (m_1 w_{z1} + m_2 w_{z2}) = 0 \qquad (A3.2-46)$$

which is often briefly stated as:

$$\Sigma m (u_x, u_y, u_z) = \Sigma m (w_x, w_y, w_z) \qquad (A3.2-47)$$

or $\qquad \Sigma m (u_x, u_y, u_z) - \Sigma m (w_x, w_y, w_z) = \Delta \Sigma m (u_x, u_y, u_z) = 0 \qquad (A3.2-48)$

where Δ stands for change or difference, and Σ denotes sum, so that equation (A3.2 – 48) states that the change in the sum of the momenta, from that before the collision, to that after the collision, is zero.

Now, if the collision is considered to take place in the S frame with the law of conservation of momentum satisfied, and then one applies the transformation equations from the S to the

S' frame, the two frames moving at constant velocity v relative to each other, it will be found that the law of conservation of momentum fails to apply in the S' frame, or putting it differently, the law is not invariant upon transformation from one frame to another.

An actual specific example for the breakdown of the law of conservation of momentum is not given here, as the algebra involved is tedious and lengthy.

Since physical laws must apply equally in all frames of reference, even when such frames are moving relative to each other at constant velocity, one can only conclude that mass, like length and time, is not an invariant quantity upon transformation between different frames of reference.

One thus needs to find quantities that are invariant under transformation. An insight into this problem may be gained by making a change in the time variables from t to τ and t' to τ' such that:

$$ct = i\tau \qquad \text{or} \qquad \tau^2 = c^2 t^2 / i^2 = -c^2 t^2 \qquad (A3.2-49)$$
$$ct' = i\tau' \qquad \text{or} \qquad \tau'^2 = c^2 t'^2 / i^2 = -c^2 t'^2 \qquad (A3.2-50)$$

where c = speed of light, and $i^2 = -1$, so that $i = \sqrt{-1}$.

Since both c and i are constants, one has: $\tau \propto t$ and $\tau' \propto t'$.

Now let two new "space-time" variables: s and s' be examined in the S and S' frames, such that they satisfy the following relations:

$$s^2 = x^2 + y^2 + z^2 + \tau^2 \qquad (A3.2-51)$$
$$s'^2 = x'^2 + y'^2 + z'^2 + \tau'^2 \qquad (A3.2-52)$$

Substituting equations (A3.2 – 49) and (A3.2 – 50) into the transformation equations (A3.2 – 19) and (A3.2 – 20) yields:

$$x' = \beta\left(x - \frac{i}{c}v\tau\right) \qquad (A3.2-53)$$

$$\frac{i}{c}\tau' = \beta\left(\frac{i}{c}\tau - \frac{v}{c^2}x\right) \qquad \text{or} \qquad \tau' = \beta\left(\tau + \frac{iv}{c}x\right) \qquad (A3.2-54)$$

Putting (A3.2 – 1), (A3.2 – 2), (A3.2 – 53), and (A3.2 – 54) into (A3.2 – 52) gives:

$$s'^2 = \beta^2\left(x - \frac{i}{c}v\tau\right)^2 + y^2 + z^2 + \beta^2\left(\tau + \frac{iv}{c}x\right)^2$$

Squaring and collecting terms involving x^2 and t^2 yields:

$$s'^2 = \beta^2\left[x^2\left(1-\frac{v^2}{c^2}\right) + \tau^2\left(1-\frac{v^2}{c^2}\right)\right] + y^2 + z^2$$

Or since by equation (A3.2 – 18), $1 - (v^2/c^2) = 1/\beta^2$, one has:

$$s'^2 = x^2 + y^2 + z^2 + \tau^2$$

Hence, the variables s and s' in equations (A3.2 – 51) and (A3.2 – 52) are identical:

$$s^2 = s'^2 = x^2 + y^2 + z^2 + \tau^2 = x'^2 + y'^2 + z'^2 + \tau'^2 \qquad (A3.2-55)$$

Finally, putting (A3.2 – 49) and (A3.2 – 50) back into (A3.2 – 55) gives:

$$s^2 = s'^2 = x^2 + y^2 + z^2 - c^2 t^2 = x'^2 + y'^2 + z'^2 - c^2 t'^2 \qquad (A3.2 - 56)$$

Alternatively, one may write equations (A3.2 – 55) and (A3.2 – 56) as:

$$s = s' = \sqrt{x^2 + y^2 + z^2 + \tau^2} = \sqrt{x^2 + y^2 + z^2 - c^2 t^2} \qquad (A3.2 - 57)$$

$$= \sqrt{x'^2 + y'^2 + z'^2 + \tau'^2} = \sqrt{x'^2 + y'^2 + z'^2 - c^2 t'^2} \qquad (A3.2 - 58)$$

These important results show that, while neither the space nor the time intervals of an event, with respect to the origins of two coordinate frames in uniform motion relative to each other, are invariant, the space-time interval of an event, relative to the origins in the two frames, as shown by equations (A3.2 – 55), (A3.2 – 56), (A3.2 – 57), and (A3.2 – 58), is invariant. This suggests that time must be regarded as a fourth dimension, leading to four-dimensional space-time coordinate frames, or four-dimensional space-time continua.

Let ds, dx, dy, dz, and dt represent small changes, or increments, in $s, x, y, z,$ and t. Then, (A3.2 – 56) may be written in the incremental form:

$$(ds)^2 = (dx)^2 + (dy)^2 + (dz)^2 - c^2 (dt)^2$$

which upon division by $(dt)^2$ yields:

$$\left(\frac{ds}{dt}\right)^2 = \left(\frac{dx}{dt}\right)^2 + \left(\frac{dy}{dt}\right)^2 + \left(\frac{dz}{dt}\right)^2 - c^2 \qquad (A3.2 - 59)$$

This equation must hold in general, and so it must hold for any fixed point in the S' frame, moving relative to the S frame with velocity v. Thus, the square of the velocity of such a point relative to the S frame is:

$$\left(\frac{dx}{dt}\right)^2 + \left(\frac{dy}{dt}\right)^2 + \left(\frac{dz}{dt}\right)^2 = v^2$$

Equation (A3.2 – 59), for such a point, may thus be written as:

$$\left(\frac{ds}{dt}\right)^2 = v^2 - c^2 \qquad (A3.2 - 60)$$

Now, for speeds v less than the speed of light c, one has $v < c$, and so $v^2 - c^2 < 0$, namely it is negative. Hence (A3.2 – 60) in terms of (A3.2 – 18) may be written as:

$$\frac{ds}{dt} = i\sqrt{c^2 - v^2} = ic \sqrt{1 - \frac{v^2}{c^2}} = \frac{ic}{\beta} \qquad (A3.2 - 61)$$

Recalling equation (A3.2 – 48), the law of conservation of momentum in three-dimensional space would be expected to be given by:

$$\Delta \Sigma m (u_x, u_y, u_z) = \Delta \Sigma m \left(\frac{dx}{dt}, \frac{dy}{dt}, \frac{dz}{dt}\right) = 0 \qquad (A3.2 - 62)$$

which says that, the change in the sum of the momenta from before an event, to that after an event, such as a collision, is zero. However, it was noted that this relation is not invariant between frames in relative translation at uniform velocity.

Since the space-time intervals, as given by equations (A3.2 – 57) and (A3.2 – 58), were found to be invariant, one might expect the expression below to be invariant:

$$\Delta \Sigma m \left(\frac{dx}{ds}, \frac{dy}{ds}, \frac{dz}{ds}, \frac{d\tau}{ds} \right) = 0 \qquad (A3.2-63)$$

But, from (A3.2 – 61): $ds = (ic/\beta) \, dt$ \qquad (A3.2 – 64)

Substituting (A3.2 – 64) into (A3.2 – 63) yields:

$$\Delta \Sigma \frac{m\beta}{ic} \left(\frac{dx}{dt}, \frac{dy}{dt}, \frac{dz}{dt}, \frac{d\tau}{dt} \right) = 0 \qquad (A3.2-65)$$

Equation (A3.2 – 65) may be split into two parts, without invalidating it, as follows:

$$\Delta \Sigma \frac{m\beta}{ic} \left(\frac{dx}{dt}, \frac{dy}{dt}, \frac{dz}{dt} \right) = 0 \qquad (A3.2-66)$$

$$\Delta \Sigma \frac{m\beta}{ic} \left(\frac{d\tau}{dt} \right) = 0 \qquad (A3.2-67)$$

The above was done since equation (A3.2- 66) so obtained appears to represent change in momentum, which begs further examination. In equation (A3.2 – 66) let m be a mass stationary at some fixed point in the S' frame, and therefore be moving with a velocity $v = u$ (dx/dt, dy/dt, dz/dt) in the S frame. Also, since the expression in (A3.2 – 66) equals zero, while ic is a constant, ic may be omitted from (A3.2 – 66), which then becomes:

$$\Delta \Sigma m\beta \, u = 0 \quad \text{or} \quad \Delta \Sigma m' u = 0 \qquad (A3.2-68)$$

where $m' = m\beta = m / \sqrt{1 - \dfrac{v^2}{c^2}}$ \qquad (A3.2 – 69)

is recognised as the new, relativistic, velocity dependent mass.

It is to be noted that as $v \to 0$, $m' \to m$,
and as $v \to c$, $m' \to \infty$.

Thus a given mass, moving with some velocity in the S frame, increases as its velocity increases, and its magnitude approaches infinity as its velocity approaches the speed of light.

Equation (A3.2 – 68) is recognisable as the new relativistic law of conservation of momentum, which is found to be invariant between frames S and S'. For velocities v so small that v^2/c^2 may be considered negligible compared with unity, one has that $\beta \to 1$, and equation (A3.2 – 68) becomes $\Delta \Sigma mu = \Delta \Sigma m (u_x, u_y, u_z) = 0$ as expected from pre-relativity classical mechanics, and given by equation (A3.2 – 48).

Now, let equation (A3.2 – 67) be examined. From equation (A3.2 – 49):
$d\tau / dt = c / i$ \qquad (A3.2–70)

Putting (A3.2 – 70) into (A3.2 – 67) gives:
$\Delta \Sigma (-m\beta) = \Delta \Sigma (m\beta) = 0$

Appendices to Chapter 3

or, again by equation (A3.2 – 18):

$$\Delta \Sigma m / \sqrt{1 - \frac{v^2}{c^2}} = \Delta \Sigma m \left(1 - \frac{v^2}{c^2}\right)^{-1/2} = 0 \qquad (A3.2-71)$$

Let now expand (A3.2 – 71) by the binomial theorem, and approximate it by the first two terms of the expansion. Also, multiply by c^2, which is permissible since the expression equals zero, while c^2 is a constant. One then obtains:

$$\Delta \Sigma \, mc^2 \left(1 - \frac{v^2}{c^2}\right)^{-1/2} \approx \Delta \Sigma \, mc^2 \left(1 + \frac{1}{2}\frac{v^2}{c^2}\right) = \Delta \Sigma \left(mc^2 + \frac{1}{2}mv^2\right) = 0$$

or $\quad \Sigma \left(mc^2 + \frac{1}{2}mv^2\right) \approx \text{constant} \approx W_t = W_o + W_k \qquad (A3.2-72)$

In equation (A3.2 – 72), $W_k = \frac{1}{2} mv^2$ is obviously the kinetic energy of a mass m moving with velocity v in the S frame, while being stationary in the S' frame. Thus, W_t would have to be the total energy possessed by mass m, and so the term W_o must be the energy possessed by mass m when at rest. From equation (A3.2 – 72) this energy equals:

$$W_o = mc^2 \qquad (A3.2-73)$$

Equations (A3.2 – 72) and (A3.2 – 73) indicate the equivalence of mass and energy.

Alternatively, the total energy W_t of a moving mass may be taken as the relativistic mass times the speed of light squared, since that also equals the sum of the rest energy plus the kinetic energy:

$$W_t = m'c^2 = mc^2 / \sqrt{1 - \frac{v^2}{c^2}} \approx mc^2 \left(1 + \frac{1}{2}\frac{v^2}{c^2}\right) = mc^2 + \frac{1}{2}mv^2 \qquad (A3.2-74)$$

where the binomial theorem was relied on, as above.

In classical mechanics the force F acting on a mass m is given by:

$$F = m \frac{du}{dt} = ma \qquad (A3.2-75)$$

where: u = velocity, t = time, and $a = du/dt$ = acceleration of the mass.

However, in relativistic terms, if a mass m' is accelerated, then both the velocity and the mass itself increases with time, and one has to calculate the force using the rule for differentiating the products of variables:

$$F = \frac{d}{dt}(m'u) = m'\frac{du}{dt} + u\frac{dm'}{dt} \qquad (A3.2-76)$$

Velocities close to the speed of light can be attained by accelerating electrically charged subatomic particles in strong magnetic fields. The results from many such experiments verify the validity of the foregoing mathematical relations for momentum, energy, the variation of mass with velocity, and the equivalence of mass and energy.

Appendix 3.3 – Photoelectric Effect - Planck's Constant

With reference to Figure 3.6 let:

h	=	Planck's constant (joule seconds)
f	=	frequency of the ultraviolet ray (cycles per second)
hf	=	energy of the photons (joules)
q	=	magnitude of the electronic charge (1.602×10^{-19} coulomb)
W_o	=	minimum photon energy required to secure electron emission from the given cathode material (joules)
W	=	kinetic energy of the electron immediately after it is emitted (joules)
	=	potential energy of the electron when it is brought to a stop (joules)
V	=	magnitude of the minimum negative anode to cathode voltage which is necessary to stop electrons from reaching the anode (volts)

The kinetic energy of the emitted electron must equal the difference: the energy of the incident photon minus the energy required to secure emission ($W = hf - W_o$). This energy is converted into potential energy ($W = Vq$), when the electron is brought to a stop. So:

$$W = Vq = hf - W_o \quad \text{from which:} \quad V = \frac{h}{q}f - \frac{W_o}{q}$$

If one varies the photon frequency f, and plots the magnitude of the stopping voltage V against the frequency, the slope of the resulting line is h/q. Thus multiplying the measured slope of the line by the electronic charge q yields Planck's constant.

With reference to Figure A3.3 – 1, suppose that in an actual experiment the stopping voltage changes from 0.65 volt to 2.3 volts, as the frequency is increased from 6×10^{14} cycles per second to 10×10^{14} cycles per second.

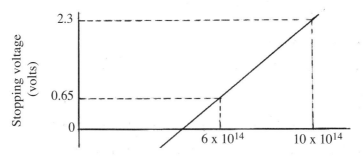

Figure A3.3 – 1

Hence, the changes in voltage and frequency are:
$2.30 - 0.65 = 1.65$ volts, and $(10 \times 10^{14}) - (6 \times 10^{14}) = 4 \times 10^{14}$ cycles per second.

Thus the slope is: $1.65 / (4 \times 10^{14}) = 0.413 \times 10^{-14}$, and Planck's constant must equal this slope times the electronic change: $h = (0.413 \times 10^{-14}) \times (1.602 \times 10^{-19}) = 6.62 \times 10^{-34}$ joule second. A more precise value of Planck's constant is $h = 6.625 \times 10^{-34}$ joule second.

Appendix 3.4 – The Bohr Atom Model for the Hydrogen Atom

With reference to Figure A3.4 – 1, let:

r	=	radius of the electronic orbit around the nucleus situated at O (metres)
v	=	electronic orbital speed (metres per second)
m	=	electronic mass (9.109×10^{-31} kilogram)
q	=	electronic charge (1.602×10^{-19} coulomb)
h	=	Planck's constant (6.625×10^{-34} joule second)
n	=	integer = 1, 2, 3, etc., to each of which corresponds a specific allowed orbit
π	=	constant = 3.1416

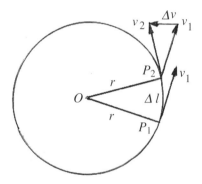

Figure A3.4 – 1

The De Broglie wavelength of the electron is:

$$h / mv \qquad (A3.4 - 1)$$

The De Broglie proposition requires an integral number n of electronic wavelengths to fit into the orbital circumference of radius r, and so:

$$2\pi r = nh / mv$$

Hence follows the Bohr requirement for possible orbits, namely:

(orbital circumference) x (electronic mass) x (electronic speed) = nh

or $\quad 2\pi rmv = nh \qquad (A3.4 - 2)$

Referring to Figure A3.4 – 1, as the electron moves around the nucleus at O, in an orbit of radius r, let it move a short distance Δl, from point P_1 to P_2, in time interval Δt. In the same time the electron's speed changes from v_1 to v_2, the corresponding change in speed being denoted Δv. If v is the magnitude of the orbital speed, and if the arc P_1 to P_2 is short enough to be regarded a straight line Δl, then one has by similar triangles:

$$\Delta l / r = \Delta v / v$$

or $\quad (\Delta l / \Delta t) / r = (\Delta v / \Delta t) / v$

But $\quad \Delta l / \Delta t = v \quad$ is the magnitude of the velocity of the electron,
while $\quad \Delta v / \Delta t = a \quad$ is the magnitude of the acceleration of the electron.

Hence, from the above $v/r = a/v$ which yields the acceleration a as:

$$a = v^2/r \qquad (A3.4-3)$$

Allowing Δl in Figure A3.4 – 1 to approach zero shows that, at any point on the orbit, the direction of the velocity is tangential to the orbit, while the acceleration, having the same direction as that of Δv, is directed toward the nucleus at the centre of the orbit. Since force equals (mass) x (acceleration), the force keeping the electron in its orbit equals:

$$ma = mv^2/r \qquad (A3.4-4)$$

This force must be supplied by the electric force of attraction between the positively charged nucleus and the negatively charged electron. It is known from many experiments that the force of attraction between two unlike charges Q_1 and Q_2 coulombs, r metres apart, is kQ_1Q_2/r^2 newtons, where k = constant = 8.99×10^9. Thus, the force of attraction between the nucleus and the electron is kq^2/r^2, where $k = 8.99 \times 10^9$, while $q = 1.602 \times 10^{-19}$ coulomb is the magnitude of the charge on both the nucleus and the electron, and r is the radius of the electron's orbit in metres. Hence, to keep the electron in orbit, one must have:

$$mv^2/r = kq^2/r^2 \qquad (A3.4-5)$$

But, from equation (A3.4 – 2), the orbital speed of the electron in the nth orbit is:

$$v = nh/2\pi rm \qquad (A3.4-6)$$

which upon substitution into equation (A3.4 – 5) yields the orbital radius:

$$r = n^2h^2/4\pi^2kmq^2 \qquad (A3.4-7)$$

Putting this back into (A3.4 – 6) gives the orbital speed as:

$$v = 2\pi kq^2/nh \qquad (A3.4-8)$$

Equations (A3.4 – 7) and (A3.4 – 8) enable the orbital radii, and the orbital speeds, to be calculated for various values of $n = 1, 2, 3$, etc. Thus $n = 1$ gives the orbital radius and the orbital speed for the innermost orbit. It is notable that the orbital radii are proportional to n^2, while the orbital speeds are proportional to $1/n$. Hence as n increases, the radii increase, and the speeds fall.

From equation (A3.4 – 8), the kinetic energy of the electron in the nth orbit is:

$$W_k = \frac{1}{2}mv^2 = 2\pi^2 k^2 mq^4/n^2h^2 \qquad (A3.4-9)$$

To find the electron's potential energy in the nth orbit, one must first determine the work done in moving an electron from the nth orbit with radius r, to infinity.

Now, the force of attraction varies nonlinearly with the radius, that is, with the distance from the nucleus, and so the product (force) x (distance) needs to be integrated:

$$\text{Work done:} \quad W = \int_r^\infty \frac{kq^2}{r^2} dr = \frac{kq^2}{r} \qquad (A3.4-10)$$

As the electron is moved further away from the nucleus, its potential energy increases, and yet the potential energy of the electron at infinity, namely when it is completely removed from the atom, needs to be regarded as zero, and so in any one orbit it is a negative quantity.

Thus, the potential energy of the electron in the nth orbit with radius r must equal:

W_p = (potential energy at infinity) – (work done in moving electron to infinity)
$= 0 - kq^2/r = -kq^2/r$

which upon eliminating r by equation (A3.4 – 7) becomes:

$$W_p = -4\pi^2 k^2 mq^4 / n^2 h^2 \qquad (A3.4-11)$$

The total energy W_t of the electron in the nth orbit is the sum of its kinetic and potential energies, as given by equations (A3.4 – 9) and (A3.4 – 11):

$$W_t = -2\pi^2 k^2 mq^4 / n^2 h^2 \qquad (A3.4-12)$$

If the electron drops from level n to level m, where $m < n$, then the energy given up by the electron, in rounded figures, is:

$$\Delta W = -\frac{2\pi^2 k^2 mq^4}{h^2}\left(\frac{1}{n^2}-\frac{1}{m^2}\right) = \frac{2\pi^2 k^2 mq^4}{h^2}\left(\frac{1}{m^2}-\frac{1}{n^2}\right)$$

$$= \frac{(2) \times (3.1416)^2 \times (8.99 \times 10^9)^2 \times (9.109 \times 10^{-31}) \times (1.602 \times 10^{-19})^4}{(6.625 \times 10^{-34})^2}\left(\frac{1}{m^2}-\frac{1}{n^2}\right)$$

$$= 2.181 \times 10^{-18} \left(\frac{1}{m^2}-\frac{1}{n^2}\right) \text{ joule.} \qquad (A3.4-13)$$

This must equal the energy of the emitted photon, and so:

$$\Delta W = hf = hc/\lambda \qquad (A3.4-14)$$

where: f = frequency of the emitted photon (cycles per second)
λ = wavelength of the emitted photon (metres)
c = speed of light (3×10^8 metres per second)

From equation (A3.4 – 14) the wavelength of the emitted photon is:

$$\lambda = hc/\Delta W \qquad (A3.4-15)$$

Thus, if an electron drops from the third orbit ($n = 3$) to the second orbit ($m = 2$), the energy of the emitted photon from equation (A3.4 – 13) is:

$$\Delta W = (2.181 \times 10^{-18}) \times \left(\frac{1}{4}-\frac{1}{9}\right) = 0.3029 \times 10^{-18} \text{ joule,}$$

and the wavelength of the emitted photon from equation (A3.4 – 15) is:

$\lambda = (6.625 \times 10^{-34}) \times (3 \times 10^8) / (0.3029 \times 10^{-18})$
$= 656.2 \times 10^{-9}$ metres, or 656.2 nanometres,

which corresponds to the wavelength of the strongest spectral line in Figure 3.10.

If subsequently the electron drops from the second orbit ($n = 2$) to the first orbit ($m = 1$), the emitted energy is:

$$\Delta W = 2.181 \times 10^{-18} \times \left(1-\frac{1}{4}\right) = 1.636 \times 10^{-18} \text{ joule,}$$

and so the emitted photon wavelength is:

$$\lambda = hc / \Delta W = (6.625 \times 10^{-34}) \times (3 \times 10^{8}) / (1.636 \times 10^{-18})$$
$$= 121.5 \times 10^{-9} \text{ metre, or } 121.5 \text{ nanometres.}$$

This is a spectral line in the ultraviolet region.

When the electron is in the innermost ($n = 1$) orbit, the hydrogen atom is in its normal, or ground, state. The diameter of this orbit may be considered the diameter of the hydrogen atom. From equation (A3.4 – 7) the radius of the innermost ($n = 1$) orbit is:

$$r = h^2 / 4\pi^2 kmq^2$$
$$= \frac{(6.625 \times 10^{-34})^2}{(4) \times (3.1416)^2 \times (8.99 \times 10^{9}) \times (9.109 \times 10^{-31}) \times (1.602 \times 10^{-19})^2}$$
$$= 0.0529 \times 10^{-9} \text{ metre, or } 0.0529 \text{ nanometre.}$$

The diameter of the innermost orbit, and so the diameter of the hydrogen atom, is twice the radius, that is 0.1058 nanometre, or in rounded figures 0.1 of a nanometre. This is the size of the hydrogen atom in its normal state.

The electronic speed in the innermost orbit ($n = 1$) from equation (A3.4 – 8) is:

$$v = 2\pi kq^2 / h$$
$$= (2) \times (3.1416) \times (8.99 \times 10^{9}) \times (1.602 \times 10^{-19})^2 / (6.625 \times 10^{-34})$$
$$= 2.19 \times 10^{6} \text{ metres per second,}$$

or $\qquad$ 0.73% of the speed of light.

Any increase of electronic mass with speed at 0.73 % of the speed of light is negligible, and may be ignored. The electronic wavelength at this speed is:

$$\frac{h}{mv} = \frac{6.625 \times 10^{-34}}{(9.109 \times 10^{-31}) \times (2.19 \times 10^{6})} = 0.332 \times 10^{-9} \text{ metre, or } 0.332 \text{ nanometre,}$$

while the circumference of the innermost orbit is:

$$2\pi r = (2) \times (3.1416) \times (0.529 \times 10^{-10}) = 0.332 \times 10^{-9} \text{ metre, or } 0.332 \text{ nanometre.}$$

Thus, the circumference of the innermost orbit is 1 wavelength long, or 0.332 nanometre, as would be expected from the De Broglie proposition.

Appendices to Chapter 6

Appendix 6.1 – The Period of a Pendulum

A pendulum consists of a small, round, solid object, often called a bob, suspended from a fixed point by a length of non-stretchable cord. With reference to Figure A6.1–1, let the pendulum be suspended from point A, and at some instant, as the pendulum is swinging, consider the centre of the bob to be located at point B.

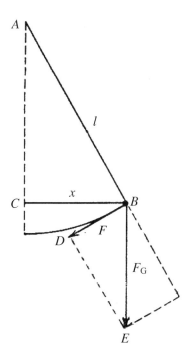

Figure A6.1–1

Let the following notation be introduced:

l = AB = length of the pendulum (metres)
m = mass of the bob (kilograms)
g = gravitational acceleration (9.807 metres / second ^{2})
F_G = BE = gravitational force acting on the bob vertically downward (newtons)
F = BD = component of the gravitational force, acting on the bob in a direction perpendicular to line AB (newtons)
a = acceleration of the bob due to force F, having the same direction as F (metres / second ^{2})
x = BC = horizontal displacement of the bob from its rest position (metres)
t = time measured from the instant when the bob is first released from its initial point of displacement (seconds)
T = period of the pendulum's oscillations (seconds)

Note that since: (force) = (mass) x (acceleration), one has: $F_G = mg$ and $F = ma$.

Appendices to Chapter 6

Since the two triangles ABC and EBD are similar, one must have:

$$BD / BE = BC / BA$$

or: $\quad F / F_G = ma / mg = a / g = x / l \quad$ (A6.1 – 1)

Thus, from equation (A6.1 – 1):

$$a = gx / l = (g / l) x \quad \text{(A6.1 – 2)}$$

If x is small compared with l, then the directions of F, a, and x, may be assumed to lie in the same line. Further, since the acceleration is the second derivative of the displacement, one has from equation (A6.1 – 2):

$$d^2x / dt^2 = -a = -(g / l) x \quad \text{(A6.1 – 3)}$$

where the negative sign arises because the acceleration a is oppositely directed to the displacement x, as measured from C.

Equation (A6.1 – 3) is a differential equation, the solution of which is known to be:

$$x = K \sin \left(\sqrt{\frac{g}{l}} \, t + \frac{\pi}{2} \right) \quad \text{(A6.1 – 4)}$$

where K = amplitude of the swing,

and $\quad \pi = 3.1416$.

It can be shown that (A6.1 – 4) is the solution of (A6.1 – 3) by substituting (A6.1 – 4) back into (A6.1 – 3):

$$\frac{dx}{dt} = \sqrt{\frac{g}{l}} \, K \cos \left(\sqrt{\frac{g}{l}} \, t + \frac{\pi}{2} \right)$$

$$\frac{d^2x}{dt^2} = -\left(\frac{g}{l}\right) K \sin \left(\sqrt{\frac{g}{l}} \, t + \frac{\pi}{2} \right) = -(g / l) x$$

which is the same as equation (A6.1 – 3), showing that equation (A6.1 – 4) is the solution of equation (A6.1 – 3). Equation (A6.1 – 4) represents a sine wave such as depicted in Figure 3.3, Chapter 3.

When one full period has elapsed, one has $t = T$, and since equation (A6.1 – 4) is periodic with period 2π, the following must hold:

$$\sqrt{\frac{g}{l}} \, t = \sqrt{\frac{g}{l}} \, T = 2\pi$$

yielding: $\quad T = 2\pi \sqrt{\dfrac{l}{g}} \quad$ (A6.1 – 5)

The length of the pendulum in terms of the period from (A6.1 – 5) is:

$$l = \frac{g}{4\pi^2} T^2 \quad \text{(A6.1 – 6)}$$

If the period is to be 1 second, that is, $T = 1$, then:

$$l = \frac{g}{4\pi^2} = \frac{9.807}{(4) \times (3.1416)^2} = 0.2484 \text{ metre.}$$

Appendix 6.2 – The Orbital Motion of the Planets

Two masses, m_1 and m_2 kilograms respectively, with a distance of r metres between their centres of gravity, attract each other with a gravitational force of F newtons, where:

$$F = Gm_1m_2/r^2 \qquad (A6.2-1)$$

In the above equation G is the gravitational constant, the value of which can be determined using a sensitive apparatus enabling the measurement of the force of attraction between suspended masses having known fixed magnitudes. The value of G is:

$$G = 6.67 \times 10^{-11} \text{ newton metre}^2/\text{kg}^2 \qquad (A6.2-2)$$

Planets move around the sun in orbits, most of which are elliptical, but may be considered circular to a good approximation. Let M and m denote the masses of the sun and one of the planets respectively in kilograms. Also, let r denote the radius of the planet's orbit in metres, and T denote the planet's period of revolution around the sun in seconds.

With reference to Appendix 3.4, equation (A3.4 – 3) gives the acceleration of an electron directed toward the nucleus in an atom. Now similarly, if a planet's speed is v metres per second in its orbit of radius r metres, then its acceleration directed toward the sun is:

$$v^2/r \text{ metres per second squared} \qquad (A6.2-3)$$

while the force causing this acceleration equals the acceleration multiplied by the planet's mass, namely:

$$mv^2/r \text{ newtons} \qquad (A6.2-4)$$

As this force equals the force of gravitation between the planet and the sun, one must have:

$$GMm/r^2 = mv^2/r \qquad (A6.2-5)$$

The circumference of the planet's orbit is $2\pi r$, (where $\pi = 3.1416$), while the time for one complete revolution, namely one period T, is the circumference divided by the speed:

$$T = 2\pi r/v \text{ seconds} \qquad (A6.2-6)$$

Substituting equation (A6.2 – 5) into (A6.2 – 6), so as to eliminate v, gives:

$$T^2 = \frac{4\pi^2}{GM} r^3 \qquad (A6.2-7)$$

Equation (A6.2 – 7) is known as Kepler's third law of planetary motion.

The Sun, the Earth and the planet Mars line up once approximately every two years as shown in Figure A6.2 – 1, with the Sun and Mars on the opposite sides of Earth.

One may select two points A and B on the surface of the Earth, in a way so that the line connecting the centre of Mars to the middle point of line AB is perpendicular to line AB. When this condition obtains, the angles α and β between the line AB and the lines connecting Mars to points A and B respectively will be equal. Measuring the angle $\alpha = \beta$ enables the distance x from Earth to Mars to be calculated as discussed with the aid of Figure A6.2–1 below. From Figure A6.2–1 one has for x:

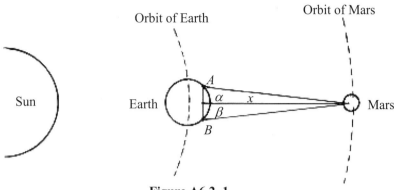

Figure A6.2–1

x = (one half of line AB) x (tangent of angle α at apex A)

It is not practicable to measure the angle α directly. However, α may be deduced from the measured angle γ between the lines connecting the centre of the arc AB on Earth to the apparent positions of Mars in the night sky as viewed from points A and B on Earth. One then has $\gamma = 180° - 2\alpha$, yielding $\alpha = (180° - \gamma)/2$, and hence the value of x, which is essentially the difference of the radii of the orbits of Earth and Mars around the Sun.

The periods of revolution T_E and T_M of Earth and Mars respectively around the Sun may be determined from astronomical observations. If the radii of the orbits of Mars and Earth are denoted by r_M and r_E respectively, then from equation (A6.2 – 7) one has:

$$\frac{r_M^3}{r_E^3} = \frac{(r_E + x)^3}{r_E^3} = \frac{T_M^2}{T_E^2} \tag{A6.2 – 8}$$

If x is known, (A6.2 – 8) is easily solvable for r_E, yielding $r_E \approx 1.5 \times 10^{11}$ metres.

Knowing the radius of the earth's orbit r_E, the radius of the orbit of any other planet can be readily calculated from its observed period of revolution using equation (A6.2 – 8), where r_M and T_M then stand for the orbital radius and the period of that other planet. The orbital speed of any planet is the circumference of its orbit divided by its period of revolution:

$$v = 2\pi r / T \tag{A6.2 – 9}$$

If at any given instant the position and the velocity, that is the speed and the direction of motion, of a planet is known, or is determined by astronomical measurements, then its position and velocity at any future instant is calculable. It is to be noted that neither the orbital radii, nor the periods of revolution, are dependent on the planetary mass.

Further, the mass M of the sun is calculable from equation (A6.2 – 7) as $M \approx 2 \times 10^{30}$ kilograms. Also, in equation (A6.2 – 1), equating m_1 and r to the mass and the radius of earth respectively, and putting $F = m_2 g$ = gravitational force on a mass m_2 at the earth's surface, then m_2 cancels, and the earth's mass is calculable as $m_1 \approx 6 \times 10^{24}$ kilograms.

Since the planetary orbits are elliptical to varying degrees, accurate calculations are more complex, nevertheless the simplified approach above offers a good approximation.

Appendix 6.3 – Table A6.3

If a coin is tossed 10 times in succession, then the outcome may be any one of 11 possibilities for the number of heads, extending from 0 head to 10 heads. Let the process be repeated 1024 times, that is to 1024 batches of 10 tosses, each batch yielding a value for the number of heads. As discussed in Chapter 6, one would expect 0 head to occur in 1 batch, 1 head to occur in 10 batches, 2 heads to occur in 45 batches, and so on. To find the mean, the variance, and the standard deviation, of these 1024 values, one may proceed as set out in Table A6.3 below.

Table A6.3

Heads or values	Number of times values occur	Sum of values	Deviations from mean	Squares of dev.	Sum of squares
0	1	0 x 1 = 0	-5	25	25 x 1 = 25
1	10	1 x 10 = 10	-4	16	16 x 10 = 160
2	45	2 x 45 = 90	-3	9	9 x 45 = 405
3	120	3 x 120 = 360	-2	4	4 x 120 = 480
4	210	4 x 210 = 840	-1	1	1 x 210 = 210
5	252	5 x 252 = 1260	0	0	0 x 252 = 0
6	210	6 x 210 = 1260	1	1	1 x 210 = 210
7	120	7 x 120 = 840	2	4	4 x 120 = 480
8	45	8 x 45 = 360	3	9	9 x 45 = 405
9	10	9 x 10 = 90	4	16	16 x 10 = 160
10	1	10 x 1 = 10	5	25	25 x 1 = 25
	Total number of values = 1024	Total sum of values = 5120			Total sum of squares = 2560
Mean = 5120 / 1024 = 5			Variance = 2560 / 1024 = 2.5 Standard deviation = $\sqrt{2.5}$ = 1.581		

Appendix 6.4 – Table A6.4

The Normal Probability Curve is calculated from:

$y = 0.3989 e^{-(1/2)(z^2)}$, where $e = 2.718282$,

and the Shaded Area = Probability P, listed for given values of the normalised deviation Z or higher.

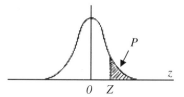

Z	0.00	0.01	0.02	0.03	0.04	0.05	0.06	0.07	0.08	0.09
0.0	.50000	.49601	.49202	.48803	.48405	.48006	.47608	.47210	.46812	.46414
0.1	.46017	.45620	.45224	.44828	.44433	.44038	.43644	.43251	.42858	.42465
0.2	.42074	.41683	.41294	.40905	.40517	.40129	.39743	.39358	.38974	.38591
0.3	.38209	.37828	.37448	.37070	.36693	.36317	.35942	.35569	.35197	.34827
0.4	.34446	.34090	.33724	.33360	.32997	.32636	.32276	.31918	.31561	.31207
0.5	.30854	.30503	.30153	.29806	.29550	.29116	.28774	.28444	.28096	.27760
0.6	.27425	.27093	.26763	.26435	.26109	.25785	.25463	.25143	.24825	.24510
0.7	.24196	.23885	.23576	.23270	.22965	.22663	.22363	.22065	.21770	.21476
0.8	.21186	.20897	.20611	.20327	.20045	.19766	.19489	.19215	.18943	.18673
0.9	.18406	.18141	.17879	.17619	.17361	.17106	.16853	.16602	.16354	.16109
1.0	.15866	.15643	.15386	.15150	.14917	.14687	.14457	.14231	.14007	.13786
1.1	.13567	.13350	.13136	.12924	.12714	.12507	.12302	.12100	.11900	.11702
1.2	.11507	.11314	.11123	.10935	.10749	.10565	.10383	.10204	.10027	.09853
1.3	.09680	.09510	.09342	.09176	.09012	.08851	.08692	.08534	.08379	.08226
1.4	.08076	.07927	.07780	.07636	.07493	.07353	.07214	.07078	.06944	.06811
1.5	.06681	.06552	.06426	.06301	.06178	.06057	.05938	.05821	.05705	.05592
1.6	.05480	.05370	.05262	.05155	.05050	.04947	.04846	.04746	.04648	.04551
1.7	.04457	.04363	.04272	.04182	.04093	.04006	.03920	.03836	.03754	.03673
1.8	.03593	.03515	.03438	.03362	.03288	.03216	.03144	.03074	.03005	.02938
1.9	.02872	.02807	.02743	.02680	.02619	.02559	.02500	.02442	.02385	.02330
2.0	.02275	.02222	.02169	.02118	.02068	.02018	.01970	.01923	.01876	.01831
2.1	.01786	.01743	.01700	.01659	.01618	.01578	.01539	.01500	.01463	.01426
2.2	.01390	.01355	.01321	.01287	.01255	.01222	.01191	.01160	.01130	.01101
2.3	.01072	.01044	.01017	.00990	.00964	.00939	.00914	.00889	.00866	.00842
2.4	.00820	.00798	.00776	.00755	.00734	.00714	.00695	.00676	.00657	.00639
2.5	.00621	.00604	.00587	.00570	.00554	.00539	.00523	.00508	.00494	.00480
2.6	.00466	.00453	.00440	.00427	.00415	.00402	.00391	.00379	.00368	.00357
2.7	.00347	.00336	.00326	.00317	.00307	.00298	.00289	.00280	.00272	.00264
2.8	.00256	.00248	.00240	.00233	.00226	.00219	.00212	.00205	.00199	.00193
2.9	.00187	.00181	.00175	.00169	.00164	.00159	.00154	.00149	.00144	.00139

Z	0.0	0.1	0.2	0.3	0.4	0.5	0.6	0.7	0.8	0.9
3.0	1.35×10^{-3}	9.68×10^{-4}	6.78×10^{-4}	4.83×10^{-4}	3.37×10^{-4}	2.33×10^{-4}	1.59×10^{-4}	1.08×10^{-4}	7.23×10^{-5}	4.81×10^{-5}
4.0	3.17×10^{-5}	2.07×10^{-5}	1.33×10^{-5}	8.54×10^{-6}	5.41×10^{-6}	3.40×10^{-6}	2.11×10^{-6}	1.30×10^{-6}	7.93×10^{-7}	4.79×10^{-7}
5.0	2.86×10^{-7}	1.70×10^{-7}	9.96×10^{-8}	5.79×10^{-8}	3.33×10^{-8}	1.90×10^{-8}	1.07×10^{-8}	5.98×10^{-9}	3.31×10^{-9}	1.82×10^{-9}
6.0	9.85×10^{-10}	5.30×10^{-10}	2.82×10^{-10}	1.49×10^{-10}	7.75×10^{-11}	4.01×10^{-11}	2.05×10^{-11}	1.04×10^{-11}	5.22×10^{-12}	2.59×10^{-12}
7.0	1.28×10^{-12}	6.22×10^{-13}	3.00×10^{-13}	1.43×10^{-13}	6.79×10^{-14}	3.18×10^{-14}	1.48×10^{-14}	6.78×10^{-15}	3.08×10^{-15}	1.39×10^{-15}
8.0	6.19×10^{-16}	2.74×10^{-16}	1.20×10^{-16}	5.18×10^{-17}	2.22×10^{-17}	9.43×10^{-18}	3.96×10^{-18}	1.65×10^{-18}	6.80×10^{-19}	2.78×10^{-19}

Z	9.0	10.0	11.0	12.0	13.0	14.0	15.0	16.0	17.0	18.0
P	10^{-19}	10^{-23}	10^{-28}	10^{-33}	10^{-39}	10^{-45}	10^{-51}	10^{-58}	10^{-65}	10^{-72}

Appendix 6.5 – The Binomial Theorem

Let: N = number of decisions, or attempts, (tosses, throws, draws, guesses etc.)
p = probability of a hit (head, six spot, correct answer, etc.)
in one decision, or one attempt
q = probability of a miss (tail, other than six spot, wrong answer etc.)
in one decision, or one attempt

Then, the "binomial theorem" (also called "binomial expansion") states:

$$(p+q)^N = p^N + \frac{N}{1} p^{(N-1)} q + \frac{(N)(N-1)}{(1)(2)} p^{(N-2)} q^2 + \frac{(N)(N-1)(N-2)}{(1)(2)(3)} p^{(N-3)} q^3$$
$$+ \frac{(N)(N-1)(N-2)(N-3)}{(1)(2)(3)(4)} p^{(N-4)} q^4 + \ldots + q^N$$

There are $(N+1)$ terms in the expansion.
In the case of coin tossing: $p = q = 1/2$, and in the case of die throwing: $p = 1/6$, $q = 5/6$.

The various terms in the expansion yield the following:
1st term = probability of N hits in N attempts,
2nd term = probability of $(N-1)$ hits in N attempts,
3rd term = probability of $(N-2)$ hits in N attempts,
and in general:
n th term = probability of $[N-(n-1)]$ hits in N attempts.
The probability of $(N-n)$ hits or more in N attempts is the sum of the first $(n+1)$ terms.

In the case when $N = 10$, $p = q = 1/2 = 0.5$, the 11 terms of the expansion give the probabilities as fractions, as listed in Table 6.5. Also, when $p = q = 1/2 = 0.5$, the terms in the expansion divided by p^N yield the horizontal lines in Pascal's triangle in Table 6.3.

For example, with the help of the binomial theorem one can find the probability P of obtaining in $N = 100$ tosses of a coin:
100 heads: $P = p^N = (0.5)^{100} = 7.89 \times 10^{-31}$,
99 heads: $P = Np^{(N-1)} q = (100) \times (0.5)^{99} \times (0.5) = 7.89 \times 10^{-29}$,
98 heads: $P = (1/2) N (N-1) p^{(N-2)} q^2 = (0.5) \times (100) \times (99) \times (0.5)^{98} (0.5)^2 = 3.9056 \times 10^{-27}$.
The probability for 98 heads or more is the sum of the above three probabilities, namely 3.985×10^{-27}.

Working from the normal curve one has: Mean = $N/2 = 100/2 = 50$,
Standard deviation = $\sqrt{N/4} = \sqrt{100/4} = 5$.
Now 98 heads or more extend from 97.5 upward on the continuous scale of the base line. Hence the normalised deviation = $(97.5 - 50)/5 = 9.5$. The corresponding probability from Table A6.4 by interpolation is approximately $P \approx 10^{-21}$.

The discrepancy between the normal curve and binomial theorem results is substantial. But, as found earlier in Chapter 6, the normal curve yields a higher probability figure, and so it underestimates the level of significance, and may be safely relied on.

The binomial theorem can also be used in cases when $p \neq q$. For example, in the case of die throwing $p = 1/6$ and $q = 5/6$. If a die is cast 100 times, the probability of obtaining 99 six spots or more is: $p^N + Np^{(N-1)} q = (1/6)^{100} + (100)(1/6)^{99}(5/6) = 7.66 \times 10^{-76}$.

Appendices to Chapter 9

Appendix 9.1 – Table A9.1
Chi-Square (X^2) Table

The table lists X^2 values for various values of the degrees of freedom DF, and various values of the probability P. As an example, if $DF = 10$ and $X^2 = 17$, then entering the line $DF = 10$ shows that $X^2 = 17$ falls between $X^2 = 16$ and $X^2 = 18.3$. Thus, the probability P lies between 0.1 and 0.05, and so fails to reach significance as $P > 0.05$.

DF	Probability P									
	0.95	0.75	0.50	0.25	0.10	0.05	0.025	0.01	0.005	0.001
1	0.004	0.10	0.46	1.32	2.71	3.84	5.02	6.64	7.88	10.8
2	0.10	0.58	1.39	2.77	4.61	5.99	7.38	9.21	10.6	13.8
3	0.35	1.21	2.37	4.11	6.25	7.81	9.35	11.3	12.8	16.3
4	0.71	1.92	3.36	5.39	7.78	9.49	11.1	13.3	14.9	18.5
5	1.15	2.67	4.35	6.63	9.24	11.1	12.8	15.1	16.8	20.5
6	1.64	3.45	5.35	7.84	10.6	12.6	14.5	16.8	18.6	22.5
7	2.17	4.25	6.35	9.04	12.0	14.1	16.0	18.5	20.3	24.3
8	2.73	5.07	7.34	10.2	13.4	15.5	17.5	20.1	22.0	26.1
9	3.33	5.90	8.34	11.4	14.7	16.9	19.0	21.7	23.6	27.9
10	3.94	6.74	9.34	12.5	16.0	18.3	20.5	23.2	25.2	29.5
11	4.58	7.58	10.3	13.7	17.3	19.7	21.9	24.7	26.8	31.3
12	5.23	8.44	11.3	14.8	18.5	21.0	23.3	26.2	28.3	32.9
13	5.89	9.30	12.3	16.0	19.8	22.4	24.7	27.7	29.8	34.5
14	6.57	10.2	13.3	17.1	21.1	23.7	26.1	29.1	31.3	36.1
15	7.26	11.0	14.3	18.2	22.3	25.0	27.5	30.6	32.8	37.7
16	7.96	11.9	15.3	19.4	23.5	26.3	28.9	32.0	34.3	39.3
17	8.67	12.8	16.3	20.5	24.8	27.6	30.2	33.4	35.7	40.8
18	9.39	13.7	17.3	21.6	26.0	28.9	31.5	34.8	37.2	42.3
19	10.1	14.6	18.3	22.7	27.2	30.1	32.9	36.2	38.6	43.8
20	10.9	15.5	19.3	23.8	28.4	31.4	34.2	37.6	40.0	45.3
25	14.6	19.9	24.3	29.3	34.4	37.7	40.7	44.3	46.9	52.6
30	18.5	24.5	29.3	34.8	40.3	43.8	47.0	50.9	53.7	59.7
40						55.8	59.3	63.7	66.8	
50						67.5	71.4	76.2	79.5	
60						79.1	83.3	88.4	92.0	
70						90.5	95.0	100.4	104.2	
80						101.9	106.6	112.3	116.3	
90						113.2	118.1	124.1	128.3	
100						124.3	129.6	135.8	140.2	

Appendix 9.2 – Table A9.2
Student's t Table

The table lists t values for various values of the degrees of freedom DF, and various values of the probability P. For example, if $DF = 10$ and $t = 2.0$, then entering the line $DF = 10$ shows that $t = 2.0$ falls between $t = 1.81$ and $t = 2.23$. Consequently, the probability P lies between 0.05 and 0.025, indicating a significant result as $P < 0.05$.

DF	Probability P									
	0.4	0.25	0.10	0.05	0.025	0.01	0.005	0.0025	0.001	0.0005
1	0.33	1.00	3.08	6.31	12.71	31.82	63.66	127.3	318.3	636.6
2	0.29	0.82	1.89	2.92	4.30	6.97	9.93	14.09	22.33	31.60
3	0.28	0.77	1.64	2.35	3.18	4.54	5.84	7.45	10.21	12.94
4	0.27	0.74	1.53	2.13	2.78	3.75	4.60	5.60	7.17	8.61
5	0.27	0.73	1.48	2.02	2.57	3.37	4.03	4.77	5.89	6.86
6	0.27	0.72	1.44	1.94	2.45	3.14	3.71	4.32	5.21	5.96
7	0.26	0.71	1.42	1.90	2.37	3.00	3.50	4.03	4.79	5.41
8	0.26	0.71	1.40	1.86	2.31	2.90	3.36	3.83	4.50	5.04
9	0.26	0.70	1.38	1.83	2.26	2.82	3.25	3.69	4.30	4.78
10	0.26	0.70	1.37	1.81	2.23	2.76	3.17	3.58	4.14	4.59
11	0.26	0.70	1.36	1.80	2.20	2.72	3.11	3.50	4.02	4.44
12	0.26	0.70	1.36	1.78	2.18	2.68	3.06	3.43	3.93	4.32
13	0.26	0.69	1.35	1.77	2.16	2.65	3.01	3.37	3.85	4.22
14	0.26	0.69	1.35	1.76	2.15	2.62	2.98	3.33	3.79	4.14
15	0.26	0.69	1.34	1.75	2.13	2.60	2.95	3.29	3.73	4.07
16	0.26	0.69	1.34	1.75	2.12	2.58	2.92	3.25	3.69	4.02
17	0.26	0.69	1.33	1.74	2.11	2.57	2.90	3.22	3.65	3.97
18	0.26	0.69	1.33	1.73	2.10	2.55	2.88	3.20	3.61	3.92
19	0.26	0.69	1.33	1.73	2.09	2.54	2.86	3.17	3.58	3.88
20	0.26	0.69	1.33	1.73	2.09	2.53	2.85	3.15	3.55	3.85
25	0.26	0.68	1.32	1.71	2.06	2.49	2.79	3.08	3.45	3.73
30	0.26	0.68	1.31	1.70	2.04	2.46	2.75	3.03	3.39	3.65
40	0.26	0.68	1.30	1.68	2.02	2.42	2.70	2.97	3.31	3.55
60	0.25	0.68	1.30	1.67	2.00	2.39	2.66	2.91	3.23	3.46
120	0.25	0.68	1.29	1.66	1.98	2.36	2.62	2.86	3.16	3.37
∞	0.25	0.67	1.28	1.65	1.96	2.33	2.58	2.81	3.10	3.29

Appendix 9.3 – Combining Test Run Results

Formulae for calculating the overall values of the mean, variance, and standard deviation, for the results of a test series from the individual test run results are given below.

Let:

$N_{A1}, N_{A2}, \ldots N_{An}$	: Numbers of active readings in test runs 1, 2, … n
$M_{A1}, M_{A2}, \ldots M_{An}$	: Means of the active readings in test runs 1, 2, … n
$S_{A1}^2, S_{A2}^2, \ldots S_{An}^2$	: Variances of the active readings in test runs 1, 2, … n

One may deliberately arrange all test runs to have equal number of readings, in which case:

$$N_{A1} = N_{A2} = \ldots = N_{An} = N$$

Then, the total combined overall mean of all the active runs in the test series is:

$$M_{AT} = \frac{M_{A1} + M_{A2} + \ldots + M_{An}}{n}$$

And, the total combined overall variance of all the active runs in the test series is:

$$S_{AT}^2 = \frac{M_{A1}^2 + S_{A1}^2 + M_{A2}^2 + S_{A2}^2 + \ldots + M_{An}^2 + S_{An}^2}{n} - M_{AT}^2$$

Given that the above are values applicable to active readings, then:

Similarly for the control readings: M_{CT} and S_{CT}^2

If the above were rotating wheel total motion readings, then:

Similarly for the incremental motion active readings: $\Delta M_{AT}, \Delta S_{AT}^2$

Similarly for the incremental motion control readings: $\Delta M_{CT}, \Delta S_{CT}^2$

In all cases the standard deviation is the square root of the variance.

The formulae for calculating student's t values, as given in Chapter 9, apply to overall test series results as well, provided that the total number of active and control readings are kept the same.

Appendix to Chapter 13

Appendix 13.1

The main nutritional constituents of the human diet are carbohydrates, fats, and proteins, all of which contribute to the sustenance of the human body. In addition small quantities of micronutrients, such as vitamins and minerals, are also needed.

The carbohydrates and fats are composed of three elements, namely carbon, hydrogen, and oxygen, but proteins contain, in addition to these, the elements nitrogen, and in some cases sulphur. The rather complex protein molecules are built of simpler building blocks called amino acids. When protein is digested, it is broken down into its constituents, from which the body builds up the type of protein molecules it needs for growth and repair.

In this building process eight amino acids are considered to be essential, in the sense that if any one is missing the building process cannot go on. It is possible to analyse protein food sources for the total protein content, and also for the amounts of the various constituent amino acids. It is also possible to estimate the daily protein requirement for humans by ascertaining the daily nitrogen loss from the human body, which then can be extrapolated to protein loss that needs to be replaced. Some results of such tests for the estimated daily requirements for adults, together with relative amino acid contents of various protein food sources, are listed in Table A13.1. The eight essential amino acids are listed at the heads of Columns 1 to 8. These columns give the proportions of the eight essential amino acids as percentages of the total essential amino acid contents for various protein food sources. The percentage figures have been rounded to the nearest whole number for clarity, even though giving them to one decimal place would have been possible and more accurate.

The first two rows represent recommended proportions of the eight essential amino acids for human nutrition from two nutritional science sources. The disparity between the two sets of figures is indicative of the extent to which expert opinion may be at variance. As human milk occupies an intermediate position between the two, while it is also the only protein source definitely meant for human consumption in infancy, it is taken to represent the ideal amino acid balance for humans.

There is better agreement amongst nutritional science sources on the daily requirement of adults for the sum total of the eight essential amino acids. The average recommendation is 4.7 grams, which is the figure adopted in Table A13.1. This means that if the eight essential amino acids in a protein food source were present in the correct proportion, the necessary daily combined intake of the eight essential amino acids would be 4.7 grams. However, if the proportion is not correct, then the essential amino acid intake needs to be increased by the factor in Column 9, so as to satisfy the daily requirement for all the essential amino acids, including the one most deficient.

Further, since protein food sources contain nonessential amino acids also, the daily protein requirement is greater than the essential amino acid requirement by a factor ranging from 2 to 5, depending on the type of protein food source. Taking both factors into account leads to the daily protein requirement in grams from various protein food sources in Column 10.

Finally, the protein content of different protein food sources varies greatly, and when this variation is also factored in, one arrives at the figures in Column 11, giving the amount of

Table A13.1

	Iso-Leucine (%)	Leucine (%)	Lysine (%)	Methionine (%)	Phenylalanine (%)	Threonine (%)	Tryptophan (%)	Valine (%)	Amino Acid Balance	Daily Requirement Protein (grams)	Daily Requirement Food (grams)
Requirement Source 1	12	18	14	13	14	9	5	15			
Requirement Source 2	15	23	17	5	7	11	5	17			
Human Milk	14	22	16	5	11	11	5	16	1.0		
Cow's Milk	14	22	18	5	11	11	3	16	1.4	15	430
Cheese Cheddar	16	22	17	6	12	8	3	16	1.5	16	62
Eggs	14	20	14	7	13	11	4	17	1.2	13	100
Chicken	14	19	23	7	10	11	3	13	1.5	18	87
Pork	14	19	21	7	10	12	3	14	1.3	16	99
Beef	13	21	22	6	10	11	3	14	1.6	18	100
Fish	13	19	23	7	10	11	3	14	1.7	21	115
Soy Beans	15	21	17	4	14	11	4	14	1.4	17	48
Peanuts	14	22	13	3	18	9	4	17	1.7	24	90
Mixed Beans	14	22	19	3	14	11	2	15	2.1	25	116
Whole Wheat	15	23	10	5	17	10	4	16	1.7	28	210
Rye	14	22	13	5	15	12	3	16	1.3	20	210
Whole Rice	13	24	11	5	14	11	3	19	1.5	20	260
Green Peas	15	22	16	3	14	13	3	14	1.9	30	450
Spinach	13	21	17	5	12	12	5	15	1.2	15	660
Potatoes with skin	14	16	18	4	14	13	3	18	1.4	21	1000
Cabbage	13	19	22	5	10	13	4	14	1.2	26	1800

protein food in grams necessary for covering the daily requirement of all essential amino acids from that protein food source alone, after allowance for imbalance has been made.

Two frequently quoted contentions claim that only animal protein food sources are capable of satisfying all the essential protein needs for human health. According to these, firstly, only animal protein food sources supply all the essential amino acids, and secondly, do so in the correct proportion. Table A13.1 clearly indicates that both of these contentions are false. Column 9 in Table A13.1 shows that plant food protein sources also supply all the essential amino acids, and some, for example spinach and cabbage are, in fact, better balanced than most animal protein food sources. Animal based diet is promoted through false claims propagated by vested interests, such as the animal husbandry and animal feed industries, the suppliers of growth promoters and antibiotics to these industries, some health professionals who benefit from the ailments resulting from the consumption of food of animal origin, and the support industries of all these.

It is true that the percentage protein content of plant protein food sources is lower in general. This, however, may well be beneficial, since consuming protein in excess of the daily requirement is suspect of being detrimental to the metabolic functioning of the human body, which has to convert the excess protein to fat, and excrete the nitrogenous by-products of this conversion. Animal protein food sources also often contain large quantities of saturated fat, which is very suspect of being the source of further complications. The consumption of food of animal origin is a very likely contributory factor to a number of serious degenerative diseases, such as arterial blockages, heart attacks, strokes, and cancer.

Thus, the eating of animals by humans is not only immoral in view of the principles put forward in Chapter 13, but it is also likely to be very deleterious to human health.